STRATEGIC MANAGEMENT

STRATEGIC MANAGEMENT

Cliff Bowman
Humberside College of Higher Education

and

David Asch
The Open University

First published 1987

Published by
MACMILLAN EDUCATION LTD
Houndmills, Basingstoke, Hampshire RG21 2XS
and London
Companies and representatives
throughout the world

Printed in Hong Kong

British Library Cataloguing in Publication Data
Bowman, Cliff
Strategic management.
1. Strategic planning
I. Title II. Asch, David
658.4'012 HD30.28
ISBN 0–333–38764–3 (hardcover)
ISBN 0–333–38765–1 (paperback)

Contents

List of figures

List of tables

List of illustrations

Preface

Strategic management as a business and management subject has developed rapidly over the past few years. The study of corporate strategy has evolved a long way from the prescriptive 'corporate planning' model of the 1960s and early 1970s. The study of strategic management, that is, how a firm is managed in a strategic sense, embraces both the formulation and implementation of strategies. Prescriptions for better strategic decision-making need to be set against more developed insights into the realities of organisational life. This book is designed to reflect this broadening scope through the overall structure of the text, in particular, through the inclusion of important recent developments.

Corporate strategy is often used as a capstone unit in many advanced business and management courses, both as an important integrating mechanism because it incorporates and develops the more functional areas, and because of a recognition that a 'strategic perspective' is a desirable attribute for all levels of management. This book is primarily aimed at post-graduate (MBA, DMS) and final-year undergraduate Business Policy/Strategic Management courses, but we hope that it will be of use to anyone who is interested in strategic management, whether or not they encounter it as a part of a formal course of study.

In writing the book it has often been difficult to decide what to include and what to leave out, and in making these judgements we have assumed that the reader will already have some prior knowledge of the main functional areas in organisations.

Brief illustrations have been included to encourage the reader to relate the concepts developed in the text to practice examples. Although no case studies as such have been included, the text can be used to support a case-based study programme.

Finally, we would like to thank Joanna Witty for her valuable contributions to Chapter 10 on Managing Change, and Liz Knight and Denise Donovan for typing (and retyping!) the drafts of the chapters.

CLIFF BOWMAN
DAVID ASCH

Acknowledgements

The author and publishers wish to thank the following who have kindly given permission for the use of copyright material:

Administrative Science Quarterly for figure from 'The Structure of "Unstructured" Decision Processes' by Henry Mintzberg, Duru Raisinghani and Andre Theorat; Basic Books Inc. for figure from 'Constraints on Strategic Choice' from *Decision Making at the Top* by G. Donaldson and J. W. Lorsch. Copyright ©1983, Basic Books; The Free Press, a Division of Macmillan, Inc. for figures from *Decision Making* by Irving L. Janis and Leon Mann. Copyright ©1977 by The Free Press, *Competitive Strategy* by Michael E. Porter. Copyright ©1980 by The Free Press and *Competitive Advantage* by Michael E. Porter. Copyright ©1985 by Michael E. Porter; *Harvard Business Review* for exhibit from 'Evolution and revolution as organizations grow' by Larry E. Greiner, HBR, July–August, 1972; William Heinemann Ltd for figures and illustrations from *Corporate Strategy and Planning* by B. Taylor and J. R. Sparkes; McGraw-Hill Book Company for figures from *The Mind of the Strategist* by Ohmae; Pitman Publishing, Inc. for table and figure from *Power in Organizations* by J. Pfeffer; Penguin Books Ltd and Stuart Slatter for figure from *Corporate Recovery: Successful Turnaround Strategies and their Implementation* by Stuart Slatter, Penguin Education. Copyright ©Stuart Slatter 1984; Prentice-Hall International (UK) Ltd for figures from *Making Management Decisions* by S. Cooke and N. Slack, 1984 and from *Strategic Industrial Marketing* by P. Chisnall, 1985; Prentice-Hall, Inc. for material from *Structure in Fives: Designing Effective Organisations* by Henry Mintzberg ©1983; *Sloan Management Review* for figure from 'Defining Strengths and Weaknesses' by H. H. Stevenson, SMR, Spring 1976. Copyright ©1976 by the Sloan Management Review Association; Stanford University Graduate School of Business, ©1977 by the Board of Trustees of the Leland Stanford Junior University for figure by C. W. Hofer; West Publishing Company for material from *Strategy Formulation* by Macmillan and *Strategy Implementation* by Galbraith and Nathanson; John Wiley & Sons Ltd for table and figure from 'Of Strategies, Deliberate and Emergent' by H. Mintzberg and J. A. Waters, *Strategic Management Journal*, 1985.

Every effort has been made to trace all the copyright-holders, but if any have been inadvertently overlooked the publishers will be pleased to make the necessary arrangement at the first opportunity.

PART I

THE FORMULATION OF STRATEGY

CHAPTER 1

Introduction

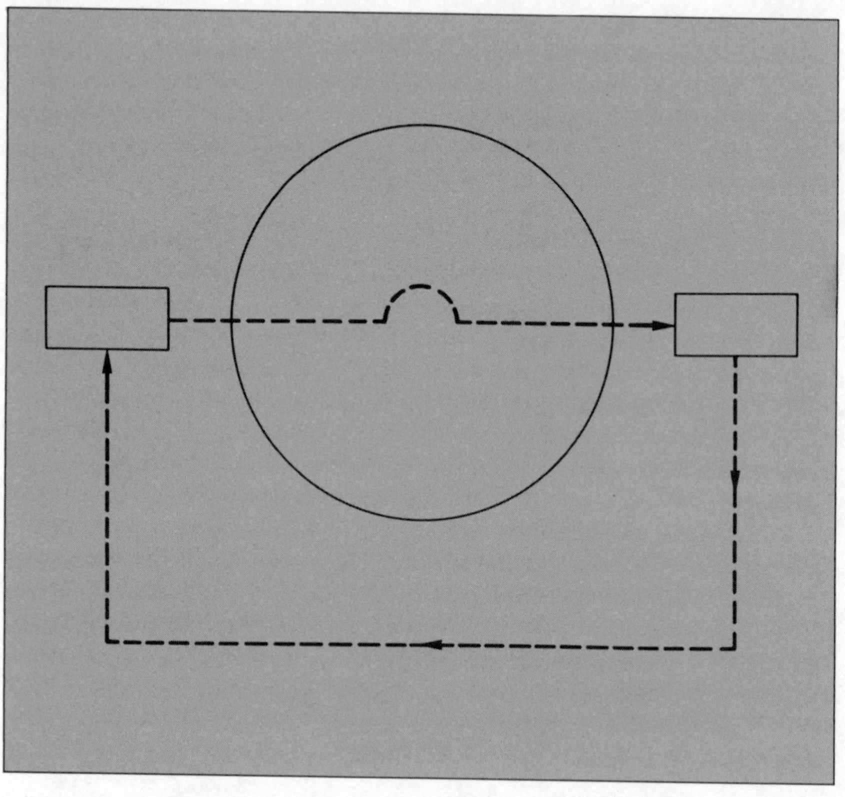

On the outskirts of Crescent City, California is a small fast-food restaurant. On a sunny day around lunch-time, it seems to be doing little trade, and on investigation it appears that closure is a distinct possibility. Why has this little business not succeeded?

This small firm is the outcome of a series of decisions made by its owners, and it would seem, with the benefit of hindsight, that either their decisions were wrong, or they have been very unlucky, or maybe the lack of success is a result of a combination of the two. The owners must have decided, first, to go into business, then to single out the fast-food trade as a likely winner; then they must have looked around for premises, negotiated and purchased them; designed the menu, the décor, the seating arrangements, the kitchen, the staffing, the opening hours, etc., etc.

Which of these decisions were crucially wrong? Was it the *location* of the restaurant (it is, in fact, directly opposite a brand new Burger Chef)? Was it the quality of the food (should they have hired the owner's brother as the chef after all)? Well, the problem could have something to do with the name they chose: 'The Tired Chicken' (what images does this name conjure up in the hungry traveller's mind?)

This book is about strategic management and the reasons for starting with this seemingly trivial example are twofold. First, we want to make the point very forcibly at the outset, that strategic decisions take many forms. In the case of this firm, no one would argue that the location decision was of strategic importance. But maybe it was the name, or the décor, which caused the restaurant to fail. So, these decisions must also be of strategic importance. This leads us to our second reason for using this example, and that is that, unfortunately, it is only *in hindsight* that many decisions appear to have been critical; at the time they were made, they were not accorded the same care as more obviously crucial decisions.

Strategic decisions and strategic management

For our purposes *strategic decisions are big decisions; decisions which significantly affect the organisation's ability to achieve its objectives*. So this includes decisions which were seen as important at the time they were made and also decisions which only in restrospect appear to have been strategic. It could include decisions about what products to sell in which markets, where to build the new factory, as well as decisions about pay systems, production processes, organisation structure, management style, and management promotions.

One strategic management problem is that most prescriptive techniques and systems for making 'better', more 'rational' decisions (for example, corporate planning) will inevitably only capture the *a priori* strategic decisions – those that are acknowledged as critical and important *before* they are made. This brings us to another problem, and that is that strategic decisions could be made at many levels in the organisation. A decision of a purchasing manager to switch to a cheaper supplier could lead to a reduction in the quality of a vital component, then to a poorer product, a dissatisfied important customer, and a loss of business. A hasty decision to discipline a fitter by a production supervisor could lead to a damaging strike.

One way in which firms try to counter this problem is to draw as many decisions as possible up to the top of the organisation where a 'strategic perspective' can be brought to bear on each decision. This is often impractical as the relevant detailed information is not available at the top; it can lead to an overload of decision-making at the apex of the firm, and a demotivated lower and middle management lacking in initiative. Another reaction is to proceduralise and routinise as many of these desicions as possible, so that with double-checking and overseeing, errors in strategic decision-making are less likely. A third response would be to spread the strategic perspective further down the organisation structure, so that this broader view can inform many more decisions.

This book is concerned with problems of, and prescriptions for, strategic management. *Strategic management is the process of making and implementing strategic decisions, or put another way, strategic management is about the process of strategic change.* A decision which has no discernible impact on the organisation, which leads to no change in the organisation, is of little interest.

We are concerned as much with the *processes* of making strategic decisions, as with the *content* of these decisions, because the process of decision-making can have considerable impact on the subsequent implementation of those decisions.

Before we introduce the model which underpins the structure of the book, we should make one further point about the nature of *strategy*. 'Strategy' usually describes a thought-out plan of action, a consciously-formulated, broadly-defined policy for achieving an objective. The term 'strategy' has been borrowed from its military use and has been applied to decisions made at the 'corporate' level of the firm. Our use of the term is much looser than this. For our purposes the strategy of a firm refers to its perceived posture with regard to its customers, competitors, employees, production processes, structure etc. This posture may only have been consciously constructed in the mind of an outside observer –

in other words, a firm can have a strategy even if no one within the organisation perceives these different postures as an integrated policy. So *all* firms have a strategy; it is just in some firms someone has consciously tried to construct the strategy, in others it has emerged as a result of a series of separate decisions which collectively have resulted in a viable organisation.

We shall now introduce our model of the processes of strategic management which will help in explaining the structure of the book.

The process of strategic management

Figure 1.1 depicts the basic model. Strategic changes come about through the interaction of the objective and subjective conditions. Let us assume that a major competitor has launched a technically superior product (a change in the objective conditions facing the firm). The senior management, who have been surprised by the launch, conclude that a swift response is required to minimise the firm's loss of market share. They perceive that their firm cannot match the technology of the compe-

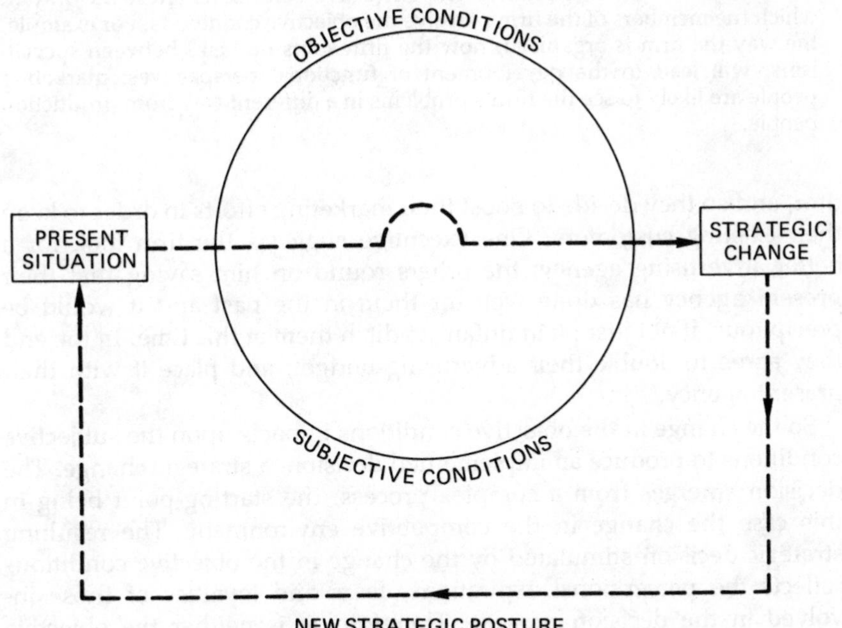

FIGURE 1.1 The process of strategic management

Notes:

The present situation: This is the state of the firm today, its current strategic posture.

Strategic change: Any adjustment to the existing strategy is a strategic change. Changes may be organisation-wide or very localised; they may be the outcome of an elaborate corporate planning process, or the change may have resulted from an ill-thought-out decision made in haste by an executive under pressure.

The 'new strategic posture' loop: The model is dynamic, implying that the process of strategic change is continuous. Today's strategic change forms tomorrow's present situation.

Objective conditions: These include the present and future states of the firm's environment, and the deployment of the firm's resources. The environment of the firm includes the competitive situation, the economic and technological environments, and the political and social context in which the firm is operating. The objective conditions, both external and internal are more amenable to systematic analysis than the subjective conditions.

Subjective conditions: These refer to the complex of social, psychological and political variables that pervade the organisation. Included here would be a wide range of conditions which have evolved and emerged from past management decisions, the external environment, leadership influence (both formal and informal), and the structure of the organisation. Some examples might be: the firm's culture; power relationships; inertia; management values, beliefs and aspirations; trust; hostility. The subjective conditions affect the way in which the members of the firm perceive the objective conditions. For example, the way the firm is organised, how the firm splits up tasks between specialisms, will lead to the development of functional perspectives: marketing people are likely to see the firm's problems in a different way from production people.

titor, and so they decide to boost their marketing efforts in order to keep their existing customers. One executive suggests the firm look for a better advertising agency: the others round on him saying that their present agency has done well for them in the past and it would be precipitous, if not just plain unfair, to ditch them at this time. In the end they agree to double their advertising budget, and place it with their present agency.

So the change in the objective conditions impacts upon the subjective conditions to produce an implemented decision, a strategic change. The decision emerges from a complex process, the starting-point being in this case the change in the competitive environment. The resulting strategic decision stimulated by the change in the objective conditions reflects the perceptions, aspirations, fears and loyalties of those involved in the decision process. Therefore, it is neither the objective conditions alone, nor the subjective conditions alone which determine the shape of strategic change. Rather, it is the *interactions* of both the subjective and objective conditions together which produce the change.

In this example, the stimulus for change originated in the objective conditions facing the firm. Strategic changes can also be instigated by shifts in the subjective conditions. Consider, for instance, the promotion to Works Manager of a more aggressive person, with new ideas and a desire to make an immediate impact. The new manager may introduce a whole series of changes in work practices at such a rate that production supervisors and operatives become confused and demoralised. This could feed through to the objective conditions through reduced efficiency, overrunning delivery dates and a loss of customer confidence.

The model provides us with a loose and adaptable framework for analysing the processes of strategic management. We believe that a broadly-drawn model is appropriate if we are to successfully explore the complexities of the subject. In particular, the differences between prescriptive and descriptive approaches to strategic management can be usefully drawn out with the aid of the model.

Prescriptive and descriptive approaches

Prescriptions for 'better' management can be traced back as far as Henri Fayol (Mullins 1985) and his suggestions for improving the administration of business organisations. The scientific-management approach of Taylor, Gantt and Gilbreth, whilst chiefly concerned with improving operating-level efficiency, has inspired a range of management disciplines concerned with telling managers how to do their job more efficiently and effectively. At the 'hard-edged', quantitative end of the spectrum are the management scientists and operations researchers, with an expanding tool kit of techniques for solving particular problems, and at the 'softer' end are the descendants of the human-relations movement proffering prescriptions about management style, job design and organisation structure.

In the 1960s the scientific-management tradition moved into the upper reaches of the firm with the emergence of systematic corporate planning. Here was a 'logical' approach to the making of the most important decisions facing the firm's management. The corporate-planning technique has been augmented by other analytical techniques (for example, the BCG matrix, structural analysis of industries) which can be used either as part of a corporate planning exercise, or as 'stand-alone' pieces of analysis. These logical methods are primarily focused on the *objective conditions* facing the firm.

There is gathering evidence that the corporate planning approach has not been successfully applied in practice by some organisations, and, more importantly, many firms do not appear to use systematic approaches of any kind in making strategic decisions. And firms that *have* used corporate planning often find problems when they come to implement the selected strategy.

The descriptive tradition in organisation research is much stronger in the sociological and socio-psychological disciplines. Perhaps because the researchers were less pressured by the need to provide solutions than those with a more obvious management orientation, they have been able to bring a more rounded, 'warts-and-all' perspective on the firm. These disciplines help us to explore the *subjective conditions* within the firm.

Hopefully, a useful synthesis is now emerging in strategic management where prescriptions for 'better' management have been thoroughly informed by a sophisticated understanding of the internal structures and processes of the organisation. And, in the same way that management theory has developed contingency approaches to management style and organisation structure (so there is no longer 'one best way' to organise, it all depends on the situation) so too may we see the emergence of contingency approaches to strategic management (see Luthans). This prospect is considered further in Chapter 14 on Models of Strategic Decision-making.

The structure of the book

Figure 1.2 locates the major chapters on our model of strategic management. Chapter 2 on Objectives spans both the objective and subjective hemispheres: here we are exploring the *raison d'être* of the organisation, what it is established to do, and the extent to which the objectives reflect the external influences on the firm, or the values and aspirations of the managers who control the organisation. Chapters 3, 4, 5, 6 and 7 are largely concerned with exploring the objective conditions facing the firm. In these chapters techniques of strategic analysis are presented which can help managers systematically to explore the external and internal environments of the firm, for the purpose of generating successful strategic options. Chapter 8 on Strategic Selection focuses on the evaluation and choice processes prior to implementation. Chapter 9 considers the more 'objective' aspects of implementation: action planning and budgeting, whereas Chapter 10 reviews the human aspects of managing change: resistance and strategies for coping with change, and

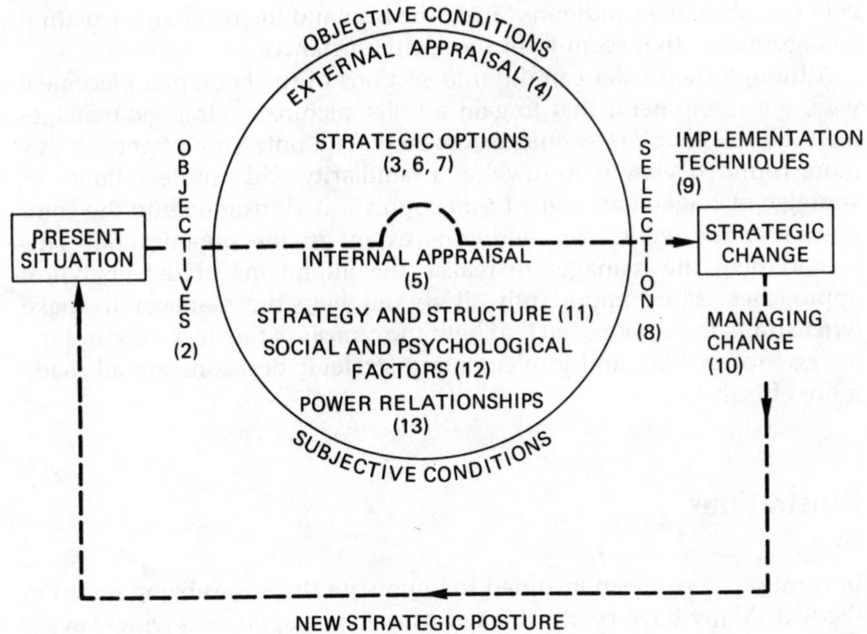

FIGURE 1.2 The structure of the book

Note: Figures in brackets are chapter numbers.

shifts the emphasis towards the subjective conditions extant in the firm. The relationships between strategy and structure, (Chapter 11), social and psychological factors influencing decision processes (Chapter12), and power relationships and power strategies (Chapter 13) complete the exploration of subjective conditions. Chapter 14 evaluates various prescriptive and descriptive models of strategic decision-making. The final chapter on Not-For-Profit Organisations considers their particular strategic management issues which, in our view, merit separate treatment.

There is one feature of the version of the model depicted in Fig 1.2 which has so far not been explained: that is the penetration of the subjective conditions into the objective conditions, represented by the bulge in the dotted line linking the present situation to the strategic change. The space represented by the bulge defines internal factors that are more open to objective analysis, for example, particular skills or capabilities the firm possesses, locations, machinery, cash resources, credit ratings, etc. This space is explored specifically in Chapter 5 on internal appraisal, and Chapter 11 which examines the interrelationship between objective conditions facing the firm and the resultant structural configurations that seem to fit these circumstances.

Although the reader can dip into sections of the book in a piecemeal way, we recommend that to gain a fuller picture of strategic management all the chapters should be covered. The only way of getting this more rounded view is to develop a familiarity with the techniques of strategic management, *coupled with* sophisticated insights into the complexity of the subjective conditions extant in the organisation. This should help the manager to realise the limitations of the analytical approaches. More importantly, it should help the manager to make *better* strategic decisions, so that both the *content* of the decisions and the *processes* of making and implementing strategic decisions are all made more effective.

Illustrations

Illustrations have been included to illuminate the issues being raised in the text. Many have been extracted from newspapers and widely available periodicals. The reason for using these sources is to encourage the reader to make connections between theory and practice, so that by reading the business press real-life examples can be constantly accessed in such a way as to strengthen the reader's insights into strategic management. The illustrations are arranged in separate boxes, so that the flow of the argument in the main body of the text is not interrupted. However, we hope that this will not discourage the reader from getting some benefit from a consideration of the examples in the illustrations.

References

Luthans, Fred (1977) *Organisational Behaviour* (New York: McGraw-Hill) pp. 441–5 for a discussion of contingency theory of leadership style.

Mintzberg, Henry (1983) *Structure in Fives* (Englewood Cliffs, New Jersey: Prentice-Hall) for a well-developed theory of organisation structure.

Mullins, Laurie J. (1985) *Management and Organizational Behaviour* (London: Pitman) ch. 3, for a review of the classical and scientific management approaches.

CHAPTER 2

Objectives

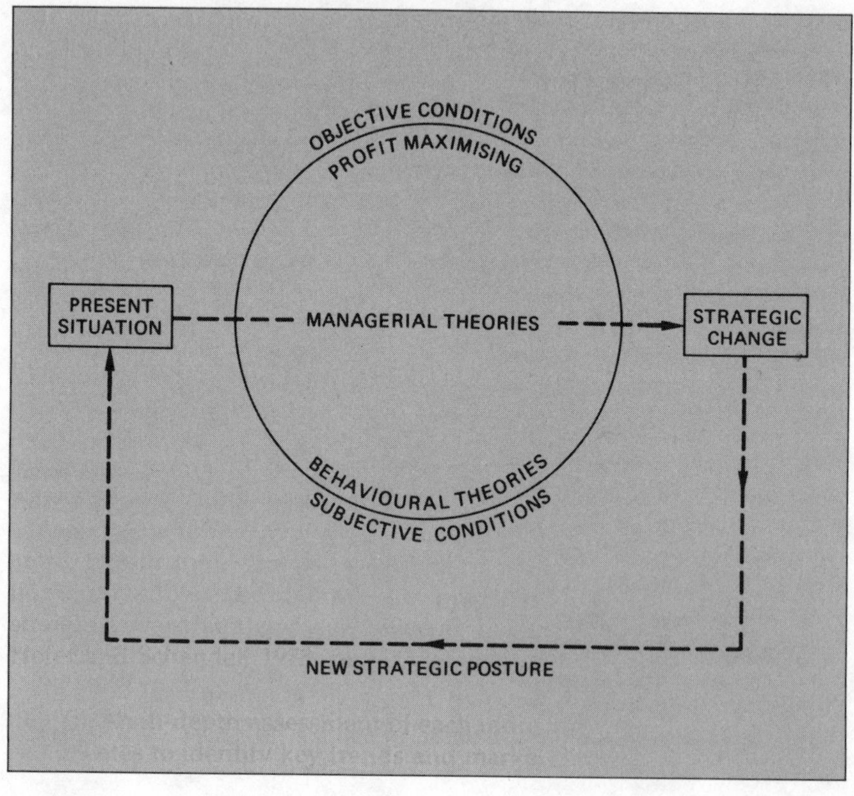

2.1 Introduction

In the introductory chapter we concluded that to adopt either a wholly prescriptive or a wholly descriptive perspective on strategic management was inappropriate and that the differences between these approaches would be considered in the context of particular topics. So, in a discussion of objectives we must distinguish between views about what the firm is *believed* to be doing, and opinions as to what firms *should* be doing. However, when consideration is given to various models of the firm's objectives, which purport to be essentially descriptive in nature, a normative element can be detected. In as much as any attempt to model the objectives of the firm is motivated by a desire to demonstrate or prove a particular point of view, we should not expect to discover an 'objective theory of objectives'! It should be no surprise that theories about objectives are inextricably linked with more widely drawn theories about the firm's behaviour. These broader models will also be considered briefly in his chapter. First, though, we should explore whether or not an organisation *can* have a goal!

2.2 Can an organisation have a goal?

What does it mean to say that an organisation has a goal? Can only people have goals? Can the goal of the organisation be regarded as something separate from the goals of various individuals who inhabit or control the organisation?

One view, a 'rational' perspective, would contend that an organisation is set up to achieve something; it is an instrument for achieving a particular end. But this picture is complicated by the existence of actions and behaviours in actual organisations which do not appear to be helping the organisation to reach the stated goal.

Reification, treating the organisation as something more than a system of interacting individuals, has been thoroughly criticised by many organisation theorists. But if people inside and outside an organisation *perceive* that the organisation has a goal and 'does things to them', then as far as their behaviour is concerned, the organisation *is* a separate and distinct entity, over and above the individuals in it.

If we can observe some consistent pattern in the decisions and actions of an organisation, then we might infer that there is some intention (or goal) driving these actions. So in what circumstances is this consistency likely to emerge? Mintzberg (pp. 246–7) identifies two sets of circumstances where 'intended consistency' is likely to emerge:

1. *An organisation with a strong ideology*: Here all the members of the organisation share a set of beliefs, for example, a religious sect, a revolutionary political group. People who wish to join have to accept the organisation's goals as their own. Clearly, we would expect a high degree of consistency in decisions emerging from this type of organisation.
2. *An organisation with a dominant influencer*: In this organisation the influencer is able to *impose* his or her goals on the organisation through the exercise of formal power. Other members of the organisation may not necessarily share these goals, they comply with them to further *their* own interests (salary, status, security).

We shall return to the 'dominant-influencer' concept at the end of the chapter, after we have considered a variety of theories about objectives. Before we focus on the firm's objectives,we shall distinguish firms from other types of organisation which can be collectively labelled as 'not-for-profit' organisations.

2.3 For-profit and not-for-profit organisations

For most of this book we will be concentrating on the *firm* in our exploration of strategic management. This is because most of the theoretical and empirical work in strategic management relates to firms rather than to other types of organisation. We believe, however, that there are particular strategic issues facing not-for-profit organisations (like charities, local authorities, universities, nationalised industries) that stem largely from their objectives, which require them to be treated as a distinct category of organisation. Whereas firms are required to make some level of profits (otherwise they cease to exist), this 'bottom-line' objective is missing for most not-for-profit organisations (NFPs).

Let us consider as an example of an NFP the UK Civil Aviation Authority. Illustration 2.1 contains extracts from the Civil Aviation Act 1982 which lays down what parliament's objectives for the CAA are. Paragraph 4 offers guidance about how the CAA amongst its other duties, should go about licensing air routes and approving fare increases. The words in italics have been highlighted to illustrate some of the problems in carrying out these objectives. Phrases like 'reasonable interests', 'economic return' and 'efficient operators' leave a lot of scope for argument and interpretation. So, in so far as objectives drive the organisation and inform its decision-making there is a good deal of ambiguity even, as in this case, where the objectives are spelt out in

ILLUSTRATION 2.1 Objectives of the Civil Aviation Authority (Excerpts from the Civil Aviation Act 1982)

4. (1) It shall be the duty of the CAA to perform its functions in the manner which it considers is best calculated -

   (a) to secure that British airlines provide air transport services which satisfy *all substantial* categories of public demand (so far as British airlines may *reasonably* be expected to provide such services) at the *lowest charges consistent with a high standard of safety* in operating the services and an *economic return* to *efficient* operators on the sums invested in providing the services and with securing the *sound development* of the civil air transport industry of the United Kingdom; and

   (b) to further the *reasonable interests* of users of air transport services.

5. (1) It shall be the duty of the CAA in exercising any aerodrome licensing function to have regard to the need to *minimise so far as reasonably practicable* -

   (a) any adverse effects on the environment, and

   (b) any disturbance to the public

   from noise, vibration, atmosphere pollution or any other cause attributable to the use of aircraft for the purpose of civil aviation.

legislation. Moreover, the problem of measuring the organisation's performance (in terms of its efficiency and effectiveness) is largely a matter of subjective judgement.

A firm's performance, in contrast, can be quantitatively measured (for instance, return on capital employed) and using this criterion a firm making baby clothes can be compared with one manufacturing nuclear-powered submarines.

We explore the specific strategic management issues of NFPs in Chapter 15. However, there are organisational and managerial aspects of many NFPs that make them appear very similar to firms (for example, many firms and NFPs have bureaucratic structures) so the reader will be able to relate a lot of the earlier material to the strategic management of NFPs.

We shall now turn to our exploration of theories of the firm's objectives, beginning with an economics perspective.

2.4 Profit maximisation

Economists, since the rise of microeconomics in the late nineteeth Century, have considered the firm to be their special area of interest. The reader may well be familiar with the elegant and elaborate structures of cost and revenue functions to be found in the introductory economics texts.

The neoclassical theory of the firm is centred on the assumption that the entrepreneur brings together the 'factors of production ' (land, labour and capital) with a view to making and selling something which the sovereign consumer wants to buy; and, as a reward for his efforts, after the other factors have received their returns, the entrepreneur might make a profit. The firm will be managed so as to 'maximise' these profits – that is, decisions about what to make, in what proportions men and machines should be combined, what price to charge, are made with this objective in mind.

This view of the firm has served economists well for many years, but it has not been without criticism:

(a) How can the entrepreneur 'maximise profits' when he cannot predict the outcome of his decisions? Moreover, no one person or group of people is smart enough to consider all the alternatives available, before selecting the maximising strategy.
(b) Will he seek to maximise profits regardless of risk?
(c) The owner-controlled firm describes only a very small portion of economic activity (and one which is probably shrinking).

In addition to these difficulties, there have been other criticisms of the wider theory based on the assumption of profit maximisation because the theory really only applies to single-product firms, and, second, firms do not have information about cost-curves and, more critically, revenue (demand) schedules upon which to base decisions.

More pragmatic economists would counter these criticisms by pointing out that the predictions based on the theory compare reasonably well with the way firms actually behave. They might also suggest that in the light of the role of the firm in society as a whole (that is, the free-enterprise, or capitalist economy) the pursuit of profit in competition with others ensures economic efficiency: so not only *do* firms effectively aim to maximise profits, they *should* do so for the benefit of society.

2.5 Managerial theories

Berle and Means' empirical investigation into the ownership and control of US business resulted in a need to reconsider the entrepreneurial view of the firm (see Wildsmith 1973 for a full treatment of this, and other managerial theories). They discovered that, for many corporations in the US, the people who owned the firm were different from those who managed it (the shares often being dispersed among a large number of passive stockholders, whilst the day-to-day decisions about the firm were being made by hired managers, usually non-stockholding).

This finding raised the question as to whether we could expect these hired managers to behave as if they owned the firm, or might they make decisions based on their own personal interests? However, we cannot rule out the fact that, either through coercion (threat of dismissal by the shareholders' representatives, the board) or through loyalty (and, possibly, the internalisation of the shareholders' interests into the way the manager sees his job) the manager may behave as if he owned the firm, thereby leaving most of the theory intact.

Nevertheless, this divorce of ownership from control creates a situation whereby the firm may be managed in a way which might not be wholly in the interests of the shareholders (see Illustration 2.2). Economists have responded to this problem by putting forward developments and refinements to the profit-maximising model. We will briefly consider four of these, revenue maximisation, managerial discretion, growth theory and managerial utility.

Revenue maximisation

The basic Baumol model is a fairly straightforward development of the profit-maximising model, and assumes that managers seek to maximise

ILLUSTRATION 2.2 On the Power of Shareholders: Dunlop

Almost half of Dunlop's equity is now in the hands of (mostly small) British shareholders. A revitalised Dunlop Shareholders Association gave Sir Michael Edwardes a lecture in director's accountability. The group urged the board to consult shareholders and employees, rather than present a non-negotiable rescue plan to the shareholders at the special meeting to be held to approve a capital restructuring of the company. Existing shareholders may salvage next to nothing from the wreckage.

The same cannot be said of some of Dunlop's former directors, who walked away with hundreds of thousands of pounds in goodbye cash. And Dunlop's new directors may have strong conflicts of interest. Put in by the banks but responsible to the shareholders, whose interests will they protect?

Directors in essence write their own contracts, fix their own salaries and at worst leave no poorer when a company fails. In theory, shareholders can butt in. But annual reports often appear barely a month before a company's annual general meeting; resolutions must be put in writing to the company at least 21 days in advance; and at least 10 per cent of thousands of shareholders must agree to it.

(Source: *The Economist*, 24 November 1984)

sales subject to a minimum-profit constraint. Profit-maximisation is seen as a poor explanation of the firm's behaviour, especially in oligopolistic industries. Scale of operations (that is, the size of sales revenue) increases the magnitude of profits which can be used to finance expansion (even though the return on capital may be unremarkable). Size also confers benefits on the management, such as bigger salaries, more prestige and status. Shareholders are rewarded with a level of dividend and reinvestment which they would consider 'satisfactory'.

Managerial discretion

O. E. Williamson's approach introduces a much stronger flavour of organisation theory than does the Baumol model. He postulates that management is interested in pursuing the following:

1. Salary
2. Security
3. Status
4. Power
5. Prestige
6. Professional excellence

(Items 2–6: Non-pecuniary goals)

The concept of 'expense preference' is used to describe the process whereby the non-pecuniary goals are achieved. Hence, the classical economists' assumption of cost-minimisation is abandoned.

(a) *Staff expenditure* contributes to the attainment of power, status, prestige and, as size is often related to security, and staff expansion, these objectives are also met.
(b) *Emoluments* These are rewards in terms of salary, but more usually in the form of cars, expense accounts, interest-free loans, etc., which the management are able to grant themselves. The non-salary perquisites have the advantage of being less visible to other members of the firm, the shareholders and the tax authorities.
(c) *Discretionary profit* In contrast to Baumol, the managers may pursue profits in excess of the minimum level acceptable to shareholders. This is because higher profits mean that more staff and emoluments can be obtained; and there is a certain satisfaction and achievement to be gained through managing a firm that has a favourable profit performance.

One interesting development of this model concerns the *structuring of organizations*. The ownership and control problem is exacerbated in large, functionally-specialised firms. Here the risks of functional managers pursuing their own, functionally-related interests are maximised. However, the trend in very large firms towards multidivisional structures, with each division being operated as a profit centre (the 'holding company' structure) may mean that the management will be forced into pursuing more or less profit maximising behaviour (see Chapter 11). So, paradoxically, the concentration of *capital* (rather than concentration within a particular industry) may be leading, through developments in organizational structures, towards a return to behaviour akin to the firm in a perfectly competitive market.

This could lead to the development of the model depicted in Figure 2.1. There is some empirical support for the managerial models presented here. Pondy (1969) in a survey of forty-five manufacturing firms,

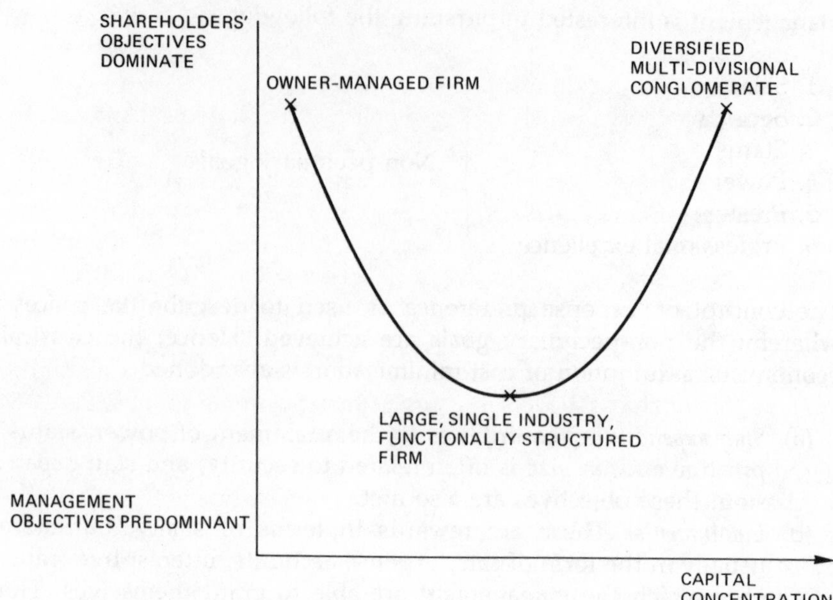

FIGURE 2.1 Objectives and capital concentration

discovered that the ratio of administrative to operating personnel increased as ownership was more divorced from management. And Wolf (quoted in Mintzberg (1983) p. 125) surveyed ten firms, with stated goals of improving profitability, that had changed their chief executives (CEOs). Five firms brought in outsiders, the other five promoted internally. All those organisations who recruited externally achieved increased profitability, which was correlated with decreased selling, general and administrative expenses. Only one of the firms that promoted internally showed profit improvement, which was not, however, linked with decreased administrative expenses.

Growth theory

Galbraith (1967) has suggested that, whereas the expansion of industry in the eighteenth and nineteenth centuries resulted in a power shift from land-owners to capitalists, the increasing rates of development in 'technology' (broadly defined) in the latter half of this century have resulted in a shift of power from owners of capital to the 'technostructure' (the management élite). Capital is no longer in scarce supply for the well-run, large organisation.

The technostructure has three objectives:

1. to make sufficient profit to secure the independent life of the organisation;
2. to achieve the maximum rate of growth;
3. to produce things which are challenging to technological ingenuity.

The technostructure designs new products, establishes levels of production and then influences the consumers to buy the products. It may also have scant regard for the wider interests of society, with regard to pollution, congestion etc. (See 2.7 'Social responsibility').

Galbraith's idea of 'countervailing power' suggests that organisations must grow large in order that they can stand up to other groups and organisations that are also increasing in size and power (Galbraith, 1967). So 'big business' begets 'big government' and big unions. Perrow (1970) observes that 'as the pond grows bigger, so does the size of the frog', so the individual manager benefits from the growth of his employing organisation. And Katz and Kahn (1966) see growth as a means of solving some awkward management problems. For example, one department may perceive itself to be disadvantaged relative to another in terms of status and promotions: it is much easier to solve this problem by *adding* resources to the disadvantaged group than by subtracting them from the privileged group.

Marx also sees the need to grow, to 'accumulate' capital, as being an inherent tendency in the capitalist system. Accumulation is a defensive strategy pursued by the capitalist so as to preserve the value of his initial investment in the face of competition and technological change. This concept is linked with the existence of economies of scale in many industries, where a downward-sloping long-run average-cost curve means that the firm that reaches the high capacity/low unit cost-point first can squeeze its rivals out of the market by undercutting their prices.

Managerial utility

Following on from the divorce of ownership from control, R. L. Marris (1964) raises the question as to the ability of the shareholder to exert influence over the management. If the chances of forcing the management to adopt different policies are slim, the best policy is to 'vote with the feet' and sell your shares to a 'raider' who is aiming to own a substantial proportion of the shares (sufficient to enable the raider to change management). So, we might expect the present management group, who should be aware of this possibility, to pursue policies which would discourage takeovers by raiders (see Illustration 2.3). Therefore the firm should be managed sufficiently well to suggest to outsiders that there are no obvious, simple and cheap ways to improve performance

ILLUSTRATION 2.3 On Vulnerability to Takeover

(1) THE DIXONS BID FOR CURRYS

Mr Kalms, Chairman of Dixons: 'Curry's business is not performing anywhere near adequately. We believe we can make dramatic improvement'.

Financial Times: 'The failure of Currys' business-computers operation lends substance to the change that tough markets have exposed strategic shortcomings; the parallel development of several retailing ideas at once within the group does not suggest a strong case of immediate direction'.

Mr Terry Curry, joint MD of Currys: 'Recent market research shows customers think we are more up-to-date than Dixons. Their offer is totally inadequate'.

(Source: *Financial Times*, 5 October 1984)

(2) REED INTERNATIONAL AND MIRROR GROUP NEWSPAPERS

The ruthless manner in which Reed plans to float MGN next year will leave MGN vulnerable to a wave of stock-market raids on its shares – and to the attentions of unwelcome predators. Once the shares are floated a predator could buy 29.9 per cent before having to make a full public takeover bid. MGN's only defence would be its recent profits performance and its board's plans for the future to keep the MGN share price too high to make it worth a bidder's while to enter the fray.

But there are benefits through not being tied to a large conglomerate: MGN chief executive Douglas Long: 'If we are on our own we are much more liable to be entrepreneurial than in a large corporation. We will not be restricted by the need for business plans and cash-flow projections, and we won't have to get through a huge layer cake full of accountants to get approval for new ideas, in a situation where you are competing for money with paint factories'.

(Source: *Sunday Times*, 16 October 1983)

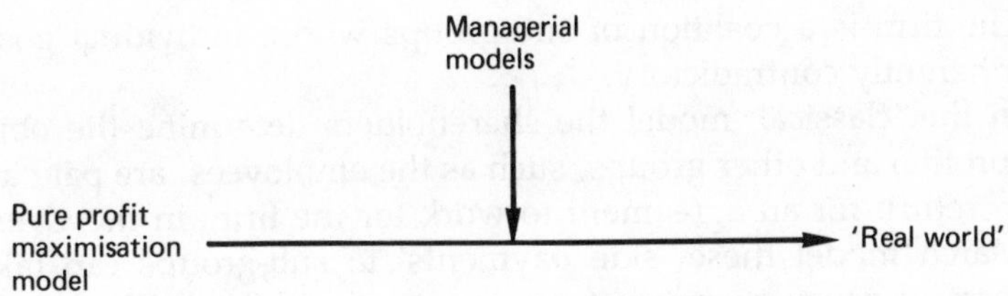

FIGURE 2.2 The objectives continuum

markedly. The stock-market valuation should reflect the real value of the firm, so as to discourage take-overs.

In addition to the concern for security from take-over, Marris includes power, prestige, salary and stock market approval as components in the managerial utility function.

2.6 Coalitions and Stakeholders

We can view the theories of the 'managerial economists' as attempts to move away from the pure profit maximising model towards an incorporation of empirical reality that begun with the Berle and Means study. (See Figure 2.2). However, the terminology, orientation and algebraic style adopted by these models is clearly descended from the neoclassical economists' tradition. So these models retain a strong economics perspective which, it could be argued, results in an exclusion of rich varieties of concepts that have been developed in other disciplines (such as sociology, social psychology, systems theory). We would argue that economists have been guilty of treating the firm and its internal workings as a 'black box', which is defensible up to a point given the 'scientific method' adopted by the discipline: that is, moving from fundamental principles towards adaptions and elaborations which cope with real-world complexities. The managerial models have succeeded in inching up the lid of the black box and as such they should be regarded as a step in the right direction.

Cyert and March's 'Behavioural Theory of the Firm' (1963) was, in a sense, freed from many of the constraints imposed by the economist's perspective. Here we have a well-developed, sophisticated model of the firm which tackles the 'human dimension' explicitly, in contrast to the rational consumer/entrepreneur/rentier, etc., of neoclassical economics. The crucial elements of the theory are:

1. The firm is a coalition of sub-groups whose individual goals are inherently contradictory.
2. In the 'classical' model the shareholders determine the objective (profits) and other groups, such as the employees, are paid a wage in return for an agreement to work for the firm; in the Cyert and March model these 'side payments' to sub-groups can take the form of *policy commitments*, not just wages. So, in the process of bargaining over side payments many of the firm's goals are determined.
3. Some of these objectives are stated in the form of aspiration-level constraints, rather than maximising constraints. (Satisficing).
4. Conflicting objectives can be dealt with by the organization dealing with each in turn (sequential attention to goals).
5. Problems lead to search behaviour aimed at finding the simple, least painful solutions first (and, if none exist, more complex solutions will be explored).
6. 'Organisational slack' is a reserve of 'fat' in the organisation that comes about through an imperfect matching (in an upward direction) between the *minimum* necessary level of resources required to maintain the coalition (deployed as inducements to sub-groups) and the *actual* level absorbed by sub-groups. Slack permits a degree of stability to obtain in the organisation during fluctuations in the environment.

The coalition concept certainly has its attractions. The picture of a rather messy process of bargaining, policy compromises and the need to tackle goals sequentially (rather than expecting some synthesis of conflicting goals to emerge) probably relates more to the reader's experience than the single-minded, all-knowing, efficient, maximising corporate person which may be conjured up in the pure economics model.

This behavioural model has been extended into an almost normative theory of the firm. We might now view the firm as consisting of different societal groupings who agree to work together to satisfy their separate interests. These stakeholders get their just rewards in a variety of forms:

Stakeholder	*Rewards*
Employees	Wages, job satisfaction, etc.
Society at large	No pollution, 'good works'
Government	Tax and rate income to enable them to do 'good works'
Managers	Salaries, status, responsibility, challenge, perks, etc.

Consumers	Useful, desirable products
Shareholders	Dividends, capital growth
Loan financiers	Interest

Therefore, as long as every stakeholder group is satisfied with the relationship between its contribution to the firm's effort and its rewards, the stakeholder coalition carries out its social and economic purpose.

This view of the firm has developed alongside the 'human relations' movement in management thinking. If we see the employee as having 'needs' which can to an extent be satisfied at work (typified by the writings of Maslow, Herzberg, Argyris, etc.) through the enlightened redesigning of jobs, organisation structures and management styles, the employee is satisfied and the firm's objectives are satisfied. The employee achieves self-actualisation through applying his effort and talent at work; the shareholders concurrently achieve their objective of profit. The other important strand in this 'consensus' perspective is the notion of *social responsibility*.

2.7 Social responsibility

The issue of some form of corporate social responsibility emerged strongly in the early 1960s and probably reached its peak in the early 1970s. In essence the concept is that the firm has a duty to conduct itself in the interests of society as a whole. This has been variously interpreted as: concern about employee safety, employment of ethnic minorities/disabled people, positive discrimination in favour of women, making and selling safe products, avoiding pollution, giving to charities, etc. (see Illustration 2.4).

Galbraith argues that the large corporation (which bears so little resemblance to the tiny firm, buffeted by the actions of cut-throat competitors and the fickle demands of the consumer idealised by some proponents of the market system) has enormous power which can be exercised in the interests of the ruling managerial oligarchy, the shareholders, consumers and the wider society. Indeed it is possible to argue that only the large oligopolistic or monopolistic corporations are in the comfortable position of being able to decide to behave in a manner other than the basic struggle for survival experienced by small firms in competitive industries.

However, there is evidence that the concern for socially responsible behaviour is no longer such an issue in the minds of corporate executives in the 1980s. Managers can look to champions of freedom like

ILLUSTRATION 2.4 On Stated Objectives

UNITED BISCUITS

Extracts from Chairman's Statement (1977):

1. **Return on Capital Employed**
   Objectives: To make a profit, before interest and tax, of not less than 20 per cent of capital employed, with a target of 25 per cent on an historical cost basis. Capital employed is defined as the total of shareholders' funds plus long- and short-term borrowings.
2. **Sales and Profits**
   Objectives: At least to maintain the increase in profits in line with the increase in sales, i.e., to maintain net profit margins.
3. **Capital Expenditure**
   Objective: To maintain the quality of existing assets by investing not less than 5p per £ sales annually and to make new investments at rates of return applicable to the risk involved to meet the Group's targeted return on capital employed.
4. **Dividends**
   Objective: That the return to shareholders should grow in line with the growth in net profit.

These objectives are designed to give security of employment and the highest possible standard of living to our employees, the best possible value for money to the consumer, and consistently reward the investor at a level which fully recognises the element of risk, while ensuring that the business remains internationally competitive.

INDIAN HEAD MILLS

Extract from the CEO's policy manual:

The company is *not* in business to grow bigger for the sake of size, nor to become more diversified, nor to make the most or best of anything, nor to provide jobs, have the most modern plants, the happiest customers, lead in new product development, or to achieve any other status which has no relationship to the economic use of capital.

> Any or all of these may be, from time to time, a means to our objective, but means and ends must never be confused. Indian **Head Mills** is in business solely to improve the inherent value of the common stockholders' equity in the company.
>
> (Quoted in Mintzberg's, 'Power In and Around Organizations', p. 280)
>
> WANG LABORATORIES
>
> **Dr An Wang**: 'I am there to impart the philosophy I value, to serve a useful purpose to society at large and to make sure that the people we serve – stockholders, employees and customers, get a fair return'.
>
> (Source: *Sunday Times*, 17 October 1982).

Milton Friedman to provide arguments as to why the most socially responsible action the corporation can do is to work flat out in the interests of its shareholders. 'Socially responsible' actions can still play a part as a public relations device, to improve the corporate image, but it is possible to imagine a collective sigh of relief emanating from boardrooms across the nation freed from the need to develop arguments, evidence and excuses about the less obviously 'social' aspects of their 'legitimate' business pursuits.

We might suggest that the concern for 'social responsibility' varies directly with the stages of the business cycle, in so far as it is perceived as a luxury born out of the good times with which firms need not concern themselves in a recession. (The influence of pressure groups and societal norms is considered further in Chapter 13 on Power).

2.8 Single or multiple objectives?

One of the problems raised by the stakeholder theory is how the management cope with the multiple objectives of the different stakeholders groups. We have mentioned one way out; the sequential attention to goals suggested by Cyert and March. It would appear to be an enormously difficult management task to make decisions about the firm's activities even within this piecemeal approach unless an implicit goal hierarchy is being operated. For example, let us assume our employees are concerned to increase their wages; let us further assume that management decide to meet these aspirations. There is obviously some implicit limit on the increase they would be prepared to grant and, we would suggest, that limit is strongly related to the requirement to make some level of profits. The same would apply to claims by other stakeholders, which, if they were met, may impinge upon the firm's ability to show a profit. Furthermore, we could envisage circumstances where some stakeholders may be very unhappy at their reward level:

(a) A monopoly supplier may be providing a deteriorating service to consumers.
(b) A monopsonist employer who may be able to enforce changes in the working conditions and remuneration to the disadvantage of employees.
(c) A government which may be distressed about the large corporation's environmental impact (pollution, destruction of natural resources) but may be unable to influence the firm because of a dependence on the corporation for various reasons (providing employment, foreign currency, etc.).

The 'floor' below which these stakeholders would refuse to co-operate may be very low, in other words, they may well have to tolerate a considerable worsening of their position. Their relatively weak bargaining position stems from their *dependence* on the firm (see Chapter 13).

We would argue, however, that for the suppliers of capital the tolerance of worsening conditions is considerably less. These stakeholders rarely find themselves in positions where there is little or no alternative outlet for the employment of their contribution. For example, their capital could be invested in another company, in government securities or sent abroad. Hence, the prudently managed coalition would be advised to place the supplier of capital at the top of any hierarchy of stakeholders' interests they may choose to construct.

There is another aspect to the 'multiple objectives' problem which does not necessarily result from the stakeholder view of the firm, which could be described as the 'means–ends' confusion. Problems arise in strategic decision-making even if the management group agree about the need for profits. At the beginning of a strategy-formulation process some planning teams may include objectives like the following:

(a) To expand our market share in the UK
(b) To maintain our leadership in the field of extrusion technology
(c) To improve the quality image of the company.

The difficulties which face this strategy-making group in the future are likely to be:

1. *Generating alternative strategies* What happens if the internal and external appraisals suggest that the firm should concentrate on foreign markets (a); or get out of extruded tubes as quick as possible (b); or that the competitive advantage held by the firm is in selling cheap and cheerful products (c)?
2. *Evaluating alternative strategies* What if strategy X meets the profit target but not, say, objective (a) above? Do the team reject it?

The management group which expands the objective statement must necessarily constrain the consideration of alternative strategies. The problem is essentially one of confusing means and ends. If the management group adopt some profit target as the key objective, then (a) to (c) above should be viewed as *strategic alternatives*, as different ways of meeting the profit target.

As an example of the means/end problem, consider the case of a company set up at the end of the last century to transport sea shells from the South Seas to be sold in England. How large would this firm be today if its objective had been the transporting of sea shells rather than the making of profits? Well, the sea-shells market has seen better days and we would justifiably expect this company to be struggling, if not to be out of business by now. In fact, today it is one of the largest companies in the world, and the only link it has retained with its original line of business is its name: Shell.

2.9 Some other issues

1. Short or long term?

Clearly, the time-scale over which profitability is to be viewed will alter the strategic decisions made by the management. They may decide to interpret the wishes of shareholders as being to secure long- or short-term profitability. This may result in the adoption of various strategies:

(a) opting for a short-time potentially highly profitable investment against a less spectacular longer-term prospect;
(b) conceding a high short-term gain resulting from an increase in specialisation for a more flexible posture yielding longer-term results;
(c) the firm may engage in a strategy of increasing market share (by, say, price-cutting) with the longer-term view of establishing a quasi-monopoly supply position.

2. Profits and risk

Risk will be explored in greater depth in Chapter 7 on Financial Strategies. Suffice it to say in this context that the risk – return relationship is a crucial aspect of objective setting. If the management group wish to act in the interests of the owners of the firm then they should attempt to ascertain their risk – return preferences. Clearly shareholders with a balanced portfolio of investments may require a firm's management to eschew low-risk, secure strategies in favour of high risk/potentially high return ventures. In these circumstances, the individual manager's 'survival' objective clashes somewhat with the shareholders' wishes.

3. Survival

Argenti would disagree with survival as the objective of the firm, inasmuch as no firm (or any organisation) exists merely to exist. Although, it is clear that *short-term* conditions and considerations (that is, times of crisis) may result in management adopting policies which seem to have abandoned the pursuit of profits in favour of mere survival, the longer-term objective must still be profit-orientated (despite the wishes of the management). So, the survival objective is related to a shorter time-horizon, as it is clear that if the firm cannot survive in the short term it certainly cannot provide profits in the longer term.

4. The firm as a hobby

There are cases where owners may sacrifice profitability (or, more realistically, higher achievable levels of profit then the firm currently realises) for a variety of reasons:

(a) they wish to remain in sole charge of the firm, so they discourage take-over bids by another firm who could increase the return on the owner's capital (the 'independence' argument);
(b) the firm provides other, non-profit, rewards (it is fun, a hobby, provides status, power, etc.).

Mintzberg (1983, p. 278) has dealt with this problem by distinguishing between *mission*, the organisation's basic function in the eyes of the world at large, and the organisation's *goal*, which is determined by its controlling influencers. So a chain of retail furniture outlets would have a mission of retailing furniture to the locality, whereas its goal may well be the pursuit of profits. In contrast, consider an owner of a small antique shop dealing primarily in furniture. Here the owner is more interested in the pleasure of handling exquisite furniture and socialising with favourite customers then in making money. Here the organisation's *mission* (to retail antique furniture) is also its *goal*.

5. Return on capital employed or return on shareholders capital?

Should the management seek to achieve a target level of return on total capital employed in the firm, or on the shareholders' proportion only? We can envisage a situation where, through loan-funded expansion the amount of profit and the ROCE were increased dramatically. But this expansion may not benefit the shareholders. Much of the profit may go to paying interest on the loans, and the massive increase in gearing may well put the shareholders' capital at greater risk.

On the other hand, such an expansion may result in a smaller overall ROCE but a dramatically increased ROSC. Clearly, the choice of performance indicator will affect the thrust of strategic thinking.

2.10 Conclusion

We believe all firms have to make profits in order to survive. Firms do not, however, 'profit-maximise' in the classical economic sense. The separation of ownership from control weakens the shareholders' influence over the firm's management, thus permitting a situation in which managerial objectives can be pursued. Managerial objectives *dominate* the profit goal only in exceptional circumstances (such as a survival crisis). At all other times the need for *some* level of profit is the intention behind many strategic and operating decisions.

Figure 2.3 describes the feasible space of the firm's objectives, between points *A* and *B*. Note that pure profit-maximisation is not feasible, neither is a circumstance where profit is not an enduring consideration in decision-making. We believe that the firm resembles most closely Minztberg's 'Dominant Influencer' goal model, where a powerful group (the owners) are able to influence explicitly or implicitly the members of the organisation, to the extent that the shareholders' interests are taken into consideration in most strategic decisions. However, the relatively straightforward picture of objectives represented in Figure 2.3 will be complicated by arguments developed in the second half of the book. An exploration of social and psychological influences on decision-makers, internal power relationships and the effects of the structure of the firm on decision processes will help to develop an increasingly sophisticated understanding of objectives and strategic management (see especially Chapters 11, 12, 13 and 14).

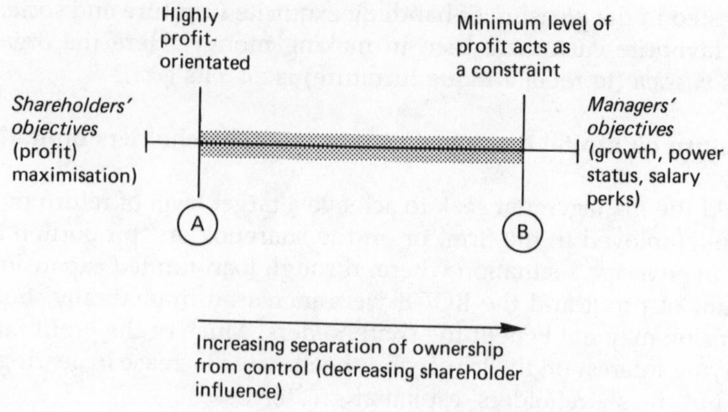

FIGURE 2.3 The firm's objectives

2.11 Summary

1. The concept of 'organisational goal' was briefly explored. Where consistency in a stream of decisions is discernible, we can infer that there is *intention* behind the decisions.
2. Not-for-profit organisations have fundamentally different objectives from firms. As such they require separate treatment with regard to strategic management.
3. The profit-maximising model has serious shortcomings when trying to explain strategic decision making in practice.
4. The divorce of ownership from control opens up possibilities for management objectives (rather than shareholder objectives) to be pursued.
5. A 'coalition' views moves us away from the rational, maximising economics perspectives on the firm. Satisficing, sequential attention to conflicting goals and organisational slack, are important features of this approach.
6. 'Social responsibility' may be a feature of (a) corporate monopoly power, and (b) boom and growth conditions in the macroeconomy, rather than a result of genuine concern on behalf of senior executives.
7. A stakeholder view of the firm poses problems with regard to hierarchies of objectives, and there are problems in confusing *means* with *ends*.

8. In conclusion, firms have to make *some* level of profit in order to exist; they do not *maximise* profits, and in some circumstances arising from weak shareholder influence, managerial goals will be important in strategic decision-making.

Further Reading

Wildsmith (1973) provides a tightly written exploration of the managerial developments of the profit maximising model. Mintzberg (1983) is number three in a planned series of texts on the theory of management policy. This is a remarkably interesting book; Part III, Chapters 15 and 16, are specifically concerned with goals.

References

Argenti, J. (1980) *Practical Corporate Planning* (London: Allen & Unwin).
Cyert, R. M. and March, J. G. (1963) *A Behavioural Theory of the Firm* (Englewood Cliffs, New Jersey: Prentice-Hall).
Galbraith, J. K. (1967) *The New Industrial State* (London: Hamish Hamilton).
Katz, D. and Kahn, R. C. (1966) *The Social Psychology of Organizations* (Chichester: Wiley) p. 101.
Mintzberg, H. (1983) *Power In and Around Organizations* (Englewood Cliffs, New Jersey: Prentice-Hall) pp. 246–7.
Marris, R. L. (1964) *The Economic Theory of Managerial Capitalism* (London: Hamish Hamilton).
Perrow, C. (1970) *Organizational Analysis: A Sociological View* (New York: Wadsworth).
Pondy, L. R. (1969) 'Effects of Size, Complexity and Ownership on Administrative Intensity', *Administrative Science Quarterly*.
Wildsmith, J. R. (1973) *Managerial Theories of the Firm* (Oxford: Martin Robertson).

CHAPTER 3

Strategy formulation

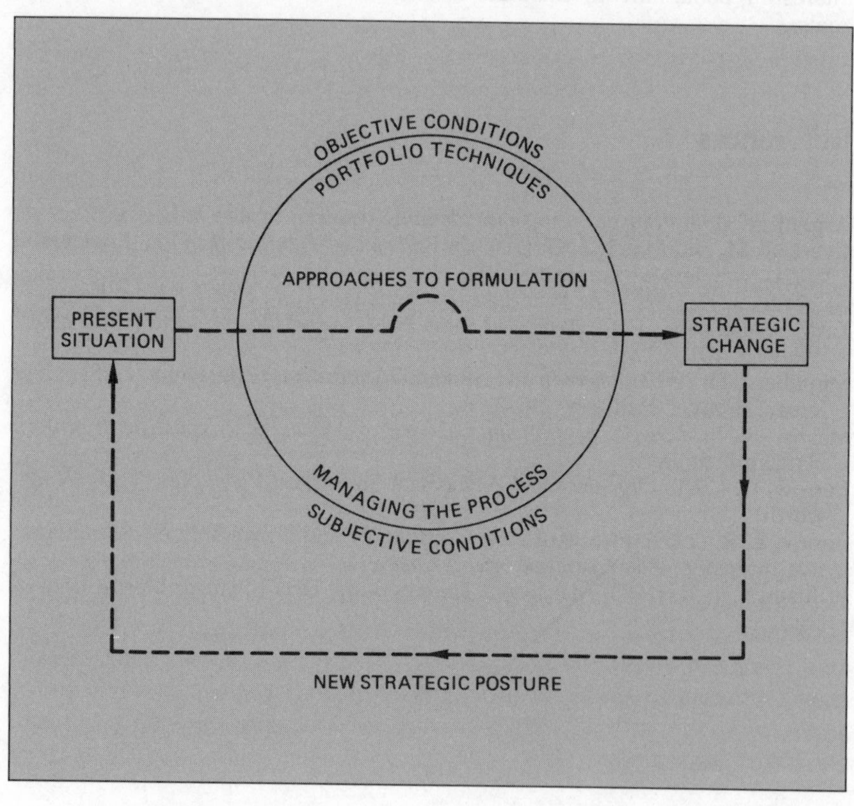

3.1 Introduction

The objectives of the organisation discussed in the preceding chapter provide an overall framework in which the formulation of a firm's strategy can be developed. In this chapter we define corporate and business level strategy, discuss approaches to strategy-formulation, review the use of models and visual representations as an aid to formulation and consider horizontal strategy. We conclude by briefly considering the management of the formulation process.

Any debate concerning strategy-formulation presupposes two fundamental issues: first, that those involved in the process, whether the process is formal and systematic, or informal and incremental, will make rational decisions. So it is necessary initially to define our use of the term rational as it applies to policy issues. Second, consideration should be given to the problem of determining whether or not a firm's involvement in evaluating strategic issues in the broadest sense is of benefit to it.

Rationality is a key concept in decision-making. Indeed a common argument is that strategic choice is and should be an entirely rational matter, where those involved weigh the objective economic evidence in a decision and make a logical choice. But as Donaldson and Lorsch (1983) argue 'strategic decisions are not the product of simple economic logic alone . . . they involve considerable uncertainty and ambiguity. To analyse these complexities top managers draw upon their experience and judgement . . . Thus to some extent their decisions always reflect non-rational considerations'. However, this situation can be reconciled by recognising that rationality has two aspects, qualitative and quantitative. A qualitatively rational decision represents an appropriate choice of alternatives for the end that is sought. Regan (1978) argues 'rationality is not therefore a separate autonomous quality, it is entirely relative to the end sought'. He also stresses that rationality is morally neutral. Qualitative rationality may also involve conflicts; for example, between subjective and objective rationality, and between personal and organisational rationality. Such conflicts arise out of problems of information and/or from goal divergence as may be the situation in personal versus organisational conflict.

Quantitative rationality is concerned with analysing what is a more as opposed to a less rational decision, which ideally concludes with perfect rationality so essentially seeking efficiency in decision-making. It is possible to argue that planning is essentially a member of the fraternity of quantitative rationality. The whole concept is, however, subject to criticism from L. E. Lindblom and the proponents of extra-rationality represented by de Bono and Dror. So we can conclude that rationality is not a concept that can be taken for granted. Problems of information, goal divergence and the psychology of the decision-maker may all lead to 'non-rational' decisions.

The variety of issues relating to the quality of decision-making in organisations are dealt later in the book, so for the remainder of this chapter, and Chapters 4–9 we will assume that the tools and techniques presented assist the firm in making better strategic decisions.

The second point which we will now consider is whether or not an evaluation of strategy benefits the organisation. It should be made clear at the outset that it is the quality of the organisation's strategy that will determine its performance and not the processes by which the strategy is formulated. Hofer and Schendel (1978, p. 11) conclude that there is evidence to suggest that the use of formal approaches to strategy-formulation is associated with superior organisational performance, especially for manufacturing companies, but with some reservations. Sutton (1983) has comprehensively reviewed the literature and concludes that:

> planning has generally led to an improvement in performance as has the pursuit of market share. Diversification need not be profitable, although it may be in closely related activities; and while mergers do not generally improve efficiency or benefit the shareholders or acquisitive firms, there may well be gains for the managers of an acquiring firm and for the shareholders of their victim.

However, Sutton's survey also identified a number of reservations concerning these conclusions. We believe that organisations which adopt some degree of formalisation, systematic analysis and structuring in the strategy-formulation process will tend to perform better than those who do not, whilst acknowledging the problems inherent in measuring such performance differences.

3.2 Corporate and business strategy definitions

Strategy can be broadly defined as the match an organisation makes between its own resources and the threats or risks and opportunities created by the external environment in which it operates. So strategy can be seen as a key link between what the organisation wants to achieve – its objectives – and the policies adopted to guide its activities. In a wide-ranging review of definitions of strategy, Hofer and Schendel (1978, pp. 16–20) conclude that disagreements over a definition hinge

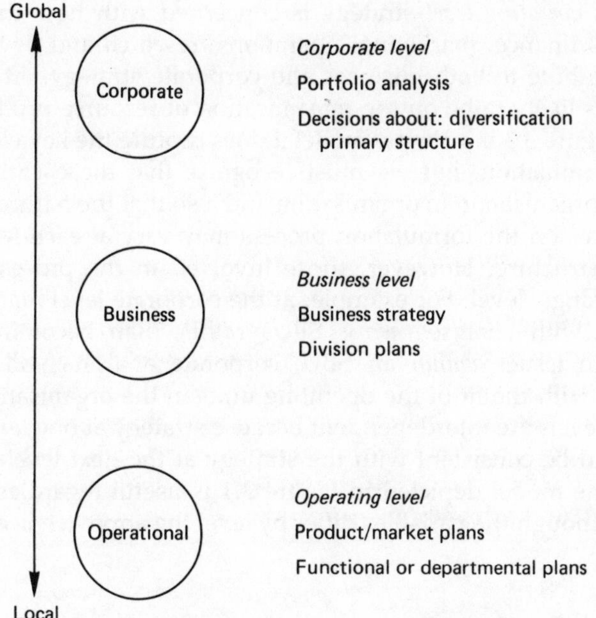

FIGURE 3.1 Levels of strategy

primarily on whether strategy should be defined broadly or narrowly, that is, whether it includes both ends and means, or ends only.

We need to recognise that an organisation can have a single strategy or many strategies, and that strategies are likely to exist at a number of levels in an organisation. Figure 3.1 illustrates the different levels of strategy formulation and the way they may vary on a global–local continuum.

Corporate strategy is concerned with the type of businesses the firm, as a whole, is in or should be in. It addresses such issues as the balance in the organisation's portfolio by directing attention to questions like the attractiveness of entire businesses, with reference to important strategic criteria, such as markets, contribution to corporate profits and growth in a particular industry. Questions concerning diversification and the structure of the firm as a whole are corporate issues.

Business strategy is concerned with how an operating unit within the corporate whole can compete in a particular market. Strategic business units (SBUs) are created at corporate level, and can be subsumed under it. The strategies of SBUs can be regarded as the parts which require and define the organisational whole.

A firm's *operating level* strategy is concerned with how the various functions – finance, marketing, operations, research and development etc. – contribute to both business and corporate strategy. At this level the focus is likely to be on the maximisation of resource productivity.

While Figure 3.1 is a simple model it does capture the key elements in strategy-formulation, but we must recognise that these variables will vary from organisation to organisation and also that the nature and type of influences on the formulation process may vary at each level in the three-tier structure. However, those involved in the process tend to focus at a single level. For example, at the corporate level managers are concerned with analyses *across* SBUs rather than becoming deeply involved in issues *within* an SBU; corporate analysts will be more concerned with the fit of the operating units in the organisation. Obviously the levels are interdependent because strategy at one level should include and be consistent with the strategy at the next level down. In addition the model depicted in Figure 3.1 is useful regardless of level because although the variables differ by level the approach is essentially the same.

3.3 Approaches to strategy formulation

Strategy-formulation can be viewed as a decision-making process which is primarily concerned with: the development of the organisation's objectives; the commitment of its resources; and environmental constraints; so as to achieve its objectives. This process has several elements that are depicted in Figure 3.2. The components in the model can be distinguished in that the first set of elements is concerned with the *identification* of a number of strategic options, while the second group deals with the *selection* of a preferred strategy or strategies.

The model is an attempt to organise and structure the formulation process, and develops our earlier construct in Chapter 1. It is not intended to give a comprehensive view of the complexity of the strategy-making process. Whilst it concentrates on the analysis of objective elements it also incorporates the key-role of values in the formulation process.

Before we discuss the model in 3.2 in any more depth the reader should be aware that there are other formulation models which have been developed (for example, Ansoff (1965), Hofer (1977)). Generally these models differ from Figure 3.2 in the more detailed nature of their construction, and the complexity with which steps in the process are considered. However, although it could be argued that we have over-

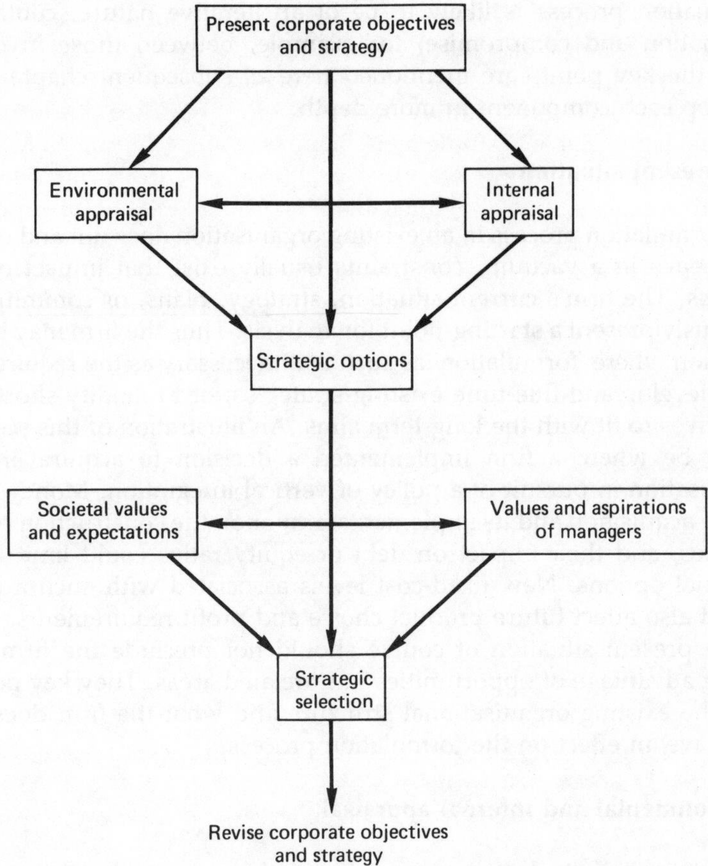

FIGURE 3.2 Strategy-formulation model

simplified the process, we believe that our model, when linked with the subsequent chapters, covers much the same ground without over-emphasising the process by which this is achieved. We also believe that those wishing to explore strategy-formulation concepts are able to build complexity into Figure 3.2 without being constrained by an over-prescriptive 'solution'.

We will now turn our attention to a brief examination of the components in the formulation model. Although each is dealt with individually, as Figure 3.2 reveals, they are interconnected. Also, while we will discuss the elements in a sequential manner, this is not to indicate that this represents the way in which the process might work in practice. Because of the interrelationship between the elements the strategy-formulation process is likely to be of an iterative nature, containing negotiation and compromise, for example, between those involved. Only the key points are mentioned here as subsequent chapters will develop each component in more depth.

The present situation

The formulation process in an existing organisation does not and cannot commence in a vacuum, constraints usually exist that impact on the process. The firm's current situation, strategy, plans, or commitments obviously present a starting-point for analysis. Thus the firm may be in a situation where 'formulation' as such is unnecessary as the requirement is to develop and fine-tune existing strategies, or to modify short-term objectives to fit with the long-term aims. An illustration of this scenario might be where a firm implemented a decision to acquire another organisation in pursuit of a policy of vertical integration. Money spent on the acquisition and its implementation, or on the construction of new facilities, and their impact on debt or equity ratios could limit future financial options. New fixed-cost levels associated with such a policy would also affect future product choice and profit requirements.

The present situation of course should not preclude the firm from taking advantage of opportunities in unrelated areas. They key point is that the existing organisational structure and what the firm does well will have an effect on the formulation process.

Environmental and internal appraisal

A firm can be viewed as an open system with respect to the environment in which it operates. It is involved in a continuous process of exchange with external parties – suppliers, customers, employees, government bodies – to obtain the necessary inputs and to disperse its output. So it competes with the other organisations for these resources. As such the environment represents a source of both opportunities and threats. Environmental appraisal is a central element in formulating strategy.

Additional analysis is required to identify strategic options, involving an appraisal of the organisation's own resources with the objective of identifying the firm's strengths and weaknesses. Such analysis will reveal the capability of the firm to counter external threats and to take advantage of presenting opportunities. An important feature of this process concerns the identification of 'distinctive competencies', that is, those things at which the organisation is particularly good in relation to its competitors.

Strategic options

The generation of strategic options is not a random process but may be stimulated, for example, by a shortfall in current performance and the level of performance expected by key decision-makers. It is also more complex than merely seeking to fit a range of variables affecting the firm and its environment.

Hrebiniak and Joyce (1984, pp. 42–9) suggest that five features affect the identification of strategic options:

- Organisational learning
- Distinctive competence and the location of slack resources
- Past performance and type of search activity
- Power differences within the organisation
- Absorption of uncertainty through politics.

Strategic selection

The method of evaluating which strategic option(s) will be selected will vary from organisation to organisation. In 3.1 we noted the effect of rational and non-rational factors on decision-makers, a theme which is explored further in Chapter 14. Later, in 3.6, we explore the management of the process of strategy-formulation, but at this point we can assert that although strategic decisions emanating from the formulation process may often be presented as utilitarian, in most cases the decisions are reached as a result of, or in spite of, a wide range of influences on those involved. Such influences will include, for example, individual needs, values and perceptions, coupled with wider societal values and expectations impacting on managers as individuals and the organisation as a whole.

The analytical techniques which are of use to decision-makers in determining which option(s) are acceptable are discussed in Chapter 8.

3.4 The use of models

Models or visual representations can be of use in understanding and evaluating a firm's current strategic position as well as identifying problems to be addressed in the future. We will discuss three portfolio matrices, the BCG growth share matrix, the nine-cell General Electric matrix, and Hofer and Schendel's product/market evolution matrix. For those firms where these constructs are not an adequate tool we will, briefly, discuss Ansoff's product/mission and diversification matrices.

Each of the three portfolio matrices have strengths and weaknesses. Any or all can be used to gain insights from different perspectives, the key being to describe completely and with analytical accuracy the firm's position, both present and future, with the objective of achieving the best performance from the portfolio as a whole from the allocation of corporate resources.

Research by Haspeslagh (1982) revealed that 45 per cent of all Fortune 500 firms and 36 per cent of all Fortune 1000 firms used portfolio analysis to some extent, and that 75 per cent of large diversified firms utilised the technique. Executives reported the following perceived benefits:

(i) a noticeable improvement in the quality of strategies at both corporate and business levels;
(ii) more selective and focused allocation of corporate resources in an environment with capital rationing;
(iii) a stronger framework for tailoring 'how we manage' to the needs of each business in the portfolio;
(iv) an improved capacity for performing the tasks of strategic management and exerting firmer control over both corporate and business level strategies;
(v) less reluctance to face the problem of marginal businesses.

Executives also noted that the use of portfolio techniques tended to: increase their understanding of the role and potential contribution of each business; assist in the construction of a rational framework for resource commitments; and helped in prescribing general types of strategies for each business unit. Overall, therefore, the technique was of use in clarifying what the firm should do with each of its businesses. Perhaps one of the most interesting findings was the shift away from emphasising short-term profit and sales objectives to competitive analysis and the achievement of long-term profit and sales targets.

We would note that many texts tend to refer to portfolio matrices as corporate strategy tools: in fact they can also be a useful analytical technique for use at the business level. While the portfolio matrices have the merit of straightforward presentation, as they develop in scope from BCG to the product evolution matrix, the variables incorporated in the axes increase. There is some evidence (see Illustration 3.1) that managers have difficulty in comprehending the nature of what the matrix represents. Business portfolio matrices do not adequately describe the strategies of firms which are either single product-line companies just commencing major diversification, or dominant product-line firms

ILLUSTRATION 3.1 The Use of Portfolio Models

The portfolio analysis techniques were examined in a diversified international company. They were the BCG matrix, the GE business screen and the Shell Directional Policy Matrix. A number of points emerged:

- The techniques were useful in assisting senior managers to define the most acceptable strategy.
- Portfolio techniques were used to evaluate the firm's own products and those of directly relevant competitors.
- The simpler BCG matrix was favoured, possibly because the technique was used to provide a decision framework as opposed to the more mechanistic use proposed in some sections of the literature.
- Management appear to believe that portfolio techniques are a *qualitative* tool which has played an important part in developing strategic thinking.
- Managers' perceptions of 'market attractiveness' and 'competitive position' vary considerably.
- BCG plots for the firm and competitors were used to help determine results of decisions rather than to generate options.
- Performing portfolio analysis on major competitors helps to deduce competitive strategy.
- The *process* proved more important than the detail of the model.
- Portfolio techniques provided a framework to structure the R & D needs of the existing portfolio.
- New product development appears to have been enhanced by the introduction of portfolio techniques in the 1970s.

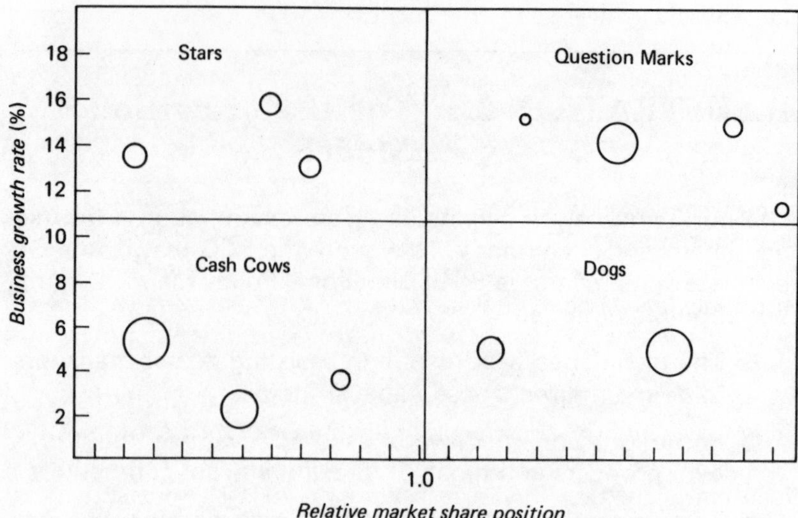

FIGURE 3.3 The BCG growth share matrix

Note: Relative market share is defined as the ratio of the firm's market share to that of its largest competitor. It is plotted on a log-arithmetic scale to be consistent with experience curve effects.

whose non-principal businesses are closely related to their principal business. It is difficult to visualise the strategies of such firms using portfolio concepts because they may not adequately capture the inter-related nature of the businesses. Actual or potential dominant product-line firms must devote attention to their diversification ventures so that they can be developed into viable units. At the same time the dominant base in such firms is still such a large part of the corporate whole that it should not be treated as just another business in the firm's portfolio. A balance needs to be struck between the efforts and resources devoted to the firm's base business and those directed toward diversification.

The BCG growth share matrix

The simplest and most publicised business portfolio matrix, depicted above in Figure 3.3, was pioneered by the Boston Consultancy Group (BCG). Each of the firm's businesses is plotted according to the growth rates of the industry or market and its own relative position in that industry, the size of each circle being proportioned to the size of business involved. In Figure 3.3 the dividing line between 'high' and 'low' market growth has been arbitrarily set at 10 per cent. The idea is to position the line so that businesses above it can be said to be in a growth phase, while those below are in a mature/saturation/decline phase. Similarly the dividing line for relative market-share should be positioned so that those businesses to the left are market leaders (though not necessarily *the* leader), while those to the right are in a trailing situation.

Relative market-share is used instead of simply market-share in the construction of the matrix because it is a better indicator of comparative market position. For example, a 15 per cent market-share is considerably stronger if the leader's share is 18 per cent than if it is 40 per cent.

Businesses plotted in the upper left quadrant are called *stars* by BCG, because they are growing rapidly and have a strong market position. As such BCG believes they probably represent the best profit and growth opportunities available. They may also be self-sustaining in terms of cash flow. These businesses should be nurtured for the long run because of the 'experience-curve' effect.

Businesses with a high market-share in a low-growth industry are called *cash cows* by BCG and are plotted in the lower left quadrant. Given this combination of low growth and high market-share they usually have an entrenched position which tends to generate substantial cash surpluses over and above that required for investment and growth. Cash cows represent a valuable resource because the cash they generate can be used to develop new stars as well as providing funds for corporate spending on overheads and dividends. Cash cows may have been yesterday's stars and could be tomorrow's dogs.

Businesses in the lower right quadrant are referred to as *dogs* by BCG because of their poor competitive position. They suffer from low growth and low market-share, and usually are not very profitable. They may not even generate enough cash to maintain their position. Consequently BCG suggest that companies should endeavour to extricate themselves from such businesses using whichever methods yield the most attractive cash-flow.

Those businesses which fall in the upper right quadrant have high market growth but a low market-share and are referred to as *question marks* by BCG. Their high growth-rate makes them an attractive market proposition, but their weak market-share means their cash-generation is low. Question marks usually have the worst cash-flow because their cash needs are high because of the high growth rate. BCG typifies such businesses as *cash hogs* and recommends two alternative strategies; to grow a question mark into a star or to divest it.

The use of the BCG matrix focuses attention on the cash-flow and investment characteristics of the organisation's businesses, and how the firm's financial resources can best be deployed to optimise the long-term strategic position and performance of the whole corporate portfolio. The firm's current position can be plotted on such a matrix and a projection made of its future position, assuming there are no major changes in its strategy. Used in such a way these two matrices can help to outline the scope and competitive-advantage elements in the company's corporate strategy as well as helping to identify some of the key strategic issues facing the firm. A BCG matrix may also help in isolating some of the basic characteristics of each SBU's strategy.

Although the BCG matrix has considerable appeal in evaluating various businesses, and may be of use in the derivation of strategic decisions, several criticisms have been made of it:

(i) A four-quadrant matrix is too simplistic, as 'high' and 'low' classifications may not be appropriate for many businesses. There is, therefore, a problem in positioning the 'average' business.

(ii) Business growth rate is not a sufficient description to describe industry attractiveness. There are some industries with high growth rates which are not very profitable because supply has grown even faster.

(iii) Business growth rate and relative market-share are not the only relevant factors in determining the standing of a business in a firm's portfolio. Other issues warranting consideration would include, for example, market size, ability to take opportunities and ward off threats, susceptibility to variations in the economy, ease of entry into and exit from the business, the existence of distinctive competencies and competitive advantages, degree of fit with other businesses held by the company and so on.

(iv) The matrix may not help in determining opportunities between SBUs because it will not indicate whether every 'star' is better than a 'cash cow' for instance.

THE BCG EXPERIENCE CURVE

As noted above the BCG growth share matrix is closely linked with another BCG development – the experience curve. The experience curve concept, which is similar to and an extension of the learning curve, states that the *overall* unit costs of making a product decline by up to 30 per cent each time the number of units produced doubles. BCG believed the results to be predictable enough to be accurately plotted, hence the experience curve (Figure 3.4).

These cost reductions can occur in a number of ways, economies of scale, value engineering and the application of innovations to reduce costs. Economies of scale can be derived from the development of specialised knowledge or skills, the ability to take advantage of indivisibilities in existing technology, the ability to spread fixed costs over increased volumes, and learning-curve effects. Value engineering can be applied in cases where the appearance and performance of a product will not be affected by the substitution of a lower cost component – the best examples of which appear in the motor industry. The application of

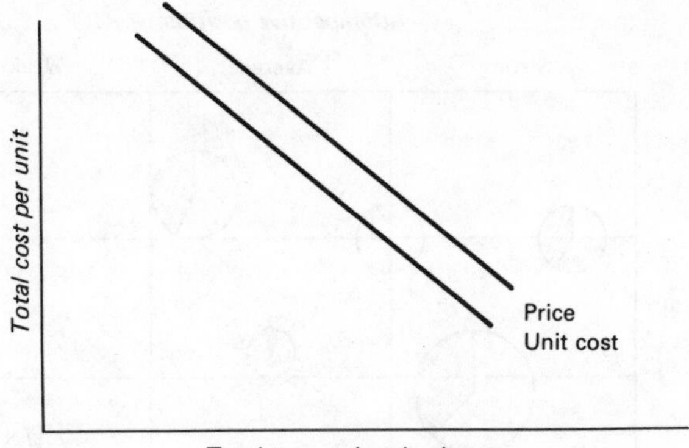

FIGURE 3.4 A typical experience curve

innovations to reduce costs may relate, for example, to the use of modern computer technology to reduce administrative costs. What should be clear is that in order to achieve any of these cost improvements management action is required; they will not occur automatically.

Hofer and Schendel (1978, p. 134) identify three major strategic implications of experience curve effects:

(i) They depict the rate at which a business should be reducing the cost of its products so allowing cost reduction proposals to be evaluated against a norm.
(ii) Experience curves may help a business develop long-run pricing policies as well as enabling a prediction to be made of the effects of short-and long-term cash-flows from following 'skim the cream' pricing as opposed to pricing for growth, or pricing for margins. Each could be compared with the firm's profit and growth objectives to determine which policy seems appropriate.
(iii) Experience curves can also be used to predict the speed with which the firm's prices of supplies should be going down with obvious implications for its purchasing policies.

Although conceptually attractive, experience curves should be used with some caution because of their strategic implications. A strategy based on sustained cost-reduction emphasises cost–price efficiency over other considerations. The business needs to be sure that the market requires low-cost goods as opposed to differentiating features (quality, service, product innovation, etc.). In addition, the firm adopting a strategy based on experience curve effects – which often results in inflexible facilities and technologies – must keep its ability to sense changes in the product, customers and technology.

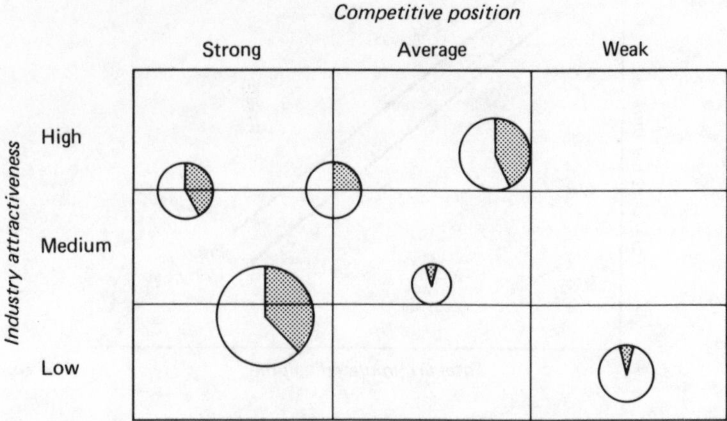

FIGURE 3.5 Nine-cell GE matrix

Hofer and Schendel (1978, p. 135) note the difficulty in obtaining the necessary cost data and that much of the evidence purporting to support the experience curve effect derives from price behaviour which is not quite the same at all. Thomas (1983, p. 167) is less than enthusiastic 'on examining the evidence from successive UK studies, and noting in passing the paucity of supporting evidence from BCG, one is bound to have serious doubts about its validity. The idea that one can posit an experience curve and hang a product policy upon it strikes one as simplistic, to say the least!'

The nine-cell General Electric matrix

An alternative matrix which avoids some of the problems of the BCG matrix is the nine-cell matrix developed by General Electric (GE). The GE matrix, shown in Figure 3.5, uses two axes to represent industry attractiveness and competitive position. In this case the area of the circles is proportional to the size of the industry, and the pie-slices within the circles reflects the business's market share. Industry attractiveness and competitive position are composite values used to plot each business's position.

Industry attractiveness is a function of a number of factors, for example, market growth-rate, market size, profitability, market structure, competitive rivalry, seasonality, cyclicality, economies of scale, technological and capital requirements and social, legal and environmental issues. The procedure involves assigning each of the factors a weight depending on its perceived importance, followed by assessing how each business compares on each factor, using a 1–5 rating scale, and then computing a weighted composite rating.

The same approach is used to measure competitive position where aspects such as market share, competitive ability, knowledge of customers and markets, technological capability, calibre of management and so on are considered. The variety of factors involved in making these assessments will be discussed more fully in Chapter 8.

The three cells in the upper left of the GE matrix where industry attractiveness and competitive position are favourable are said to be the businesses where a strategy of growth and development is appropriate. As such, businesses in these areas should be given priority in the allocation of corporate resources. The three cells in the lower right-hand corner, however, are those businesses where a strategy of divestment is appropriate. The three diagonal cells, from the lower left to the upper right, should be treated as a holding-type strategy and would not, therefore, rank as a priority in resource terms.

The use of the GE matrix allows for intermediate rankings between high and low and between strong and weak. Furthermore, unlike the BCG matrix it includes consideration of a wide range of relevant strategic variables. Finally, the focus of the matrix can help in channelling resources to those businesses which combine medium-to-high industry attractiveness with an average-to-strong competitive position; the belief being that these represent areas where there is a higher probability of an improvement in performance. Again, the firm's future position can be forecast and the present and forecast matrices used to describe the firm's scope and competitive position as well as identifying some important strategic issues facing the firm.

Attractive though the GE matrix may appear, it only offers a general prescription in strategic terms, and as Hofer and Schendel (1978, p. 33) point out the matrix takes no account of the positions of new businesses that are just starting to grow in new industries. Such businesses may well be about to emerge as winners because the product/market is entering the take-off-stage.

The product/market evolution matrix

The better to identify the developing winner, Hofer and Schendel suggest a fifteen-cell matrix in which businesses are plotted in terms of their competitive position and their stage of product/market evolution depicted in Figure 3.6. As with the GE business screen, circles represent the sizes of the industries involved, and the pie-wedges represent the market-shares of the businesses involved. Future positions can be plotted and used to identify major strategic issues.

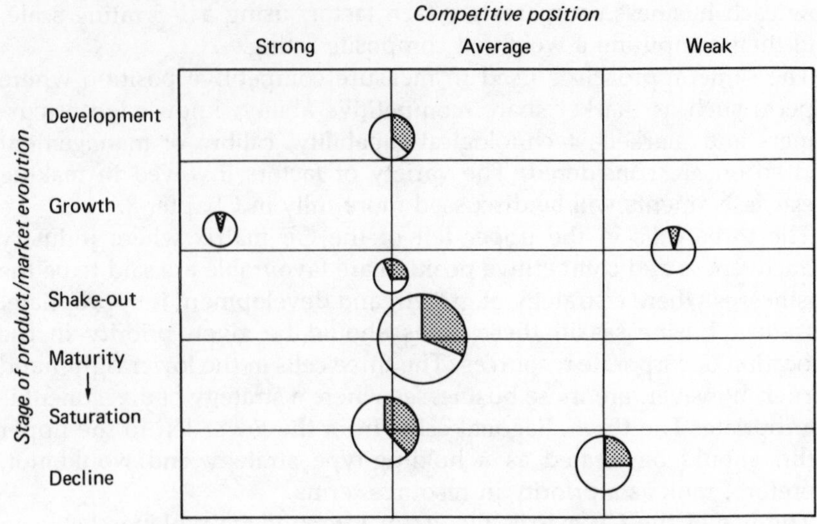

FIGURE 3.6 The product/market evolution matrix

Constructs for actual or potential dominant-product-line firms

Ansoff (1965) developed two constructs which we can use to visualise the strategies for actual or potential dominant product-line firms. First, the product/mission matrix depicted in Figure 3.7 can be used to indicate changes the firm has developed, and plans to develop through changes in scope. Such a matrix is useful in conceptualising differences in expansion such as market- or product-development, and diversification which entails more risk since it involves departure from familiar products and familiar markets. The decision to diversify or not represents a major milestone in a firm's development.

If the firm wishes to consider diversification in more depth then

Mission \ Product	Present	New
Present	Market penetration	Product development
New	Market development	Diversification

FIGURE 3.7 Product/mission matrix

	New Products	
Products / *Customers*	*Related technology*	*Unrelated technology*
Same type	Horizontal diversification	
Firm its own customer	Vertical integration	
Similar type	Marketing and technology related concentric diversification	Marketing related concentric diversification
New type	Technology related concentric diversification	Conglomerate diversification

FIGURE 3.8 A diversification matrix

Ansoff's diversification matrix is a useful tool for describing the *type* of diversification intended. There are some brief pertinent points we can make concerning diversification at this stage in order fully to understand the use of the matrix depicted in Figure 3.8.

Horizontal diversification involves moves within the firm's existing environment, which means that marketing synergy is a key issue, since this strategy will not tend to enhance the firm's flexibility. Ansoff also argues that vertical integration, by its very nature, increases the firm's dependence on a particular economic environment.

Indeed Ansoff concludes that both vertical integration and horizontal diversification offer only limited potential and contribute little to flexibility or stability. Concentric and conglomerate diversification differ in their degree of synergy with the firm's present business. We can see that concentric diversification has some commonality with existing businesses either through marketing or technology or both, whereas conglomerate diversification has none. Clearly the decision as to the diversification strategy, if any, which a firm should adopt is of central concern in strategy formulation. Chapter 6 will explore these issues in greater depth.

3.5 Horizontal strategy

Porter (1985, p. 318) defines horizontal strategy as a 'co-ordinated set of goals and policies across distinct but interrelated business units'. He goes on (p. 319) 'Without a horizontal strategy there is no convincing rationale for the existence of a diversified firm because it is little more than a mutual fund. Horizontal strategy – not portfolio-management – is thus the essence of corporate strategy'. In the light of what we have discussed in the preceding section this view is perhaps contentious. However, important issues are raised by Porter which will be of use in strategy-formulation. The relationships among and between business units, and an organisation's ability to exploit them are likely to provide a driving force to ensure that, overall, the firm performs better than the sum of the parts.

Porter identified four interconnecting forces which he believes will accelerate this trend in the 1990s (Porter, 1985, pp. 320–3):

- Diversification philosophy is changing with a shift in emphasis towards related diversification. Corporate portfolios have been reduced with more attention being paid to 'fit', so that unrelated or marginal business units have been sold off. Peters and Waterman refer to the process of staying with a core of related businesses as 'stick to the knitting' (Peters and Waterman 1982, pp. 292–305).
- Emphasis is shifting from growth to performance because of a more difficult environment caused by slower growth and growing global competition.
- Technological change is proliferating interrelationships and making them more achievable particularly in electronics and information technology. The development of new technologies enables activities to be shared across business units. The growing sophistication of information systems may also act to open up possibilities for interrelationships.
- Multipoint competition is increasing as more and more firms seek out and pursue interrelationships between business units. Multipoint competitors are firms that compete with each other in a number of related business units.

Three broad types of interrelationship are identified (pp. 323–63) and discussed in detail; here we will just note the main points:

- *Tangible interrelationships* derive from opportunities to share activities among related businesses. They may lead to competitive advantage if sharing lowers costs or enhances differentiation.
- *Intangible interrelationships* involve the transfer of managers' knowledge between businesses which may be generically similar in terms of the *type* of buyer or the *type* of process and so on.
- Competitive advantage is obtained through the transfer of

generic skills or knowledge from one unit to another.

- *Competitor interrelationships* arise from the existence of rivals that actually or potentially compete with the enterprise in more than one industry. Such multipoint competitors necessarily link industries together because action in one area may have implications in another. The three types can occur together, but each type leads to competitive advantage in a different way.

The formulation of horizontal strategy involves a number of analytical steps which lead from the above (Porter, 1985, pp. 368–75). Figure 3.9 overleaf provides a simple framework for the first step of identifying interrelationships. The main steps are:

(i) identify all tangible interrelationships;
(ii) trace tangible interrelationships outside the boundaries of the firm;
(iii) identify possible intangible interrelationships;
(iv) identify competitor interrelationships;
(v) Assess the importance of interrelationships to competitive advantage;
(vi) Develop a co-ordinated horizontal strategy to achieve and enhance the most important interrelationships;
(vii) create horizontal organisational mechanisms to ensure implementation.

The above obviously involves a considerable effort and subtle interpretation and judgement by the management. Unlike portfolio techniques there is little empirical evidence to cite in support of Porter's ideas. Nevertheless they do represent an important and creative step forward in thinking about alternate methods of strategy-formulation. The interested reader is strongly recommended to pursue this area by reading the relevant parts of Porter's book, *Competitive Advantage*.

3.6 Management of the formulation process

Firms will approach the task of formulating strategy differently depending on the nature of the organisation itself, in terms of its culture, management style and so on, and the environment(s) in which it operates. Some organisations have a very formal approach, others informal. As Quinn (1980) reported, the earliest signals for strategic change did not come from the formal structures but from highly diffuse and informal sources, such as top managers' feelings or beliefs. Indeed Quinn noted that informal methods and processes are both effective and widely utilised.

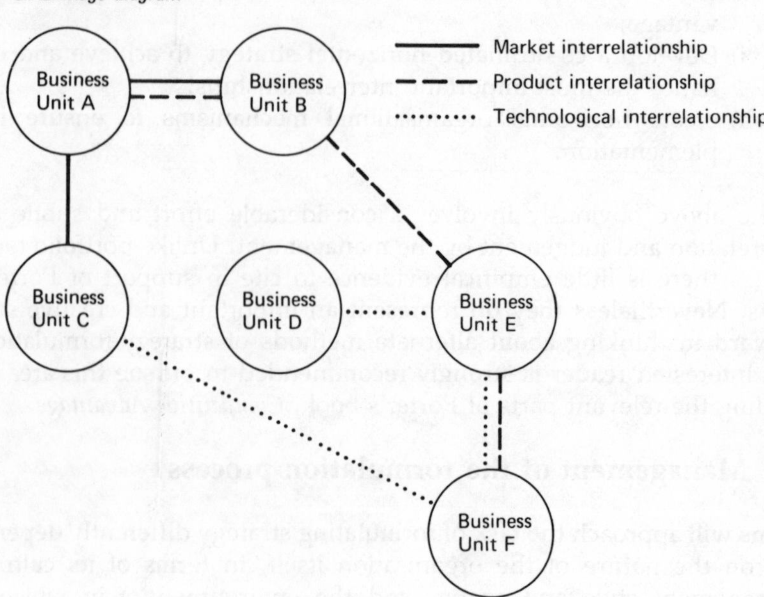

FIGURE 3.9 Tangible interrelationships in a diversified firm

Source: Porter, M. E. (1985) *Competitive Advantage* (New York: Free Press) p. 369.

This indicates that no single method for formulating strategy can be prescribed. Regardless of the process used the objective is to determine as realistically as possible the future state of the firm. Ultimately the objective is to ensure that better decisions are made now to ensure future success, partly by reducing uncertainty. The process itself may well lead those managers involved into questioning fundamental assumptions, altering values, and conditioning them to changes that will affect the future success of the firm's strategy.

McLellan and Kelly (1980) identified four different approaches to strategy formulation which we discuss below.

Bottom–up approach

Formulation takes place at the business unit level and is passed upwards for approval and aggregation with other units' strategies. Consequently corporate strategy is a composite of all the business units' strategies. As a result corporate strategy may lack coherence, unity and consistency, which does not fit the environmental and resource demands facing the firm as a whole.

At the business level, strategy is geared to match its particular circumstances with the focus being on existing areas of activity and consolidation of its position. Large numbers of business-unit managers tend to be involved, with corporate managers exerting downward influence on the assembly of strategy. Because of this informal involvement corporate approval is usually forthcoming.

Top– down approach

In this case strategy-formulation is viewed as the province of corporate managers. Strategy reflects, therefore, their judgement about how to achieve corporate objectives, and any inconsistencies and conflicts between SBUs are settled at the corporate level. This approach tends to result in a unified, coherent strategy which explicitly states corporate direction and performance targets. The corporate strategy is then broken down into individual strategies and guidelines for each unit for implementation.

Interactive or negotiated approach

Both business unit and corporate managers jointly formulate business strategy and corporate strategy, with influences moving upward and downward. The formulation process is participative and negotiated reflecting the link between corporate expectations and SBU managers' knowledge of their specific businesses. Negotiations and deliberations may be lengthy and exhaustive but this may be compensated by the speed of the approval and implementation stages.

The Corporate manager's role is to shape the pattern of the separate SBU strategies into a corporate portfolio of strategies compatible with corporate resources, objectives and direction. Any conflicts between corporate strategy and a business unit's proposed strategy are resolved through negotiation.

Semi-autonomous approach

This approach is distinguished by relatively independent strategy-formulation activities at both corporate and business levels. At the corporate level formulation and re-evaluation is virtually continuous with the focus on identification of new directions for the firm, the evaluation of emerging threats and opportunities, decisions about which new businesses to enter, which existing businesses to divest, and what priorities to attach to those businesses remaining in the corporate portfolio. The emphasis of the corporate level lies in evaluating the portfolio of SBUs and trying to improve the performance of the portfolio as a whole.

At the business-unit level, strategy is formulated to suit each unit's particular set of circumstances and objectives. The SBU's strategy is submitted for corporate approval and is normally subject to a formal periodic review, often annually.

These and other approaches to the formulation process can be observed in practice. Which one a firm uses is largely a matter of management preference, but Chapter 14 (models of strategic decision-making) will explore the view that certain contingent conditions (such as the firm's environment, its production technology) can effectively constrain the management's choice of strategic decision-making processes.

3.7 Summary

Strategy-formulation involves the interaction of a number of different perspectives embracing conditions currently existing, and projections for future conditions, within and external to the organisation. In this chapter we have focused the bulk of our discussion on the 'objective' side of our model of strategic change. However, it is apparent that perceptions of objectivity will differ, thus the techniques and analysis presented here are subject to individual and group subjectivity.

Nevertheless, as our discussion of the main portfolio techniques revealed, the use of such matrices is, of necessity, overlaid by subjective criteria. The same sort of subjective conditions are also likely to exist in horizontal strategy-formulation. This interplay between objective and subjective conditions should be regarded as a benefit, if it reveals that those managers involved in the process are utilising the variety of models discussed in this chapter to formulate strategies that enable the organisation to progress in such a way that it meets its objectives in spite of (or because of) the external and internal conditions prevailing. Having introduced some key tools, we will discuss further the formulation of strategy within the framework of the model depicted in Figure 3.2, in succeeding chapters.

Further reading

Part II (Chapters 4, 5, and 6) of Abell and Hammond, *'Strategic Market Planning* (Englewood Cliffs, New Jersey: Prentice-Hall, 1979) provides a comprehensive discussion of portfolio techniques.

Horizontal strategy is dealt with in depth in Porter's, *Competitive Advantage* (New York: Free Press, 1985) chapters 9, 10, 11 which are well worth reading for those interested in diversified firms.

References

Ansoff, H. I. (1965) *Corporate Strategy* (Harmondsworth: Penguin).

Donaldson, G. and Lorsch, J. W. (1983) *Decision Making at the Top* (New York: Basic Books).

Haspeslagh, P. (1982) 'Portfolio Planning: Uses and Limits', *Harvard Business Review*, vol. 60, no 1, January - February, pp. 58–73.

Hofer, C. W. (1977) *'Conceptual Constructs for Formulating Corporate and Business Strategies* (Boston: Intercollegiate Case Clearing House) p. 4.

Hofer, C. W. and Schendel, D. (1978) *Strategy Formulation: Analytical Concepts* (St Paul, Minnesota: West).

Hrebiniak, L. G. and Joyce, W. F. (1984) *Implementing Strategy* (New York: Macmillan).

McLellan, R. G. and Kelly, G. (1980) 'Business Policy Formulation: Understanding the Process', *Journal of General Management*, vol. 6, no 1, Autumn, pp. 38–47.

Peters, T. J. and Waterman, R. H. (1982) *In Search of Excellence* (New York: Harper & Row).

Porter, M. E. (1985) *Competitive Advantage* (New York: Free Press).

Quinn, J. B. (1980) *Strategies for Change* (Homewood, Illinois: Irwin).

Regan, D. E. (1978) 'Rationality in Policy Making: Two Concepts Not One', *Long Range Planning*, vol. 11, October, pp. 83–8.

Sutton, C. J. (1983) 'Does Strategy Pay?', *Managerial & Decision Economics*, vol. 4, no 3, pp. 153–9.

Thomas, R. E. (1983) *Business Policy* (Oxford: Philip Allan), 2nd edn.

CHAPTER 4

External appraisal

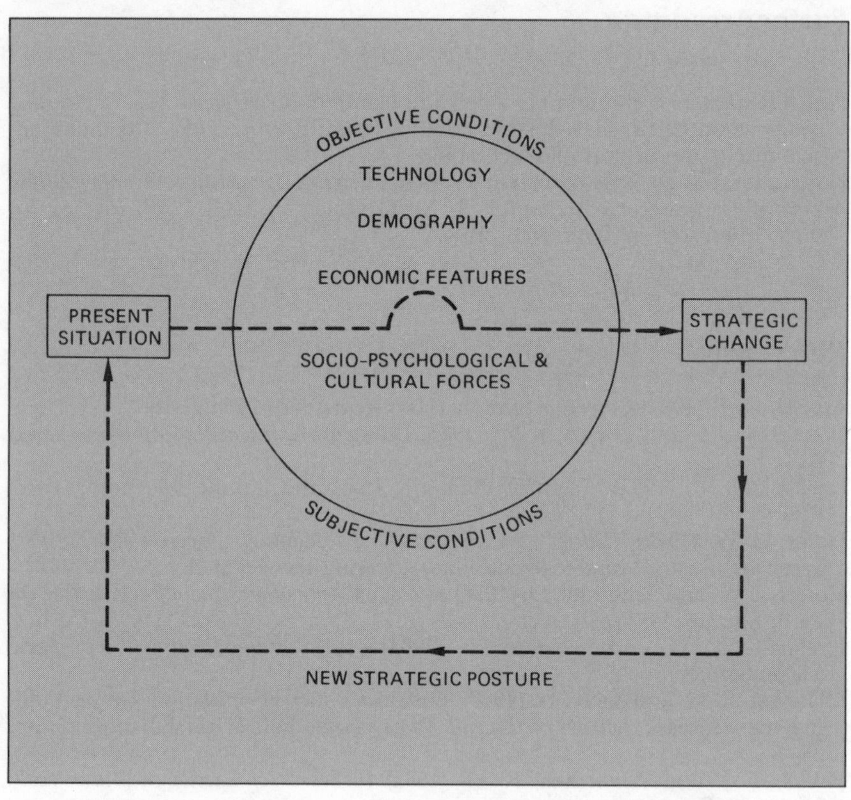

4.1 Introduction

Both this chapter and Chapter 5, Internal Appraisal, are concerned specifically with the objective conditions faced by the organisation. Analysis of the situation confronting the firm is often very complex, hence we will consider external or environmental influences in this chapter, followed by a review of the firm's resources in Chapter 5. It should be realised that such a neat divide is often not the case in practice as not only will environmental forces help to shape strategic decisions but also such decisions may impact on parts of the external environment. Readers should also remember that our strategic analysis is interdependent and that what is required is an understanding of the complex issues involved – their links and relative importance – plus an acknowledgement that these will change over time and show substantial differences from one firm to another.

There is one further point to make which relates to the scope of external appraisal. While we recognise the importance of an organisation's economic environment it is important to realise that external appraisal for strategic decisions is more than just an assessment of the firm's immediate sector of the economy. The behaviour of the economy as a whole, together with the effect of social, technological and political factors, is an important input to our analysis of the external influences affecting the future development of the organisation. Figure 4.1 identifies the main external environmental influences indicating the scope of the problem faced by an organisation in appraising it's environment.

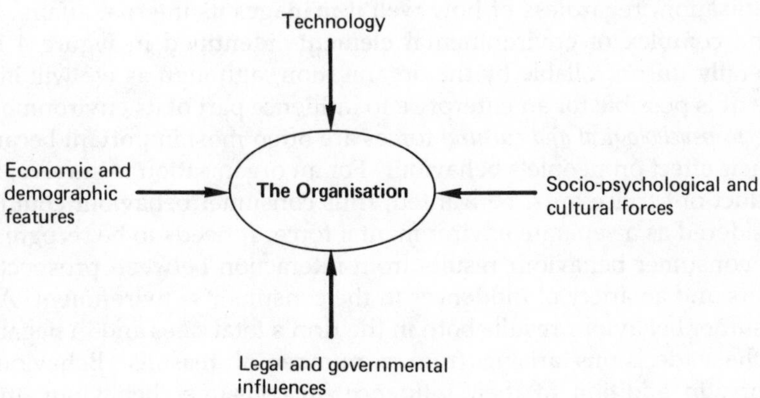

FIGURE 4.1 Environmental influences affecting organisations

These factors will be reviewed in an attempt to aid our understanding of the complexities and interrelationships with which an enterprise's management must grapple in order both to predict future trends and also the better to understand key features which affect the success or otherwise of the firm.

There are two further aspects to this problem. First, the effect of changes in the environment may go further than the products or services offered, as external events can influence, for example, the supply and attitudes of labour, the utility of plant and equipment, the supply of raw materials, the ability to raise additional capital, or render existing technology obsolete and so on. Events taking place outside the organisation should be monitored as these will affect the future of the entity. After all, most institutions have systems for measuring and reporting on internal events on a daily, weekly, monthly or annual basis.

Second, we should also recognise that the relationship between the organisation and its environment is a two-way affair, because in addition to the enterprise reacting to changes in external factors, the environment itself will react to the enterprise. This is particularly evident if the organisation introduces technological innovation causing major changes in the environment. In addition we must expect that managers may not always fully appreciate the impact of forthcoming changes or may be unwilling to recognise that significant changes are taking place. Changes in the organisation's environment as well as posing threats to existing operations may present opportunities for the enterprise to develop in the future. In our consideration of the wide spectrum of environmental influences we can be certain only of *change*. Failure to respond to such changes may result in the ultimate failure of the organisation, regardless of how well it manages its internal affairs.

The complex of environmental elements identified in Figure 4.1 is generally uncontrollable by the organisation, although as we will illustrate, it is possible for an enterprise to influence part of its environment.

Socio-psychological and cultural forces are often most important because of their effect on people's behaviour. For an organisation to survive, the product or service must be wanted, thus consumer behaviour could be considered as a separate environmental force. It needs to be recognised that consumer behaviour results from interaction between prospective buyers and a variety of influences in the consumer's environment. Also consumer behaviour results both in the firm's total sales and in negative purchase decisions arising from a number of reasons. Behavioural factors, in addition to their influence on consumer behaviour affect organisations internally, that is, the employees and management as reflected in our strategy-formulation model in Chapter 3. Group behaviour is of particular interest and its effect on decision-making is examined in Chapter 12. Any environmental appraisal must recognise the influences that 'reference', for example, may have on the behaviour of managers, employees, customers, suppliers and competitors with the objective of determining the effect of changes in the enterprise.

Consequently this chapter will start with a brief discussion on the need and importance of environmental appraisal, and then move on to consider the broader economic, socio-political and technological influences so assisting our understanding of the wider environment in which the organisation operates. When some 'feeling' for these key influences has emerged we are then in a position to analyse the firm's more immediate economic environment by drawing on Porter's *Competitive Strategy*. At the conclusion of this chapter we will discuss how the preceding analysis helps to identify opportunities and threats to the firm.

While there is general agreement that environmental appraisal is a crucial element in the formulation of an organisation's strategy there is little consensus as to the *method* which should be adopted. Quinn's research (noted earlier in Chapter 3) showed that, although many firms formally assessed external influences, the earliest signs for change emerged in diffuse and informal ways. Whichever method is used the objective of the process is to determine the possible future condition of the external factors impacting on the organisation, so enabling better decisions concerning future developments to be made. Clearly certainty cannot be achieved, but uncertainty can be reduced.

4.2 The need for external appraisal

Organisations do not exist in a vacuum, they are part of a complex world. Management should be continually aware of the external forces which not only influence demand for existing products and services but also create opportunities for new products and services. It can be argued that this is the case whether the organisation is profit-orientated or 'not-for-profit'.

Wide social forces also influence the behaviour of people, for example, the increase in leisure-related activities has not only created new products and services but has also affected life-styles. Thus interest in leisure will affect product-planning, and attitudes of employees. In a similar way the attraction found in simplicity and convenience has led to significant increases in products offering such benefits. The increase in sales of microwave ovens from 15 000 in 1975 to 1 million in 1984 is but one example of this trend.

Technological forces are often the most apparent and dramatic. However, it often happens that a breakthrough which receives widespread publicity, perhaps because of its implications for the public at large, has been the subject of research for many years in a variety of institutions (hospitals, companies, universities). If those firms affected by the breakthrough only become aware of it through the widespread publicity then it may be too late to respond. A further feature of technological change is the reduction in time between scientific discovery and commercial application, best exemplified in the continuing innovation in microcomputers.

Management must, therefore, be aware of relevant technological developments and they must assess their impact. Some innovations may create new industries, as well as destroying others. But recognition is required of the fact that technological change may affect areas other than products. An innovation which becomes a major product-feature for the seller presents a decision to prospective customers of the equipment.

A new development may affect not only the manufacturing or servicing process but also the personnel function (obtaining and/or training personnel to operate the new equipment, how to shed redundant labour) and the finance functions (how to finance the new equipment). The advance in computer technology has had a major influence on information for management decision-making. An aspect of this is evident in Illustration 4.1 where modern computers have enabled Kwik-Fit substantially to reduce administrative staff while enhancing the enterprise's ability to respond to competitive forces in the market place.

Various *legal and governmental* factors may constrain a firm's actions in respect of changes in the environment. For some organisations such influences may be all pervasive, for others less so. In general the impact of government is far-reaching and increasing. To take the pharmaceutical industry as an extreme case for example, government influences the:

- composition of the product;
- development of the product;
- processing of the drug;
- labelling on the package;
- pricing of the product (for NHS prescription products);
- amount to be spent on advertising and promotion (for NHS drugs);
- hiring of employees;
- wages paid;
- factory design;
- accounting practices; and so on.

ILLUSTRATION 4.1 Technological Change at Kwik-Fit

Kwik-Fit, the tyre and exhaust replacement company, has achieved the state of paperless retailing. The firm which used to employ 110 administrative staff to run 90 depots now runs 260 outlets with a staff of 28. Not many more will be needed when the company's target of 400 depots is reached.

Invoices, quotations, stock control, payroll, marketing and promotion, management performance, local pricing policies are all handled on a £2m computer system. 'We went from the position that the depot manager is king', said Mr Farmer, the Kwik-Fit chairman. 'The head office and administration are just support staff.' The terminal at the depot provides the customer with a quote on tyres, batteries, shock absorbers or exhaust systems. A sale is punched out on the terminal and the only printed copy given to the customer. At the end of each day stocktaking and administration take about ten minutes and during the night the head office computer automatically dials each depot to note the daily sales and parts sold.

A viewdata system enables regional managers to examine depots in terms of their sales performance. For example, they are able to see if an outlet is selling a high enough proportion of wheel-balancing with tyre changes, and whether battery sales targets are being met. Supplies are also linked in to the system as it is essential for close links to be maintained on substantial contracts for supplying parts.

Local sales patterns can be analysed to determine the appropriate level of local sales. It adapts, for example, to the high proportion of Vauxhall car parts near Luton, or Ford near Dagenham. A regional manager can report a local competitor with a special offer and the system will see if Kwik-Fit can match, or better, the offer and determine what price rises in other areas will be needed to compensate for the special discount.

(Source: *Financial Times*, 18 October 1984)

It is beyond the scope and interest of this book to go into the detail of the numerous laws and regulations which affect organisations. But management must be aware of these constraints, actual and potential, and seek out the implications for the enterprise from legal advisers.

Economic forces are clearly of vital concern to the enterprise. The overall economic climate tends to determine, in a broad way, the opportunities for organisations, because an expanding economy provides scope for many firms as well as for the establishment of new firms. A recession can bring about failure, as evidenced by the increase in the number of firms being liquidated in the early 1980s. Even so a generally depressed economy may still provide opportunities for some. Poor economic conditions, in addition to influencing demand for goods and services, may also have other secondary effects. For example, if the stock market is depressed a planned share-issue may have to be postponed, or an increase in lending rates may make an expansion programme too expensive.

An important problem for management to overcome in assessing the effect of the economy is to distinguish between short-run phenomena and more fundamental changes in the economy overall. So the firm must identify factors likely to affect demand in the short run as well as those influencing the enterprise's ability to meet expected future demand in the long term. Increases in the firm's cost of capital may well interfere with plans to construct additional capacity, thus limiting its ability to satisfy projected future demand..

In addition to the general economic situation each organisation is part of a sub-environment, being the industry of which it is a member. Analysis of the industry involves consideration, first, of those firms producing similar products and, second, of those producing substitutes. A number of features require appraisal as the firm must be aware of:

- economic features influencing operations (for example, availability of materials, capital and labour);
- the technological state of the industry, including the extent of commitment to research and development;
- pricing;
- marketing and advertising features;
- the cost structure of the industry.

In addition changes in other areas, such as distribution, should be appraised.

A further aspect of assessing the industry in which the entity operates concerns competitor appraisal, allowing comparisons to be drawn with the organisation's own products policies and tactics so assisting in the evaluation of relative advantages and disadvantages. The picture drawn of competitors could be as extensive as for the firm itself.

The prediction of the multitude of economic factors is problematic, professional economists rarely agree and sometimes appear to fail to detect developments which with hindsight seem obvious. One aspect of the environment which can be predicted with a high degree of accuracy for time-periods exceeding normal planning horizons is the composition of the population. *Demographic* projections by their nature have relatively high accuracy; once a segment of the population is born its growth can be projected and its size estimated over time.

Although broad demographic forecasts are concerned with major segments of the population, changes within the population require assessment as they influence the demand for goods and services. The increase in the number of people living alone, for example, created a new segment of the house construction market for firms like Barratt.

We can conclude by suggesting that from an analytical perspective it seems useful to examine general economic and demographic conditions, specific industry conditions and the particular entity's situation. A major managerial problem that must be recognised is the tendency to deal with day-to-day operations to the exclusion of an assessment of the future. Such myopia may lead to the neglect of significant environmental changes and to questionable assumptions.

It is not possible to be prescriptive on how analysis of environmental factors should be undertaken. At the heart of the matter are two issues; first, it should be of constant concern and second, it must become sensitive to the implications for the enterprise. Some steps in achieving this are obvious such as reading newspapers, general or professional journals and attendance at conferences.

Research in this area is thin. Aguilar found that top managers' sources of information about the environment were personal experiences, journals, reports, books, professional meetings, industrial conferences, colleagues, board members, friends and employees. Thomas reported effective use of formal 'environmental scanning' in nine large organisations. But the desirability of setting up such separate environmental appraisal units was questioned by Stubbact in a study of twelve organisations, 'effective environmental scanning depends on the judgements and interpretations of general managers familiar with these environments'.

4.3 Forecasting the environment

Given the complexity of the organisation's environment it is clear that consideration of *all* forces is required. Some aspects of some areas may be amenable to quantification, others will not. It is necessary to over-

Figure 4.2 The scope of environmental forecasting

Source: Wilson, I. H. (1977) 'Forecasting Social and Political Trends' in Taylor and Sparkes, *Corporate Strategy and Planning* (London: Heinemann, 1977) pp. 96–117; amended.

come an over-reliance on 'rational' models and to accept as valid supposedly subjective judgements concerning the future. This is not to argue that such an approach is any less rigorous, indeed by questioning what are often implicit assumptions by making them explicit, managers are able to subject the assumptions to critical examination and to establish points at which such predictions can be checked against events, allowing modification to take place if necessary.

The more complete approach to environmental forecasting is depicted in Figure 4.2. This broad outlook encompassing the forces identified in the preceding section provides the framework for our discussion of forecasting.

Socio-political forecasting

The importance of changes in the social and legal political environment to all organisations has already been discussed, but it is worth reiterating that change in this segment causes change in economic and technological environments. The socio-political arena is particularly susceptible to non-quantitative appraisal methods, two of which will be discussed, based on Ian Wilson's article in Taylor and Sparkes (pp. 96–117) prior to a brief consideration of scenarios and Delphi techniques.

The *probability-diffusion matrix* is a method which provides a useful starting-point in a difficult area of analysis. Its use – and Wilson observes that its principal purpose should be to stimulate improvement as opposed to using it blindly – involves gathering information, analysing the information, reaching informed judgements, assigning mathematical probabilities and taking the analysis as far as is realistic given the nature of the tool.

In his discussion of the probability-diffusion matrix Wilson notes:

> In predicting developments over a decade it is more meaningful to talk in terms of degrees of relative probability than of certainty or 'inevitability' . . . assigning probability to a trend or future event is a matter of judgement after weighing the known data and cross-checking with informed opinion. A further cross-check can be run by plotting the predictions along a probability axis so that their relative positions are made apparent. It is also helpful to assess the probable diffusion of a trend or event . . . Again plotting the predictions along a diffusion axis makes explicit, in a co-ordinated fashion, the relative weightings assigned in separate judgements.

The combination of the two axes into the matrix shown in Figure 4.3 enables a check on the internal consistency of a large number of predictions to be made. An event might fall anywhere on the matrix, the position depends on the probabilities assigned by those involved. For example, the probability of single-digit inflation for the remainder of the 1980s could occur in the upper right sector of the matrix, indicating a

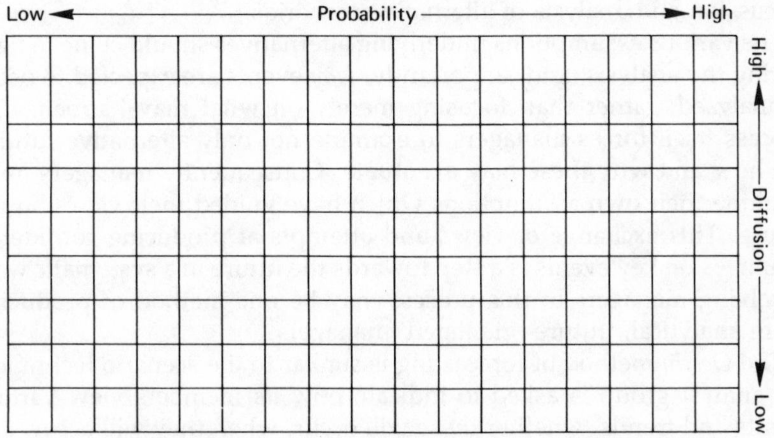

Figure 4.3 Probability-diffusion matrix

high probability of occurrence and high diffusion of this probability over the relevant population, say the UK in this instance.

The second method of forecasting is the *values profile* which involves constructing a profile of values for a particular population, young people in the EEC for example. Again Wilson provides a succinct examination of the technique.

> Like the probability-diffusion matrix, this chart should be viewed not as a precise scientific measurement but merely as a useful way of looking at the future. Like the matrix it contains plottings that are meant to be indicative – pointing the way to a more comprehensive study – rather than definitive. To point up the possible attitude changes as dramatically as possible the chart has been made up of contrasting pairs of values. Each society and generation has tended to seek its own new balance between these contrasting pairs, with the weight shifting from one side to the other as conditions and attitudes change.

The result of responses to questions posed to the subject population about a range of topics gives a profile of the values of that population. This profile can indicate, to an extent, how that population may react to alternative choices. As such it is one aid in developing an enterprise's strategy.

Scenarios are a method used to explore the probability of possible future developments and changes and to identify the interaction of uncertain future trends and events, particularly causal relationships and key decision-points. Scenarios are generated by experts, panels, or managers who draw up future situations encompassing various dimensions of an entity, an industry, or a society. The central point is the discussion and analysis of alternative scenarios.

The various assumptions underlying alternatives should come to light during the analysis, and, importantly, *why* events are expected to occur is analysed, rather than focusing merely on what may happen. The process itself forces managers to examine not only alternative futures but how and why these may eventuate. Consequently managers must examine their own assumptions which have guided their views on the future. This exchange of views and attempts at producing confidence estimates on key events is a step towards the future in a systematic way. Involving managers in this process may be one method of producing more analytical, 'future-orientated' managers.

The *Delphi* method of forecasting is similar to the scenario technique. An analyst group is asked to indicate how its members view various events and trends, whether these will occur, when they will occur, and the likelihood of occurrence. The information is then summarised, aggregated and presented as feedback to the group, each member of which can then compare his/her prediction with the 'average'. The individual group member may then modify their first prediction, and the process is repeated. Ultimately this iterative process may result in consensus from the group about future events and trends.

Technological forecasting

Because technological change often develops because of changes in the socio-political arena, which alter needs, consumer behaviour and so on, the features noted in the preceding section need to be kept in view in any appraisal of the technological environment.

Committed analysis is required to investigate changes in the technological environment which involves categorising and putting in order of priority information concerning possible effects, and then drawing conclusions about the most probable and important features. Forecasting technological change is primarily achieved by analysing competitive behaviour. Consequently there is requirement to define competition, including potential competitors from both public and private sectors, as well as giving consideration to other industries. Information on state-of-the-art developments may be obtained from technical journals, seminars and research papers. Technological forecasting may take a more structured form as noted by Gordon Wills. In his article he reports that scenarios and the Delphi technique have been used in predicting technological information. He also notes that morphological analysis, which involves a systematic analysis of a technology into its basic parameters, and which provides rigour and a fresh orientation on customary technologies, is a valuable tool acclaimed by both scientists and research and development managers. Wills concludes by advocating that the evaluation of technological change should not be limited to specialists but should include marketing, sales and personnel people, for example, because one is seeking technological opportunity and creative insights regardless of their source.

Economic forecasting

Economic forecasting is more susceptible to quantitative analysis than are other aspects fo the organisation's environment. Nevertheless the economy is still susceptible to influence by factors, such as government policy and international influences, which can distort the most thorough and logical mathematical techniques.

Forecasting techniques in this area may range from individual judgement to highly complex and sophisticated econometric models. Cooke and Slack (1984) classify forecasting models and techniques into:

	Non-causal	Causal
Objective	Time series analysis	Regression Econometric models
Subjective	Hunch	Individual expert opinion Group expert opinion (e.g. Delphi)

Figure 4.4 A classification of some forecasting methods

Source: Cooke, S. and Slack N. (1983) *Making Management Decisions* (Englewood Cliffs, New Jersey: Prentice-Hall) p. 386.

(a) subjective and objective;
(b) causal and non-causal.

Subjective methods involve judgement and intuition, whereas objective techniques have specified and systematic procedures so that the results produced are capable of replication whoever uses them. Non-causal techniques use past values to predict the future so assuming that the underlying causes of events will continue to shape events in exactly the same way in the future. Causal methods attempt to make predictions on the basis of causal relationships, so if the cause – effect relationship between variables can be modelled then predictions of the factors which influence a forecast will allow the forecast to be made. Figure 4.4 classifies some of the more common techniques.

'Time series' examines historic data over time and then uses the analysis to forecast future behaviour. Regression models use statistical techniques to determine the 'best fit' expression which describes the relationship between the variable being forecast and other variables. Econometric models consist of a set of regression equations which describe complex cause – effect relationships which are then solved simultaneously allowing a more realistic representation of the relationships.

There are a number of dimensions to the problem of using and utilising any one of the number of forecasting models and techniques. First we need to recognise that forecasts are not better than the assumptions on which they are based, hence the more explicit and specific the assumptions, the better it is for forecasting purposes. Second, judgement plays an important role in predicting the future. However sophisticated the technique may be, imperfect data will always give imperfect results. So recorded data should be viewed in the light of the analyst's knowledge and understanding of the market in which he operates. Third, although the pace of change is increasing it is important to recognise that major trends change only gradually. Finally, in recognising that most organisations use a number of forecasting techniques it is important to ensure that assumptions, say about the growth in GDP or changes in inflation rates, are consistent in all the models used.

In the economic arena, therefore, the firm will be attempting to predict both macroeconomic phenomena and more specific microeconomic phenomena with a view to forecasting the future position of the industry in which it operates. So the firm will need to have a view of future events, and how such events shape the firm's immediate economic environment, by considering, for example, how changes in general consumer spending, investment spending and movement in the business cycle will affect the firm. As Sparkes (1977) notes

> The business planner is much more concerned with the 'unconditional' forecast, which incorporates the changes in policy the government may be likely to introduce. Gauging the timing of changes in government policy so as to anticipate the development of the business cycle is perhaps the most difficult aspect of the whole task.

Evaluation of forecasts

The performance of forecasting models is not impressive. Hogarth and Makridakis (1981) found that, while the overall performance of forecasts was poor, in certain situations some forecasting techniques perform quite well: 'simple mechanistic methods, such as those used in time-series forecasts, can often make accurate short-term forecasts and even outperform more theoretically elegant and elaborate approaches used in econometric forecasting'. Cooke and Slack (1984) have observed that, even recognising the problem of judging success because of the time between the forecast and the event, long-term forecasting methods are more amenable to an objective causal approach.

Perhaps more importantly the *process* of forecasting provides those involved with valuable insights into the nature of events as well as providing a vehicle for communication between decision-makers. Also, even though a particular technique was incorrect in predicting what would happen, it does not necessarily mean that it was also incorrect in predicting what would not happen. The importance of the process should not be underestimated. Fahey *et al.* (1977) noted that some firms included line-management as part of teams engaged in environmental analysis. In this way they were involved in the process of environmental

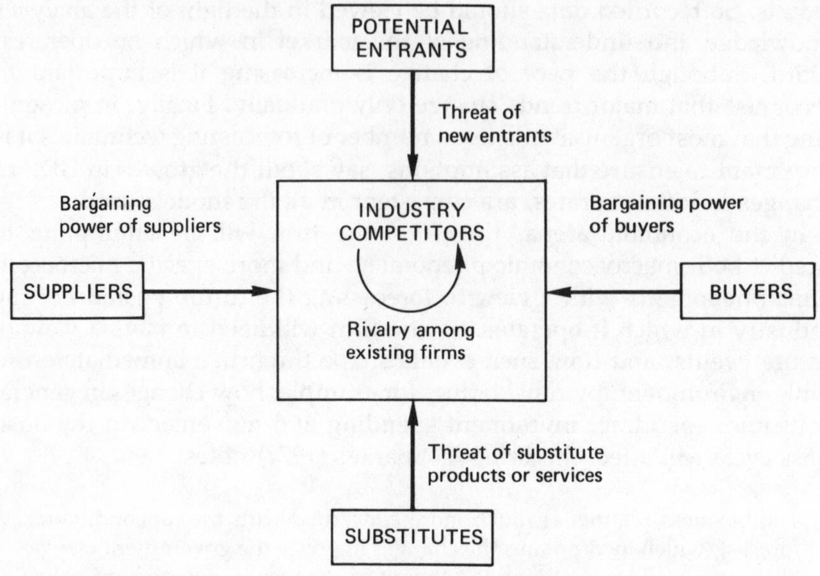

Figure 4.5 Forces driving industry competition

Source: Porter M. E. (1980) *Competitive Strategy, Techniques for Analysing Industries and Competitors* (New York: The Free Press) p.4.

and futures-forecasting, so enhancing the integration of forecasting efforts into strategic decision-making.

4.4 Structural analysis of industries

Having reviewed the broad environmental forces which influence organisations it should be clear that most of the factors examined are significant in a relative way. This is because these forces usually affect all firms in the industry. We will now consider the more immediate environment in which the enterprise operates by using Porter's book *Competitive Strategy : Techniques for Analysing Industries and Competitors* (1980) to provide a framework for a more detailed examination of the industry (or industries) relevant to the firm.

Porter identifies five basic competitive forces, (Figure 4.5) which determine the state of competition and its underlying economic structure. It is necessary to identify the *key* structural features so that the strength of the competitive forces and hence industry profitability can be determined. The essence of the analysis is to identify the sources of each force to enable the organisation to develop a strategy which builds upon opportunities while avoiding threats. Drawing on Porter's work we will deal with each of the five competitive forces.

An important feature of the model shown in Figure 4.5 is the recognition that competition in an industry goes beyond the immediate competing firms. All five forces determine the intensity of competition and profitability. Therefore, identification of the strongest force(s) is critical in strategy-formulation.

Threat of new entrants

The threat of new entrants is a function of both barriers to entry and the reaction from existing competitors that an entrant can expect. Barriers to entry arise out of six main sources:

Economies of scale act as a barrier to entry by requiring the entrant to come in on a large scale, risking strong reaction from existing competitors, or alternatively to come in on a small scale accepting a cost disadvantage. Scale economies may be present in nearly every function of the enterprise. Businesses in diversified firms may be able to achieve economies of scale if they are able to share operations or functions. In this way related diversifications around a common core (of operations or functions) may remove volume constraints imposed by the size of a particular industry.

Product differentiation creates a barrier to entry by forcing entrants to incur expenditure to overcome existing customer loyalties. Such expenditure often involves losses in the start-up phase and may take considerable time. An investment in a brand name may be particularly hazardous, since it will have little or no value if entry fails.

Capital requirements may create a barrier if there is a need to invest or commit substantial resources in order to compete, especially if the capital required is for unrecoverable upfront advertising or research and development. It is important to recognise that resources may also be required for working capital (inventory, debtors, etc.) and losses in the start-up period, which, taken together, may be larger than the capital costs of, say, plant and equipment.

Switching-costs, that is the one-off cost to a buyer of changing from one supplier to another, may be a barrier to entry. Switching-costs could include the cost of new ancilliary equipment, product redesign, employee retraining and so on. An example of switching-costs operating as an entry barrier would be the cost to the NHS of changing the supplier of oxygen and other gases from BOC. Another could be the retraining and spare-parts stockholding costs an airline would incur if it decided to introduce a new aircraft into an existing fleet of common aircraft types.

Access to distribution channels can be a barrier to entry because of the new entrant's need to obtain distribution for its product. A new entrant may have to persuade the distribution channels to accept its product by providing extra incentives which reduce profits. Occasionally this barrier to entry may be insurmountable unless the firm creates an entirely new distribution network.

Cost advantages independent of scale may be enjoyed by incumbents in an industry which a new entrant may not be able to replicate. Such factors may include:

- proprietory product technology maintained through patents or secrecy;
- favourable access to raw materials where incumbent firms have tied up the most favourable sources using long-term contracts;
- favourable locations may be enjoyed by established enterprises prior to the market bidding-up prices to their full value;
- learning or experience curve effects may be enjoyed by incumbents (see Chapter 3).

In addition to these six features, government policy may be a barrier to entry, for example, through the use of the Monopolies Commission. More subtle governmental restrictions may derive from environmental pollution standards which effectively increase the capital required for entry to the industry.

The expectations by the potential entrant of existing firms' reactions will also influence the threat of entry. Where existing firms are expected to react vigorously entry may be deterred. The following conditions are likely to signal retaliation by existing firms in the industry, and may act as a deterrent:

- a history of vigorous retaliation to new entrants;
- established firms with substantial resources to retaliate;
- established firms with great commitment to the industry and highly illiquid assets employed in it;
- slow industry growth, which limits the ability of the industry to absorb a new entrant without depressing the performance of established firms.

The *entry-deterring price* is an interesting hypothetical concept advanced by Porter as the prevailing structure of prices which balances the potential rewards from entry with the expected costs of overcoming entry barriers and risking retaliations. So, where the current price level is above the entry deterring price, potential entrants will forecast above-average profits from entry, and hence will enter the industry.

In considering barriers to entry from a strategic perspective it is crucial to recognise that the conditions noted above will change and that a firm's own decisions may have a major impact. Also some organisations may possess the resources or key skills which will allow them easily to overcome entry barriers, as the ability to share costs, for example, may enable an enterprise to achieve low-cost entry to an industry. Tangentially many of Porter's ideas are supported by evidence from other sources and it is perhaps useful to summarise one view of the threat of new entrants as observed by Peters and Waterman:

> The real barriers to entry are the 75-year investment in getting hundreds of thousands to live service, quality and customer problem solving at IBM, or the 150-year investment in quality at P & G. These are the truly insuperable barriers to entry, based on people capital tied up in ironclad traditions of service, reliability and quality.

Rivalry among existing firms

Rivalry among existing firms may manifest itself in a number of ways – price competition, new products and increased levels of customer service. Rivalry occurs because one or more firms see the opportunity to improve their position or perhaps feels the pressure. Competitive moves by one enterprise normally affect its competitors, so inciting retaliation or counter-moves. Firms, in the majority of industries, are mutually dependent, and this process of action-then-reaction may not leave the initiator, or the industry as a whole, better off.

The degree of rivalry in an industry is a function of a number of interacting structural features:

Numerous or equally balanced competitors may create instability because where there are a large number of firms some may believe they can make competitive moves without being noticed, and where there are relatively few but relatively balanced firms (in size and resources) they may be prone to conflict and possess the resources for sustained and vigorous retaliation. On the other hand where an industry is dominated by a small number of firms there is little possibility of mistaking relative strength and the leader(s) can impose discipline.

Slow industry growth means that firms seeking to expand have to gain market-share from others in the industry. Thus competition tends to be more intense than in a growing industry where results may be a function of keeping up with industry growth.

High fixed costs create pressure for firms to fill capacity which may lead to price-cutting when excess capacity exists. The important feature here is fixed costs relative to value added as those firms who purchase a significant proportion of costs in external inputs (that is, low value added) will be under pressure to break even.

Lack of differentiation or *switching costs* tend to occur when the product is seen as a commodity, the buyer's choice being based, therefore, on price and service leading to intense price and service competition. Differentiation provides a defence in this instance as buyers have loyalties to, or preferences for, a particular seller.

Capacity augmented in large investments may disrupt the industry supply/demand balance, especially if there is a risk of bunching capacity additions. This is a particular problem where economies of scale indicate large capital increments as is the situation in the manufacture of chemicals for example.

Diverse competitors because they have differing goals and differing strategies may not be able to read competitor's intentions, and their decisions may run counter to others in the industry. So a firm viewing a market purely as an outlet for surplus capacity may well adopt strategies completely at odds with a firm viewing the market as a primary outlet. Foreign competitors may often increase the diversity of an industry in a similar way.

High strategic stakes make an industry more volatile if firms perceive the industry as strategically important to them. In such cases profitability may be sacrificed to achieve success in order to enhance a firm's overall corporate strategy.

High exit barriers keep firms in an industry even when low returns are earned. When exit barriers are high, excess capacity stays, firms hang on and the profitability of the industry as a whole may be low. Exit barriers arise for a number of reasons:

- dedicated assets which are highly specialised to the business with low liquidation values;

- exit costs including resettlement, redundancy agreement, spare-parts capabilities;
- strategic interrelationships between the business unit and other parts of the firm such as shared facilities, access to financial markets and so on;
- emotional barriers caused by management's unwillingness to make exit decisions because of loyalty to employees, identification with a particular business, etc.,
- government and social restrictions involving discouragement of exit because of concern for the impact on a required economy or unemployment.

As with the threat of entrants the intensity of rivalry between competing firms will change over time. As an industry matures rivalry intensifies (because of slower growth) leading to declining profits and a shake-out. Technological change may raise the relative level of fixed costs leading to a more volatile situation. Many features which determine the intensity of competition are part of the economies of the industry. Nevertheless the firm may be able to make certain shifts in posture to improve its position by increasing product differentiation, or raising buyer's switching costs for example.

Threat of substitutes

All firms in an industry compete with other industries offering substitute products or services. Substitutes effectively limit the returns in an industry by limiting prices, so influencing the industry's overall elasticity of demand. Identifying substitutes involves seeking out other products which perform the same function as the industry's product. Often an industry may have to take collective action to improve its position as one firm's initiative may be insufficient.

The substitutes which warrant attention are those which are subject to trends improving their price-performance trade off with the industry's product, and those produced by industries earning high profits. A degree of subtlety is also required in the analysis of potential substitutes as they may arise from businesses seemingly remote from the industry. For example, the already highly-competitive, and highly-profitable, food-retailing industry may be entered by one of the large profitable oil companies – BP who are experimenting with 'Food Plus' stores in Leicester with plans for a network of 60–70 stores, developed out of its successful experience with the same concept in Australia. So the pressure on the independent and small co-operatives is likely to intensify as the supermarket chains compete for the large markets and the oil companies exploit the convenience shopping trade with the financial and physical resources to represent a significant threat.

Bargaining power of buyers

Buyers, in negotiating for improved service, better quality and lower prices compete with an industry and by such actions reduce profitability. The power buyers hold is a function of a number of factors and is likely to be high when:

- there is a concentration of buyers especially if they purchase a large proportion of the sales;
- the product purchased is a significant part of the buyer's costs when they are likely to seek alternative suppliers;
- the product is undifferentiated or the buyer faces few switching-costs, buyers may play one supplier off against another;
- the buyer earns low profits so creating a need to lower purchasing costs, conversely very profitable buyers may be less price-sensitive;
- there is a credible threat of backward integration by the buyer if satisfactory prices, quality, etc., cannot be obtained;
- the product is not important to the quality of the buyers product.

These factors change with time and the firm's choice of buyer-groups should be regarded as an important element in strategic decision-making. It is possible, by exercising buyer-selection, for an enterprise to enhance its strategic position by choosing buyers who do not have the power to exercise adverse influence.

Bargaining power of suppliers

Suppliers can exert power over firms in an industry by raising prices or reducing the quality of purchased goods and services, so reducing profitability. The conditions which tend to make suppliers powerful are similar to those making buyers powerful, and supplier-power is likely to be high when:

- there is a concentration of suppliers as opposed to a more fragmented source of supply;
- there are no substitute products to contend with;
- the industry is not an important customer of the supplier group, in which case the supplier need have little regard for the future of customers;

- the supplier's product is an important input to the buyer, because if such an input is crucial to the success of the buyer's output then the buyer is less likely to be price-sensitive;
- switching-costs from one supplier to another are high or the supplier's products are differentiated, which in both cases reduces the ability of buyers to play one supplier off against another;
- there is a credible threat of the suppliers integrating forward if they do not achieve the prices, and hence profitability they seek.

It is important to recognise that *labour* is a supplier, and may exert a considerable degree of power in some situations. The factors noted above should also be applied in analysing the degree of influence of labour with the addition of consideration of the degree of organisation and whether the supply of scarce labour skills can be expanded. The power of buyers and suppliers over the firm is considered further in Chapter 13 on Power.

Structural analysis and strategy

Having identified the forces influencing competition in an industry the firm is in a position to consider its own position in relation to the underlying causes of each of the competitive forces. Porter (1980) argues that an effective strategy should be designed to establish a defendable position *vis-à-vis* the five competitive forces involving three possible approaches:

- positioning the enterprise in such a way that it has the best defense against the competitive forces, which in effect means matching the firm's strengths and weaknesses (which we discuss in Chapter 5) to a given industrial structure;
- influencing the balance of forces by altering their causes so improving the organisation's relative position. This involves utilising structural analysis with a view to identifying key factors and so the places where action to influence the balance will yield the greater pay-off;
- forecasting changes in the factors underlying the five forces and responding accordingly, so exploiting change by the selection of an appropriate strategy prior to competitors' recognition of the change.

4.5 Opportunities and threats

Building on our analysis so far concerning the nature of the environment and of the structural features of the industry we are now able to identify environmental issues that may have an impact on the firm. However, because of the diverse nature of organisations and the wide variety of environmental factors the identification which follows is necessarily broad rather than a detailed prescription. It should however be of some assistance in achieving a degree of *focus* in deliberation on strategy-formulation. As we have already noted in our introduction to this chapter consideration of external environmental features is but one part of the overall appraisal of an organisation's situation, and in our later consideration of some of the issues (for example, Chapter 6 on Strategic options) we will be giving more detailed analysis to many of the issues raised earlier in this chapter.

The first aspect we consider in looking at opportunities and threats is the extent to which an enterprise's strategy matches, or does not match its environment. Thus an organisation's environment may have changed, but the strategy has not. This can often occur when a relatively stable industry becomes more volatile but the firm does not alter its strategy. Alternatively, or additionally, the structure of an organisation is not suited to the new conditions prevailing in the environment, which may be the situation where different organisational structures are required to cope with a more dynamic volatile situation. (The links between the structure of the firm and its environment are considered in Chapter 11.)

As with many situations management must assess the change in the environment, in relation to the nature of the firm, to determine whether the change is permanent or merely a short-term phenomenon, and the speed and extent of the change – that is, is it likely to affect a large section of the firm? Change in the wider environment may significantly affect the structure of the industry. For example, the balance in the competitive forces may be altered because barriers to entry have been reduced by technological innovation, which may require an incumbent organisation to undertake a fundamental strategic shift to maintain position.

The fact that an organisation's strategy does not match its environment may not lead to an immediate threat, unless it is unable to respond. Whether or not a firm is capable of change and can manage the process are considered in Chapter 10.

An external appraisal would form an important part of any systematic approach to strategy-making. All corporate planning models include an external or environmental appraisal. However, managers inevitably monitor the environment even if they are not attempting a structured approach to strategic planning. The key issues to which managers should address themselves are:

1. Could we benefit from a more systematic analysis of our firm's environment?
2. How can we make sure that vital environmental information is reaching the right people, in the right form at the right time (and this may well include quite junior levels of management)?

The issues raised in (2) are likely to require tailor-made solutions – the information system needs to match the particular circumstances of the organisation. One problem that must be avoided is information overload – a swamping of managers with so much irrelevant data that the nuggets of vital information are lost.

The second aspect which requires consideration is the strength of the firm relative to the environmental changes it faces. The next chapter deals in detail with the analysis of the internal position and what we are concerned with here is some indication of whether the firm is capable of handling environmental change given strengths in some areas and weaknesses in others.

Strengths of an organisation depend on a wide variety of factors. For example, a firm may have a record of successful product innovations involving substantial changes in work practices, organisational structures entry into new markets and so on, indicating that it is well-placed, or was well-placed in the past, to handle change. Its key strength therefore, may, not be its product innovations but the fact that it has a flexible posture.

4.6 Summary

External appraisal encompasses a broad sweep of the variety of environmental influences which affect organisations. Because enterprises may be crucially influenced by external forces, and because decisions made by the firm may influence its environment it is necessary for managers to understand the key influences which affect the organisation.

We have discussed a number of forecasting methods, such as the probability-diffusion matrix, scenarios, technological and economic forecasting, and concluded that while forecasting may not have an impressive record, the process may well provide valuable insights for those involved. A review of industrial structure utilising the framework developed by Porter allowed us to focus on those issues more directly related to, and perhaps capable of influence by, the entity. This type of analysis – broad environmental then more focused on the particular industry concerned – is designed to allow managers to develop a view on those opportunities present, and on those threats posed, in the environment.

Further reading

Readers wishing to utilise the concepts introduced on the structural analysis of industries should read Porter (1980) chapters 1, 2, 3 and 7. Cooke, and Slack, (1984) provide a straightforward account of the use of a variety of forecasting techniques. Taylor (1977) includes some excellent material to which reference is made in the chapter, for example, Wilson's paper on forecasting social and political trends.

References

Aguilar, F. J. (1977) *Scanning the Business Environment* (New York: Macmillan) p. 11.

Cooke, S. and Slack, N. (1984) *Making Management Decisions* (Hemel Hempstead: Prentice-Hall).

Fahey, L. and King, R. (1977) 'Environmental Scanning for Corporate Planning', in McCarthy D. J. *et al. 'Business Policy and Strategy: Concepts and Readings'* (Homewood, Illinois: Irwin, 1983) pp. 130–43.

Hogart. R. M. and Makridakis, S. (1981) 'Forecasting and Planning: An Evaluation', *Management Science*, vol. 27, pp. 115–38).

Peters, T. J. and Waterman, R. H. (1982) *In Search of Excellence* (New York: Harper & Row).

Porter, M. E. (1980) *Competitive Strategy* (New York: Free Press).

Quinn, J. B. (1980) *Strategies for Change* (Homewood, Illinois: Irwin).

Sparkes, J. R. (1977) 'Monitoring the Economic Environment' in Taylor, B. and Sparkes, J. (1977). *Corporate Strategy and Planning* (London: Heinemann) pp. 61–74.

Stubbact, C. (1982) 'Are Environmental Scanning Units Effective?', *Long Range Planning*. June, pp. 138–44.

Thomas, P. S. (1980) 'Environmental Scanning – The State of the Art', *Long Range Planning*, February, pp. 20–8.

Wills, G. S. C., (1977) 'Forecasting Technological Innovation', in Taylor, B. and

Sparkes, J. *Corporate Strategy and Planning* (London: Heinemann, 1977) pp. 75–95.

Wilson, I. H. (1977) 'Forecasting Social and Political Trends', in Taylor, B. and Sparkes, J. *Corporate Strategy and Planning* (London: Heinemann, 1977) pp. 96–117.

CHAPTER 5

Internal appraisal

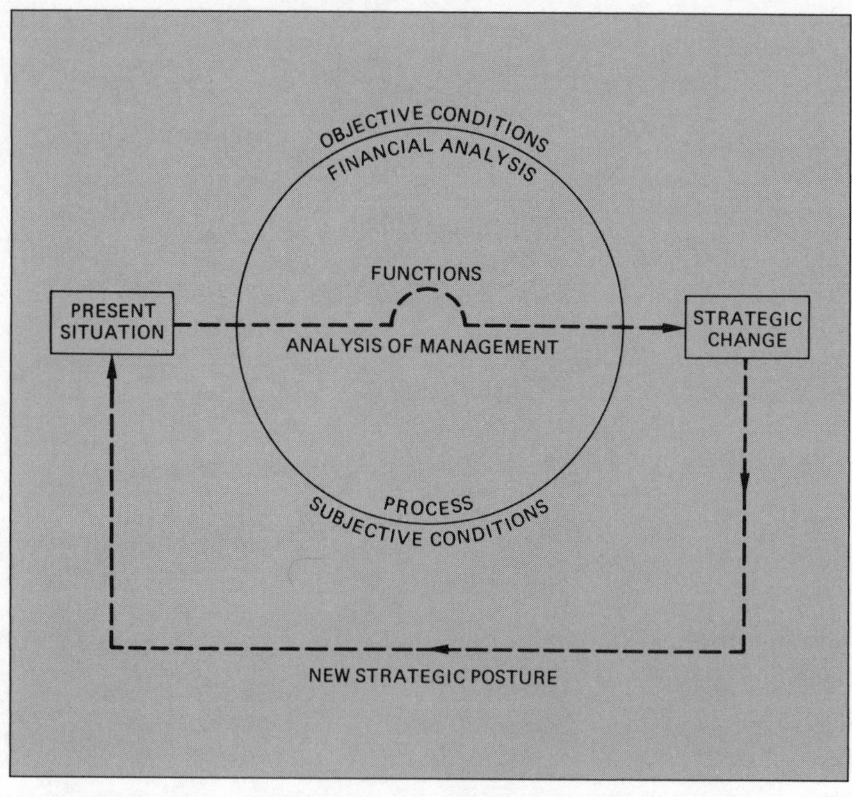

5.1 Introduction

In this, the second stage, of the strategic analysis of the firm we consider the objective conditions which exist within the organisation. The assessment of the internal position is of importance in evaluating the enterprise's capabilities in the light of its resources. So we should be in a situation to judge the organisation's capability in view of its resource profile, and as a consequence of our external appraisal, to decide what it ought to be doing considering the environment in which it is operating.

For the internal analysis to be effective, the *process* must be underpinned by a strategic view, preferably in a creative manner, which will allow multidimensional insights to be obtained. In the process of strategy-formulation the objective of internal appraisal is to produce a picture of the organisation, its resources and capabilities which provides a segmented and integrated internal perspective of the strengths and weaknesses of the firm as a whole. This chapter, and the preceding chapter on external appraisal, taken together provide a comprehensive consideration of organisational analysis.

Our discussion of internal appraisal will commence with a consideration of the role and process of internal analysis followed by a review of the parts or functions in the organisation which require evaluation. We conclude by discussing the assessment of the entity's resources in terms of key areas, balance and flexibility.

5.2 The role and process of internal appraisal

Our model of the strategy-formulation process (Figure 3.2 in Chapter 3) indicated the importance of the impact of the present situation in which the enterprise finds itself. We argued then that not only was the current position a result of past decisions but also that it represents a starting-point for analysis. Therefore, to determine the current position involves consideration of the firm's resources, the business(es) the firm is in, what its objectives are, and how well it achieves them. The results of this analysis are crucial elements in determining the firm's future strategy. Further, internal appraisal not only indicates what resources the firm has but also evaluates how well they have been used by management. This may also lead to a judgement on how well resources may be used in the future by the same management. The scope of internal analysis is more than just identifying and tabulating the organisation's resources. It involves appraising management's utilisation of resources, its formulation and implementation of strategy as well as its performance in the various functions.

Analysis of resources involves an examination of all areas of the enterprise with a view to reaching conclusions based upon facts, opinions, observations and any other available evidence, assessed in terms of the firm's strategy. Hofer and Schendel (1978, p. 145) expound the view that the process involves three stages:

- development of a profile of principal skills and resources;
- comparison of this resource profile with the product/market requirements to identify strengths and weaknesses;
- comparison of the strengths and weaknesses with major competitors to identify areas where significant competitive advantage exists.

However, they then go on to admit that in practice this process is dynamic and interactive and that the presumed linear progression may not be followed. Indeed this could be seen as an advantage since it may lead to insights which might be overlooked by a structured and more bureaucratic analysis.

Before proceeding to discuss what should be analysed and why, we need to consider the limitations to an objective assessment of the organisation's resources. In Chapter 3 we referred to the fact that strategic decisions, because of their complexity, are often analysed utilising managers' experience and judgement. Stevenson (1976) found that an individual's cognitive perceptions of strengths and weaknesses were strongly influenced by factors associated with both the individual and the organisation's attributes. 'Position in the organisation, perceived role, and type of responsibility so strongly influenced the assessment that the objective reality of the situation tended to be overwhelmed.' Stevenson's study indicated that there were a variety of influences which impinge upon the manager as he analyses strengths and weaknesses. These influences are shown diagrammatically in Figure 5.1.

In addition Stevenson's research found that most attributes were both strengths and weaknesses because of the ambiguity of the definition process. This reinforces our view that management needs to apply judgement to develop a useful tool for action, judgement that needs to be exercised in the context of the decision process in the organisation.

Further to these results, and of relevance to the analysis of resources, is Stevenson's conclusion that managers use different criteria in defining strengths and weaknesses. He identified three types of criteria:

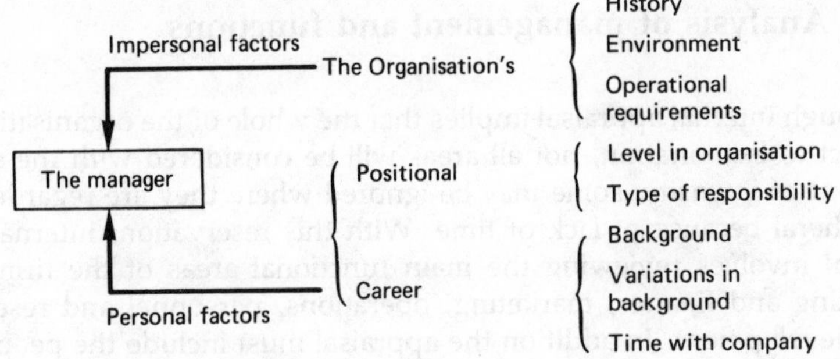

FIGURE 5.1 Factors which influence a manager in defining strengths and weaknesses

Source: Stevenson H. H. (1976) 'Defining Corporate Strengths and Weaknesses', *Sloan Management Review*, Spring, pp. 51–68.

- Historical – past experience of the organisation
  intracompany comparisons
  budgets
- Competitive – direct and indirect competition
  other companies
- Normative – consultants' opinions
  rules of thumb
  managements' understanding of management literature
  opinion

Historical criteria were used to identify strengths and normative criteria to identify weaknesses. The use of historical criteria for evaluating strengths occurs because managers are constantly searching for improvements in previously identified problem areas, so the base from which these improvements are made is the standard by which the current attributes are judged. Conversely with weaknesses the organisation's current position is only a step on the way to where the managers wish it were. The gap between the current position and the goal reflects a normative judgement of what ought to be. To conclude, it is important to remember that the items being evaluated are not specific events; they are directions, strategies, policy commitments and past decisions. The process of defining strengths and weaknesses can provide a link in a feedback loop so allowing managers to learn from the success or failure of the policies they initiated.

5.3 Analysis of management and functions

Although internal appraisal implies that the whole of the organisation is subject to examination, not all areas will be considered with the same amount of intensity; some may be ignored where they are regarded as peripheral because of lack of time. With this reservation, internal appraisal involves reviewing the main functional areas of the firm, accounting and finance, marketing, operations, personnel and research and development. In addition the appraisal must include the people in the organisation as this aspect will affect the areas and is probably the most important part of the entire analysis.

Implicit, therefore, in our appraisal of the functional areas is an evaluation of their management. There is a caveat, however, in that it is necessary to distinguish between how well management performs its functions and with what results. Such a distinction is necessary because the results alone may not reveal the whole picture. For example, the success of Jaguar Cars in 1984 and 1985 is probably due in part to the relative decline of the £ sterling against the US dollar making exports to America more profitable. Because of the importance of appraising, the people in an organisation in a strategic manner, we will consider this broad over-arching aspect first and then go on to discuss the analysis of the various functions.

Human resources

One result of conducting an internal analysis will be an assessment of the top management in the entity. In evaluating and assessing individual functions and their managers valuable insights can be obtained concerning the top managers under whose aegis the events occurred. In analysing top management, results of all types – not just financial results – provide a valuable backdrop. The point is not that financial results are unimportant, but that other results of activities are also important. Another crucial aspect to consider is whether the results achieved were planned and measured against a predetermined objective. Although an assessment of top management would probably commence with a review of the organisation's results, in terms of sales, profits, research and development, morale and so on, a complete analysis should incorporate aspects which are less capable of quantification like the type of leadership exhibited in the various departments, the response of supervisors to their managers, and of the workforce to their supervisors. There is one other point of relevance to understanding the significance of the results achieved which is that some appreciation should be obtained of the problem faced by management in putting the results in perspective.

Human resources are present throughout the organisation, and although our consideration of the main functional areas will include analysis of this element, it should also be considered in its own right so that a judgement can be made as to whether the people in the entity are a resource and strength or a weakness in the future development of the organisation. Some of the key issues to be considered in this context would be:

- the relationship between individuals and the enterprise;
- the impact of informal groups and whether they are supportive to the formal organisation;
- the degree of management sensitivity to human behaviour;
- morale in the organisation, and the health of the organisational climate;
- the qualifications and expertise of personnel given the present, projected activities of the entity;
- the organisation's policy in respect of hiring, placement in the entity, and training of individuals;
- the organisation's relationships with trade unions represented in the firm;
- the firm's position, relative to competitors, in respect of pay, promotion, fringe benefits and so on;
- the attention devoted to the people in the firm both in formal terms, such as the personnel department, and in terms of the organisation's overall philosophy;
- the extent to which human resources are considered strategically in the firm by their consideration in the context of formulating and implementing strategic decisions.

The importance of analysing the human resources of the organisation should not be understated, even though in some respects it is perhaps a more problematic area in which to form judgements. As we will see later the implementation phase is crucially dependent upon the people who will be required to put the decisions into action.

Accounting and finance

The financial area is often a good place to start an internal appraisal because an insight into the financial situation can give a perspective on the state of the organisation fairly quickly. In addition, for most entities financial resources are the most flexible as they are generated by activities of the whole firm and are directly convertible into other types of resources. An organisation's financial statements provide a wealth of information concerning the present situation and the results of operations over time.

A useful starting-point for analysis is the calculation of ratios; a comprehensive selection of ratios is provided in the appendix to this chapter. True analysis, however, requires looking behind the figures to ascertain what is actually represented. Drawing quick conclusions is to be resisted as the information *must* be related to the situation in which the enterprise is, in terms of its competitive environment or stage of development. Furthermore a comparative analysis, say with industry averages or competitors, will considerably enhance the utility of the information derived from ratios. Valuable though this is it should be realised that financial statements only provide historic information, some of which may be from a relatively distant past. The balance-sheet position relates to a specific past date and may not necessarily always reflect a realistic picture of the firm if, for example, it was drawn up at a low point in a trading cycle. The profit and loss statement reveals the results of past operations for a specific period. As such these statements show what has happened and what the situation was but that is all. It is tempting to extrapolate the data into the future but this presupposes that past conditions will remain similar. There is one other important aspect of financial statement analysis which requires addressing and that is that any consideration of the results must take account of the fact that most financial statements are not adjusted for inflation. This can have a marked impact on profitability ratios in particular by producing quite dramatic reductions. This can be simply illustrated by comparing the return on shareholders equity for Reckitt & Colman in 1983 which on the traditional historic-cost basis was 18 per cent, but on an inflation-adjusted basis was 6 per cent.

Results, though somewhat outdated, are important because they indicate the financial consequences of past decisions and conditions. Much can be learned by reviewing accounting and finance about management which goes beyond this area providing useful and necessary insights into how the organisation is managed. Financial information is a vital element in such functions as planning and control and communication. The adoption of a strategic view incorporating the financial status of the entity provides a broad background for subsequent areas of analysis and if the analysis of the financial area is combined and interrelated to the others it may well enable new perspectives to be drawn as well as allowing a deeper and more fundamental analysis to be undertaken. Some of the key areas to be addressed in a consideration of the finance and accounting function would include:

- the financial results and financial status of the firm;
- the link between financial budgets and the overall strategic and operating plans;
- consistency between divisional (or sub-unit) budgets and overall organisational budgets;
- the process of budget-preparation and whether management across the organisation is involved;
- utilisation (or otherwise) of forecast profit and loss statements, balance sheets and cash-flow projections;
- the information prepared for management control, in particular which managers receive reports and the reports' appropriateness and timeliness;
- the attitude of managers to planning and control reports and whether such documents are utilised as a motivational element in the entity;
- the utilisation by management of control reports for evaluation of performance and formulation of strategy; in particular whether the reports compare actual results with budgets or standards and whether corrective action is taken.

This analysis is important to strategy not only because it evaluates the financial resources of the organisation and how well they have been and are being utilised, but also because they reveal important facets concerning the way the firm is managed and the systems used in the management process. This is key information in the task of assessing the appropriateness of past, present and future strategies as well as their implementation.

Marketing

Because the marketing function of the organisation represents the most important interface between the entity and its external environments Chapter 4 has already included many vital aspects which would normally be included in a review of the marketing area. Marketing, in encompassing market research, sales forecasting and promotions activity represents a vital communication link between the organisation, whether profit-orientated or not, and the outside world. It does this essentially by considering changes in economic, technological, social and other environments, and bringing such knowledge into the entity as well as making information about the enterprise available to customers and potential customers.

Since our previous chapter on external appraisal discussed the key external influences this section will focus on important issues relevant for analysing the marketing function, particularly its links with other functional areas, in a strategic context. Perhaps its two most important internal interrelationships are with operations and research and development. The way in which the marketing area relates and communicates with these functions, and vice versa, is crucial as much of the information required for decisions emanate from marketing personnel. For example, the sales forecast provides a starting-point for the preparation of financial budgets and production-planning, while information from market research may be of crucial importance in new product development.

In analysing the effectiveness of marketing communication and information attention must be paid to the role of marketing in the organisation and the extent to which management adopts a marketing perspective. This would entail careful observation and the collection of information, whether it is factual such as sales and profits by product group, or more qualitative like the length of product life-cycle or percentage market share, as well as opinions, all of which need to be placed in a strategic context. In appraising the marketing function crucial areas for consideration would include:

- the use made of market research and the extent to which it influences product development;
- the relative position of each product group in terms of sales and contributions to profits;
- the market share of each product group and its stage in the product life cycle;
- the distribution channels used and the extent to which new distribution developments may indicate a need for change;
- the relationship, if any, between sales price and sales volumes; the pricing policy pursued by the firm;
- important competitive features which may include quality, price, service and delivery, and the extent to which such features are appropriate given the structure of the industry;
- the extent to which the marketing area is aware of competitors' moves, technological change and environmental aspects relevant to the firm.

This sort of information allows assessment of the area as to its strengths and weaknesses which can then lead to an evaluation of the firm's marketing strategy and whether the propounded strategy is being followed. The controls utilised in the function, some of which of course may already have been considered in the analysis of the accounting and finance function, and the performance of managers will all have been the subject of scrutiny and judgement which may lead to suggestions concerning the role of marketing in the firm.

Operations

The preceding discussion of the marketing area indicated the importance of links with the operations function because of the latter's reliance on information from sales forecasts. In fact these connections go further to ensure that the enterprise produces a product, manufactured and designed with the selling-price in mind, in the volume and at the place to ensure that the market is satisfied. Also, management of the function is normally expected to produce the product or service within predetermined cost limits as well as meeting financial budgets. It is worth remembering that the operations function whether in a manufacturing or service organisation probably controls, and has responsibility for, more resources (physical, human and financial) than any of the other functions.

Further to considering the above relationships the links between operations and research and development may be fundamental to the successful development of products in terms of cost, quality and effectiveness.

Appraisal of the operations function, which may include production, engineering, purchasing and distribution of the product would probably include:

- production planning and control and their interface with both marketing and production;
- information received from sales and marketing, accounting, quality control and so on with particular regard for its usefulness in managing the function;
- production costs, in absolute and percentage terms, and their movement relative to sales prices, plus identification of causes of cost changes; the entity's record on experience curve effects;
- the use of performance standards and the exercise of cost control; control over key cost elements (for instance, labour, material, packaging);
- stock levels in relation to output and sales and the relationship between levels of raw material stocks, work in progress and finished goods stocks;
- plant and equipment, their adequacy, age, state of repair and level of investment in relation to industry norms; the nature of these assets, the degree of dedication and flexibility are aspects of particular interest;

- the extent of automation/computerisation of production facilities, and the enterprise's policy on replacement should be considered along with developments in production process;
- communications between all facets of the operations function and other areas of the firm, and the organisation of the function including, for example, purchasing and materials management;
- the reputation of the firm as a producer coupled with the requirements of industry and environmental conditions.

As with the other functions it is important in considering the operations functions to adopt a strategic perspective to endeavour to achieve an insight into how the area coalesces with the other functional areas. The conduct of this sort of analysis will of necessity involve appraising management of the function both as a group and individually.

Research and development

Research and development is normally relevant in efforts to improve products, introduce and develop new products, and improve or enhance production processes. For those organisations not involved in these areas, such as retailers, research and development is unlikely to have much importance. In this section, therefore, we are concerned with research and development in its strategic influence on products and processes. For many organisations research and development is crucial to survival, let alone success. There are numerous examples of enterprises which today produce only a few of the products of a decade ago, and the pace of change, as we saw in the preceding chapter, is increasing. The importance of research and development should not be underestimated. *The Economist* reported in 1982:

> Japan's universities train 10 times as many engineers as Britain's. Its industry spends as high a proportion of the country's GNP on research and development as almost any western nation. It employs more people on research and development than Britain, France and West Germany put together (*The Economist*, 19 June 1982).

As with the other functions considered earlier the objective of assessing research and development is to determine its effect on the firm's strategy. This is dependent upon the past record of research and development in product and process innovation for example, and perhaps more importantly upon the future expectations for research-and-development-driven innovation. A further aspect relates to how research and development is perceived in the entity's external environment. So an appraisal of research and development would include:

- industry expenditure on R & D, and the firm's commitment to R & D;
- the nature of the product and whether it calls for continual development, or whether the nature of the market or competition requires such development;
- the nature of the production process and whether it calls for further enhancement;
- the return to the firm for a product breakthrough including an evaluation of the risk – return trade-off;
- the resources that the firm can devote to R & D, analysed between projects or products and whether the spread of effort is too broad or sufficiently focused;
- the record of the firm in terms of new or improved products or processes, and the present state of likely innovations for future exploitation;
- the way in which R & D is organised, in particular its links with marketing and operations, and the manner in which creativity is encouraged;
- links between the organisation and other R & D organisations such as universities or hospitals, and whether the firm has any R & D joint ventures with other bodies.

R & D is probably the hardest area in which even to attempt an objective appraisal. It is also, in many respects, one of the easiest areas to 'trim' or 'cut' in periods when profits are under threat, if only because the benefits from the development of new products may take many years to materialise. This is certainly the case in one organisation with which we are familiar where inception to exploitation of a product takes at least ten years so that it would be possible to make better profits by effectively closing down the firm and employing just one person to open the mail and bank the royalties on past innovations. In this instance the firm would 'survive' for about eight years and then cease to function.

To conclude, however problematic it may be, an attempt must be made both to evaluate R & D, and on the results of sound analysis to determine whether it is a strength upon which the firm can build future success, or a weakness requiring a strategy designed to focus attention on other stronger parts of the organisation.

5.4 Assessment of resources

Having completed the analysis of the functional areas it is important to recognise that resources have no value if assessed in a vacuum. The manner in which they are to be used imparts a value to them, it is therefore only possible to assess whether a resource is a strength or weakness in relation to identified features of the environment in which it operates. When the organisation uses outside bodies to perform some activities, such as market research or R & D for example, then the assessment needs to encompass these features as well. The objective of the process is to identify strengths which the firm can utilise in its strategy and weaknesses which need to be overcome to avoid the possibility of failure. Clearly this process involves management judgement of opportunities and threats presented in the environment(s) where the firm operates, or may wish to operate in the future, linked – indeed inextricably bound – to the entity's strengths and weaknesses (see Illustration 5.1).

Earlier in this chapter we noted how differing attributes, historic and normative, were used to identify strengths and weaknesses. In addition to these features changing over time as the organisation develops, the environment also will change which may indicate that a feature that was once considered a weakness may, in differing circumstances, be assessed as a strength. Thus the manager must be cognisant of the fact that as the product/market evolves the bases of competition in the industry may change. A simple example can illustrate this point. Suppose that in the past an organisation identified higher-than-average labour turnover, caused by the use of casual part-time labour, as a weakness. If the industry is entering a period of decline, or substantial technological advances have taken place in process technology, then competing firms may be required to shed labour. In such a situation the existence of a casual part-time labour element may well be viewed as a strength since it makes the transition to a smaller workforce more easily achievable.

Assessment of strengths and weaknesses also leads to the ability to evaluate any competitive advantages that a business may have in relation to the competition. A comparative analysis of the firm's strengths and weaknesses with those of competitors may identify areas in which strengths provide an advantage capable of sustaining a competitive strategy, or weaknesses which competitors may be able to exploit. Further to identification of competitive advantages an attempt should also be made to assess what distinctive competences, if any, the firm may possess. The assessment of distinctive competences, or unique resource deployments, is notoriously difficult not just because not all firms will have distinctive competences but also because the identification of utility may be problematic. Thus if an organisation is seeking to diversify it would be necessary to analyse and judge whether the proposed industry is attractive enough to warrant entry and exploitation, and crucially whether the organisation itself has the ability to

ILLUSTRATION 5.1 Strengths and Weaknesses of Reckitt & Colman plc

STRENGTHS

Personnel and Industrial Relations – industrial relations have generally been good, with a move towards flexible work practices enabling operating divisions to meet seasonal demand fluctuations. The group has a good record of looking after employees, based on founder's Quaker traditions.

Capital Structure – sound financial policies and a progressive reduction in loan capital in the late 1970s early 1980s allowed for a successful rights issue in 1984 to fund a major acquisition.

Geographic Coverage – world-wide operations with major markets in the UK, Europe, North America, Latin America, Australasia and Asia, and Africa helps to insulate the company from the effects of a recession in a particular area.

Product Range – wide and balanced with a focus on products which are generally immune from the effects of a downturn in activity has allowed the firm to increase profits during the recession of the early 1980s.

Brand Names – the names of Colmans, Robinsons, Dettol, Harpic and Brasso, are well-known and perceived as being associated with quality products.

WEAKNESSES

US Market – the company has experienced problems in penetrating this large market and has taken a long time to acquire a suitable vehicle to enable expansion to take place.

Acquisitions – there is a query over the ability of the firm to acquire a suitable company to allow further development (for example, the failure of the Nicholas–Kiwi bid in 1984). It may take some years to incorporate Airwick fully into the group given the lack of experience of take-overs and mergers.

Power of Buyers – the large multiple retailers (for example, Sainsbury, Tesco, Boots, etc.) have considerable power and require 'own label' brands which compete with the company's

ILLUSTRATION 5.1 *continued*

own branded products. Some pharmaceutical products are subject to DHSS regulations on profits.

Promotions – costs of promoting products to compete with supermarkets and other well-known brands (such as Kia Ora) can be very high due because of the intensity of the competition.

- The above is an example of an analysis of a company's strengths and weaknesses at a corporate level, and is by no means exhaustive. Individual divisions (Food and Wine, Household, Pharmaceutical, for example) would also need to analyse their own position relative to the industry in which they operate.
- This illustration also reveals the use of differing attributes, historic and narrative for assessing strengths and weaknesses respectively. Thus personnel and industrial relations are regarded as a strength based on the company's record, whereas expectations are used to assess the company in respect of its acquisition policy.
- Furthermore, depending upon the perspective adopted, we can see how issues described as either strengths or weaknesses could be interpreted. For example, the company's problems with acquiring a suitable vehicle to expand its penetration in the US market, exemplified by the failure of the Nicholas–Kiwi bid, could well be regarded as a strength as it avoided the possibility of paying more than the acquisition was worth, as well as avoiding the consequences of the board adopting a 'macho' stance on the issue.

compete effectively in the new industry. Hofer and Schendel (1978, p. 151) believe that this issue should be explored prior to assessing industry's attractiveness, so that the firm's distinctive competences are used to screen prospective industries.

There are a number of methods of assessing the firm's resources including portfolio analysis which we discussed in Chapter 3 and to which we will refer again in Chapter 8 on strategic selection. Portfolio analysis can be a useful tool for assessing the *balance* of resources in the firm. Earlier in this chapter we referred to the importance of analysing the management of the organisation to enable judgements to be made concerning their ability to manage the organisation effectively in a strategic manner. We have also referred to the importance of assessing those features or functions of the firm which are capable of exploitation to provide some competitive advantage over rivals.

There is now a need to put the preceding analysis together in such a way that it becomes usable for the strategist. Clearly the issues discussed so far do not in reality take place in a rather sterile environment; in practice such analysis is often triggered by the realisation that the organisation faces a problem in a particular area or with a particular product. So to draw together much of what has been presented so far we are using Ohmae's issue diagram (Figure 5.2) as an example of an approach to the analysis of a strategic problem, and much of what follows is based on Ohmae's thinking expressed in *The Mind of the Strategist* (1982) pp. 23–35.

The issue diagram takes the overall problem and divides it exhaustively until the emergent sub-issues are manageable and capable of analysis. In this way problems can be broken down so that, individually, they become manageable. Suppose that a firm is concerned about the profitability of Product *A*. Two basic issues are involved in increasing its profitability:

1. Can profitability be improved at the present selling price by increasing efficiency *internally* (that is, through cost reduction)?
2. Can more profit be gained *externally* (that is, from the market)?

If product costs are thought to be too high then the first question might concern product design. But even if the product is over-designed and so more costly than those of competitors, before instituting any change the needs of consumers requires analysis, plus an assessment of the impact on profits of selling at a higher price to reflect costs is needed. This might lead to a campaign to persuade customers that product *A* represents top quality at a top price. But if this is not possible then the product would need to be the subject of value analysis and value engineering, to enable product *A* to compete in the market. The techniques of value analysis and value engineering, and the design function, do not exist in a vacuum, for if all competing products suffer in the same way the application of such change may result in damaging alterations to the market's perception of the product, in other words, all products in the market may suffer from over-design and low-profit margins. Alternatively variable costs may be suspected as being too high or the issue diagram may reveal a number of areas requiring action or analysis,

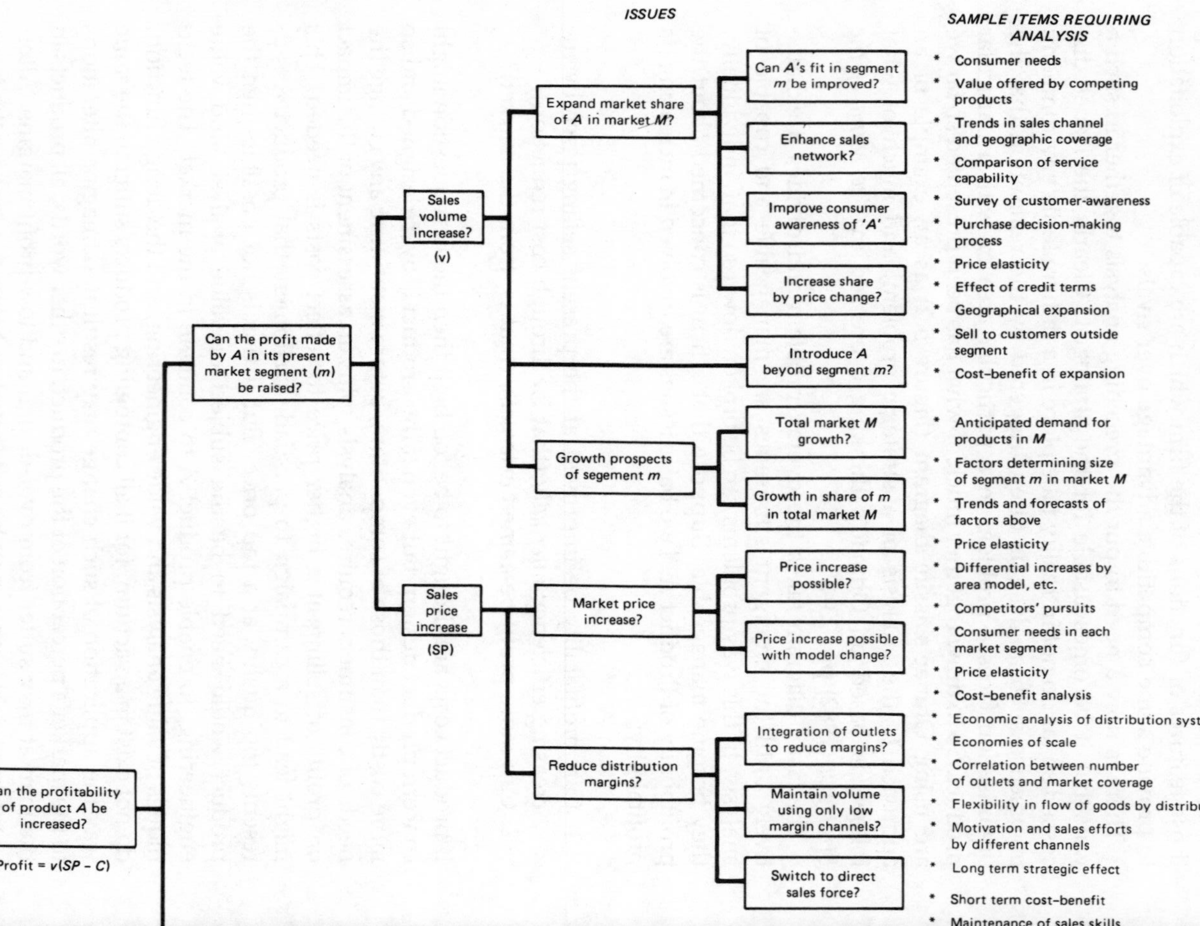
ISSUES
SAMPLE ITEMS REQUIRING ANALYSIS
Can the profitability of product A be increased?
Profit = v(SP – C)
Can the profit made by A in its present market segment (m) be raised?
Sales volume increase?
(v)
Sales price increase
(SP)
Expand market share of A in market M?
Growth prospects of segement m
Market price increase?
Reduce distribution margins?
Can A's fit in segment m be improved?
Enhance sales network?
Improve consumer awareness of 'A'
Increase share by price change?
Introduce A beyond segment m?
Total market M growth?
Growth in share of m in total market M
Price increase possible?
Price increase possible with model change?
Integration of outlets to reduce margins?
Maintain volume using only low margin channels?
Switch to direct sales force?
* Consumer needs
* Value offered by competing products
* Trends in sales channel and geographic coverage
* Comparison of service capability
* Survey of customer-awareness
* Purchase decision-making process
* Price elasticity
* Effect of credit terms
* Geographical expansion
* Sell to customers outside segment
* Cost–benefit of expansion
* Anticipated demand for products in M
* Factors determining size of segment m in market M
* Trends and forecasts of factors above
* Price elasticity
* Differential increases by area model, etc.
* Competitors' pursuits
* Consumer needs in each market segment
* Price elasticity
* Cost–benefit analysis
* Economic analysis of distribution system
* Economies of scale
* Correlation between number of outlets and market coverage
* Flexibility in flow of goods by distribution channels
* Motivation and sales efforts by different channels
* Long term strategic effect
* Short term cost–benefit
* Maintenance of sales skills

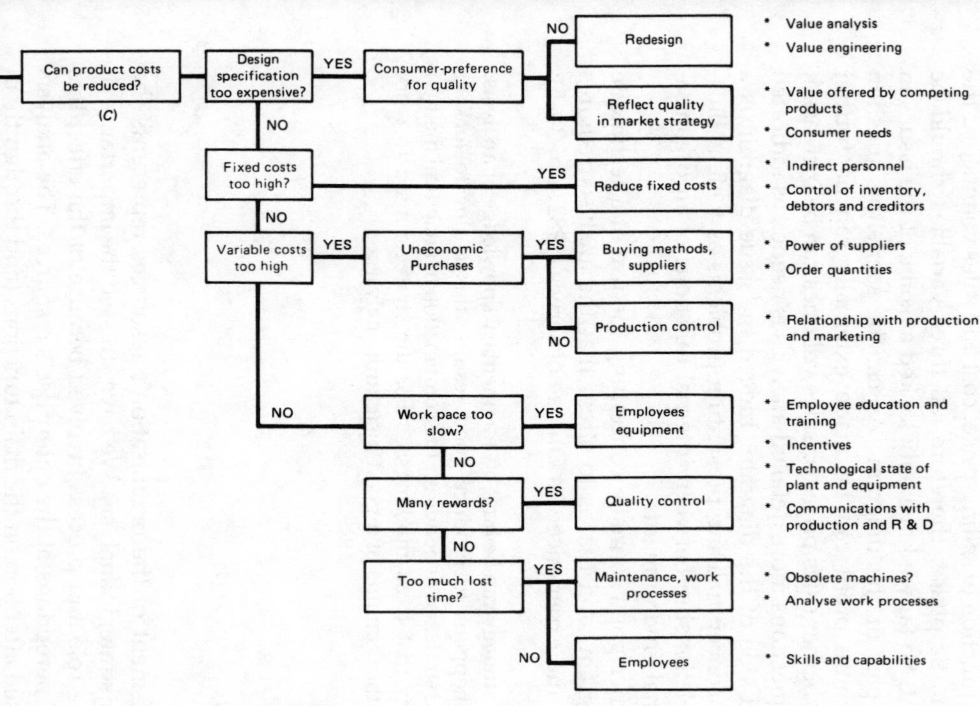

FIGURE 5.2 Sample issue diagram

Source: Ohmae (1982) pp. 24, 28, 30–33 (adapted).

employee training, purchasing methods and so on. It also avoids a leap from a symptom, variable costs to one possible diagnosis, cost of purchases, which would only serve to reduce the probability of solving the problem.

In fact this represents, of course, only part of the required analysis because profit is a function of selling-price, cost and sales volume. At the start of the diagnostic phase, therefore, all three variables should be given equal weight. So far we have only looked at some of the issues in the product-cost part of the diagram. As can be seen, the question whether or not more profit can be made externally can be further subdivided into whether sales prices or sales volumes can be increased. To answer these questions more detailed analysis is needed as indicated on the right-hand side of the diagram. Indeed the issue diagram is a useful method of conceptualising presenting-problems as well as illustrating the interrelationship between internal functions of an organisation and its external environment.

There is one other point to make concerning the use of a technique like the issue diagram, and that is to stress that the analysis requires considerable skill and experience. As Ohmae observes (1982, pp. 34–5):

> No proper business strategy can be built on fragmentary knowledge or analysis. If such a strategy happens to produce good results, this is due to luck or inspiration. The true strategist depends on the combination of analytical method and mental elasticity that I call thinking . . . For the strategic mind to work creatively, it needs the stimulus of a good insightful analysis.

5.5 Summary

An internal assessment of the organisation's resources represents the second part of our strategic analysis. We have stressed the importance of understanding the role and process involved because of the effect this has on managers' pereptions of the enterprise's resources. The analysis of resources focused attention on the main functions (and through them the managers in the organisation):

- human resources
- accounting and finance
- marketing
- operations
- R & D.

The assessment of the resources, to allow a view to be taken of the entity's strengths and weaknesses, concluded by considering the use of the very detailed issue diagram. This technique allows a strategic perspective while breaking down a problem into understandable, and hence manageable, chunks. Nevertheless to obtain a meaningful, insightful analysis requires those involved to apply their background knowledge and creativity.

Having completed the strategic analysis we are now in a position to start examining what options may be available to the organisation in the light of identified resources (Chapter 6) as well as being able to think about evaluating and selecting a suitable strategic option (Chapter 8).

APPENDIX: A summary of some financial ratios, their calculation and interpetation

Ratio	*Calculation*	*Interpretation*
Profitability ratios		
1. Gross profit margin	$\frac{\text{Sales} - \text{Cost of goods sold}}{\text{Sales}}$	An indication of the total margin available to cover operating expenses and yield a profit
2. Net operating margin	$\frac{\text{Profits before taxes and before interest}}{\text{Sales}}$	An indication of the firm's profitability from current operations without regard to the interest charges accruing from the capital structure
3. Net profit margin (or return on sales)	$\frac{\text{Profits after taxes}}{\text{Sales}}$	Shows aftertax profits per £ of sales. Subpar-profit margins indicate that the firm's sales prices are relatively low or that its costs are relatively high or both

Ratio	*Calculation*	*Interpretation*
4. Return on total assets	Profits after taxes / Total assets OR Profits after taxes + Interest / Total assets	A measure of the return on total investment in the enterprise. It is sometimes desirable to add interest to after-tax profits to form the numerator of the ratio since total assets are financed by creditors as well as by shareholders; hence it is accurate to measure the productivity of assets by the returns provided to both classes of investors
5. Return on shareholders' equity (or return on net worth)	Profits after taxes / Total shareholders equity	A measure of the rate of return on investment in the enterprise
6. Return on ordinary shares	Profits after taxes – preference dividends / Total equity – par value of preference shares	A measure of the rate of return on investment which the owners of ordinary shares have made in the enterprise
7. Earnings per share	Profits after taxes – preference dividends / Number of ordinary shares outstanding	Shows the earnings available to the owners of ordinary shares
Liquidity ratios		
1. Current ratio	Current assets / Current liabilities	Indicates the extent to which the claims of short-term creditors are covered by assets that are expected to be converted to cash in a period roughly corresponding to the maturity of the liabilities

Ratio	*Calculation*	*Interpretation*
2. Quick ratio (or acid test ratio)	(Current assets – Inventory) / Current liabilities	A measure of the firm's ability to pay off short-term obligations without relying upon the sale of its inventories
3. Inventory to net working capital	Inventory / (Current assets – current liabilities)	A measure of the extent to which the firm's working capital is tied up in inventory
Gearing (leverage)		
1. Debt to assets ratio	Total debt / Total assets	Measures the extent to which borrowed funds have been used to finance the firm's operations
2. Debt to equity ratio	Total debt / Total shareholders' equity	Provides another measure of the funds provided by creditors versus the funds provided by owners
3. Long-term debt to equity ratio	Long-term debt / Total shareholders' equity	A widely used measure of the balance between debt and equity in the firm's overall capital structure
4. Times-interest-earned (or coverage ratios)	(Profits before interest and taxes) / Total interest charges	Measures the extent to which earnings can decline without the firm becoming unable to meet its annual interest costs
5. Fixed charge	(Profits before taxes and interest) / (Total interest charges + lease obligations)	A more inclusive indication of the firm's ability to meet all of its fixed charge obligations

Ratio	*Calculation*	*Interpretation*
Activity ratios		
1. Inventory turnover	$\frac{\text{Sales}}{\text{inventory of finished goods}}$	When compared with industry averages, it provides an indication of whether a company has excessive or perhaps inadequate finished goods inventory
2. Fixed assets turnover	$\frac{\text{Sales}}{\text{Fixed assets}}$	A measure of the sales productivity and utilisation of plant and equipment
3. Total assets turnover	$\frac{\text{Sales}}{\text{Total assets}}$	A measure of the utilisation of all the firm's assets; a ratio below the industry average indicates the company is not generating a sufficient volume of business given the size of its asset investment
4. Debtor turnover	$\frac{\text{Annual credit sales}}{\text{Debtors}}$	A measure of the average length of time it takes the firm to collect the sales made on credit
5. Average collection period	$\frac{\text{Debtors} \times 365}{\text{Total sales}}$	Indicates the average length of the time the firm must wait after making a sale before it receives payment
Other ratios:		
1. Dividend yield	$\frac{\text{Annual dividends per share}}{\text{Current market price per share}}$	A measure of the return to owners received in the form of dividends

Ratio	*Calculation*	*Interpretation*
2. Price-earnings ratio	Current market price per share / Aftertax earnings per share	Faster growing or less risky firms tend to have higher price – earnings ratios than slower growing or more risky firms
3. Dividend payout	Annual dividends per share / Aftertax earnings per share	Indicates the percentage of profits paid out as dividends

Further reading

The analysis of financial statements is comprehensively covered in texts such as, Sizer, J. (1979) '*An Insight to Management Accounting*' (Harmondsworth: Penguin), or Gitman, L. J. (1982) *Principles of Managerial Finance* (New York: Harper & Row).
Corporate Strategy by Ansoff (Penguin 1968) is still of interest for those seeking a discussion of capability profiles (Chapter 5) or internal appraisal (Chapter 8).

References

Hofer, C. W. and Schendel, D. (1978) *Strategy Formulation: Analytical Concepts* (St Paul, Minnesota: West).
Ohmae, K. (1982) *The Mind of the Strategist* (New York: McGraw-Hill).
Stevenson, H. H. (1976) 'Defining Corporate Strengths and Weaknesses', *Sloan Management Review*, Spring, pp. 51–68.
'The Innovative Japanese', *The Economist*, 19 June 1982, pp. 5–31.

CHAPTER 6

Strategic options

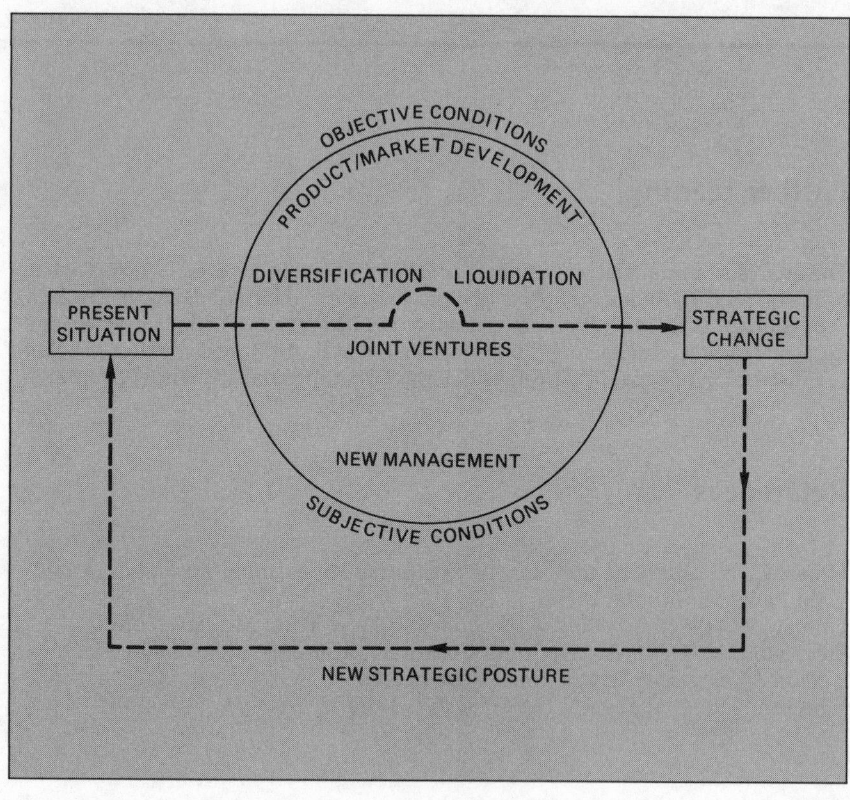

6.1 Introduction

The previous two chapters were concerned with exploring the issues inherent in a strategic appraisal of the organisation primarily by considering the objective conditions prevailing, and expected to prevail, in both the environment and the resources controlled by the enterprise. In this chapter we consider the main strategic options which are open to the firm in pursuit of its objectives. Because of the range and complexity of the options involved we intend to approach the chapter in three broad strands. First we consider the *ways* in which an organisation may seek to achieve its ends, ranging from liquidation to diversification. We then discuss the *means* by which these can be attained. The concluding section will deal with *turnaround* situations.

Our rationale for separating the discussion of the options in this way is that the variety of alternatives from which an enterprise is able to choose benefits from a separate discussion, and having chosen a particular alternative management then has a further choice in the method by which the alternative is adopted. We recognise that in practice it will not always be feasible to separate out the discussion in this way. Similarly, as our previous chapters have indicated, the options available to the firm may be considerably reduced as a result of past decisions, prevailing environmental circumstances, or as a result of the type of management in the firm and so on. Because of the experience of industry in the UK in the past four years, and the growing body of literature, it seems pertinent to devote some space to the particular considerations involved in managing turnaround situations.

There is one other point to make which is that the choices open to an organisation arise because its internal and external conditions are *changing*, so it needs to develop just to stand still. Consequently our emphasis is not limited to discussions of strategies for growth, but is more on *development* which is seen as fundamental if the enterprise is to survive.

6.2 Alternative ways of strategic development

The literature contains a variety of ways in which an organisation may seek to develop. Hofer and Schendel (1978, pp. 162–77) identify six generic business options whereas Ohmae (1982, pp. 99–135) identifies four alternatives. Perhaps the easiest way of conceptualising the options available to the enterprise is to use Ansoff's product/mission matrix which we discussed in Chapter 3 (Figure 3.7) and to adapt it as we have

Product / *Mission*	*Present*	*New*
Present	Market penetration Consolidation Liquidation	Product development
New	Market development	Diversification

FIGURE 6.1 Product/mission matrix

done here in Figure 6.1. These identified options will be discussed in turn; generally they conform to those noted both by Hofer and Schendel, and Ohmae, the differences referring to the breadth, or otherwise, of definition. In a similar way they include the key elements of Porter's (1980, pp. 35–40) three generic strategies – cost advantage, differentiation and focus. Both Hofer and Schendel, and Porter stress the importance of the state of product/market evolution in considering options.

Although we will deal with each of these strategic options individually it is likely that an organisation may well need to consider more than one. Also the options discussed relate essentially to *businesses* so where an enterprise contains several discrete business units it is inevitable that various options would be considered in the firm as a whole and that the key issue from a corporate viewpoint may well be that of determining which units to resource. The allocation of normally scarce resources to business units will be raised in Chapter 8 when we discuss the evaluation of the strategies open to the organisation.

Market penetration

Market penetration as a strategy refers to gaining market-share for the business involved, and usually entails fundamental changes to the

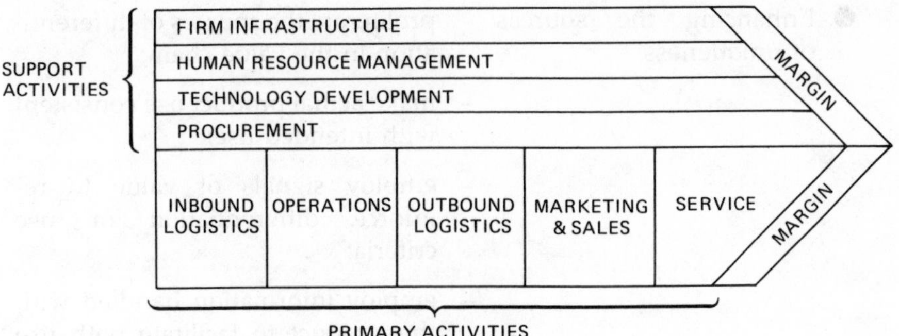

FIGURE 6.2 The generic value chain
Source: Porter (1985) p. 37.

competitive position. However, before we consider the implications of this option further, the ease with which this option can be pursued is a function of the nature of the market and its situation. In general if the market is expanding it may be easier to increase market-share because all firms involved will be either still growing, or unable to meet the increased demand. In static situations this may not be the case and, as we saw in Chapter 3, experience-curve effects make penetration by low market-share competitors problematic. In a declining market the key question may well be whether the firm should stay in it, rather than seek an enhanced share. Market penetration can be achieved in two ways – differentiation or cost leadership. As we noted earlier (Chapter 4) both can be enhanced by focusing the strategy effectively. Porter (1985, pp. 150–63) advocates that differentiation is achievable in two ways, first by becoming more individual in performing its existing activities and second by reconfiguring its value chain in such a way that enhances its individuality. In both cases the organisation must control the cost of differentiation so that it translates into superior performance.

Porter (1985, pp. 36–9) defines the value chain, depicted in Figure 6.2, as a collection of activities that are performed to design, produce, market, deliver and support its product. The value chain and the way an organisation performs individual activities are a reflection of the organisation's history, strategy, implementation of strategy, and the economics of the activities themselves.

The relevant level for the value chain is the business unit and differences between competitor value chains are a key source of competitive advantage. According to Porter (1985, pp. 154–60) successful differentiation may be achieved by:

- Enhancing the sources of uniqueness
  - proliferate the sources of differentiation in the value chain;
  - make actual product use consistent with intended use;
  - employ signals of value to reinforce differentiation or use criteria;
  - employ information handled with the product to facilitate both use and signalling.
- Making the cost of differentiation an advantage
  - exploit all sources of differentiation that are not costly;
  - minimise the cost of differentiation by controlling the cost-drivers;
  - emphasis forms of differentiation where the firm has a substantial cost advantage in differentiating;
  - reduce cost in activities that do not effect buyer value.
- Change the rules to create uniqueness
  - shift the decision-maker to make a firm's uniqueness more valuable;
  - discover unrecognised purchase criteria;
  - pre-emptively respond to changing buyer or channel circumstances.
- Reconfigure the value chain to be unique in entirely new ways
  - reconsideration of distribution and selling approach;
  - control of product quality, for example, by backward integration;
  - adoption of new process technology.

The sustainability of differentiation is a function of its perceived value to buyers and the lack of imitation by competitors. Differentiation can be eroded where competitors copy the firm or overtake the bases on which differentiation was founded, or where buyers' needs or perceptions change.

The value, in a strategic sense, of cost advantage depends on its sustainability, which will be present if the bases of the cost advantage enjoyed by the firm are difficult for competitors to imitate or replicate. Cost advantage exists if the organisations cumulative cost of performing all value activities is lower than competitors', or potential competitors', costs. Porter (1985, p. 99) identifies two ways in which a firm may gain a cost advantage:

1. control cost-drivers – a firm can gain an advantage with respect to the cost-drivers of value activities representing a significant proportion of total costs;
2. reconfigure value chain – a firm can adopt a different and more efficient way to design, produce, distribute, or market the product.

Successful cost-leaders usually derive their advantage from multiple sources within the value chain. There are two crucial issues warranting comment here. First, it is important to appreciate that we are referring to *total* costs, (not just product or manufacturing costs) which are generated by activities such as marketing, service, research and development and so on. As Porter argues 'An examination of the entire value chain often results in relatively simple steps that can significantly reduce cost position'. Second, cost advantage may affect differentiation so a choice may need to be made between improving relative cost position and sustaining all or part of differentiation.

So, in terms of enhancing the enterprise's position in the market, it should be clear that we need to treat with some caution panaceas like increasing marketing activity, or improving productivity by investing in capital equipment. In the first case an increase in marketing activity, unless it is allied to changing buyers' awareness or perceptions of the product and takes account of the relative power between the firm and the buyer, is unlikely to be successful as it not based on a thoroughly thought-out view of the product as a whole. Investment in equipment to improve productivity as a strategy ignores other, important elements in the value chain, as well as raising barriers to exit. As such it may, particularly where heavy expenditure is involved or where to achieve the desired reductions in product-cost necessitates the utilisation of full capacity, restrict the firm's future strategic options by its impact on cash-flows, selling prices, relationships with employees and so on.

Consolidation

In our introduction to this chapter we noted the necessity for organisations to adapt to changing circumstances. Consequently a strategy of consolidation does not imply that the firm does nothing; indeed the pressure for change may be such that this option is as radical in its own way as any other.

Much of the discussion on market penetration applies equally to consolidation. Given that the entity wishes to remain with its present range of products and markets the stage of product/market evolution is of crucial importance. Where a market is growing rapidly the consolidation option implies that the firm wishes to grow at the same rate and so maintain its market share. Such a strategy means, generally, that the firm must invest (in equipment, infrastructure, people, etc.) often substantial sums to keep pace, for if it does not then market share may decline and the firm could end up with a cost structure higher than its competitors.

The strategic focus then may shift as the market reaches maturity. With a reduced rate of growth the need for investments declines and competition tends to stabilise. Instead the firm should direct its attention to market segmentation and asset utilisation in order to increase the return on investment. Hofer and Schendel (1978, pp. 166–9) refer to this as a profit strategy as the organisation seeks to alter resource deployments the better to fit current needs and to exploit possible synergies which may not have been developed earlier because of the pressure on managers' time and resources.

Care needs to be exercised in measuring growth rates to ensure that the rate of growth of sales is measured either in units or deflated pounds. Sales expressed in current prices may be misleading because of the effects of inflation.

Liquidation

Liquidation or divestment strategies are often overlooked, or just not recognised as alternatives to consider. Liquidation is an option when the business concerned is in a declining industry or where, as a unit, it is no longer seen as appropriate for the attainment of corporate objectives. The concept of 'fit' in a strategic sense is discussed in Chapter 8. Whatever the rationale underlying the option, the goal is to maximise cash inflows while deliberately withdrawing from the business involved. Illustration 6.1 shows that divestment can generate significant inflows and allow management to attend to products and markets with more potential. It also indicates the main features of liquidation or divestment strategy. We can identify two methods of divestment, early liquidation or the adoption of a harvesting strategy. Early liquidation assumes that the enterprise can maximise its recovery from the business early in decline rather than by harvesting and selling it later. The earlier the business is sold would normally maximise the sales value because the uncertainty concerning the subsequent decline is greater, and may not be seen as such by the prospective purchasers. It is conceivable that in some situations early liquidation of the investment prior to decline may be more advantageous. However, early liquidation runs the risk that the forecast of decline will be proved incorrect. Early withdrawal from the market would allow competitors to make more profits, or lower losses than would otherwise be the case. This is likely to be true, except if withdrawal is accomplished using a management buy-out which may further intensify competition, but hardly represents a rational reason for continuation. What does appear to be clear is that an early liquidation forces management to confront exit barriers like image or interrelationships with other business units in the firm.

ILLUSTRATION 6.1 The Disinvestment Boom

The strength of the disinvestment movement is a phenomenon of equal significance to the US acquisition boom of 1981. Seldom before have so many corporations restructured and redeployed their assets in such far-ranging ways. The sell-offs often represent a complete reversal of the past policies and reveals that US strategists are becoming more sensitive to their limitations and more critical of conglomerate type linkages.

Contemporary divestments originate due to factors such as high interest rates, inflation, over-capacity in mature industries, corporate hunger for new technologies, investors' bearishness about the shares of conglomerates, the ascendancy of return of investment as a priority, the decline of seeking after growth, pronounced imbalances between industries, changes in corporate strategy fashions, and so on.

American Can is a fairly typical case. For over a decade it has been seeking a winning diversification formula, in glass containers, forest products, printing, pharmaceuticals, publishing, aluminium recycling, mail order retailing – mostly without success. The firm announced plans to increase its rate of return by severing over a fifth of the firm, its profitable wood and paper products enterprise for a reported US$ 900m.

ILLUSTRATION 6.1 *continued*

Inflation not only raises the cost of borrowing it also affects stock-market valuations, so stimulating redeployments to boost stock prices. A number of recent restructurings seem to have had this goal in mind. Seagram's sale of its **Texas Gulf Petroleum** division to **Sun Oil** caused the stock price to rise in a spectacular fashion. The presumed undervaluation of corporate assets by the stock market lies at the heart of much recent merger activity, so firms have been bidding up take-over candidates to premiums in the belief that acquisition is cheaper than creating the business from scratch. This is because the business buyer considers current replacement cost of the assets acquired whereas the investor, not being interested in replacement, values stocks in relation to returns on other investments.

Sellers usually tend either to be inadequately capitalised (perhaps with too much loan capital in view of current interest costs), or to have small market shares, or both. Behind many cases of redeployment is the issue of technological or market leadership. Diversified companies are deciding in which businesses they are leaders and are getting out of the others. As the disinvestment boom has gathered momentum it has undermined the intellectual arguments for spreading business risk through diversification. One reason for this is that the use of portfolio matrixes designed to balance the firm, say 'stars' with 'cash cows', is that it can not spread the risk in the same way as a diversified portfolio of stocks. This is mainly because businesses are subject not only to random setbacks but also to attacks by competitors who are able to focus all their resources and energies on one set of activities. In using the portfolio approach corporate management abrogated to itself the role of allocating capital, which the stock market probably does for the better.

(Source: *Management Today*, January 1982, pp. 46–9, 100)

A *harvest strategy*, in which the organisation seeks to optimise cashflow by reducing or eliminating new investment, cost reductions and reducing maintenance while capitalising on whatever residual competencies the firm has, may precede liquidation. Tactics in harvesting, or milking, the business could include reducing the product range, elimination of small customers, and eroding service in terms of delivery time, speed of repair and so on. In considering harvesting as an option Porter points out that it places great demands on management because of problems with employee morale and retention, suppliers' and customers' confidence, and the motivation of executives. 'Classifying a business as a dog to be harvested, based on portfolio planning techniques is not a great motivating device either' (Porter, 1980, p. 270).

Market development

Market development, as the matrix in Figure 6.1 implies, involves the business in exploiting existing products in new market areas. This option means that the organisation is retaining the security of its existing business and utilising its distinctive competencies in the development of new market areas. Generally this can be achieved by entering new *segments* of the market, and/or *international* exploitation of the product.

Segmentation of a market can be achieved in a variety of ways. Chisnall (1985, p. 169) identifies four principal factors which influence the opportunities for effective segmentation:

1. identification – to enable specific subsectors to be identified;
2. measurability – allowing reasonable estimates of consumption patterns to be built up;
3. accessibility – the ability of the organisation to direct its marketing efforts at a particular segment;
4. appropriateness – relates the suitability of specific segments to the enterprise's resources.

Segmentation of a market recognises several demand schedules relating to the supply of goods or services so encouraging differentiation, which may help smaller specialist organisations to cater for the needs of relatively small markets.

Kotler (1980) identified two features which determine whether a firm considers exporting as an option; *push*, caused by the lack of opportunities in the home market because prices are depressed or controlled in some way by government intervention, and *pull* due to increasing opportunities for the sake of its products abroad. In Figure 6.3 Chisnall (1985) neatly sums up most of the issues concerned. To conclude, the importance of segmentation and the concurrent development of niches should not be underrated. Peters and Waterman (1982) found that successful American firms, such as 3M, Digital and Hewlett Packard, all had a strategy of developing particular market segments. Furthermore, although we have focused our discussion on exporting, for many

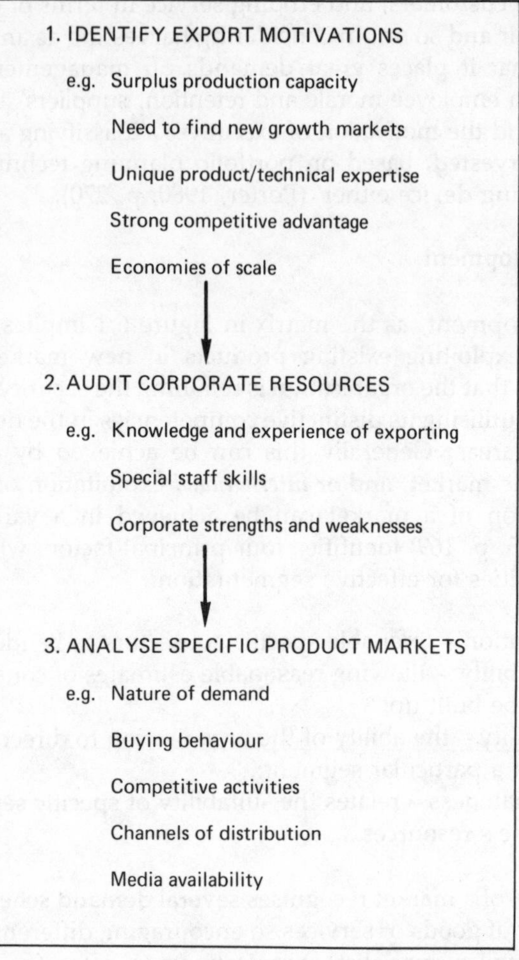

FIGURE 6.3 Steps in evaluation of export opportunities

Source: Chisnall, P. M. (1985) *Strategic Industrial Marketing* (Englewood Cliffs, New Jersey: Prentice-Hall) p. 242.

organisations it may be more appropriate to use virtually identical arguments to expand into other geographical parts of the UK where they do not currently operate.

Product development

Product development is an option of product innovation for existing markets. This may involve new product types derived from technical development or adaptations and improvements. This option should be built upon the firm's particular competence in such areas as R & D or innovation for example. In some industries, computing is perhaps the best current example, product development may be vital if the enterprise is to survive. This strategy does mean that the entity requires a high commitment to R & D, or in some cases a high perceived commitment. It does not always follow from this that it is necessary to be first with a new development, however. Indeed the history of the UK is littered with innovations which have been developed, and then exploited successfully elsewhere.

Product-innovation can have a major impact on an industry's growth by allowing it to serve new needs or by improving its position in respect of substitutes. It may also enhance differentiation. Such features should be recognised, as should the fact that product development, in a very broad way, may impact on reductions in product costs, quality enhancement, and design for a particular market segment. Another aspect of an organisation's commitment to technology generally may be its effect in the manufacturing process which could also lead to lower product costs, improved quality control, faster deliveries, and process developments designed to tune the value chain to a lower cost of serving a particular segment or to raise buyer value.

Diversification

Diversification as a strategic alternative implies that the organisation will develop into areas beyond both current products and markets at the same time. Chapter 3 introduced the various options that this implies and here we intend to focus our discussion on the two main types of diversification, related and unrelated.

Related diversification moves the enterprise from existing markets and products while remaining within the same industry and encompasses vertical and horizontal integration. Vertical integration may mean developing into activities relating to inputs to the present business (backward integration) such as a manufacturer becoming involved in distribution. Horizontal integration refers to a move into activities which are complementary to or competitive with the organisation's present activities, such as a retailer of electrical goods expanding into sales of microcomputers.

Porter (1980, pp. 302–15) discusses the benefits and costs of vertical integration which we have summarised below. Most of the points raised would also apply equally well to horizontal integration. Benefits may be derived from:

1. *Economies of integration*
   - Economies of combined operations – efficiencies can be achieved

by putting operations together, to reduce for example, handling and transportation costs, and to utilise spare capacity.

- Economies of internal control and co-ordination – integration may reduce costs of scheduling and co-ordinating operations; adjacent location facilitates co-ordination and control.
- Economies of information – integration may negate the necessity for collection of information concerning the market. The cost of obtaining information, which may itself flow more readily through an organisation, can be spread over all parts of the enterprise.
- Economies of avoiding the market – integration may permit savings on some of the marketing, negotiating, and transaction costs of the market. Advertising, for example, may be unnecessary.
- Economies of stable relationships – given the stability of the relationship more efficient specialised procedures including dedicated specialised systems, special packaging and so on, can be developed which would not be feasible where both buyer and seller face the risk of discontinuity or increased pressure by an independent party.

2. *Technology*

While the economies of integration form the core of likely benefits the ability to achieve familiarity with technology (backwards or forwards) that is crucial to the success of the business represents an important potential benefit. For example, many computer manufacturers have integrated backwards into microchip manufacture so gaining from an enhanced understanding of this important technology.

3. *Supply/demand assurance*

Vertical integration assures the organisation of supply in a tight period or an outlet for its products in a period of low demand. Assurance of supply and demand does not provide protection from market changes but does reduce uncertainty concerning their effects.

4. *Offset bargaining power*

Where the firm is dealing with suppliers and buyers who wield significant power it may be advantageous to integrate which might lower supply costs or increase selling prices in addition to eliminating the costs involved in combating practices used to cope with powerful suppliers or customers.

5. *Enhanced ability to differentiate*

Vertical integration, by placing control of a larger slice of value added under managements control, can improve the ability of the firm to differentiate.

6. *The elevation of entry and mobility barriers*

If integration achieves any of the foregoing then the integrated firm has a competitive edge over the unintegrated entity. Consequently the unintegrated firm must integrate or face a disadvantage, and the new entrant is forced to enter as an integrated firm or face a similar disadvantage.

7. *Entering a higher-return business*
Integration may enable a firm to increase its overall return on investment if the proposed structure offers a return higher than the firm's opportunity cost of capital.

The strategic costs of integration derive mainly from:

1) Cost of overcoming mobility barriers
Integration requires the organisation to overcome mobility barriers caused by cost advantages from technology, material sources, economies of scale and so on which can, therefore, represent a cost.
2) Increased operating leverage
Vertical integration increases the proportion of the firm's costs which are fixed, because the firm bears the fixed costs associated with the backward or forward operation. So, since sales of the forward business are derived from the backward business, fluctuations in either affect the whole. This increases operating leverage, thus exposing the enterprise to greater cyclical changes in earnings thereby increasing business risk. (Chapter 7 discusses the link between operating and financial leverage.)
3) Reduced flexibility
Vertical integration means that the firm's ability to compete is partly tied to the competence of its own supplier or customer to compete. Problems making this service inappropriate or of high cost increase the cost of change-over to another supplier or customer. Integration may increase the degree of dedication of the firm's assets which, when linked with other issues (strategic interrelationships, for example), raises exit barriers.
4) Capital requirements
Integration utilises capital resources which have an opportunity cost whereas dealing with a third party uses their resources. Therefore integration must yield a return at least equal to the opportunity cost of capital for it to be a viable option. Post-integration capital requirements may also restrict the strategic flexibility of the enterprise because of the requirement to preserve the overall entity.
5) Balance
The productive capacities of the forward or backward parts of the organisation must be held in balance because excess capacity or demand means that these units enter the market, implying that they would be buying or selling from competitors who may be

reluctant to deal with the firm. The risks of imbalance are not so great when a ready market for inputs and outputs exist.

6) Dulled incentives
Incentives may be dulled where the unit sells or buys in-house. Even if the firm's policy is to allow outside transactions, the onus is on management which may make arm's length deals difficult. The pressure of a troubled unit may affect others in the firm who may take or indirectly subsidise it by accepting lower quality or higher price goods than would otherwise be the case.

7) Different management requirements
Despite being related businesses can be different in structure; in technology and in management. For example, there are considerable differences between the control of production and control of retailing. Management capable of managing one part of the firm may be unable to manage another effectively. This may represent a major cost as well as increasing the degree of risk.

Any assessment of the benefits and costs of related diversification must be analysed both in terms of the present environmental structure and in view of the future state of the industry. Economies which may appear minimal at inception may well be considerably larger as the industry grows to maturity, or a reduction in the rate of technological change may remove problems associated with being committed to an internal supplier.

Unrelated diversification takes the organisation into quite different industries which probably bear little or no relation to each other. In fact this conglomerate strategy may be said to be profit-driven, as Illustration 6.2 reveals. However, while profit is clearly an important aspect there are other reasons why a firm might wish to adopt the option. It may represent an optimal route out of an industry in decline or overdependence on a single product-market area. Other possible reasons for considering unrelated diversification include:

1. Utilisation of excess cash, or a cash-rich firm acquiring a firm with a poor cash position but significant profit opportunities, such as the rumoured merger of cash-rich GEC with British Aerospace.
2. The need to balance a highly geared (leveraged) firm with a debt-free company so balancing the capital structure and increasing borrowing capacity.
3. Moving into industries which are countercyclical to smooth out sales and profits, which is akin to spreading risk.
4. Acquiring any organisation providing its profit opportunities exceed some minimum level.

ILLUSTRATION 6.2 The Rise in Popularity of the British Conglomerate

It seems to be the age of reborn British conglomerates. They are different from their predecessors in that they are managerially driven. They are perceived by the stock market to have the quality of superstar management. This makes it possible for them to grow very rapidly, by using the support of their banks, and their own paper, to acquire sleepy or lack-lustre firms which can be made to produce significantly improved results.

Today's conglomerates are very different from the asset-stripping predators of the 1960s and 1970s. After the initial shock- treatment of a bid, a management clear-out and a re-structuring of a target company the conglomerate tends to stay with its acquisitions and build them back up again. **British Ever Ready** had its back to the wall when **Hanson** took it over in 1981 but last year raised its profits 50 per cent to £32m.

BTR has an aggressive pursuit of profitable growth which has taken it into new markets where there is seemingly little industrial logic. When BTR acquired **Thomas Tilling**, another conglomerate in 1983 city institutions in supporting BTR made it apparent that only with outstanding management skills at the top does a conglomerate deserve to survive. BTR's success has been to maximise profit from its business using a highly-decentralised management philosophy which has given managers a high degree of autonomy. Like Hanson Trust BTR makes money from mundane products which had not been optimised by previous managers.

Another type of conglomerate is the mature firm seeking to secure its future. These are not run by superstars but do have enormous cash flows. **BAT**, one of the world's largest tobacco companies, in recognising that the tobacco industry had reached maturity, has utilised its high cash-flows to diversify. Some of its diversification ventures, such as retailing, were not particularly successful. Others, such as the purchase of **Eagle Star** for nearly £1 billion and **Hambro Life** for £600m are the result of finding a home for its huge cash-flow.

ILLUSTRATION 6.2 *continued*

The stock market's enthusiasm for conglomerates is partly a function of the rise in the stock market which has helped their rapid recent growth. A big premium is built into the shares of Hanson and BTR because of the City's faith in the abilities of management stars, which in itself is a weakness. Lose Lord Hanson from his company and the City may wonder what it has left, with disastrous consequences for the ratings.

(Source: Peter Rogers, Margareta Pagaro and Hamish McRae in the *Financial Guardian*, 22 January 1985)

Many of the reasons are evident in practice as Illustration 6.2 shows. Synergy is often quoted as a reason for unrelated or conglomerate diversification. Simply stated, synergy may occur when the combined effect of activities is greater than the sum of the parts, i.e. $2 + 2 = 5$. This would be a rationale for option 1 above, for example, an application of financial synergy. However, as Ansoff (1984, p. 81) notes although there has been much criticism of the perceived lack of synergy resulting from mergers this has been due to corporate managements' lack of attention to ensure that SBU managers realised the potential. Indeed, Ansoff asserts, 'under stress, and/or recession synergistic firms were more resistant and maintained better performance than the conglomerates'.

Perhaps the biggest problem of unrelated diversification is the ability (inability) of corporate managers to cope with the range of problems in a widespread diversified firm. This is similar to the problem with integrated organisations mentioned earlier when effective management in one sphere is not necessarily a prerequisite for success in another. Indeed this may lead to negative synergy, $2 + 2 < 4$, where corporate management may mismanage a unit particularly where there is a high degree of turbulence and the critical success factors are different from the historic antecedents in the firm (Ansoff, 1984, p. 82).

Diversification in practice

At the commencement of this section we indicated that diversification was likely to be a more risky alternative for an organisation when compared with product or market penetration. On one dimension this view is supported by Biggadike's research in America (Biggadike 1979) where he found that on average corporate ventures suffer severe losses through their first four years of operations. He found that, on average, it takes eight years to reach profitability. Lest this seem too disheartening for potential diversifiers, Biggadike's further analysis tended to confound the conventional wisdom of starting small and building; he suggests emphatically that to avoid such long periods of loss *large-scale* entry is required. He concludes by recommending that new ventures should be resourced to enable them to attain a good market position from the start, and that as long as market share is improving it should be financed. If on the other hand new business gains profit at the expense of market share resources should be withdrawn because profits from a low-market-share business represents tomorrow's dog.

On a macro-level Reed and Luffman (1984) researched extensively into the strategy and performance of British industry for the decade to 1980. While their research is too detailed and comprehensive to discuss in this book some of the findings are very relevant:

- During the period of diversification the diversifiers out-perform those companies where there is little change and those who reduce the extent of their portfolio, in terms of returns to shareholders, growth in sales and use of capital.
- Those in the most highly-rated category were unrelated diversifiers or conglomerates, where they found contrary to established theory, that shareholders received a higher return at a lower risk.
- Those companies which reduced their portfolios gave the lowest return to the shareholders at a high risk with the lowest growth in sales.
- Large companies achieved significantly greater increases in ROCE than others.
- Two groups, (the agriculture, food and tobacco industry, and stable conglomerates) achieved high returns and low risks, and their results, again contrary to theory showed that diversification benefits both managers and shareholders.

6.3 Alternative means of strategic development

In the preceding section we outlined the variety of ways that an organisation could utilise in its development. With all of these options, except probably unrelated diversification, there are different means that could be adopted to achieve the objective:

- internal development
- acquisition
- joint venture

Before we consider each of these alternatives it should be apparent that organisations may adopt any one, or combination of methods, and the choice may be a function not just of weighing up objective factors such as risk, cost, pace of change and so on, but also of the values and attitudes of the strategic decision-makers. Also the firm may not, in reality, have any choice in the means by which it develops because there may be no suitable candidates for acquisition or joint venture, or the firm may be one of very few operating in a particular area, and so on.

Internal development

Internal development is often conceived of as a 'natural' move for an organisation especially when it is considering product development or market development. Certainly it has the benefit of spreading the cost of moving into new areas while at the same time enabling the enterprise to develop the knowledge and skills necessary to exploit the opportunities presented. Further, it seems logical, on the surface at least, to develop sequentially, which is another implication of this method, to avoid an early overcommitment to an area.

However, internal development usually involves the creation of a new entity in an industry involving new production capacity and a new sales force for example. So in considering internal development the enterprise must consider the cost of overcoming structural entry barriers and the risk of retaliation by firms already in the industry. Furthermore, the new capacity's effect on the supply–demand balance must be considered.

Internal development has the distinct advantage of minimising disruption to other activities as the rate of change is generally slower. It also avoids the possibility of acquiring people and organisational cultures which may be incompatible, as the firm would be able to build up its own team. Key features in considering the advantages of internal development derive essentially from a structural analysis of the industry (see Chapter 4). Porter (1980, pp. 344–5) identifies the following points which make internal development a viable option:

- The industry is in disequilibrium, as in a new, rapidly growing, industry where the competitive structure is not well established.
- Where slow or ineffective retaliation may be expected, perhaps because the cost of retaliation outweighs the benefits.

- The firm has lower entry costs, for example, because of the relationship between existing skills to the new business.
- The entity has distinctive ability to influence industry structure by increasing barriers for firms attempting to enter later for example.
- Entry will have a beneficial effect on the firm's existing business by enhancing the firm's image, improving the distribution network and so on.

Acquisition

There are many reasons why an organisation may prefer acquisition as opposed to internal development as a means of strategic development. Often the most important features are time and money. The acquisition of an existing firm provides quicker entry into the market while, at the same time, sidestepping many of the entry barriers. Also, as already noted, internal development may disturb the supply–demand balance in the industry which would be avoided by acquisition of a firm already competing in the industry.

It is often believed that entry by acquisition is more costly than internal development, particularly as the cost of acquisition is not spread in the same way. This raises a number of issues, many of which may challenge the 'conventional wisdom' of this assumption. First, as Illustration 6.1 revealed, it may be cheaper to acquire a firm with its productive capacity, personnel, distribution networks and so on because the replacement cost of the assets may well be higher than the cost of buying the items piecemeal. Associated with this point is the fact that the acquisition of another entity does not always involve an actual *cash outlay*, because the acquiring organisation may issue its own shares or loan stock in full, or partial, consideration of the value placed on the target firm. So if the firm did issue its own shares the only cash outlay would be for the costs of issuing the shares, and then in following years the need for an increased dividend to service the enlarged capital base. The firm must recognise, however, that increasing capital in this way dilutes existing members' interests so they may not be as enthusiastic for such a development as the management. The second issue which warrants comment is that by acquiring an organisation established in the target industry means that the firm effectively enters the market with the benefit of this experience, in other words it is already some way down the experience curve so may derive benefits from efficiencies which would be difficult to achieve quickly by internal development.

As we noted in our discussion of internal development, perhaps the biggest problem in managing an acquisition is the ability to incorporate it and integrate its activities in such a way that the economics of the transaction are justified.

Joint venture

Joint ventures represent another method by which an organisation, in co-operation with others, can develop. There are three main avenues for which joint ventures may be appropriate. Where an activity does not represent an economic size for one firm, it may for several because the sum of the individual elements is above some threshold level of activity. North Sea Oil development, and the Alaskan pipeline are examples where corporate joint ventures were successful because not only was a single company unable, say, to fill the pipeline, but also for a single oil company, large and powerful though it may be the financial implications of such an undertaking would probably have had adverse affects on other aspects of its business. The involvement in this case of all the companies means that the risk was shared, the pipeline economically viable, and the value of the companies' Alaskan Oil reserves enhanced.

Joint ventures are also often brought about by political necessity. Many third-world countries have insisted that foreign companies have a domestic partner if they are to receive the necessary approval for the proposed activity. Apart from this obvious political pressure there may be situations in which a local partner is invaluable in helping to surmount language and cultural barriers.

The third type of joint venture is when independant organisations contribute their differing, but complementary, abilities to a jointly-owned business. In such situations each contributes its particular talents which when combined create an enterprise quite different from the partners. An example of companies pooling their talents in this way is the European Strategic Programme of Research in Information Technology (ESPIRIT) where companies have contributed to pre-competitive research. Thus under the ESPIRIT umbrella GEC, Plessey, Bull (France), and AEG (W. Germany) are jointly exploring a project in computer-aided design of silicon chips. This type of approach not only reduces the risk and heavy financial burden of such research, but also aids co-operation between partners in other areas.

6.4 Turnaround strategies

Turnaround strategies are relevant where a business worth saving is in decline. What is interesting about turnaround strategies is that the analysis of why an enterprise is in decline and whether a turnaround will lead to recovery, contains many of the features we have already discussed so that we should be in a position to recognise the symptoms of a turnaround situation prior to its advent. In this section we will briefly discuss the causes and symptoms of decline, and the main elements of a successful recovery strategy. This implies two important features, first that symptoms only indicate what may be at fault so what is required is identification of the fundamental problem(s) or causes leading to the decline. Second, that having identified the principal causes and considered the possible recovery strategies that could be implemented it may well be a situation where turnaround is not possible in which case the liquidation option discussed earlier would seem an appropriate course of action.

In this section we will draw heavily from Stuart Slatter's *Corporate Recovery* (Slatter, 1984) in which he studied forty turnaround situations. Because turnaround situations are so complex we only summarise the key points arising from Slatter's comprehensive work. The reader who is interested in an in-depth analysis of the subject is recommended to read Slatter's book.

Causes and symptoms of decline

Slatter identified eleven factors which were the principal causes of decline (pp. 25–52). They were:

- poor management
- inadequate financial control
- competition
- high cost structure
- changes in market demand
- adverse movements in commodity prices
- lack of marketing effort
- big projects
- acquisitions
- financial policy
- overtrading

Of these, two were major causes of decline in those firms examined and occurred twice as frequently as any other single factor. These were lack of financial control and inadequate top management, mainly the chief executive. The salient features of these two causes are noted below. In addition a crisis appears more likely when an organisation, already weakened by poor management and lack of control, is subjected to changes in demand for its products, price competition and adverse movements in commodity prices.

Inadequate management plays a major role in causing a decline because of incompetence or lack of interest in the business. Slatter emphasises, however, that defects in the composition and methods of operation of the management team are factors worthy of consideration. The five main factors indentified were:

- One-man rule which characterises many failing firms.
- Combined chairman and chief executive, because there is no effective watchdog over the CEO's activities.
- Ineffective boards of directors where key decisions were poorly made.
- Neglect of core business because management devotes its resources to new business development.
- Lack of depth where adequate management skills below the chief executive are missing.

Inadequate financial control often means that management is unable to identify those parts of the enterprise which are losing cash, or those which are generating cash. Poor information systems for the provision of costs, budgets, cash-flows and so on characterise firms in decline. Four common problems found were:

- Poorly-designed management accounting-systems which produce the wrong information, poorly-presented information and are too complex.
- Poor use of management accounting, in other words, are the reports used to assist decision-making and are they understood?
- Organisation structure hinders effective control, thus over-centralisation was found to make effective control difficult, as was the high level at which control was exercised in a hierarchical structure.
- Overhead allocations distort costs so misleading management as to the cost of operating in a particular market.

Symptoms of decline are often easier to detect than their underlying causes, particularly for the outsider. There are a multitude of symptoms; the major ones are noted in the next list which is by no means exhaustive. It is important to realise when interpreting figures from an organisation's financial statements that they should be adjusted for the effects of inflation, otherwise the real state of affairs may be obscured. In considering the features we mention it should be noted that many of the financial ratios have been mentioned in our earlier chapter on internal appraisal. The major symptoms of decline noted by Slatter (1984, pp. 55–7) were:

- Decreasing profitability reflected in a decline in profits before tax and interest, or as a percentage of sales and a reduction in ROI.
- Decreasing sales volume, analysed with accepted industry criteria such as sales per employee, or sales per square foot and so on.
- Increase in debt evidenced by a rise in the level of gearing.
- Decrease in liquidity, measured by the current and acid-test ratio plus the inventory, debtor and creditor situation.
- Divided policy, where a reduction indicates the need to conserve cash.
- Accounting practices where delays in publishing accounts or the use of generally unacceptable accounting policies are often symptoms of decline.
- Management turnover at a rapid rate may indicate disagreement at the higher levels.
- Management fear leading to effective incapacitation was found to be a common characteristic of firms in decline.
- Declining market share indicates that the enterprise is not effectively competing in the industry.
- Lack of strategic thinking characterises many organisations in need of a turnaround.

As can be seen many, if not all, of the causes and symptoms of decline are capable of identification during a thorough, systematic, and objective analysis of the organisation discussed in the preceding chapters.

Successful recovery strategies

Slatter (1984, pp. 78–101) identifies ten generic strategies which are commonly used in combinations in successful turnarounds. Many of the key elements in each have already been covered earlier, or will be discussed later, so here we will only briefly consider each in turn:

- *Change of management*, often a new chief executive is required to revitalise and provide new perception for the organisation.
- *Strong central financial control*, is a prerequisite for a successful turnaround because of the need to impose strict financial controls.

- *Organisational change and decentralisation* may be needed if the firm is highly centralised to start with, this could be a 'trade-off' for the centralised financial controls needed.
- *New product-market focus* will be vital if competitive forces are a contributory factor in decline.
- *Improved marketing*, particularly elements of selling and pricing because poor management rarely seems to have a sound marketing plan.
- *Growth via acquisition*, specifically related diversification, while surprising, is commonly used by stagnant firms, but may not be feasible if the organisation is in a crisis situation.
- *Asset reduction* may be an integral part of reorientating the product-market focus because as the firm cuts out products, customers or whole units the assets can be liquidated.
- *Cost reduction strategies* are designed to increase product profitability and hence cash flow.
- *Investment strategies* involve either reducing costs by asset replacement or at promoting growth.
- *Debt restructuring* applies to firms where the gearing ratio is too high, and involves either restructuring the firm's capital in agreement with the firm's lenders (for example, converting short-term to long-term debt) or raising additional finance.

The way that the strategies are combined to produce an effective recovery strategy will vary according to features like the cause of decline, its severity, past strategy, industrial structure, cost price, attitudes of stockholders and so on. Because there is normally more than one cause of decline many generic strategies may have to be combined. In fact Slatter is quite emphatic on this point 'the average number of generic strategies employed in successful turnarounds is considerably greater than the average number of factors causing decline' (Slatter, 1984, p. 104). Illustration 6.3 shows how some strategies have been implemented, for example improved marketing, asset reduction, cost reduction and investment as a combination to turn a car giant in decline around.

As we have already noted many of the options in this section have already been discussed so a comprehensive analysis, albeit of necessity a quick analysis, of the organisation and the options open to it should lead to an objective consideration of the key issues for a turnaround.

Figure 6.4 represents a useful if simplistic model for determining if the situation the enterprise is in is recoverable. Whether or not the adopted recovery strategies are successful is subject to the quality of their implementation which we discuss in Chapter 9.

ILLUSTRATION 6.3 Fiat Recovers its Way

Almost back in profit after five years **Fiat** is joining the ranks of other recovering motor firms. Fiat, Italy's largest private company, is Europe's fourth biggest car producer (behind **Volkswagen**, **Renault**, and the **Peugeot** Group) and returned to profitability largely without state subsidies. State assistance takes the form of limiting imports of cheap small cars, which is just as well because the company's recovery is based on small cars.

Aggressive cost-cutting and ending a long period of poor labour relations means the company is making profits even though its home market, which took over two thirds of its sales last year, is shrinking. On sales of L10.4 trillion expected profits are L30 billion–L40 billion compared with 1982's loss of L80 billion and 1981's loss of L254.4 billion.

Last year Fiat sold most of its loss-making car operations in South America outside Brazil and has all but abandoned the US, Spain and South Africa. Fiat's only big car-making centre outside Italy is now Brazil, although Fiats are produced under licence in many countries. Profits come from:

- *Higher productivity* The workforce is 25 per cent smaller than four years ago and annual output per worker has risen from 14.8 cars in 1979 to almost 25 today. Absenteeism is down to 5–6 per cent from 20 per cent.
- *More automation* Fiat bought a robot system to build the Ritmo/Strada in 1978, it now has some 600 robots and plan 300 more by 1985.
- *Fewer suppliers* Suppliers of die-parts now number 600 instead of 1000, and component suppliers are down to 1500 instead of over 2000. This has improved quality and slowed the increase in prices of parts.
- *Fewer car types* Plans are well advanced to reduce the number of car underbodies from ten to six and engines from 32 to 24 by 1986. Four basic body types are already out.
- *Simpler cars* The new Uno has a third fewer components and 50 per cent fewer welds (most performed by robots) than its predecessor, the **127**.

ILLUSTRATION 6.3 *continued*

The cost of producing a Fiat this year is 9–10 per cent lower than in 1982. Four years ago the company had to sell 1.5m cars to break even, today it makes money out of 1.1m.

Fiat entered joint projects earlier than most car manufacturers. It builds a light truck and has designed an engine with Peugeot, a car underbody and components were designed with **Alfa Romeo**, and it makes **Lancias** for **Saab**. Fiat now seeks partners for its new energy-saving automatic transmission (the cvt), so it is talking to **Ford** and **General Motors**.

(Source: *The Economist*, 19 November 1983, pp. 74–5)

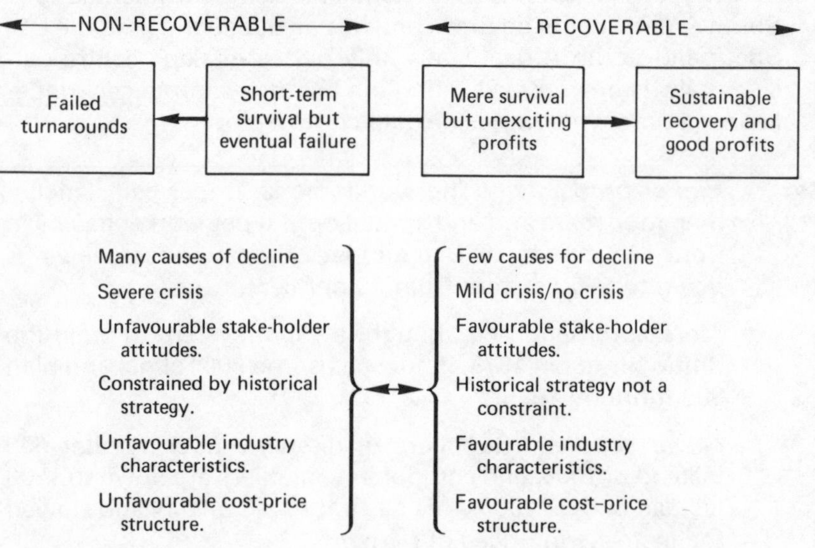

FIGURE 6.4 Factors determining the feasibility of recovery

Source: Slatter, S. (1984) *Corporate Recovery* (Harmondsworth: Penguin) p. 116.

6.5 Summary

This chapter has discussed the main options which an organisation may seek to explore in attempting to meet its objectives. Not all the avenues discussed will be relevant or (as we will see in Chapter 8) viable for consideration because of constraints caused by either the environment or the resource position of the firm. Nevertheless the fact is that there is a wide range of alternative ways of strategic development which when linked with the three means by which such options can be implemented means that an enterprise should be able to select a strategy suitable to its own needs.

In discussing the ways that are open to an organisation (market development, acquisition and joint ventures) it is necessary to recognise that in most instances the type of strategic change discussed is likely to occur slower rather than faster. There are two exceptions to this: first, acquisition because this is often a means by which a new area is developed quickly, and second, in a turnaround situation where if the change is too slow the organisation itself may cease to exist.

Our discussion of the options which may be available to an organisation has naturally involved an element of evaluation as we considered the advantages of the alternatives. This will be explored in more detail in Chapter 8.

Further reading

Strategies appropriate for differing stages of industry evolution see Porter, M. E. (1980) *Competitive Strategy* (New York: Free Press) Chs 9, 10, 11, and 12.

For the relationship of diversification to performance see Reed, R. and Luffman, G. (1984) *The Strategy & Performance of British Industry, 1970–80* (London: Macmillan) Chs 5, 6, and 7.

Turnaround strategies are discussed in Slatter, S. (1984) *Corporate Recovery* (Harmondsworth: Penguin) Chs 2, 3, 4, and 5.

References

Ansoff, H. I. (1965) *Corporate Strategy* (Harmondsworth: Penguin).

Ansoff, H. I. (1984) *Implanting Strategic Management* (Englewood Cliffs, New Jersey: Prentice-Hall).

Biggadike, R. (1979) 'The Risky Business of Diversification', *Harvard Business Review*, May–June, pp. 103–11.

Chisnall, P. M. (1985) *Strategic Industrial Marketing* (London, Prentice-Hall).
Hofer, C. W. and Schendel, D. (1978) *Strategy Formation: Analytical Concepts* (St Paul, Minnesota: West).
Kotler, P. (1980) *Marketing Management: Analysis Planning and Control* (Englewood Cliff, New Jersey: Prentice-Hall).
Ohmae, K. (1982) *The Mind of the Strategist* (New York: McGraw-Hill).
Peters, T. J. and Waterman, R. H. (1982) *In Search of Excellence* (New York: Harper & Row).
Porter, M. E. (1980) *Competitive Strategy* (New York: Free Press).
Porter, M. E. (1985) *Competitive Advantage* (New York: Free Press).
Reed, R. and Luffman, G. (1984) *The Strategy and Performance of British Industry, 1970*–80 (London: Macmillan).
Slatter, S. (1984) *Corporate Recovery* (Harmondsworth: Penguin).

CHAPTER 7

Financial Strategies

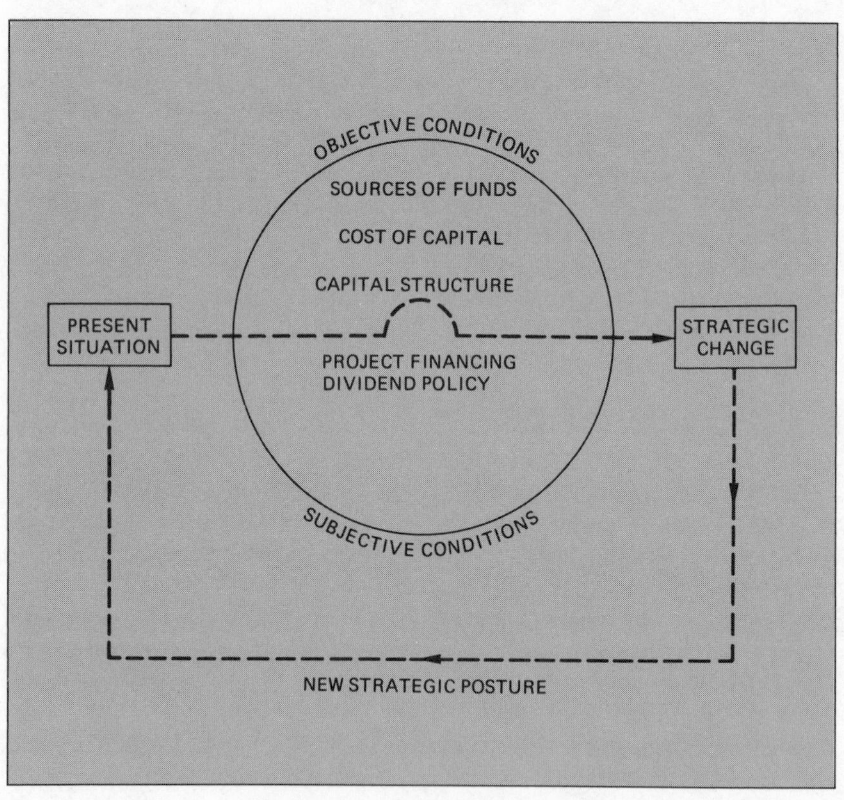

7.1 Introduction

So far we have considered the objectives of the enterprise, a comprehensive strategic analysis of the situation faced by the firm and the variety options open for the firm's future development. We have already seen (Chapter 5) that the financial statements are one of the crucial documents used by both management and owners, or potential owners, to evaluate the success or otherwise of the enterprise. Indeed Lee and Tweedie's research shows the importance of the annual report as being *the key document* used by institutional investors in evaluating corporate performance (Lee and Tweedie, 1981). Furthermore, Briston and Dobbins estimate that the institutional investors combined will own over 50 per cent of the quoted equities in UK-registered companies by 1977 and over 70 per cent of UK equities by 1990 (Briston and Dobbins, 1978). Therefore the picture presented in financial statements is of vital concern to those involved in formulating a suitable strategy for the organisation.

Virtually every project undertaken by an organisation is designed to generate future cash-flow benefits, which may add to the capital market-valuation of the firm. However, since each project normally requires investment expenditure, which ultimately derives from the owners' claim on assets, unless their assessment of the benefits exceeds the investment required, no net positive benefit will be generated. Indeed such an undertaking could be described as unprofitable because it will not result in any net increase in the market value of the firm.

In recognising that future investment requires funding, whether internally generated or externally obtained, the first part of the chapter will focus on the sources of funds available to the firm, followed by a discussion on the effect of the capital structure on the firm. We will endeavour to show that the choices made in the method of funding can have a significant impact on the degree of risk perceived by the owners (or potential owners).

Finally, we will analyse alternative methods of project-financing which enable the firm to undertake ventures of a particularly capital-intensive nature for which traditional methods of financing are inadequate (or involve too great a degree of risk).

It is important to note that the financial aspects of strategy considered in this chapter are an integral part of the strategy-formulation and implementation process. Subtle and complex financial policies count for nothing if the firm does not have the right products aimed at the right markets, the appropriate operations strategy, the correct organisational structure, etc. Success for the firm comes about through the matching of all these strategic components to produce a coherent whole. Illustration 7.1 shows the increasing importance of the financial aspects, plus a warning of over-reliance on financial information.

7.2 Sources of funds

Most funds employed by established firms are internally generated, but external sources of finance are a vital resource required from time to time by nearly all organisations, including those in the public sector such as local authorities or central government. The clearing banks provide the bulk of short-term funds, although some bank loans are available for up to ten years. Table 7.1 summarises the sources and uses of funds by UK companies for the four years 1977 to 1980.

TABLE 7.1 Companies – sources and uses of funds

	£m			
	1977	*1978*	*1979*	*1980*
Sources				
Capital issues	1573	2943	1182	2341
Short-term borrowing	4282	4748	10142	2761
Retained income	12111	13458	17903	13856
Other	(959)	(656)	(1297)	(966)
Total sources	17007	20493	27930	17992
Uses				
Expenditure on fixed assets, etc.	8143	10608	12477	14561
Increase in current assets and investments	8864	9885	15453	3431
Total uses	17007	20493	27930	17992

Source: *Annual Abstract of Statistics* no. 119 (London: HMSO 1983).

This confirms the American findings of Donaldson and Lorsch (1983, p. 52) who noted that management preferred internally-generated funds supplemented by loan capital. The rationale for this policy was that such funds could be relied on with a high degree of certainty, and so were seen as *assured* or *plannable* sources of funds. Logical though this may appear it is important to realise that the UK statistics give only a global position which may mask substantial variations, and Donaldson and Lorsch considered only major industrial companies. As Illustration 7.2

ILLUSTRATION 7.1 The Role of Finance within an Organisation

The gravitation or real power towards the mandarins of finance has given them clout at the top and throughout the fabric of the typical corporation. In the late 1970s one third of the chief executives in the top 800 US corporations originated from the finance function. The increasing preponderance of financial specialists at the top is a function of greater product, geopolitical and technological diversity and complexity which requires more centralised control. Also many manufacturing corporations have increasingly become financial institutions.

Based on the healthy profits of the 1950s and 1960s the typical corporation extended itself both geographically and, in an effort to achieve stability of earnings and financial soundness, diversified into new products and processes to compensate for cyclical declines in the original enterprise. Nearly all established firms strove to insulate themselves from the periodic slumps of demand and prices in any one product by calling upon the countervailing forces in totally different markets. This urge to be above the fray of economic battles and uncertainties sprang from a basically financial cast of mind; a yearning for insurance and certainty through what appeared, on paper, to be a prudently mixed portfolio. The centralised control of conglomerates' varied portfolio of businesses was based on financial performance, financial reporting, financial adjudication, financial language and symbolism, financial diagnosis and financial remedy.

From being predominantly accountants who had recorded business outcomes, the finance mandarins in large companies became first the interpreters and later the shapers of events. Their status was greatly assisted by the increasing importance of outside financing in the 1970s. As inflation became pronounced in the 1960s and 1970s, debt gearing was always repaid in cheaper dollars. Because the advantages from these paper transactions greatly improved corporate earnings, the finance experts could now claim to be direct profit-creators. As external funding increased so did the banking expertise of the typical manufacturing corporation. Its executives became adept and

ILLUSTRATION 7.1 *continued*

ubiquitous at issuing commercial paper. Off-balance-sheet lease financing is another complex area that was mastered.

A bold archetype of the corporate finance department is to be found at **Dow Chemical**. 'It used to be that the controllers kept the books, today they are part of management decision-making' says a Dow source. Dow's finance boss, **Robert Kyle**, exudes a rugged confidence, 'I personally have handled many billions of dollars. We're all big leaguers here. We're big boys who are comfortable with doing megabuck deals on our own'.

'Our financial plan', explains **J. C. Penney's** finance chief, 'develops guidelines for return on investment, earnings per share objectives and hurdle rates; which end up affecting and impacting the operating plans of the company'.

It is alleged that preoccupation with financial performance diminishes innovation and inhibits adequate levels of costly but essential investments in the future. 'Dependency on short-term financial measurements like return on investment for evaluating the performance of managers increases the structural distance between those entrusted with exploiting actual competitive opportunities and those who must judge the quality of their work', write professors **Robert H. Hayes** and **William Abernathy**.

(Source: *Management Today*, August 1982, pp. 54–7)

TABLE 7.2 Advantages and disadvantages of share capital and loan capital

	Advantages	*Disadvantages*
Share Capital	No fixed charge or legal obligation to pay a dividend No maturity date Issue of equity increases credit worthiness Easily marketable	Extension of voting rights High issue costs Dividend payable not tax deductable. May increase cost of capital.
Loan Capital	Known and often lower cost No dilution of equity Interest payable is tax deductible	Increase in risk, which may cause value of equity to fall Need for repayment Limit to amount of funding obtainable

ILLUSTRATION 7.2 Aidcom

Aidcom was created as a two-man design firm in 1959. It grew steadily through the 1960s and 1970s under the chairmanship of James Pilditch, who also owned by far the largest part of the company. By that stage, Pilditch had two problems. The first, common to many founders of private firms, was how to realise some personal capital from what was by now a sizeable enterprise. The second, a private obsession, was how to ensure long term continuity in a sector where in the past firms have always risen and fallen with the fortunes of their original creators.

Pilditch first backed AID into a shell company trading under rule 163(2). That enabled him to make the first major acquisition (of a market research company, not to mention the group's new chief executive, Jeremy Fowler). Rechristened Aidcom the company transferred to the **USM** in the first fortnight of the new market. Since then, the group has added financial services, microelectronics and computer graphics to the design and market research core; pushed turnover up from £1.6m to £8.5m; and grown from a staff of 60 people to over 400.

Aidcom managers are unanimous in their conviction that this remarkable advance would have been impossible without the explosion of energy released by going public. 'We had lots of qualitative ideas before going public, but no notion of how that process would crystallize them. If someone had said three years ago that we'd be turning over £8m in 1983, I'd have laughed at them', says **Fowler**.

Chief among the benefits has been the ability to raise finance for expansion. But there are internal advantages too. At the same time as allowing the founder to claim his nest-egg, a market for the shares has 'released other peoples ambitions' by means of a staff equity stake. Public status has enabled Aidcom to attract high-calibre outsiders to give balance and strength to what was previously a very design-orientated board. Aidcom believes that working for a public company is also a help for recruitment lower down the line.

Companies like Aidcom have been an important educational force on the city. 'A few years ago it was all about tangible assets – factories full of machine tools, things like that. We've

ILLUSTRATION 7.2 *continued*

proved that the virtues of service companies can be just as solid. Just because we're people based, not asset based, we don't have those kinds of peaks and troughs'. The USM having served its considerable purpose, Aidcom is now preparing to graduate to a full listing in the next few months – something it had long intended to achieve.

(Source: *Management Today*, February 1984, pp. 48–49)

reveals, for small companies the injection of finance for expansion can transform the business in a multitude of ways. The two main sources of finance – ordinary shares and loan capital – are briefly discussed below. Table 7.2 (p. 142) summarises the advantages of issuing equity or loan capital. We shall conclude by considering leasing as another funding option available to the enterprise.

Ordinary shares

Ordinary shareholders have legal control of the company by virtue of their voting rights. They are also entitled to any residual income, that is, the amount remaining after all other expenses such as loan interest and corporate taxes have been paid. As they are last in order of priority on liquidation, the capital they contribute provides a cushion for creditors if losses occur. Shareholders are the ultimate owners and have ultimate control and, as we discussed in Chapter 2, it is reasonable to assume that the company is managed on their behalf. It has been claimed that shareholders tend to be passive and rarely exercise the control inherent in their position. However, they can always sell their shares as a last resort if they are dissatisfied with the results of management policies; furthermore, in recent years, we have seen the emergence of 'ginger groups' of shareholders who attend the annual general meeting with the intention of challenging the directors' position, or altering policies pursued by the board.

Because of some of the disadvantages of issuing ordinary shares, many existing firms wishing to raise new equity do so by using a *rights issue*. In effect a rights issue is an offer to sell to existing shareholders a given number of new shares as a proportion of their present holding. An issue of 'one for every two held' means that one new share is offered for every two shares already held. Obviously, the new shares must be offered at a price equal to or less than the current market-price or shareholders would prefer to purchase shares in the open market.

Loan capital

Although the term 'loan capital' can refer to long-term fixed income securities, loan stock or debentures all have one thing in common and that is lack of control, in other words, long-term debt carries no voting rights. However, in the event of the firm defaulting on the terms of the loan, the holders may take effective control, often by the appointment of a receiver.

Loan capital can take many forms:

(i) it may be secured on certain assets of the company, often known as a mortgage debenture;
(ii) it may be secured on all the assets of the company, other than those pledged to mortgage debentures that is, it has a floating charge;
(iii) it may be unsecured, having no security in which case it would rank after mortgage debentures and those with a floating charge in the event of a liquidation.

For an investor, debt may be favourable as it usually has a definite maturity date, as well as giving priority in terms of interest and in the event of liquidation. The holder of debt obtains a fixed return unrelated to the level of earnings. However, during inflationary periods holders of debt may suffer a loss in real value as the purchasing power of the interest payment is eroded. Later, in Section 7.3, we discuss the firm's optimal capital structure, and any decision concerning the use of debt or equity involves an implicit judgement about the firm's actual debt ratio in relation to the optimal.

At this point it is pertinent to consider why a firm may offer such a wide variety of long-term debt, or equity, and why investors are interested in such variety. The rationale for such a wide range of choice relates to different investors having different risk–return trade-off preferences. This can be illustrated by Figure 7.1 which depicts the hypothetical trade-off for a company offering a range of investment opportunities compared to risk-free investment government securities. There is another broader issue linked with the use of ordinary shares as a source of funds and that is their social impact. Weston and Brigham argue that firms financed by equity are less vulnerable to a downturn in performance (sales and earnings) because there are no fixed charges the payment of which may cause the firm to go into liquidation. Against this, they point out that equity prices fall during the recession causing a rise

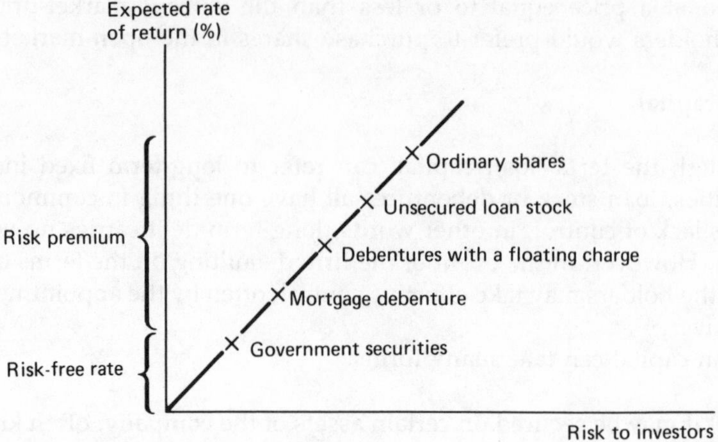

FIGURE 7.1 Investors' risk–return trade off preferences

in the cost of capital, which in turn reduces investment, so aggravating the problem. Conversely, in an expanding economy share-prices rise, thus reducing the cost of capital, and stimulating investment which may add to the developing inflationary boom. Thus Weston and Brigham conclude that because of its effect on the cost of capital equity financing may tend to amplify cyclical fluctuations (Weston and Brigham, 1979).

Leasing

In general, organisations are interested in *using* buildings, plant and equipment, not in owning them *per se*. One alternative to the purchase of an asset is to lease it. The value of leased assets in the UK. has shown dramatic growth since the entry of the major clearing banks into the market after 1972, coupled with a change in capital allowances for plant and equipment in 1971 with a 100 per cent first-year allowance being introduced. In the five years from 1976 to 1980 the volume of leasing accounted for 12.4 per cent of all new capital investment in plant and equipment in the UK. Leasing is a form of debt-financing which provides for the effective acquisition of the asset. Unlike debt- or equity-financing, leasing is typically identified with particular assets. Also, compared with debt, a lease has an advantage if the user has financial problems because, if the lessee does not meet his obligations, the lessor – as the legal owner of the asset – has a stronger legal right to reclaim the asset. The risk to the lessor is less than other financing sources used in the acquisition of assets.

A common misconception is that leasing allows the use of an asset without the firm having recourse to its own funds. However, lease

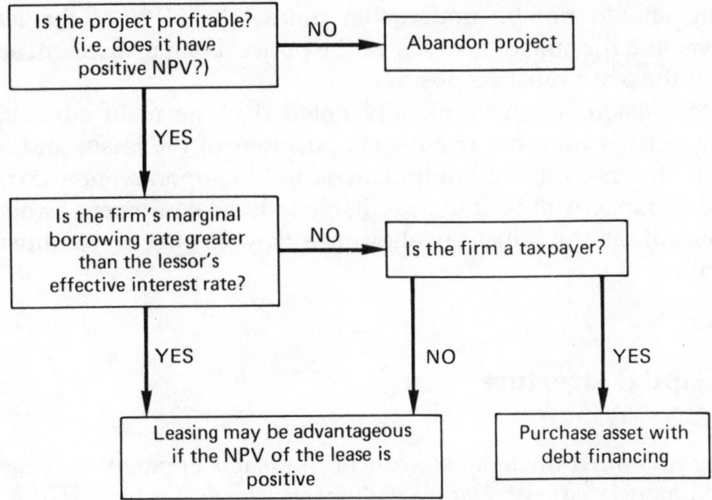

FIGURE 7.2 Fundamental issues in analysis of leasing decisions

payments are based on the price of the equipment plus an interest factor, and it is also unlikely that the lessor would advance a loan for the total cost unless the proposed lessee had other assets or equity to support the loan. Furthermore, although historically lease commitments did not appear on the balance sheet, such data was disclosed in the notes to the accounts.

An intelligent analyst will take account of the effect of lease obligations in assessing the sensitivity of the firm's earnings to changes in revenue. The main advantage in leasing derives from the tax position of the lessor or lessee.

,The use of discounted cash-flows to evaluate a lease-or-buy decision – that is, as though it were a capital budgeting decision – is critically dependent on the discount rate used. The decision to lease is primarily a *financing decision* and it is therefore necessary to estimate the lessor's interest rate and to compare that cost with the marginal borrowing rate of the lessee. If the lessee uses a discount rate greater than the marginal borrowing rate, the apparent attraction of the leasing alternative is inadvertantly enhanced. Figure 7.2 represents a useful, if simplified, model as it focuses attention on the fundamental issues in our analysis of a leasing decision.

Leasing is a financial decision which is contingent on the investment decision. This raises two questions:

(i) Is leasing profitable for the project?
(ii) Is the project profitable using lease finance?

Leasing should not be undertaken unless the NPV of the lease is positive, and the sum of the NPV of the project as an investment and the NPV of the lease must be positive.

In conclusion, we have already noted that the main advantage in leasing derives from the relative tax positions of the lessor and lessee. Thus if the user of the equipment is in a temporary non-taxpaying position, it may well be more profitable to lease equipment rather than purchase it, as the initial tax allowance may be effectively unused for some time.

7.3 Capital structure

Having identified the main sources of funds it is apparent that each has its own associated cost. Before we explore the cost of different sources we need to consider the problem of the mix of sources of capital: that is, the relationship between debt (loan capital) and equity, known as gearing or leverage.

It should be clear that there are some fairly loose constraints. For example, the number and value of mortgageable assets limits the amount of secured borrowing. Similarly, debt must bear a reasonable relationship to equity if it is to be issued on acceptable terms. *The costs of the various elements of capital depend on market prices, which reflect an overall assessment of the firm's prospects*. This might depend, amongst other things, on its capital structure. We can define *capital structure* as the permanent financing of the firm, represented by long-term debt, preference shares, and equity (which includes ordinary shares, retained earnings and any capital reserves). This excludes short-term credit.

Gearing

Probably the best way to understand the effect of gearing is to analyse its impact on profitability under various gearing conditions. For example, assume a firm has the stream of profits before dividends or interest set out below (ignoring taxation):

	Year 1	*Year 2*	*Year 3*	*Year 4*	*Year 5*
Profit	£50 000	£60 000	£50 000	£70 000	£60 000
Change over previous year (as percentage)		20	–17.6	40	–14

We may assume that the variations in profit are unpredictable and therefore represent the degree of risk inherent in the trading situation, that is, the commercial risk. In the absence of debt finance the commercial risk is borne by the equity-holders. Let us now assume that the firm is financed partly by equity and partly by debt which involves interest charges of £10 000 per annum:

	Year 1	*Year 2*	*Year 3*	*Year 4*	*Year 5*
Profit (as previously)	£50 000	£60 000	£50 000	£70 000	£60 000
Percentage change over previous year		20	–17.6	40	–14
Interest on debt	£10 000	£10 000	£10 000	£10 000	£10 000
Available to equity	£40 000	£50 000	£40 000	£60 000	£50 000
Percentage change over previous year		25	–20	50	–18

The presence of debt with its fixed annual interest payment increases the changes in the amount available to owners.

The commercial risk identified earlier has been exacerbated by the introduction of debt, that is, there is an additional element of financial risk. Even though our analysis of the effect of gearing is oversimplified to an extent, we can draw some conclusions from it. First, under any given financial structure the return to equity-holders increases with improved earnings levels. Second, these returns are magnified as gearing is increased, so increasing the degree of change in earnings. If used successfully gearing increases the returns to the owners of the firm. But if gearing is unsuccessful it may result in inability to pay fixed charge obligations and ultimately result in severe financial difficulties.

Financial gearing and operating gearing

Many organisations have some control over production methods; that is, they can use either a highly automated process with its associated high fixed costs but low variable costs or, alternatively, a less-automated process with lower fixed costs but higher variable costs. If the enterprise chooses to use the method involving a high level of automation its break-even point is at a relatively high sales level, and changes in the level of sales have a magnified effect on profits, in other words, the degree of *operating* gearing is high. This is the same effect as that produced with financial gearing in that the higher the gearing factor the higher the break-even sales volume and the greater the impact on profits.

The degree of *operating gearing* can be defined as: *the percentage change in operating profits associated with a given percentage change in sales volume.* Operating gearing can be calculated using the following formula:

$$\text{Degree of operating gearing} = \frac{S - VC}{S - VC - FC}$$

Where S represents the level of sales (quantity x value), VC is total variable cost, and FC is total fixed cost.

For example, let us suppose that a firm has a level of sales of £100 000, total variable costs of £50 000 and total fixed costs of £20 000. Its degree of operating gearing would be:

$$\frac{100\,000 - 50\,000}{100\,000 - 50\,000 - 20\,000} = 1.67 \text{ or } 167 \text{ per cent}$$

Therefore if sales increase by 100 per cent, profit increases by 167 per cent. Operating gearing affects earnings before interest and taxes (EBIT), whereas financial gearing affects earnings *after* interest and taxes, that is, the amount available to equity. Financial gearing will intensify the effects on earnings available to equity after the effect of operating gearing has been taken into account.

The degree of *financial gearing* can be defined as: *the percentage change in earnings available to equity that is associated with a given percentage change in earnings before interest and taxes* (EBIT). An equation has been developed for calculating the degree of financial gearing:

$$\text{Degree of financial gearing} = \frac{EBIT}{EBIT - I}$$

where $EBIT$ is earnings before interest and taxation and I is interest paid.

Thus in our earlier example we can compute the degree of financial gearing if we now assume that further debt is required involving interest payments (I) of £5000. The degree of financial gearing would be:

$$\frac{30\,000}{30\,000 - 5\,000} = 1.2$$

If $EBIT$ were to increase by 100 per cent this would result in an increase of 120 per cent in the amount available to equity. We can combine operating and financial gearing to reveal the overall effect of a given change in sales in earnings available to the owners as follows (which in effect merely reflects the addition of the interest cost to fixed costs):

$$\text{Combined gearing effect} = \frac{S - VC}{S - VC - FC - I}$$

which for our example would be:

$$= \frac{100\,000 - 50\,000}{100\,000 - 50\,000 - 20\,000 - 5\,000}$$

$$= 2 \text{ or } 200 \text{ per cent}$$

Therefore if sales change by 100 per cent this would cause the earnings available to equity investors to change by 200 per cent.

In this example the combined gearing effect of 2 was obtained from a degree of operating gearing of 1.67 and financial gearing of 1.2 but clearly other combinations would have produced the same effect. It is possible to make trade-offs between financial and operating gearing.

The concept of the degree of gearing allows an organisation to predict the effect of change in sales on the earnings available to ordinary shareholders, in addition to revealing the interrelationship between financial and operating gearing. The concept can be used to predict, for example, that a decision to finance a new plant and equipment with debt may result in a situation where a small change in sales volume will produce a large variation in earnings, whereas a different operating and financial gearing combination may reduce the effect on earnings.

In addition there are a number of underlying factors (discussed in Chapters 4 and 5) relating to the capital structure which require consideration:

- Future sales – their stability and rate of growth.
- Competitive structure – industry structure and its impact on profitability.
- Asset structure – the type and nature of assets held.
- Management attitudes – their views and perceptions of risk and control.
- Institutional attitudes – particularly whether this is consistent with managements.

7.4 The cost of capital

We have demonstrated that the capital structure can affect the size and riskiness of the firm's earnings, and therefore its value. In making decisions concerning the organisation's capital structure it is essential to appreciate the elements involved in the cost of capital and how this is influenced by financial gearing.

We will consider the cost of equity, the cost of debt, and weighted average cost of capital, concluding with a brief review of the effect of gearing on the cost of capital. Preference share capital will not be considered because it is so rarely used and as such does not form a major source of funds. Also the nature of preference capital is very similar to debt, with the exception of the taxation implications.

The cost of equity is clearly related to the rate-of-return equity shareholders consider satisfactory. The problem is to identify this rate. Two approaches will be considered, the Gordon growth model (sometimes also known as the Gordon – Shapiro model) and the capital-asset pricing model. Both approaches are complementary rather than competitive and theoretically should produce the same answer if all measurements involved could be made with perfect precision.

The Gordon growth model commences with an expression for the valuation of equity expressed in discounted cash-flow terms:

$$V = \frac{D_1}{(1+i)_1} + \frac{D_2}{(1+i)_2} + \frac{D_j}{(1+i)_j}$$

where V is the value of the equity concerned, and D_1, D_2, etc., are cash returns to the owner (usually dividends) which are assumed to be paid at annual intervals, and i is the cost of equity.

The rationale for the model is that if the discount rate represents the minimum acceptable rate of return, the present value of dividends will represent the maximum price that an investor would be willing to pay for the security. In the event of the price falling below the maximum, buyers are likely to move in to restore the price. Therefore the price can be assumed to equal the present value of future dividends.

As the price of the security is known it should be possible to solve the equation for i, *providing* some method can be found for predicting investors' dividend expectations.

Gordon suggested that a reasonable approximation might be obtained by assuming a constant rate of growth in dividends, which then reduces the above valuation equation to:

$$V = \frac{Do\,(1+g)}{i-g}$$

Where Do is the last dividend actually paid and g is the growth rate.

To find the cost of capital we can rearrange this equation:

$$i = \frac{Do\,(1+g)}{V}$$

This model has the advantage of being simple and direct. However, as Mullins has pointed out, two of its assumptions limit its usefulness. First, the assumption of a constant perpetual growth rate in dividends would not apply to firms where g may be greater than i. Similarly, it could not be applied to a company not paying a dividend. Second, to collapse the present value formula to the simple expression assumes that the growth rate g is less that i otherwise the equation would be invalid. Mullins goes on to argue that the model is in error in using the company's estimate of growth as opposed to the market estimate (Mullins, 1982).

The capital-asset pricing model (CAPM) is a relatively new development of modern financial theory that has achieved a degree of acceptance; for example, it has been used in cases before the Mergers Commission in the UK and cases before the regulatory agencies in the USA. CAPM is based upon portfolio theory which recognises an individual's dislike of risk. Being risk-averse, investors require a higher rate of return on a higher risk security. Given the recognition of risk aversion, portfolio theory then recognises the effect of diversification. Investors, by spreading their investments in a range of securities, diversify so as to reduce the risk. The reduction in risk arises from the selection of the investments – the *portfolio*. CAPM assumes that risky stocks can be combined so that the portfolio is less risky than its components. The power of diversification to reduce risk is dependent upon the relationship between the returns of individual investments. If alternatives do well together and badly together, diversification will do little to reduce risk.

We can extend our analysis of risk to recognise two key elements inherent in assessing risk. First, it is virtually impossible to diversify in such a way as to eliminate risk completely since some element of risk is inevitable in any investment. This element of risk is *systematic risk*, which is related to the overall movement of the stock-market and as such is non-diversifiable. Second, there is an element of risk involved in an investment which is peculiar to the firm involved. This element can be defined as *unsystematic risk*, which can be diversified away. Unsystematic risk itself is a function of not only the nature of the firm's industry, but also, its degree of operating gearing, its diversification and so on (its business risk) and the degree of financial gearing employed (its financial risk).

Figure 7.3 illustrates the concept of the use of diversification to reduce unsystematic risk. Given that investors are assumed to be risk-averse, which implies that they require compensation for taking on risk, we can use a simple equation to express the relationship between risk and return:

$$R = F + \text{risk premium}$$

where R is the rate of return expected on a particular security and F is the risk-free rate (for example, in government securities).

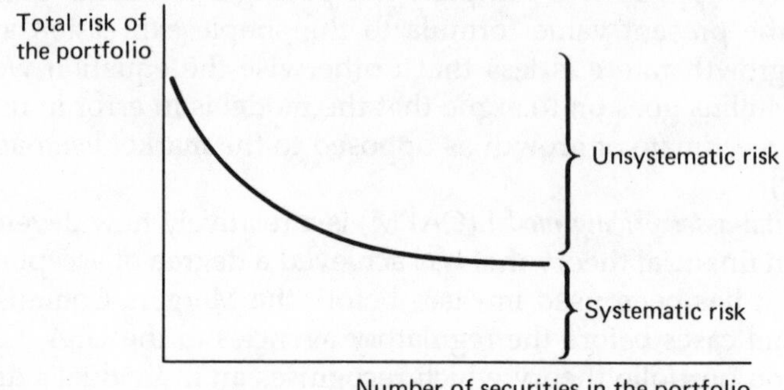

FIGURE 7.3 Diversification to reduce unsystematic risk

The CAPM recognises that unsystematic risk can be diversified away and uses beta (β) as the measure of systematic risk. Beta is derived from the correlation between the returns in the market portfolio and the returns in the security under consideration, and represents the power of diversification to eliminate the risk of the security concerned. The risk premium of a security is a function of the risk-free premium on the market, that is the difference between the risk-free rate (F) and the average rate of return expected in all securities in the market (M), and varies directly with the level of beta. The capital-asset pricing model expresses this as:

$$R = F + \beta (M - F)$$

An example may help to clarify the significance of the beta factor. Empirical studies indicate that 1.6 is a high value for beta which would mean that the price changes for the security concerned average 1.6 times market-wide changes. Thus if the market goes up 10 per cent the security would go up 16 per cent. Similarly if the market goes down by 10 per cent the security would go down by 16 per cent. This type of security would contribute little to reducing portfolio risk. A low value for beta would be 0.3. When the market goes up by 10 per cent the security with that beta would only rise by 3 per cent, and would therefore be effective in reducing portfolio risk.

The CAPM illustrates how returns on a security should be related to beta. If we assume that the risk-free rate is 10 per cent and that the

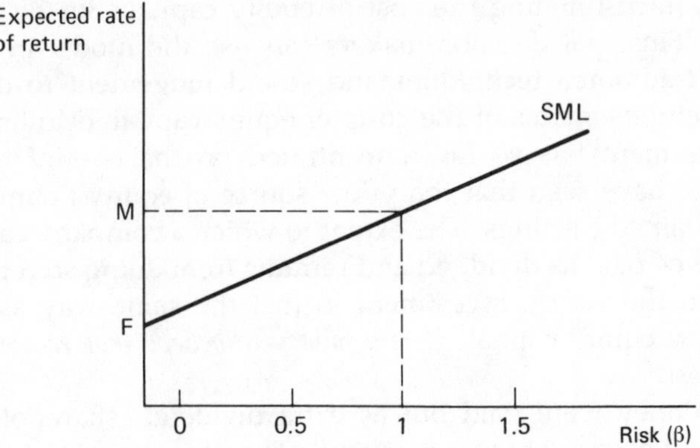

FIGURE 7.4 The security market line (SML)

market as a whole offers a return of 20 per cent the return on a security with a beta of 1.6 should be:

$$R = 10 + 1.6\ (20 - 10)$$
$$= 26 \text{ per cent}$$

The return on a security with a beta of 0.3 should be:

$$R = 10 + 0.3\ (20 - 10)$$
$$= 13 \text{ per cent}$$

The relationship between risk and expected return is called the security market line (SML) which is represented graphically in Figure 7.4. We can use the CAPM to estimate the cost of capital (the minimum required rate of return) for a company's shares. Independent estimates are required for the risk-free rate, the return on the overall market, and beta. The formula then provides the required return.

There are problems involved in the application of the CAPM. The model relates to expected returns for the future which cannot be directly observed. As a result, expected returns on the market portfolio have to be inferred from returns actually earned in the past with adjustments for factors such as changes in the general level of interest rates. Similarly, beta should be estimated for expected future returns, but in reality it has to be estimated form historic data. The risk-free rate is usually estimated from the yield available on a short-term government security.

However, the use of CAPM to estimate the cost of equity capital has the advantage of being based on a careful and well-developed theory. As Mullins observed 'We should not rely on CAPM as a precise algorithm for estimating the cost of equity capital. But he goes on to conclude 'Financial decision-makers can use the model in conjuction with the traditional techniques and sound judgement to develop realistic, useful estimates of the costs of equity capital' (Mullins, 1982).

The argument has so far concentrated on the cost of new equity capital. We have seen that the prime source of equity finance for most firms is retained earnings. The extent to which a company earns money that could be paid as dividend and refrains from doing so represents an increase in the equity investment in just the same way as if it were raising new equity capital. *It is a fallacy to believe that retained earnings entail no cost.*

If the money were paid out as extra dividend, shareholders could invest it and earn a rate of return on it. Therefore the firm must earn an equivalent rate of return to justify retaining the money in the owners' best interests. Basically, we can infer that the rate of return required on retained earnings is the same as that required on new capital. However, new capital gives rise to issue costs unlike retained earnings. This can be allowed for by inflating the estimates of outlays for projects to be financed by new share issues.

A further problem in estimating the cost of equity relates to an allowance for inflation. Inflation must be treated consistently in both the estimated returns from the investment under consideration and in setting the required rate of return. A simple example may help the reader to appreciate the impact of inflation. If we assume that investors require a return of £115 after one year for an outlay of £100, the aggregate required return of 15 per cent is known as the money rate of return. If we further assume that inflation is expected to be 6 per cent we can argue that the return has a purchasing power of £115 ÷ 1.06 = £108.5. The required rate of return net of inflation (the real return) is 8.5 per cent per annum. The discount rate in present value calculations should be set in money terms if cash-flows are estimated in money terms and in real terms if the cash-flows are estimated in real terms.

Clear thought must be given to whether the estimates of the cost of capital represent estimates in money or real terms. This depends on estimates of growth rates, because if growth is estimated in real terms the resultant cost of capital is in real terms. And if the growth is estimated in money terms, then the cost of capital is in money terms. Clearly this is a critical issue in evaluating the feasibility of strategic options in Chapter 8.

Cost of debt

The cost of debt capital – that is, capital raised from the issue of debentures, loan stocks and so on – does not present us with the sort of conceptual problems encountered with estimating the cost of equity. In the case of debt, the amount receivable by the investor is known as it is set by the contract. The investor is not certain to receive this return as the firm may become bankrupt. But it is reasonable to assume that the contractual return will be paid in estimating the interest cost of the capital. A simple equation will provide the cost of debt:

$$Rd = \frac{r}{MV}$$

where *Rd* is the cost of debt, *r* is the interest cost, and *MV* is the current market value of the debt.

In estimating the cost of debt an adjustment should be made for corporation tax. The amount of interest paid is deducted from earnings in computing the corporation tax liability. Therefore if the basic cost of debt is *r* per cent and the rate of corporation tax is *T*, the after-tax cost of debt becomes:

$$Rd = \frac{r\,(1 - \mathrm{T})}{MV}$$

For example, if a company is paying £10 000 per annum on debt capital with a current market value of £100 000 and a corporation-tax rate of 50 per cent, the after-tax cost of debt is:

$$= \frac{10\ 000\ (1 - 0.5)}{100\ 000} = 5 \text{ percent}$$

Since the contractual obligations to holders of debt capital are invariably expressed as actual money sums (and not at constant prices) the basic estimate of the cost of debt will in effect include an allowance for inflation. Where cash-flow estimates have been made in terms of constant prices, the effective cost of debt should be expressed in real terms. For example, if a firm raises debt capital at 14 per cent with a corporation-tax rate of 50 per cent, and inflation expected at a rate of 6 per cent, then the rate of return in real terms is 1 per cent.

The weighted average cost of capital

Having reviewed the methods for calculating the cost of specific sources of financing, we can now consider the techniques for determining the overall cost of capital to be used to evaluate prospective investments. It is clear that debt and equity should not be looked upon independently. It would be inappropriate to relate different sources of capital to different investment projects and argue that the cost of capital is low for some projects, financed by debt, and higher for others, financed by equity. It is a matter of chance whether a particular project is financed by one type of capital or the other and the costs of the various types are related because of the risk element discussed earlier.

The solution is *to regard the various sources of finance as contributing to a pool from which all investments are financed*. The cost of capital should be taken to be the weighted average cost of the various individual sources, weights used being in proportion to the market values of the respective classes of capital. The calculation of the weighted average cost of capital, after the calculations of the specific sources, is relatively simple:

Source	*Market Value*	*Proportion (%)*	*Cost (%)*	*Weighted Cost (%)*
Equity	£4 500 000	60	17	10.2
Debt	£3 000 000	40	7	2.8
	£7 500 000	100		13.0

The effect of gearing on the cost of capital

It can be argued that the cost of equity and the cost of debt are determined independently. If the cost of equity is higher, as we would expect because it represents a more risky investment, then the more highly geared a company becomes the lower its cost of capital. A limit to this process must be recognised, otherwise all firms would be debt-financed. At some stage the proportion of debt makes the firm's level of risk to the potential lender increase, as does the risk to holders of equity. This increased level of risk naturally causes an increase in the overall cost of capital. We can generalise, therefore, and assume that a rational organisation will employ as much debt as is feasible. This argument can be graphically presented as in Figure 7.5. This suggests that the average cost of capital declines rapidly with debt over a certain range and then begins to rise rapidly.

The traditional view just described has been challenged by a view which hypothesises that, except at extreme levels of gearing, the capital structure has no effect on the overall cost of capital. This theory, first developed by Modigliani and Miller (MM) in 1958, effectively argues that the total value of the firm depends on its expected performance and its risk, and is completely independent of the way in which it happens to be financed. The MM approach is depicted graphically as shown on Figure 7.6. The details of the MM theory are rather complex (and algebraically rigorous); its effects have been succinctly summarised as:

> *The average cost of capital is constant in a world with no taxes, but declines continuously with increases in debt when corporation tax is considered*. Thus the

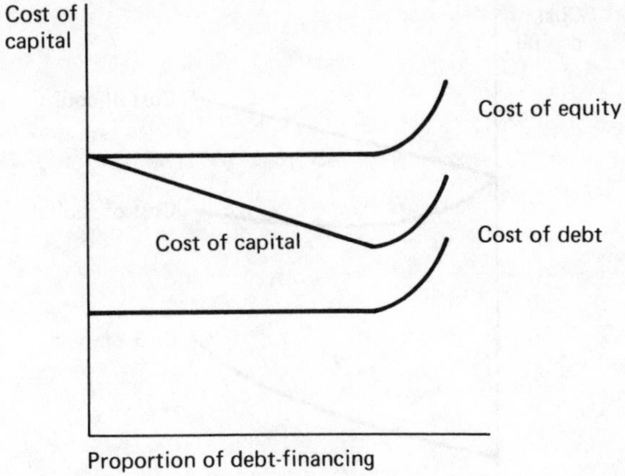

FIGURE 7.5 Feasibility of debt financing

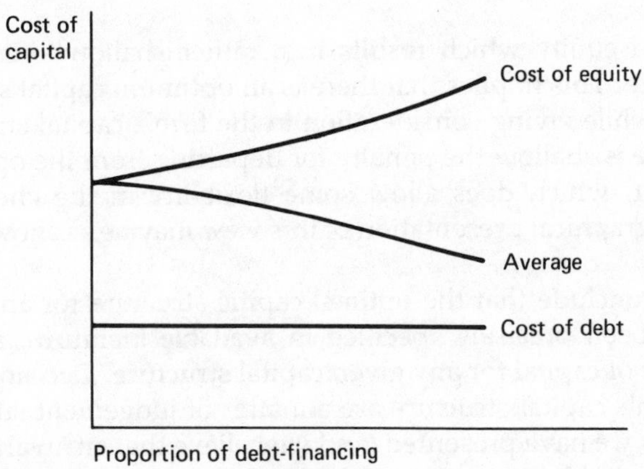

FIGURE 7.6 The Modigliani and Miller (MM) theory

MM model suggests that a firm that pays no corporation tax need not worry about its capital structure, while a firm that does pay tax should take on as much debt as it can (Weston and Brigham, 1979).

While the logic of the MM model is not in doubt it has been heavily criticised for the simplifying assumptions on which it is based.

At this point in the debate, it may well be of value to consider some mid-point between the traditional and MM views which generally reflects the way in which firms behave. This compromise view basically argues that as the degree of financial gearing increases so does the cost

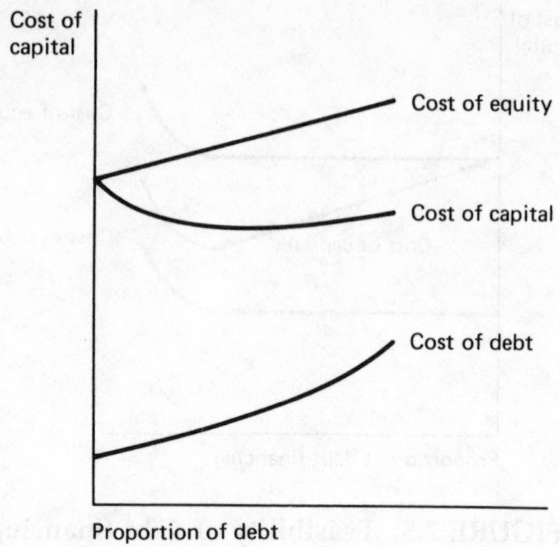

FIGURE 7.7 A compromise between traditional and MM views

of debt and equity which results in a rather shallow average cost of capital curve. This implies that there is an optimum capital structure, so it is worthwhile giving consideration to the firm's capital structure. But as the curve is shallow the penalty for departing from the optimal point is not great, which does allow some flexibility in the choice of new finance. A graphical presentation of this view may be as shown in Figure 7.7.

We can conclude that the optimal capital structure for an actual firm has never been precisely specified in available literature, nor has the precise cost of capital for any given capital structure. Decisions concerning the firm's capital structure are a matter of judgement supported by the analysis we have presented (and we believe that an awareness of the theoretical considerations is useful in such analysis). The cost of capital, and the effect of gearing is a very complex area which we have merely sought to introduce. The references at the end of the chapter and the further readings suggest sources that can be followed up if the reader requires a more thorough analysis.

7.5 Dividend policy

Dividend policy determines the division of earnings between payments to shareholders and reinvestment in the firm. Dividends represent the

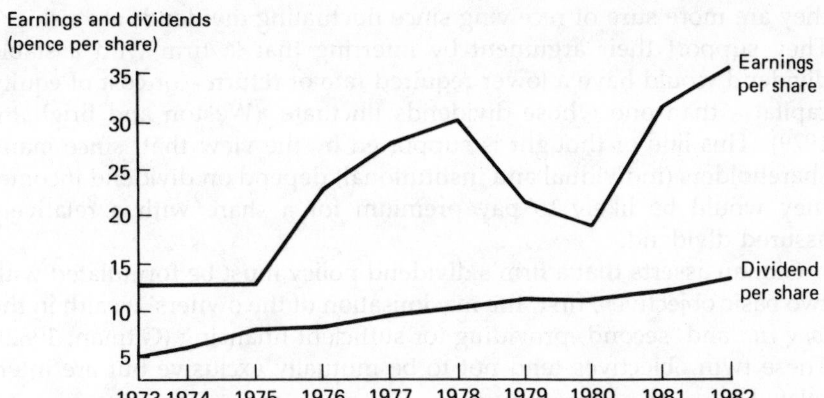

FIGURE 7.8 Dividends and earnings, Reckitt & Colman plc

owners' *current* return on their investment. Retained earnings, as we have already shown, are one of the most significant sources of funds. The extent of internal financing will be determined by the firm's dividend policy.

Three main factors can be identified which impact on dividend policy, the legal position, growth, and shareholder considerations.

Dividend policy observed

There is a general tendency for firms to pursue a stable dividend policy which means a stable money sum per share each year. Earnings on the other hand represent the annual profits attributable to equity. Profits may fluctuate but dividends are usually more stable, and tend only to increase with a lag after earnings rise. Dividends are only increased when the increase in earnings appears unsuitable. This is illustrated in Figure 7.8 where the earnings and dividend patterns of Reckitt & Colman plc over a ten-year period are charted.

We can see that, whereas the dividend per share has grown steadily over the period (from 5 per share to 15 per share) the earnings per share have shown significant variability. The firm has essentially adopted a stable dividend policy. Interestingly, over the period, dividends as a percentage of earnings have increased from 38 per cent to 45 per cent, although as the graph shows there is considerable variability (that is, over 50 per cent in 1979 and 1980, and less than 30 per cent in 1977 and 1978).

Weston and Brigham argue that a stable dividend policy tends to lead to higher share prices because 'investors value more highly dividends they are more sure of receiving since fluctuating dividends are riskier'. They support their argument by inferring that 'a firm with a stable dividend would have a lower required rate of return – or cost of equity capital – than one whose dividends fluctuate' (Weston and Brigham, 1979). This line of thought is supported by the view that, since many shareholders (individual and institutional) depend on dividend income, they would be likely to pay premium for a share with a relatively assured dividend.

Gitman asserts that a firm's dividend policy must be formulated with two basic objectives, first, the maximisation of the owners' wealth in the *long run* and, second, providing for sufficient financing (Gitman, 1982). These twin objectives tend not to be mutually exclusive but are interrelated.

A problem associated with the objective of wealth maximisation relates to the owners' understanding of the objective of dividend policy. If the owners do not appreciate the implications of the dividend policy adopted, their actions may cause the share price to fall. To counter this, it is management's responsibility to ensure that owners are aware of the objectives and implications of dividend policy, so that the market reaction is favourable.

Unless sufficient financing is available to implement acceptable projects, the desired wealth maximisation will not occur. Dividend payments should be regarded as a required outlay, after which the remaining funds can be reinvested in the firm. Therefore, in planning future needs, the retained earnings availability must be forecast on an *after-dividend* basis, particularly as the market is likely to react adversely to the non-payment of cash dividends.

Three of the most commonly used dividend policies are: *stable dividend per share, constant payout ratio,* and a *low regular dividend plus extras.* Most firms adopt the policy of paying out a stable money sum per share each year, in other words, a steady dividend per share. Few firms pay out a constant percentage of earnings because of the degree of variation in earnings. However, the relationship between earnings and dividends is important and often represents a factor in the decision on what dividend policy to adopt. As a compromise, a firm could adopt the low regular dividend plus extras policy which does provide some flexibility. It would however leave investors somewhat uncertain as to the dividend they can expect.

A firm can make a non-cash dividend pay-out in the form of a scrip dividend. A scrip dividend is effectively a transfer to the shareholder of a number of shares without the shareholder paying any cash for the shares. This preserves the firm's liquidity, and the share price would not fall provided there are sufficient profitable investment opportunities and that the number of shares is not too large. Although shares are not cash, they can be converted by the owners to cash by sales in the market.

In concluding these sections on sources and costs of capital we would reiterate that these issues do not relate to financial matters alone. The ability of a firm to utilise successfully the capital markets for external funding can have a number of equally, and sometimes more important benefits.

7.6 Alternative methods of project financing

In the previous sections we concentrated on fairly traditional strategies that the firm can deploy to optimise its use of its financial resources. However, recent years have seen industrial projects undertaken requiring huge amounts of capital. The situation has been further exacerbated by inflation, high interest rates, 'state of the art technology' (for example, in North Sea oil development), sometimes coupled with remote locations; all of which conspire to tax the financial capacity of the largest firm. In addition, the developmental nature and foreign location of such investments increase the financial risk in the venture to such an extent that its outcome may well have an enormous impact on the investing firm.

One solution to this problem is to structure the investment as a joint venture which we discussed in Chapter 6. So if the inherent managerial problems can be overcome research suggests that:

> project financing can be a vehicle for enjoying the amount of debt available to a new undertaking as well as for managing the sponsor's exposure to the associated risks. This technique is usually applied to extremely large natural resource and energy investments costing hundreds of billions of dollars (Wynant, 1980).

However, there is no reason why the same strategy should not equally apply to situations where the financial needs are not excessive but risks are great.

The first feature of project-financing is that the venture is segregated from the sponsoring firm's assets and liabilities. Second, the project's economic prospects coupled with the sponsor's and third parties commitment provides the support for extensive debt which has limited recourse to the sponsoring parent company. Several characteristics distinguish project-financing from traditional arrangements:

(i) The venture is established as a separate entity relying heavily on debt-financing, sometimes for up to 80 per cent of the capital requirement, this borrowing being linked directly to the assets and cash-flow potential of the venture.
(ii) Third party (suppliers, customers, government agencies, etc.) and the sponsoring parent firm are the important elements of credit support. The sponsor's guarantees to lenders generally does not cover all the risks involved.
(iii) For balance-sheet purposes the liabilities of the project are differentiated from the parent's other 'normal' obligations.

In opting for this kind of package the sponsoring organisation is making a trade-off between the desired risk exposure and the anticipated returns. The risk assessment of the sort of venture which may require project financing would include, for example, overspending on start-up costs, higher-than-anticipated operating costs, volatile market conditions, and for foreign ventures, high political risks. Project-financing will allow some of the risks to be transferred to other parties. It may also allow the parent company to retain its financial flexibility as off-balance-sheet debt is regarded more favourably than direct debt by many analysts. Indeed Wynant's research revealed that 'for most institutions, indirect liabilities are not formally or at least not fully included in their analysis of a company's financial position' (Wynant, 1980).

An extension of the concept of project-financing may well relate to the costs of research and development. In an economic downturn research and development (R&D) expenditure is often reduced because it is treated as a discretionary cost, that is, as a revenue expense it reduces reported profits. Such cutbacks may often be self-defeating because the expenditure may be necessary to maintain for example;

(i) the firm's product leadership;
(ii) its competitive edge in product quality or new products.

The problem is that the R & D expenditure is high risk with no guarantee of success which must be balanced against the other financial problems facing the firm. Some of the problems of R & D are summarised in Illustration 7.3.

An *R & D partnership* is a method of funding the necessary expenditure. Under such an arrangement the inventor transfers the rights to innovations created by R & D effort to a partnership in return for funding. In this way the inventor retains control over the R & D, and the expenditure is not classified as an expense, thus reducing profits, because it relates to the partnership. The investors in the partnership,

ILLUSTRATION 7.3 Research & Development – Investing in Roulette?

In the pharmaceutical industry research and development expenditure presents a wide range of problems. Most firms deal with a range of products from prescription drugs sold to the National Health Service (NHS), to 'consumer'-orientated products sold through retailers and chemists. As a result research and development will be involved, for example, in both seeking new drugs – that is, 'pure' research – and in improving the process of manufacture of other products – that is, process development is financed from profits – consequently R & D is essentially a discretionary cost whose level of operation and expenditure must be determined by management on the basis of cost–benefit.

The issue of determining profitability from drug sales is also complicated by the control exercised by the Department of Health and Social Security (DHSS) over the level of profits allowed on sales to the NHS. Simply stated, the DHSS lays down the level of profitability allowed, expressed in terms of 'Return on capital employed', the calculation of which is subject to certain expense limits: marketing costs, for example, are limited to a percentage of turnover. A manufacturer can charge any price for a product, provided that the overall profit remains within DHSS parameters. In the event that a profit exceeds that allowable by the DHSS, then the 'excess profit' may be 'clawed back'.

New drugs may take many years (ten is not uncommon) to develop and only a very small percentage pass succesfully through a battery of tests culminating in clinical trials. The whole process has been described as 'investing in roulette' and can be depicted diagramatically as follows:

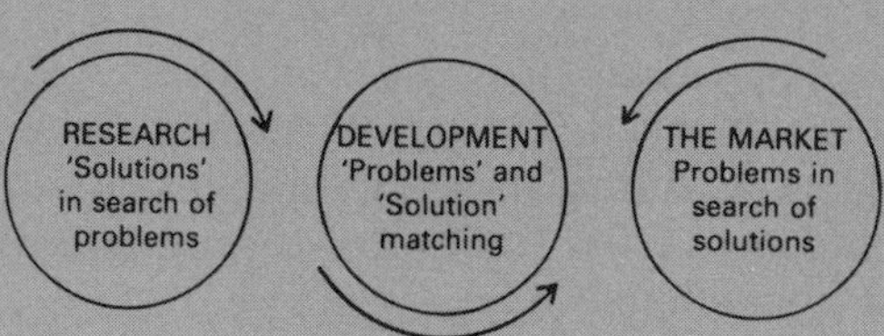

ILLUSTRATION 7.3 *continued*

Essentially the key to an R & D success is to match each of these spinning wheels so that the research can be developed through the problem perceived by the market. This will limit the uncertainty to the products development cycle.

In fact a prescription drug market product has a product life-cycle in the same way as any other product, with individual life-cycles being subject to a long product-life-cycle with one product (or solution) being superseded by subsequent products (or solutions). However, a key difference in the market controlled by the DHSS with its stringent regulations is that longer-running life-cycles are supported by patent/copyright law; thus, effective entry barriers are erected to new firms seeking to exploit the opportunities.

(Source: Asch D. C. and Kaye G. R., unpublished research)

that is, those parties providing the funds, receive a return in the form of royalties. From the inventor's point of view the arrangement can be very profitable without the need to dilute shareholders' equity or the need to obtain debt-financing.

The details of an R & D partnership arrangement, as with project financing, are very complex and require considerable patience and expertise to be successful. But an R & D partnership does represent a creative way of financing such expenditure. To conclude:

> The popularity of R & D partnerships has increased in the past few years. Using a partnership arrangement with investors, many companies have found a good way to finance new product research; and investors have found them attractive because of the high returns (Hardy, 1984).

7.7 Summary

Our discussion of financial strategies has highlighted a number of crucial issues for the formulation and implementation of strategy. Strategic management of the enterprise cannot take place without a consideration of points like:

- the differing sources of capital;
- the capital structure, and cost of capital of the enterprise;
- the effect of dividend policy.

We concluded with a brief mention of alternative financing methods which organisations may be able to utilise in the future as well as, or in place of, the more traditional methods discussed earlier. It is important to recognise the pivotal role played by the finance function not only in its own right but also in the way that it presents an image of the organisation to the external world.

Further reading

There are a number of financial management texts which develop issues raised in this chapter in more detail. For example Gitman (1982) and Weston and Brigham (1979) both referred to in the text. Franks and Broyles, *Modern Managerial Finance* (Chichester: Wiley, 1979) has the advantage of being a UK-based text.

References

Briston, R. J. and Dobbins, R. (1978) *The Growth and Impact of Institutional Investors* (London: The Institute of Chartered Accountants in England and Wales).

Donaldson, G. and Lorsch, J. W. (1983) *Decision-Making at the Top* (New York; Basic Books).

Gitman, L. J. (1982) *Principles of Managerial Finance* (New York: Harper & Row) 3rd edn.

Hardy, John W. (1984) 'Financing with R & D partnerships reduces risk', *Management Accounting*, January, pp. 56–9.

Lee, T. A. and Tweedie, D. P. (1981) *The Institutional Investor and Financial Information* (London: The Institute of Chartered Accountants in England and Wales).

Modigliani, F. and Miller, M. H. (1958) 'The cost of capital corporation finance and the theory of investment', *American Economic Review*, June pp. 261–97.

Mullins, D. W. (1982) 'Does the capital asset pricing model work?', *Harvard Business Review*, January–February, pp. 105–14.

Weston, J. F. and Brigham, E. F. (1979) *Managerial Finance* (London: Holt, Rinehart & Winston, 6th edn (British edn).

Wynant, L. (1980) 'Essential elements of project financing', *Harvard Business Review*, May–June, pp. 165–73.

CHAPTER 8

Strategic selection

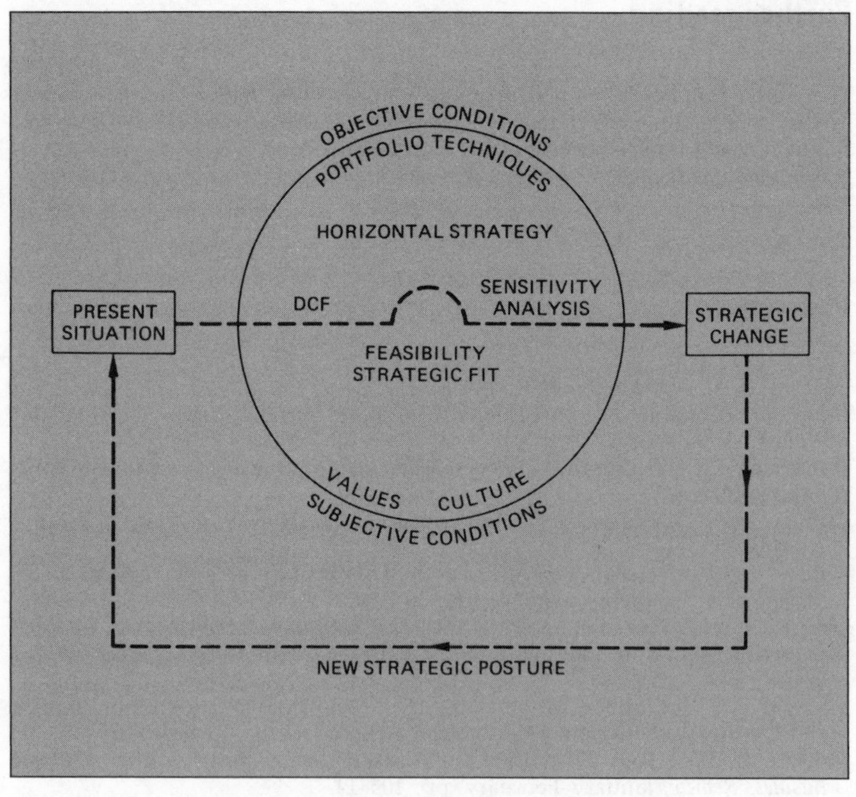

8.1 Introduction

Chapter 6 considered the array of alternatives open for strategic development. This chapter is designed to analyse how the firm may choose between these options. It will, therefore, examine the considerations of a thorough strategic evaluation which provides the basis for strategic selection.

There are two key features of this process which need to be addressed. First, Quinn (1980, pp. 15, 58, 196) has noted the variety of an all-embracing corporate-wide formulation process; a process which he found typically to be fragmented, incremental, and the product of consensus for action by management. Strategy tends to emerge incrementally as the result of internal and external changes, considering the future, gathering information, sensing problems, developing responses to *ad-hoc* crises, acquiring a 'feel' for strategically relevant factors, their interrelationships and importance. Strategic evaluation and selection, therefore, do not necessarily involve management in setting aside time for a comprehensive review as many major strategic decisions seem to emerge gradually rather than from periodic analysis followed by a decision. Indeed Quinn goes on to argue (1980, p. 203) that the most effective process seems to be one where management concentrates its attention and resources on a few critical strategic thrusts as a conscious, pro-active approach to change management. The formal analysis such as that discussed in this and earlier chapters is conducted and contributes to the outcome, but does not represent the whole process.

The second point we wish to make is that the process of evaluation and selection does not provide a set of procedures leading to the 'right' selection. Strategic selection is not a precise analytic process, intangible situational factors, creativity and judgement must be integrated with the objective realities discussed in earlier chapters. So, strategic selection is not a technique; it is a managerial responsibility.

We divide our discussion of strategy evaluation and selection into three sections, evaluation at the corporate level, evaluation at the business level, and finally we consider some other techniques which may be used in the selection process. As we indicated in Chapter 3 the distinction between corporate and business level strategy can and does become blurred, and the issues we raise in each of these sections could be, and have, been applied throughout organisations.

Underlying our discussion throughout this chapter are three criteria – fit or suitability, feasibility and acceptability. The concept of fit, sometimes referred to as suitability or consistency, expresses the degree to which the proposed development relates to key features identified as a result of the strategic analysis phase. The extent to which the option takes advantage of corporate strengths and presenting opportunities while meeting the objectives are key elements; as are the match between more subjective issues such as management values and organisational culture.

For example, C. & J. Clark, shoe manufacturers and retailers, have built upon a very strong brand image of quality footwear to develop not only retail outlets (from 200 shops in 1973 to 1440 shops in 1983) but also into other parts of the industry such as shoe-making machinery, components and accessories. Development has been restricted to wealthier countries for which their products are designed and specified. In so utilising its key corporate strength turnover and profits have quadrupled in the past decade.

The feasibility of an option has already been discussed in the process of identifying alternatives in Chapter 6. Recall, for example, that in our consideration of whether the organisation should develop internally or by acquisition an important aspect was a judgement concerning entry barriers and how they could be overcome or otherwise. At this stage the shape of the option should be a little clearer and hence capable of evaluation against more objective criteria. Such an evaluation would include, for example, whether the organisation has the financial resources to fund the development, whether it can cope with the predicted reactions from competitors and so on. The determination of whether or not a particular strategic option is acceptable depends on objective measures like profitability, risk, relationships with outsiders (suppliers, labour, customers and government, for example) and the degree of change required in the enterprise. At one level it is reasonably easy to test acceptability – by using projected financial statements, for instance – but underlying these objective conditions are subjective issues such as the cultural norms of the organisation, resistance to change (see Chapter 10), and outside or environmental perceptions of the proposed developments.

Strategy selection at the corporate level

Our discussion of strategic evaluation at the corporate level will focus upon the use of two models we discussed earlier in Chapter 3 – portfolio analysis and horizontal strategy. For our discussion on portfolio analysis we will use the nine-cell GE matrix, reproduced below in Figure 8.1. Recall that this matrix, while overcoming most of the criticisms of the BCG matrix, has the advantage of being simpler to use than the product/market evolution matrix.

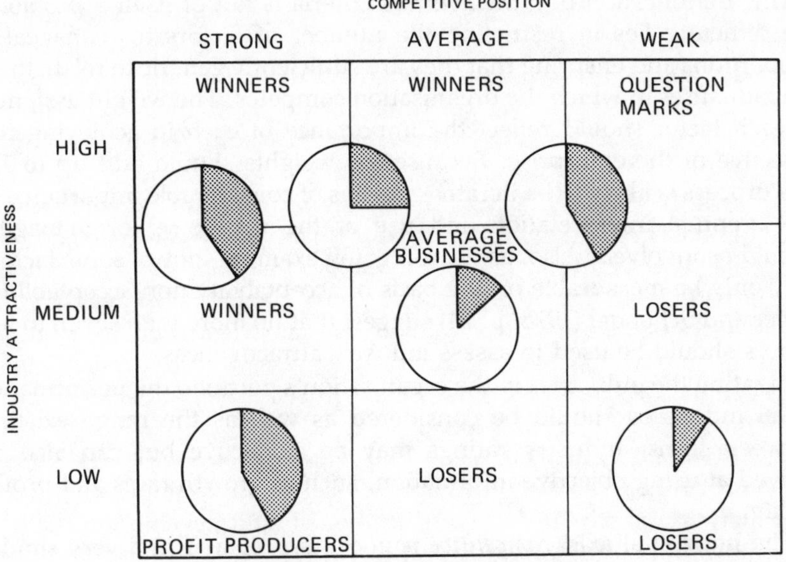

FIGURE 8.1 Nine-cell GE matrix

8.2 Portfolio analysis

The vertical axis in the matrix *industry attractiveness*, is a composite weighting of a number of factors illustrated below. The actual process involves assigning each factor a weight according to its perceived importance, then rating how the business compares to each factor using a one (very unattractive) to five (very attractive) scale. The composite value is a function of the weight and rating assigned to each factor.

Industry attractiveness factor	*Weight*	*Rating*	*Value*
Market size	0.18	4	0.72
Projected rate of market growth	0.15	4	0.60
Profitability	0.20	3	0.60
Competitive structure	0.10	3	0.30
Cyclicality	0.10	2	0.20
Technological requirements	0.07	1	0.07
Social and environmental factors	Acceptable	—	—
Opportunities	0.20	4	0.80
	1.0		3.29

The identification of attractiveness criteria is not of itself a problem, the difficulty lies in restricting the number of factors to manageable proportions and ensuring that they are sufficiently generic to relate to all the industries in which the organisation competes. The weight assigned to each factor should reflect the importance of each in achieving the objective of the enterprise. Because the weights should add up to 1.0 this process is likely to be iterative. As it is of considerable importance to the eventual interpretation and use of the matrix senior managers should be involved. Also, as the foregoing example shows, some factors may only be measurable on the basis of acceptability/non-acceptability. Hofer and Schendel (1978, p. 74) suggest that no more than seven to ten factors should be used to assess industry attractiveness.

In rating the industries in the organisation's portfolio the performance of all industries should be considered as well as the range existing between firms. Industry ratings may be subjective but can also be arrived at using objective information, such as growth rates and profitability.

The horizontal axis, *competitive position*, is prepared in a very similar way first, by, identifying the key success factors, which are those variables which may be influenced by the firm's decisions, the problem being not to identify such factors but to weight them. Second, the factors must be weighted, which, in the same way as with the vertical axis, is likely to be an iterative process. It is likely that there are a relatively small number of factors (for example, market share, product quality, effectiveness of distribution) which will have an impact on relative competitive position. Third, the factors are rated, often by considering the position relative not only to the industry average but also to the strongest and weakest firms in the industry.

As we noted in Chapter 3 the GE matrix prescribes strategy as grow and build for the 'winners', divestment for the 'losers', and consolidation or hold for the average (or profit) producer. This apparently straightforward strategic evaluation is not the whole process. In fact Hofer and Schendel (1978, pp. 71–86) identify six other features:

(i) An in-depth assessment of each industry where the entity operates to identify key trends and market direction, the nature and strength of competition, crucial technological developments, materials and labour-supply costs and conditions, capital requirement, and projected profitability with the intention of determining how worthwhile it will be to have a strategic interest and stake in the industry.

(ii) An assessment of the enterprise's competitive position in each industry and how the business ranks in terms of the important features identified as underlying competitive success.

(iii) Identification of the opportunities and threats in each business.

(iv) Consideration of what corporate resources and skills could improve the competitive strength of each business unit.

(v) A comparison of short-term profit potential and risk with long-term profit and risk for each business in the portfolio.

(vi) Assessment of the portfolio as a whole to determine the balance between winners, potential winners, losers, question marks and so on.

The strength of this sort of procedure is its systematic approach to evaluation. However, this must not be allowed to blind us to the fact that much of the content in the aforementioned six points, and in the construction of the matrix itself, is subject to (unintended) bias on the part of those charged with putting the 'facts' together. Thus in practice we have a mix of objective and subjective information. Having already considered the first two points it is worth devoting a little time to the remainder to develop an overall view of the firm's business.

Although *opportunities and threats* will have been considered in assessing industry attractiveness it is useful to focus attention on how specific opportunities and threats might affect the competitive position of each business. This will enable a better view of the potential benefits and risks to be obtained for each business because of the variability in an enterprise's ability to cope with or to counter threats and to develop or exploit opportunities.

A realistic appraisal of the organisation's *resources and skills* that could significantly affect its competitive position in an industry is of particular importance if the business is considered to be in a less than favourable competitive position, and/or improvement in a key success area is indicated. The crucial issue is to determine whether the entity's distinctive competencies are translatable into developing a competitive advantage so making a business more viable. Having assessed each business in the portfolio in terms of industry attractiveness, competitive position, opportunities and threats, and availability of particular skills and resources, the next step is to compare and rate their *relative attractiveness*. This really means more than drawing up a matrix of spurious utility, involving as it does a searching examination of some underlying details, and consideration of intangibles. Two features are important: first, the difference in assessment of short-and long-term attractiveness and second, comparing these assessments across a portfolio that has a good strategic fit and the effect this may have in changing relative rankings.

Balance in the portfolio refers to the mix of businesses. For example, if the portfolio contained too high a proportion of 'losers' or mature or declining business then corporate growth may be too low. Alternatively the firm may need to strike a balance between the 'cash cows' and the resource requirements of 'developing winners'.

Gap Analysis

The last stage of the corporate strategy evaluation processs involves determining whether the projected performance of the businesses in the portfolio as a whole meets the corporate objectives. Where a gap between the projected performance and objectives exists then changes must be considered in order to bridge the divide. Hofer and Schendel (1978, pp. 93–100) identify a number of ways of closing the gap between the projected levels of performance:

- Change the strategies of some (or all) business units; this may also involve a degree of change in the unit's level of investment with consequential effects at the corporate level.
- Add new businesses to the corporate portfolio where the focus would be on whether to diversify rather than how. The strategic issues raised would include whether or not the new business fits in a strategic, structural, and cultural way, the opportunity costs of acquisition, specific features required in a new business (for example, cash- or profit-generation). One way of assessing fit would be to plot the proposed business on the matrix which would determine whether the candidate fulfils its corporate expectations.
- Delete some businesses from the portfolio, particularly those in a weak competitive position, or in a relatively unattractive industry. In addition businesses in an industry which does not 'fit', so that management is unable to manage them effectively or adequately, would also be candidates for deletion. Remember that we considered this in Chapter 6 and noted that divestment should be conducted in such a way as to maximise the enterprise's cash inflow.
- Change business-unit political strategies, either by involving competitors so enhancing the attractiveness of the industry as a whole, or by involving other parties (not competitors) so improving the unit's competitive position within the industry. A business might join forces directly or indirectly with others (customers, suppliers, competitors, unions) to achieve results neither party would achieve on its own.
- Changing the objectives is an obvious way of closing the gap, but

only after all other feasible alternatives have been tried. On occasion, say when a fundamental shift in the economic environment has occured, then changing the objectives to bring them more into line with the new reality may be necessary.

8.3 Horizontal strategy

Portfolio analysis is often used to select the industries in which the firm should compete. It does not address the issue of how the strategies of business units in the organisation should be co-ordinated. As we noted in Chapter 3 co-ordinating business-unit strategies can contribute to competitive advantage. Horizontal strategy co-ordinates the goals and strategies of related business units and encompasses both existing units and the selection of new industries. Porter (1985, p. 365) states 'An explicit horizontal strategy should be at the core of group, sector and corporate strategy'.

Tangible and intangible relationships are important in evaluating diversification because where the preferred method is through internal development, these relationships may allow the firm to overcome entry barriers more economically than for an organisation where such interrelationships do not exist. In the case where diversification is through acquisition, entry may also be facilitated because the acquired unit may have greater value to the organisation where interrelationships exist than it does to either the present owners or other potential bidders lacking similar interrelationships. A crucial feature which the analysis of business-units' interrelationships highlights is that their presence means that diversification, however, achieved, benefits those existing units having interrelationships with the new business.

Diversification should be evaluated, therefore, by analysing tangible interrelationships and recognising that the benefits flow both to new and existing business units. Porter (1985, pp. 376–8) identifies three types of tangible interrelationships depicted in Figure 8.2.

Market-oriented diversification seeks to sell new products to common buyers' channels or geographic markets to exploit the benefits of market interrelationships. *Production*-oriented diversification seeks to produce similar products with shared activities. *Technology*-based diversification seeks to develop or enter industries based on similar core technologies. Each of these broad strands may lead an organisation in different directions. It should not be overlooked that the greatest potential for enhancing the strategic posture of the enterprise is when several value activities can be shared. Thus the firm should seek to combine the three

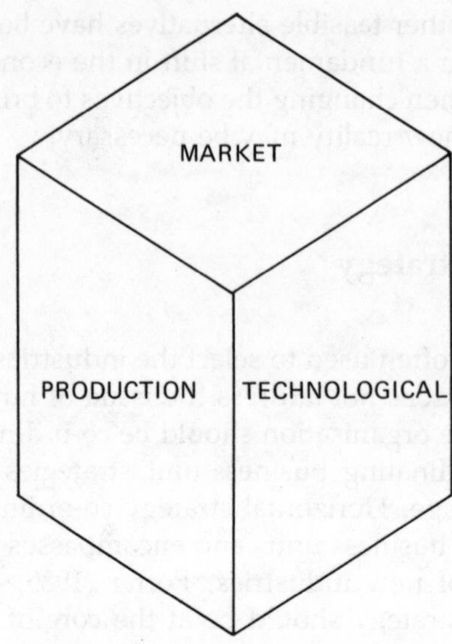

FIGURE 8.2 Tangible interrelationships

types instead of regarding them as mutually exclusive. By increasing tangible interrelationships simultaneously the firm should enhance its position.

Diversification through the exploitation of tangible interrelationships may not always be possible, in which case the strategy should recognise the importance of intangible interrelationships. Since intangible interrelationships involve the transfer of generic skills there are likely to be more opportunities for their development, but assessing which intangible interrelationships will enhance competitive advantage is a subtle process. Careful and thorough analysis of the industries where generic similarities appear to exist is required prior to embarking on a diversification strategy based on intangible relationships.

Porter (1985, pp. 78–80) notes that diversification based on intangible interrelationships should also be perceived as a potential *beach-head* which can ultimately be used to generate new opportunities based on tangible interrelationships. He hypothesises that intangible interrelationships with clusters of tangibly related business units may provide the foundation of a new cluster. So, a seemingly unrelated diversification strategy requires evaluation to ascertain what potential benefits may accrue to the enterprise because of the opportunities created by potential beach-heads.

8.4 Strategic selection at the business level

A meaningful assessment of a firm's, or business unit's strategy requires an understanding of those features which determine success as well as assessing which elements will ensure future success. This involves considering strategically important issues emanating both from the environment in which the business operates and the resources to which the business has access. At this stage, therefore, our concern is with identifying and assessing those features which are likely to have a strategic impact and which we discussed in Chapters 4 and 5 (External and internal appraisal).

Strategy evaluation is inextricably linked to an industry's unique blend of issues and problems, because the question of the strategy's adequacy to deal with such problems and issues is fundamental to evaluation. Specific strategic issues in industries will vary widely, but as our analysis in Chapter 4 indicated it is possible to identify some broad features relevant to evaluation such as:

- changes in government policies
- changes in general economic conditions (inflation, unemployment, growth, interest rates, etc.)
- expected movement in demographic trends relevant to the industry
- the industry's position to meet challenges from substitutes, its ability to meet anticipated future needs of customers, its capability to counter emerging threats or exploit opportunities and so on.

In considering such issues and the options available for dealing with them different people may perceive the same situation differently, and reach different judgements about what the key issues and problems are. Even so, it is probably better to have such differences developing out of serious and committed analysis as opposed to differences arising without consideration of the strategic problems faced by the firm.

Because competitive forces shape strategy, and because the strategy of rivals (within and outside the industry) shape competitive forces, evaluation should also consider the questions arising out of the structural analysis discussed in Chapter 4. In evaluating the strategic options relative to competitive forces we would add an important caveat. The analysis required tends to focus on 'hard' or quantitative *data*. To transform this into usable *information* for strategic decisions requires perceptive judgement, not just data accumulation. For example, it may be believed that barriers to entry (economies of scale, differentiation, switching costs, etc.) are sufficient to deter new entrants. However, Yip (1982) in a study of nearly 800 markets, found that markets with high entry barriers were no less likely to be entered than those with low barriers. Interestingly, he found that although new entrants usually had a worse position than incumbents, profit-to-sales margins declined by around 7 per cent for existing competitors.

In addition, and as a function of the interrelated nature of the organisation and its competitors to the industry, any evaluation process should include an examination of the enterprise's competitors. Porter (1980, pp. 47–74) sets out a framework for competitor analysis which allows a response profile to be prepared. The main components of this competitor analysis include:

Future goals At all levels of management and in multiple dimensions *Current strategy* How the business is currently competing *Assumptions* Held about itself and the industry *Capabilities* Both strengths and weaknesses	*Competitors' response profile* Level of satisfaction with current situation Likely moves or strategic shifts Vulnerability What will provoke retaliation by the competitor?

Porter argues that in addition to this, a sophisticated strategist should also use the framework for self-analysis as this may assist in understanding the conclusions which competitors are likely to draw. It should also be appreciated that the term 'competitors' may also include *potential* competitors.

A *SWOT analysis* (internal strengths and weaknesses, and external opportunities and threats) can be a useful way of drawing together and appraising the organisation. In Chapter 5 we gave an example of an organisation's strengths and weaknesses (Illustration 5.1). Here it is important to emphasise that for evaluation purposes we should focus on strategy-related strengths, weaknesses, opportunities and threats. SWOT analysis is not just a set of four lists, because in a strategic way some strengths may be of less importance than others, or some opportunities may be more sensible to pursue than others. Illustration 8.1 outlines the issues that may be included in a SWOT analysis. This sort of technique can be of use in helping to screen options, so an option which maximised a strength would be preferable to one which did not.

ILLUSTRATION 8.1 The SWOT Analysis

INTERNAL

STRENGTHS	**WEAKNESSES**
Distinctive competence	Obsolete facilities
Market leader	Lack of management depth
Economies of scale	Lack of key skills/competences
Cost advantage	Weak image in market
Quality of management	R & D lagging behind competitors
Financial resources	Lack of financial resources
Product differentiation	Competitive disadvantage
Record of innovation	Lack of breadth in product line
Reputation	Poor record of implementation
Insulation from competitive pressure	Lack of strategic direction

EXTERNAL

OPPORTUNITIES	**THREATS**
New markets or market segments	Entry of new competitors
Add new products, complementary products	Substitute products
Diversify into related products	Low market growth
Vertical integration	Government policies
Market growth	Degree of vulnerability to business cycle or recession
Competitor complacency	Power of suppliers, customers, etc.
Demographic changes	

Note: Remember, Chapter 5 demonstrated that historic criteria tend to be used for evaluating strengths, and normative criteria for evaluating weaknesses.

However, three considerations may ultimately assume pivotal importance in strategic selection. These issues, timing, risk/reward and contribution to objectives are often crucial in determining which strategy to adopt. A number of techniques for evaluating the *contribution* of a proposed strategy will be discussed in the next section of this chapter. The contribution made may be of particular importance when the primary concern is to restore a shortfall in performance.

Timing considerations were raised in our discussion of strategic options in Chapter 6 mainly in terms of the difference between internal development and acquisition. But the timing dilemma relates also to risk/reward trade-offs and whether the market is ready for the strategies contemplated. In addition, Tilles (1969) identifies the lead-time between action and result and a consideration of what the appropriate time-horizon should be as important issues. In fact Tilles argues that timing is one of the more difficult aspects of strategic planning because it involves a knowledge of both the industry and the organisation. The focus of management attention, whether short or long run tends to prompt the selection of a strategy which improves performance within the preferred time-horizon.

Risk–reward considerations tend to the obvious; the profitability versus risk trade-off is straightforward. The issue for the decision-maker, individual or group is considered in Chapter 13, and the next section will discuss how risk may be incorporated in some evaluation techniques. However, although risk is often regarded as a critical concept, Donaldson and Lorsch (1983, pp. 64–6) found that managers rarely include risk in their choice of specific objective criteria because senior management appeared to believe that risk can be modified by managerial wisdom and skill. So Donaldson and Lorsch assert 'If top managers are comfortable with the risk parameters their goals system implies, they will make a decision without having had to ask a question' (1983, p. 66).

To conclude, any evaluation and selection process should incorporate an assessment of the quality of the strategic-formulation process. While acknowledging that a rigorous, comprehensive process does not provide an effective strategy it may at least ensure that all the appropriate sections of the organisation were consulted. The experience of those managers involved, the reliability and accuracy of the underlying techniques used to prepare the strategy can all be evaluated. An explicit consideration of the formulation process may also assist organisational learning so that those involved not only become more aware of the process itself, but also enhance their understanding and appreciation of what constitutes a strategic issue in their involvement.

8.5 Other selection techniques

There are several analytical techniques that can be used to aid management in the selection process. Generally the techniques are primarily concerned with assessing feasibility and acceptability. In this section we are primarily concerned with the contribution that each method can make to the process of strategic selection.

Discounting techniques

Profitability is an important aspect of evaluation, particularly when related to the required investment. There are a number of ways of measuring profits and investment, the most sound being discounted cash-flow (DCF) techniques. Illustration 8.2 provides a simple example of the use of DCF which also serves to highlight some of the issues involved in using the technique.

An essential feature of the DCF technique is the recognition that cash received today is worth more than cash received in a year's time, because today's pound can be invested to earn a return during the intervening period. Rappaport (1979) notes that DCF criteria apply equally to internal investment, like additions to existing capacity and to external investment like acquisitions. However, Rappaport points out that the cash-flow stream of a prospective acquisition may well differ from the candidate's cash-flows as an independent entity because of operating economies or new post-acquisition investment opportunities. In addition he advises that the acquirer's own cost of capital may be inappropriate as the degree of risk may well differ. These points serve to illustrate some of the issues involved in using DCF to evaluate options.

In a later article Rappaport argues convincingly that conventional accounting measures are inadequate for evaluating strategic options and that DCF criteria should be used in an attempt to measure the economic value to shareholders of alternatives strategies. The shareholder value approach involves five analytical steps:

- Estimation for each business unit and the corporation of the minimum pre-tax operating return on incremental sales needed to create value for shareholders.
- Comparison of maximum acceptable rates of return in incremental sales with rates realised during the past five years and initial projections for the next year and the five-year plan.
- Estimation of the contribution to shareholder value of alternative strategies at the business unit and corporate levels.

ILLUSTRATION 8.2 An Example of the Use of DCF for Strategic Selection

Year	Annual net cash flow	Discount rate (10%)	Discounted cash flow
0	(20 000)	1.000	(20 000)
1	5 000	0.909	4 545
2	10 000	0.827	8 270
3	14 000	0.751	10 514
4	14 000	0.683	9 562
5	14 000	0.621	8 694
	Net present value (NPV)		£21 585
	Internal rate of return (IRR)		40%
	Payback period		2.3 years

Notes

(i) Cash flow can be defined as: (Earnings before interest and tax [EBIT] × [1 − tax rate]) plus depreciation and any other non-cash charges less capital expenditure less cash required (or generated) for increases in working capital.

(ii) The discount rate would normally be the firm's cost of capital (see Chapter 7)

(iii) The IRR is the discount rate that causes the NPV of a project to just equal zero. If a project's IRR is greater than the cost of capital, the project is acceptable; otherwise it should be rejected.

(iv) The payback period is the number of years required for a firm to recoup the initial investment.

- Evaluation of the corporate plan to determine whether the projected growth is financially feasible in the light of anticipated return on sales, investment requirements per dollar of sales, target capital structure, and dividend policy.
- A financial self-evaluation of the business unit and corporate levels (Rappaport, 1981).

This represents a very sophisticated approach to the use of discounting techniques. In practice, the most widely-used evaluative technique is the pay-back method found to be used by nearly 80 per cent of firms (Pike, 1982, p. 44). Pike found that 'the main justification given for pay-back was its simplicity in calculation and comprehension'. Pike also noted that over 90 per cent of the firms using multiple criteria included pay-back as a method. In contrast to the popularity of the pay-back method was the finding that just over half of the firms surveyed used IRR, and less than 40 per cent used NPV; the reasons for non-use of such techniques being lack of understanding of discounting methods by managers, constantly-changing hurdle-rates, and that they are not necessary when pay-back periods are short. (Pike, 1982, pp. 52–3).

Although discounting techniques are widely heralded as being conceptually sound, particularly as they allow the user to adopt a longer time-perspective than, say pay-back does, they do need to be used with caution. We have already pointed out both in this section and Chapter 7 some of the difficulties involved in selecting a discount rate, a crucial element in the process. It is interesting to note, therefore, that Pike's survey found that most respondents used a rate of 15 per cent (Pike, 1982, p. 26) and as Thomsen demonstrates, such a rate means that nearly half the total time-horizon is effectively included in the first four years. Thomsen shows for example, that at a discount rate of 15 per cent, the whole of the twenty-first century counts the same as 7.7 months in 1984. As a consequence he argues that present value calculations are inappropriate for strategic planning purposes because high rates bias results toward the near future (Thomsen, 1984).

Another major problem with any discounting technique is the difficulty in forecasting cash-flows with any degree of confidence. One danger here is that the intricacies of the discounting technique might deflect critical attention from the cash-flow forecasts being manipulated.

Break-even analysis

Break-even analysis is a useful and relatively straightforward way of enabling a strategy to be evaluated in terms of acceptability and feasibility. Its value lies in the fact that it focuses attention on key issues in the decision process. For instance, Illustration 8.3 raises questions concerning:

- the probability of achieving the market penetration required to break even as a minimum requirement, at the proposed selling price;
- the degree of dedication of the mechanisation, and its effect on

ILLUSTRATION 8.3 The Use of Break-even Analysis for Strategy Evaluation

An organisation was contemplating introducing a new product. There were two alternative methods of production, one known as method *A* involved a high degree of mechanisation, while the other, known as method *B*, did not. To evaluate each alternative the following estimates were collected:

	Method A £	*Method B* £
Selling price per unit	10	10
Variable cost per unit		
Materials	3	4
Labour	1	2
Other	1	1
	5	7
Contribution per unit	5	3
Fixed costs	£500 000	£240 000
Break-even point (units)	500 000 ÷ 5	240 000 ÷ 3
	= 100 000 units	80 000 units

As the market size for this particular product was estimated at 1m units, the market share required just to break even would be 10 per cent for method *A* and 8 per cent for method *B*. This information could be depicted graphically as shown opposite:

the firm's ability to respond in other areas to different demands, that is, the impact on the flexibility of the organisation;

- whether the cost assumptions are valid and achievable and whether the required volumes can be produced;
- whether the firm has the financial resources to provide the capacity, skilled labour, and materials to operate the plant;

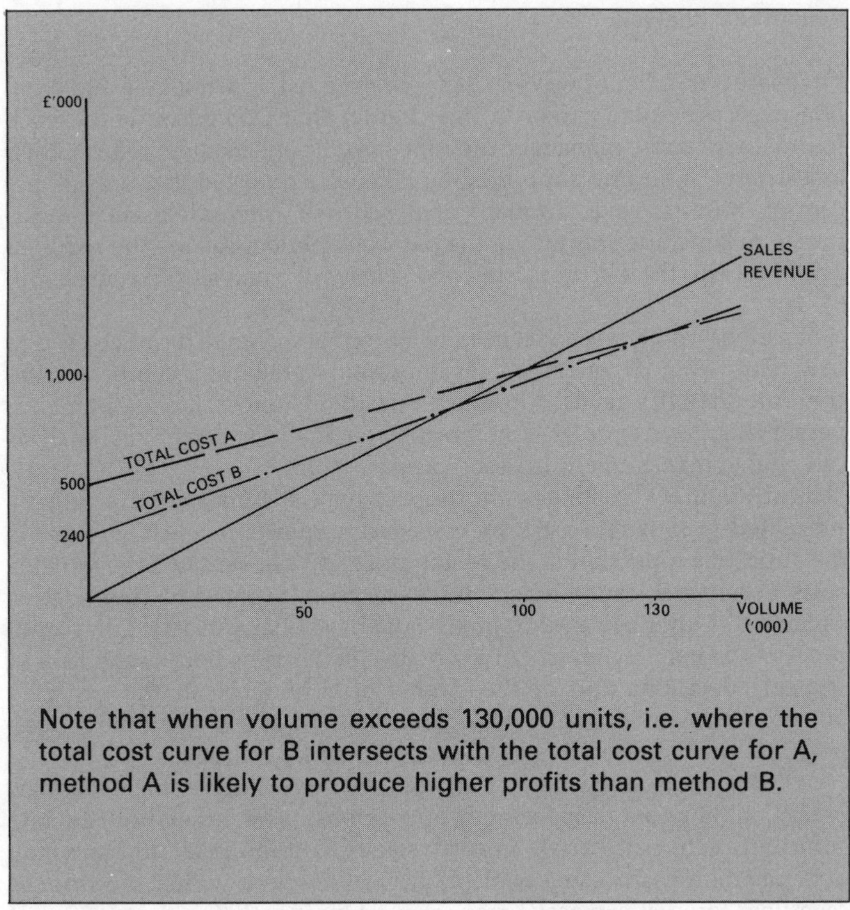

Note that when volume exceeds 130,000 units, i.e. where the total cost curve for B intersects with the total cost curve for A, method A is likely to produce higher profits than method B.

- the degree of operating gearing of each method (refer back to chapter 7). *A*'s operating gearing is 600 per cent while *B*'s is 300 per cent indicating the extent to which changes in sales volume at the given price are likely to affect profits.

The principal drawback involved in using break-even analysis is its assumption of linearity. As the graph in Illustration 8.3 demonstrates the model assumes that both revenues and costs are straight-line relationships which may not in reality be true. Despite this caveat it is a useful tool for helping to select between alternatives and for focusing attention on important areas.

Sensitivity analysis

There are a number of ways of incorporating risk in strategy-evaluation. However, we noted earlier in this chapter that Donaldson and Lorsch found that many managers did not specifically include risk in their assessment, a finding supported by Pike who reported that only 37 per cent of those surveyed formally analysed risk. Methods used to incorporate risk include shortening the pay-back period, raising the required rate of return (the discount rate), and sensitivity analysis (Pike, 1982, pp. 61–4).

Sensitivity analysis can be used in a number of ways. It can be used to deal with 'what if?' questions for important variables; it can be used to compute the NPV using differing assumptions (most likely, optimistic, pessimistic, for example). Like break-even analysis, sensitivity analysis can enable management to assess key variables.

Illustration 8.4 considers the impact on the information originally presented in Illustration 8.3 by considering questions such as: what is the effect of a reduction in the selling price of 5 per cent; what if variable costs are 10 per cent higher and fixed costs 5 per cent higher than estimated? Other key assumptions could be similarly tested. This sort of process will help management to obtain a better view both of the risks of strategic decisions and of the degree of confidence in the expected outcome. Sensitivity analysis is a good method of assessing the robustness of a proposal to adverse changes in the key variables.

Cash-flow forecasts can be an important element in assessing a strategic option. Although a proposal may appear profitable it may not generate sufficient cash, particularly in early stages, to fund itself and so many depend upon cash being available from elsewhere within the firm. A cash-flow forecast can assist management by identifying the amount of cash needed by a project, and – of equal importance – when such funds may be required. As with all forecasting techniques a cash-flow forecast is subject to the key assumptions underlying its preparation, which in effect could be subject to a degree of magnification, because it is only prepared as a result of previous assumptions, for example, concerning the level of demand, expected sales volumes, values, etc.

Illustration 8.5 provides an example of a cash-flow forecast based on some of the information first presented in Illustrations 8.3 and 8.4. This sort of forecast is particularly amenable to programming on a micro-computer so allowing the robustness of the results to be tested as earlier assumptions are altered.

ILLUSTRATION 8.4 The Use of Sensivity Analysis for Strategy Evaluation

Management estimate that given the level of marketing activity proposed, they should achieve a 12 per cent share of the market (of 1m units). Based on the original assumptions (Illustration 8.3) this would generate a profit of £100 000 if method *A* were adopted or £120 000 if method *B* were chosen. They now wish to consider each alternative in the event that:

(i) unit selling prices are 5 per cent lower than expected;
(ii) variable costs are 10 per cent higher and fixed costs are 5 per cent higher than projected.

		Method A £	*Method B* £
(i)	Selling price per unit becomes	9.5	9.5
	Variable costs	5.0	7.0
	Contribution per unit	4.5	2.5
	Fixed costs	£500 000	£240 000
	Break-even point	111 111 units	96 000 units
(ii)	Selling price	10	10
	Variable costs become	5.5	7.7
	Contribution per unit	4.5	2.3
	Fixed costs	£525 000	£252 000
	Break-even point	116 667 units	109 565 units

The above and further analysis would serve to confirm a view that Method *B* is particularly sensitive to changes in variable costs and contribution which is a function of its contribution to sales ratio. For example, originally its break-even represented 8 per cent of the estimated market which in (ii) above has now risen to very nearly 11 per cent, a change of nearly 30 per cent whereas method A involves a movement from 10 per cent to

ILLUSTRATION 8.4 *continued*

just under 12 per cent of the market, a change of little less than 20 per cent.

The point is that this sort of information can direct management to consider the key elements and so provide a sounder basis for the exercise of judgement in deciding between the two alternatives.

ILLUSTRATION 8.5 The Use of Cash-Flow Forecasts

	YEAR 1	2	3	4	5	(£,000)
Cash Receipts						
From operations	100	300	330	363	400	
Cash Payments						
Purchase of fixed assets	800	200	—	—	—	
Increase in working capital – inventory	150		15	17	18	
debtors	200		20	22	24	
creditors	(30)		(3)	(3)	(4)	
	1120	200	32	36	38	
Net cash flow	(1020)	100	298	327	362	
Cumulative	(1020)	(920)	(622)	(295)	67	

Key assumptions involved in the preparation of the above are:

- Steady increase in volume growth of 10 per cent per annum
- Price–cost relationships remain stable over time.

ILLUSTRATION 8.5 *continued*

- Payment for fixed assets delivered and installed in year 1 is completed in year 2.
- Inventory estimated at 3 months stocks, debtors at 2 months sales and creditors allow 1 month credit.

The cash received from operations represents the contribution, less fixed costs, and depreciation is added back as it is non-cash expense.

On this basis management is now aware of the cash requirements for this proposal, and therefore able to judge whether the organisation is able to fund it (whether internally or through the issue of new capital). In addition, management should become aware of associated issues like whether there is sufficient suitable storage space for the extra inventory required and whether existing office systems will be able to cope with the increase in debtors and so on.

Corporate modelling

Corporate models differ from the techniques considered so far in that they are able to incorporate many, if not all, of the methods in this section. Their comprehensive nature is their strength, but also their weakness because of the nature of their underlying assumptions. Cooke and Slack define corporate models as those which utilise both conventional accounting measures and relationships, and deterministic simulations over a fairly long time-scale (Cooke and Slack, 1984, p. 161). They go on to point out that the objective of corporate models, which are often known as financial models, is to explore the effect of different combinations of variables rather than the relationships between the variables, such as price and demand. As long as this is understood then such models have much to offer because of their ability to present a more holistic picture than might otherwise be the case. The danger lies in overlooking the assumptions which provide the foundation for the model itself.

In an extensive literature review Shim and McGlade found that corporate financial modelling has become commonplace in US businesses. Such tools also allowed managers to consider new alternatives rapidly and to adjust variables. Financial planning, and *pro forma* balance-sheet statements were found to be the most common applications and the models proved to be useful for 'what if?' questions, sensitivity analysis, simulations and so on. They also reported that top management was consistently involved in the process of using models and in their definition and implementation. (Shim and McGlade, 1984).

Given the recent advances in computer technology and the growing sophistication of software packages for both mainframe and personal computers we can expect the use of models to increase. Furthermore, as they become linked into, and then develop out of an organisation's management information system access to the data by management will be enhanced. When such a database includes both internal and external information its strategic value to the firm could be significant.

8.6 Summary

In our discussion of strategic evaluation we focused on the uses of a number of techniques:

- portfolio techniques and horizontal strategy for corporate level problems;
- SWOT analysis, discounting techniques, break-even analysis, sensitivity analysis and corporate modelling.

The consideration of the above objective conditions in reality takes place against a backdrop of subjective issues. In addition the techniques discussed are but tools for use, where appropriate, (and where understood!) in helping managers to decide whether the options under consideration are suitable, feasible and acceptable.

To conclude, the evaluation process is not necessarily a straightforward linear progression and end-piece of the strategy-formulation phase. The evaluation and selection of strategic option may well become entangled in both the formulation and implementation part of strategic management.

Further reading

For a full, and interesting, exposition of the importance of interrelationships see Porter (1985) Chapters 9, 10, and 11. Hofer and Schendel (1978) provides a thorough discussion of strategy evaluation. Readers wishing to familiarise themselves with the financial techniques discussed in this chapter should read the relevant chapters of a suitable text, such as Franks, J. R. and Broyles, J. E. (1979) *Modern Managerial Finance* (Chichester: Wiley), or Gitman, L. J. (1982) *Principles of Managerial Finance* (New York: Harper and Row).

References

Cooke, S. and Slack, N. (1984) *Making Management Decions* (Englewood Cliffs, N. J.: Prentice-Hall).
Donaldson, G. and Lorsch, J. W. (1983) *Decision Making at the Top* (New York: Basic Books).
Hofer, C. W. and Schendel, D. (1978) *Strategy Formulation: Analytical Concepts* (St Paul, Minnesota: West).
Pike, R. H. (1982) *Capital Budgeting in the 1980s* (London: ICMA Occasional Paper).
Porter, M. E. (1980) *Competitive Strategy* (New York: Free Press).
Porter, M. E. (1985) *Competitive Advantage* (New York: Free Press).
Quinn, J. B. (1980) *Strategies for Change* (Homewood, Illinois: Irwin).
Rappaport, A. (1979) 'Strategic Analysis for more Profitable Acquisitions', *Harvard Business Review*, July–August, pp. 99–110.
Rappaport, A. (1981) 'Selecting Strategies that Create Shareholder Value', *Harvard Business Review*, May–June, pp. 139–49.
Shim, J. K. and McGlade R. (1984) 'The Use of Corporate Planning Models: Past Present and Future', *Journal of the Operational Research Society*, vol. 35, no 10, pp. 885–93.
Thomsen, Torben C. (1984) 'Dangers in Discounting', *Management Accounting*, January, pp. 37–9.
Tilles, S. (1969) 'Making Strategy Explicit', in Ansoff, H. I. *Business Strategy* (Harmondsworth: Penguin pp. 180–209).
Yip, G. S. (1982) 'Gateways to Entry', *Harvard Business Review*, September–October, pp. 85–92.

PART II

THE IMPLEMENTATION OF STRATEGY

CHAPTER 9

Making the strategy operational

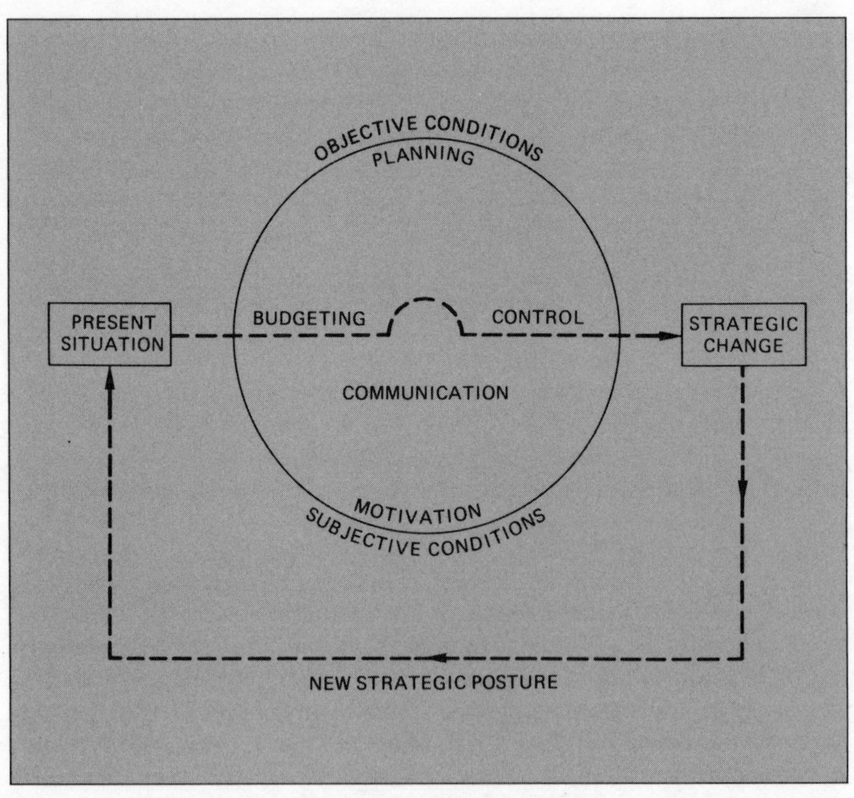

9.1 Introduction

This chapter is our first step towards achieving the implementation of the desired strategy. In common with much of the previous discussion on strategy-formulation, the chapter will focus upon objective conditions prevailing in the implementation phase. The subjective conditions which influence the implementation, and hence also formulation of strategy will be developed in depth in succeeding chapters. So these subsequent chapters will debate the issues involved in the management of change, strategy and structure, power and so on.

Strategy implementation is crucial to effective strategic management. It is management's responsibility to ensure that an appropriate strategy is both formulated and implemented, for without the latter, precise formulation is of little use to the organisation. It is interesting to note that 'Most of the time and effort of most managers is spent on strategy implementation, and the amount of this activity increases as the observer moves from top management to lower levels' (McCarthy *et al.*, 1983, p. 362).

Although we focus on objective conditions it is necessary to recognise that these are also affected by subjective criteria. Discussion of the use of budgeting as a planning-and-control technique would be incomplete without a consideration of communication and motivation for example. The chapter commences with a discussion of the use of planning and budgeting as an implementation device followed by a look at issues involved in control in a strategic sense. Behavioural issues in control are then briefly discussed.

The importance of people in the implementation process should not be underrated. Indeed Peters and Waterman continually refer to the importance of the organisation's employees, for example, in Chapter 8, Productivity through People (Peters and Waterman, 1982). Illustration 9.1 stresses both the scope and importance of implementation and goes on to suggest one method of implementation.

Before we address the issues in more detail there is one further point to make which relates to the use in this chapter of the word *planning*. Planning in this context is a method of *implementing* the formulated strategy. The planning and control system in an organisation represents the main approach through which the strategic objectives and policies (and plans) are translated into specific, measurable and attainable goals and plans.

9.2 Planning and budgeting

The process involved in formulating strategy, the marriage of objectives and the method by which these will be achieved, constitute the strategy or policy to be pursued by the organisation. Management will also need to develop an awareness of how well the chosen policy is performing, so 'the system' includes a monitoring phase for evaluation purposes. It has been argued that this type of planning and control system is in fact a single process (Anthony and Dearden, 1980, p. 5). While we will treat each separately for the purpose of discussion it should be recognised that there are continuous interrelationships in what is in effect an overall system, and that the planning-and-control system is part of the strategic management of the entity.

The planning part of the system is concerned with the more immediate future and does not normally involve new objectives since the plans are drawn up in order to achieve the organisation's strategic objectives. This phase involves the interpretation of the broader strategic policies derived during the formulation of strategy and their translation into more specific shorter-range plans. As such it is a process which involves managers at all levels in the organisation because the plans demand broad support and significant detail. Management at all levels translate the strategic thrust of the organisation into management objectives for specified time-frames.

This process requires active participation throughout the enterprise, and should be structured in such a way as to gain involvement from all involved. A planning and control process requiring the participation of all levels of management in the development of future plans builds in an important motivational force. The planning and control systems necessary for implementation does not necessarily indicate the existence of a highly formalised and documented procedure. Less formal procedures may be more than adequate, with perhaps one proviso – a belief in rumour or the grapevine could be dangerous.

The budget is the common method for implementation as it should encompass the communication of attainable goals while engaging the participation and support of all levels of management. It also provides information for evaluation. The function of budgeting, in converting strategy into an action plan, requires:

- planning
- co-ordination
- control
- replanning.

ILLUSTRATION 9.1 How to Implement Strategy

Top-class strategies are worth nothing if they cannot be implemented: better a first-class implementation procedure for a second-class strategy than vice versa. Strategies will not exist unless the organisation's managers have thought through what needs to be done, when and by whom, using which resources, to achieve what objectives. To be meaningful not only must the strategy specify its implications, but also it should be communicated to, agreed to, and supported by, management. Problems of successful implementation tend to focus on how well, or otherwise, the existing organisation responds and how adequate, or otherwise, its reporting proves to be. The problems seem to derive from:

1. implementation of the chosen strategy cuts across traditional organisation units;
2. information monitoring implementation is inadequate;
3. the organsation resists change;
4. payment systems are geared to past achievements rather than future goals.

Project management techniques can be applied to assist the successful implementation of strategies by focusing management's attention on achieving strategic objectives. Typically this may involve:

1. allocating clear responsibility and accountability for the success of the overall strategy project;
2. limiting the number of strategies pursued at any one time;
3. identifying actions to be taken to achieve the strategic objective, allocating detailed responsibilities for the actions – and getting agreement to them;
4. identifying a list of 'milestones', or major intermediate progress points;
5. identifying key performance measures to be monitored throughout the 'project' and creating an information system to record progress.

The chief executive is the *lynchpin* as without his commitment to strategic development the planning and implementation process will not work.

(Source: *Management Today*, November 1982, pp. 51–3, 104)

Budgeting has become crucial to the planning and control process because it converts all elements of an enterprise's plans into financial numbers. At one level this is crucial for comparing results of disparate areas or functions, but its utility may be diminished if the process itself is inadequate in some way. This is an issue to which we will return in a later section.

Figure 9.1 illustrates some of the more common budgets which may be prepared and indicates some interrelationships. There are several points which emerge from a consideration of Figure 9.1. First, each of the budgets may be divided into smaller segments. Thus the direct labour budget, for example, may well be broken down into a variety of departments or sections. Furthermore, the final figure appearing is likely to be a function of (at least) the numbers employed, their grading, expected pay scales, overtime earnings, anticipated sickness levels, etc. Thus the preparation of the direct labour budget is likely to involve production management, personnel and the accounting function. The second point is that the budgets are interrelated so that a change in one element has an effect elsewhere. So in addition to a fairly obvious impact on cash and purchasing, a decision to reduce raw material stocks may well have an effect on production rates and labour also. The third and final point we would wish to make is that the process is not static. The individual budgets leading up to the overall master budget is, normally, a series of continuous budgets which incorporates a feedback system permitting managerial evaluation.

The *planning* phase of the budget should not be merely an estimate based on previous performance. The budget should be designed to articulate in greater detail the agreed strategic direction of the organisation, consequently the budget should be congruent with the strategy and may well use (indeed should use) the same future-orientated information in its preparation. For example, the more detailed analysis required will often entail segmenting elements into controllable or non-controllable costs. The variability of future revenues and costs will be subject to further analysis in an attempt to identify causal relationships. The last stage will entail the preparation of a projected income statement and balance sheet to ensure that the aggregate detailed action plan meets predetermined criteria, such as return on investment or profit levels.

The *co-ordination* of budgets requires the dovetailing of individual elements to ensure internal consistency. The classic case which often arises is to ensure a reasonable achievable match, for example, between sales, production, and stockholding budgets. This represents a crucial communication link between differing functions and operations because it forces management to recognise the relationship of their particular

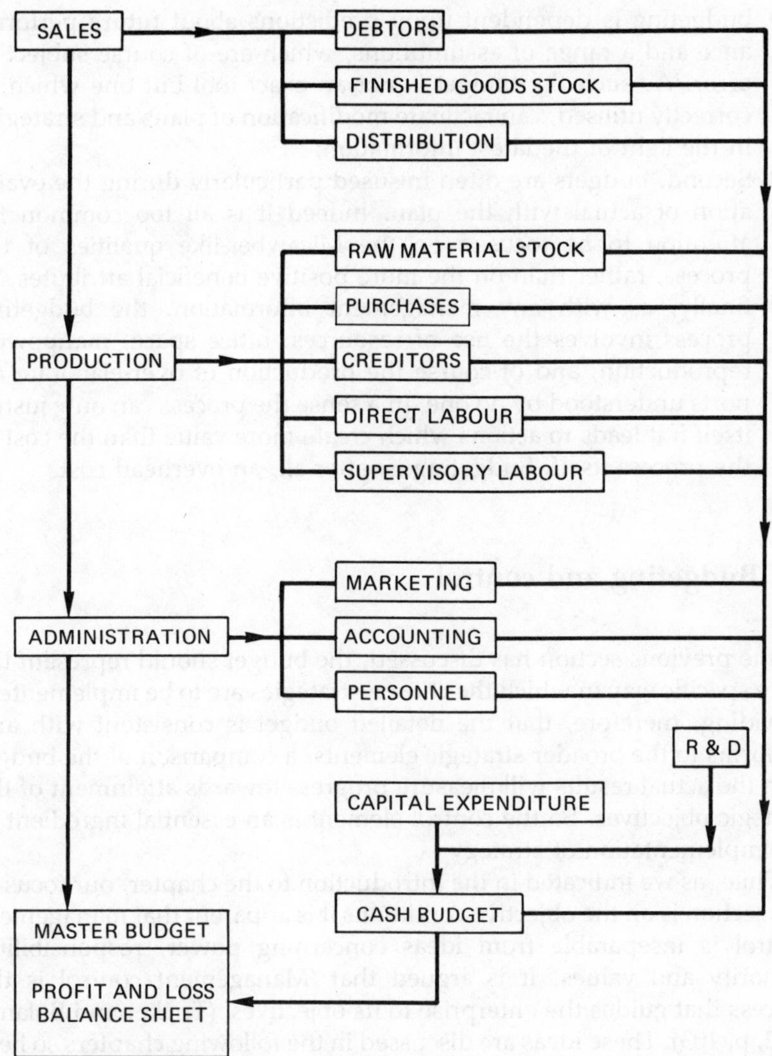

FIGURE 9.1 Budgets and their interrelationships

function to others, and to the organisation as a whole. The co-ordination of the budgets in effect determines the iterative nature of the process. A properly-prepared budget enables responsibility to be assigned and creates a situation where motivation and goal congruence is enhanced.

Before directing our attention to the control element of the process it is worthwhile identifying some areas where problems are inherent in budgeting:

- budgeting is dependent upon predictions about future performance and a range of assumptions, which are of course subject to error. As such the budget is not an exact tool but one which, if correctly utilised, can facilitate modification of plans and strategies in the light of the latest information;
- Second, budgets are often misused particularly during the evaluation of actual with the plan. Indeed it is all too common for attention to be focused on the Micawber-like qualities of the process, rather than on the more positive beneficial attributes,
- finally, as with any management information, the budgeting process involves the use of resources, office space, manpower, reproduction, and of course the production of over-elaborate reports understood by no one. In a sense the process can only justify itself if it leads to actions which create more value than the cost of the process itself. Budgeting is, after all, an overhead cost.

9.3 Budgeting and control

As the previous section has discussed, the budget should represent the more specific way in which the chosen strategies are to be implemented. Providing, therefore, that the detailed budget is consistent with and conforms to the broader strategic elements, a comparison of the budget with the actual results will measure progress towards attainment of the strategic objectives. So the control element is an essential ingredient in the implementation of strategy.

While, as we indicated in the introduction to the chapter, our focus in this section is on the objective conditions it is apparent that management control is inseparable from ideas concerning power, responsibility, authority and values. It is argued that 'Management control is the process that guides the enterprise to its objectives' (Tricker and Boland, 1982, p. 103). These ideas are discussed in the following chapters so here we will concentrate on some of the important mechanisms of control.

For control to be effective a suitable *communication* system must exist. The communication system in most enterprises has both formal and informal features, which in some reflect the complexity of the organisation's operations and its environment. Formal measures would include, for example, written policy statements, procedural manuals, job descriptions, formal meetings and so on. Informal measures would include informal gatherings, say between supervisory staff and employees. An effective communication network is an invaluable tool enabling strategy implementation to take place in an efficient manner.

Fundamental to the exercise of control is reporting appropriate information at an appropriate level. This implies that reports should be directed to those responsible for neither controlling costs or generating revenue. Revenues and/or costs must be attributable to a particular manager's efforts and must be controllable by that person. The application of this *responsibility* concept is the basis of planning and control. Normally the responsibility, say for a department, is assigned to an individual manager, to whom reports on the costs of running the department are sent. Where a department only incurs cost (for example, an accounting or personnel department) it would normally be referred to as a *cost centre*. A manager responsible for income as well as cost is also, therefore, responsible for profit and can be said to manage a *profit centre*.

Most organisations are broken down into profit and cost centres which develop their own detailed budgets. To be useful such budgets need to be broken down into their key components with a system designed to feed results of operations to the appropriate manager. There are two preconditions for responsibility-reporting to be of use. First, the budget should not be an imposed control. It should be accepted by managers who should have participated in its preparation. This is an issue to which we will return. Second, where a manager is considered to be accountable for costs then those costs should be controllable by that person. Responsibility-reporting is unlikely to be of use if managers are held responsible for costs over which they exercise no, or only partial, control. This sort of situation can occur in organisations whose costs are allocated and/or apportioned, and in enterprises where interdivisional transfer prices are arbitrarily set.

The reporting system provides the necessary *feedback* of results for comparison to the plan. Naturally there will be a time-lag between event and report. This delay should be acceptable in terms of a trade-off between the cost of reducing the delay and the benefits to subsequent management action. The reports effectively close the loop and allow the exercise of control (see Figure 9.2).

As a general rule the reports received by managers at different points in the hierarchy will differ in terms of both the degree of detail and the time period to which they relate. Thus a managing director of a unit may receive a report summarising the results of a division for the past month while the production manager may receive a report detailing the output, material usage, labour efficiency and so on for the past week. The managing director's report is likely to allow a more direct comparison between results to date and the division's strategic objectives, so allowing implementation of the present strategy to proceed.

In looking at control Goldsmith and Clutterbuck found that controls

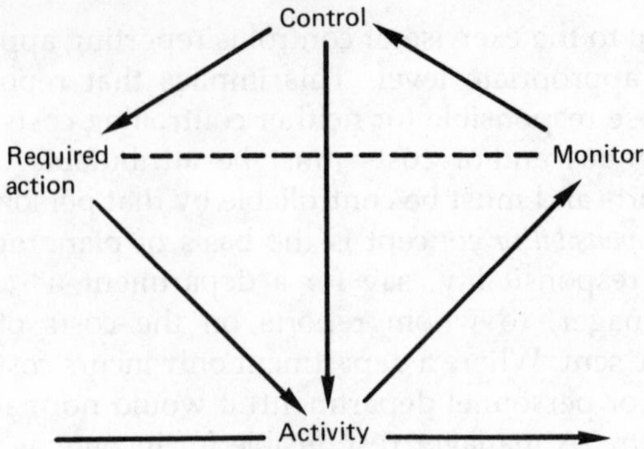

FIGURE 9.2 The control loop

were often very simple. Top managers tended to concentrate on a small number of key ratios or results of particular significance to their business. They quote that Lord Weinstock receives all his information on the giant GEC on three sheets of paper. The speed of all the reporting is another issue which they found to be common in successful UK companies. Numerous examples are quoted by the authors, but the focus is on tight financial controls, constant feedback of results, close attention to planning, and setting high standards and expecting people to stick to them (Goldsmith and Clutterbuck, 1984, pp. 47–58).

The results reported to management reflect historic performance. This can only be of use if, in evaluating what happened against what was planned, it influences future decisions. The reports need, therefore, to integrate the past with the future to provide a perspective on what may eventuate.

Designing reports for management to enable them to control more effectively the direction of the organisation is made both easier and harder with the burgeoning growth of computerised management information systems. Computerisation has tended to lead both to speedier production of information and to the generation of masses of detailed data. Management requires *information designed to assist decision-making and control* which effectively limits it in terms of its relevance. One way of determining relevance is to report only on deviations from expectations, in other words, *exception reporting*. This allows managers to concentrate on important variations from the plan; information relating to events conforming to the predetermined plan are screened out. Insignificant variations may not be reported, so a 5 per cent variance in an expense item may not be considered worthy of attention. The degree of latitude in such matters will tend to vary according to the expectations of the managers in the organisation. What may be considered significant in one enterprise may not be considered as such in another.

'Planning and control are both concerned with expectations. Planning is concerned with future expectations and control in ensuring organisational response to changes that occur when what were future expectations become present expectations' (Machin and Wilson, 1979). This sort of perception is important to the exercise of control because the budget or plan cannot control; people, managers control. Deviations from the budget (future expectations) are to be expected; the focus needs to be not on how accurate the forecasts were, but on unexpected results to see if the entity should alter its strategy in the light of this experience, and in what ways. Controllable variations from the plan warrant investigation to see how they occurred.

The comparison of actual results with the plan is of an historic nature – what is being reported has already happened. This review, focusing as we have indicated on significant deviations should be used to provide managers with important insights concerning future implementation. The review may indicate that some of the earlier assumptions were incorrect or that unexpected events made the original plan unattainable. A strategic perspective is crucial in reviewing performance for two main reasons. First, the budget or plan should not be used as a constraining force which stultifies creativity or enthusiasm. Second, management should recognise that the plan is not 'cast in stone'; subsequent events may well make it redundant as a tool for both strategy-implementation and operational control. The relationship between short- and long-term plans is crucial here, because when the organisation decides to redraw the plan it will need to draw not only upon management's previous experience, but also what has been learnt so far about implementing the chosen strategy. So changes, say, in short-term budgets to make them a more effective vehicle for control, will need to feed through in a strategic sense to ensure that they are still consonant with the overall strategy. If the changes are brought about by unexpected environmental changes, then the alteration to the short-term budgets may effectively indicate other changes required to match the strategy to the 'new' environment.

9.4 Budgeting and motivation

In order to implement strategy the organisation needs to have a reasonable commitment to the achievement of the goals by those charged with ensuring that the enterprise succeeds. So motivation on the part of those managers is a most important part of implementing strategy.

Motivation may be accomplished by the reward–punishment system, part of which may be linked to the planning–control system. A motivation system may use positive (bonuses, promotion, etc.) or negative (demotion, etc.) incentives. The establishment of a motivation system that blends the attainment of personal aspirations with goals of the organisation is a problematic task.

Cooper and Makin, having reviewed the literature and various theories on motivation summarised them by saying that clear and moderately difficult goals should be set that are accepted by the person concerned. They also noted that valued rewards should be made upon achievement of goals, and rewards should be made through an explicit and fair system. They concluded:

> All of these terms will depend upon subjective judgements and hence the only source of objective information is the people concerned, and perhaps the only way of obtaining the correct information is by asking them. Never assume that people's perceptions of the same thing are the same . . . Participation is perhaps desirable, therefore, because more than anything else it is a source of information for all parties (Cooper and Makin, 1984, p. 114).

Once the budget is recognised to be an element that helps to motivate people in the organisation attention must be paid to individual and group needs and values (these factors are discussed in more detail in Chapter 12). When these elements are incorporated in the overall planning and control process then the resulting budget is likely to fulfil its function as an aid to employees' motivation. Consequently it should serve the implementation of strategy. If the process of developing plans and budgets, and their associated control systems, is properly conceived and utilised, involving *real* participation by all levels of management, then it becomes an indispensable motivational element in strategy-implementation.

This view is confirmed by some recent American research which identified five features for successful strategy-implementation; it also serves to illustrate that the variety of issues involved in strategy implementation, including motivation, are closely interrelated:

1. Communication – clear communication with all employees concerning the new strategic decision. Communication is two-way, permitting and soliciting questions about the formulated strategy, issues to be considered, or potential problems that may occur.
2. Start with a good concept or idea – no amount of time and effort implementing a poorly-formulated strategic decision can rescue it. The idea must be fundamentally sound.

3. Obtain employee commitment and involvement – this builds on the first two and suggests that employees and managers should be involved right from the start in the formulation process. Involvement and commitment should be developed and maintained throughout the implementation process. Where people are involved with the detailed implementation planning, commitment typically increases.
4. Provide sufficient resources – of money (as a failure to provide sufficient funding may lead to failure), of manpower, of technical expertise, and of time (as sufficient time and attention by top management is needed to implement the new plan).
5. Develop an implementation plan – likely problems and their contingent responses should be addressed early rather than relying on optimism. The plan must strike a balance between too much and too little detail.

Alexander concludes that successful implementation involves the prevention of problems occurring in the first place, followed by quick action to resolve problems that do occur. He also notes that successful implementation involved doing things that help to promote success rather than just problem-prevention (Alexander, 1985).

9.5 Implementing recovery strategies

The issues we have discussed so far are of course equally relevant to an organisation in need of recovery. However, as may be evident the time-dimension for action may be considerably shorter and the action required may of necessity be more radical. Chapter 6 discussed the options open to an organisation in decline. Here we wish to indicate some of the key items involved in implementing a recovery strategy based on Slatter's book *Corporate Recovery*. As earlier discussions will have clarified, the state of product–market evolution may dictate the strategy (and its associated implementation) required, or the degree of competition may indicate that certain measures require rapid implementation. All we will endeavour to do here is to introduce the first steps in the process, the further reading will indicate sources for those interested in understanding the process in more depth.

Slatter (1984, pp. 129–52) identifies eight actions (gain management control; establish and communicate credibility with stakeholders; assess existing managers and replace if necessary; evaluate the business; develop action plans; implement organisational change; motivate employees and improve budgeting systems) which require a successful turnaround manager's *immediate* attention.

Generally, a new chief executive is the starting-point and speed of action is essential in the early days. Indeed the eight points identified by Slatter are recommended to be initiated immediately regardless of the situation. These eight actions are briefly discussed below in roughly the order in which they should be attacked, but several may need to be implemented simultaneously.

1. GAIN MANAGEMENT CONTROL

The crucial first step is to gain financial and management control by ensuring that the turnaround manager's appointment, normally to the board, is legal. The other steps would be:

- the development of cash-flow forecasts, because cash control is vital in a crisis situation. 'Quick and dirty' forecasts may dictate the type of strategy subsequently implemented;
- centralise cash control so that *all* cash and loan facilities are centrally controlled. This has proved to be the most successful means of gaining control;
- expenditure controls should be immediately implemented over capital and revenue items. For example, all cheques should be signed by the turnaround manager. The point about much of the action taken here is not its effect on cash-flow, but more its impact on employee attitudes;
- inventory controls should be introduced if they are not already in existence. Control should be simple and focused on high value items;
- debtor controls which includes an aged analysis and review of credit policy are crucial steps because the firm's debtors may provide a very quick way of improving short-term cash-flow;
- improved security may be necessary in an organisation where control systems were lax, in order to stem losses resulting from theft.

2. ESTABLISH AND COMMUNICATE CREDIBILITY WITH STAKEHOLDERS

Public relations is an important feature of the turnaround manager's job because co-operation from the stakeholders is necessary. The turnaround manager must establish credibility, which may be conditional on the departure of previous management, or the manager's own personality, persuasiveness, negotiating skills, etc.

The main stakeholders with whom new management needs to communicate very early on in the turnaround would include the banks (often the most influential stakeholder), suppliers, unions, customers and employees.

3. ASSESS EXISTING MANAGEMENT AND REPLACE IF NECESSARY

Because recovery takes place through the existing management structure one of the early tasks must be an evaluation of these managers to see if new management is required. A variety of methods could be used, from face-to-face interviews to psychological tests. Such decisions are often made quickly. Perhaps more importantly the method of implementing management changes signals to those interested the intentions of the turnaround manager. Illustration 9.2 gives one brief example of the extent to which management changes were deemed necessary in a turnaround situation.

4. EVALUATE THE BUSINESS

The turnaround manager's problem-diagnosis will probably have commenced prior to appointment. This will give a 'feel' for the principal causes of decline and hence of the recovery strategy required. Because speed is of the essence 'rule of thumb' measures are often used as there is little or no time for detailed analysis. The key to successful recovery is the identification of the issue(s) critical to survival.

Chapters 4 and 5 discussed strategic analysis and the sorts or issues raised there are equally applicable here. However, the turnaround manager may have particular difficulty in getting at the facts because truisms to existing management may turn out to be a myth.

5. ACTION PLANNING

When a recovery strategy has been identified an appropriate action plan which provides a framework for implementation must be drawn up. This will help to focus attention on the small number of issues which produce the greatest benefit (cash-flow and/or profit) as well as communicating what the crucial issues are to everyone in the organisation. The plan, though formal, should be short and simple.

6. IMPLEMENT ORGANISATIONAL CHANGE IF APPROPRIATE

Where divisionalisation and decentralisation are appropriate facets of turnaround strategy then organisational change is necessary. This is

ILLUSTRATION 9.2 All Change at British Leyland

One of the first steps taken by Michael Edwardes was to reduce the size of the board of directors by asking ten people to retire. This was all undertaken during the first afternoon of his appointment. The restructuring of the board was seen as a vital step and was completed in a matter of days. There was only a six man board from his appointment in 1977 to 1981.

Top managers were psychologically assessed, starting with the top 300. By 1981 in depth assessments had been conducted on 2000 managers. Of the top 300 managers, 60 were recruited externally and the remainder were found within the company. The 240 were assessed and appraised and no less than 150 managers found themselves in new positions, often because of the need to get 'line' people into 'managing' jobs and 'staff' people into basically advisory jobs.

Replacing senior executives was done by promoting those whose track record was good, whose psychological assessment confirmed their potential, and who had years of energy and drive ahead of them. At the same time outsiders were recruited to accelerate a change of attitude. The mix of external recruits and the best of those who had worked in the company produced a heady mixture of determined people.

(*Source:* Michael Edwardes, *Back from the Brink* (Pan, London, 1984) pp. 49–77)

often associated with new top management; where existing management remains they must sink or swim in the new culture. Such a change must be clearly communicated to *all* employees to explain its rationale and expected benefits.

7. MOTIVATE MANAGEMENT AND EMPLOYEES

Invariably the implementation of a recovery strategy will mean change. In the next chapter we discuss in-depth the management of change. We have already, albeit briefly, discussed motivation earlier in this chapter in the context of planning and control. The issue here really is to communicate effectively with all levels in the organisation. In a turnaround situation this often means that the burden falls to the turnaround manager who may have to communicate direct further down the organisation than may be usual in a healthy firm, because the management and culture inherited may not be used to open communication.

8. INSTALLATION OR IMPROVEMENT OF BUDGETARY SYSTEMS

The turnaround manager will be unable to gain full control until an effective budgetary system is in place. A complex system is not required, simplicity is the key if managers are to be familiar with their budgets and variances. The earlier sections of this chapter have discussed the issues involved in planning and control which are all equally applicable here.

These eight actions were identified by Slatter as the means to implementing the organisational and control strategies required in a turnaround and in planning what other strategies may be required to achieve recovery. While primarily concerned with these eight steps, the turnaround manager may also be simultaneously implementing cost-reduction, asset-reduction and revenue-generating strategies prior to the completion of the evaluation and action-planning phases. The time-pressure may be such, and the strategies so obvious, that implementation begins immediately with virtually no analysis.

9.6 Summary

In concentrating mainly on the objective conditions which affect the implementation of strategy this chapter has discussed how the organisation's planning and control system can contribute to successful implementation. The widespread use of budgeting techniques and the importance of control has been emphasised.

The discussion of planning and control focused on the use of budgeting in terms of planning the use of organisational resources to achieve the strategic objective(s), and then to utilise the agreed plan to control operations to ensure that the plan was met. The integrated nature of the process – that is, the link between strategy, plan, and control – was stressed, thus establishing the key link between strategy and control. Although not emphasised in this chapter we have, of necessity, discussed motivation in the context of control. Managers, not budgets, exercise control, to ensure that the firm stays with the plan, or changes it, if appropriate. We would wish to reinforce the integrative nature of the process by reminding readers that control cannot exist without planning, which itself cannot exist in a meaningful way without a strategic objective – all of which requires the systems and objectives to be accepted by those charged with managing the organisation.

Indeed the integrative nature of the process is perhaps best illustrated by the final section on the implementation of recovery strategies which vividly demonstrated the link between objective conditions (for example, cash balances) and subjective conditions (for example, suitability of managers) required for successful implementation.

Further reading

For a quick, readable survey of motivation theories read Chapter 5 in Cooper and Makin, (1984) *Psychology for Managers* (London: Macmillan). The implementation of recovery strategies is very well argued in Slatter (1984), ch 6–10. Alexander (1985) provides an interesting picture derived from research in the USA.

References

Alexander, L. D. (1985) 'Successfully Implementing Strategic Decisions', *Long Range Planning*, vol. 18, no 3, pp. 91–7.

Anthony, R. N. and Dearden, J. (1980) *Management Control Systems: Text and Cases* (Homewood Illinois: Irwin) 4th edn.

Cooper, C. L. and Makin, P. (1984) 'Motivation at Work', in Cooper, C. L. and Makin, P. (eds) (1984) *Psychology for Managers* (London: Macmillan, pp. 94–117.

Edwardes, M. (1984) *Back from the Brink* (London: Pan Books).

Goldsmith, W. and Clutterbuck, D. (1984) *The Winning Streak* (London: Weidenfeld & Nicolson).

McCarthy, D. J., Minichiello, R. J. and Curran, J. R. (1983) *Business Policy and Strategy* (Homewood, Illinois: Irwin).

Machin, J. L. J. and Wilson, L. S. (1979) 'Closing the Gap between Planning and Control', *Long Range Planning*, vol. 12, April, pp. 16–32.

Peters, T. J. and Waterman, R. H. (1982) *In Search of Excellence* New York: Harper & Row).

Slatter, S. (1984) *Corporate Recovery* (Harmondsworth: Penguin).

Tricker, R. I. and Boland, R. J. (1982) *Management Information and Control Systems* (London: Wiley) 2nd edn.

CHAPTER 10

Managing change

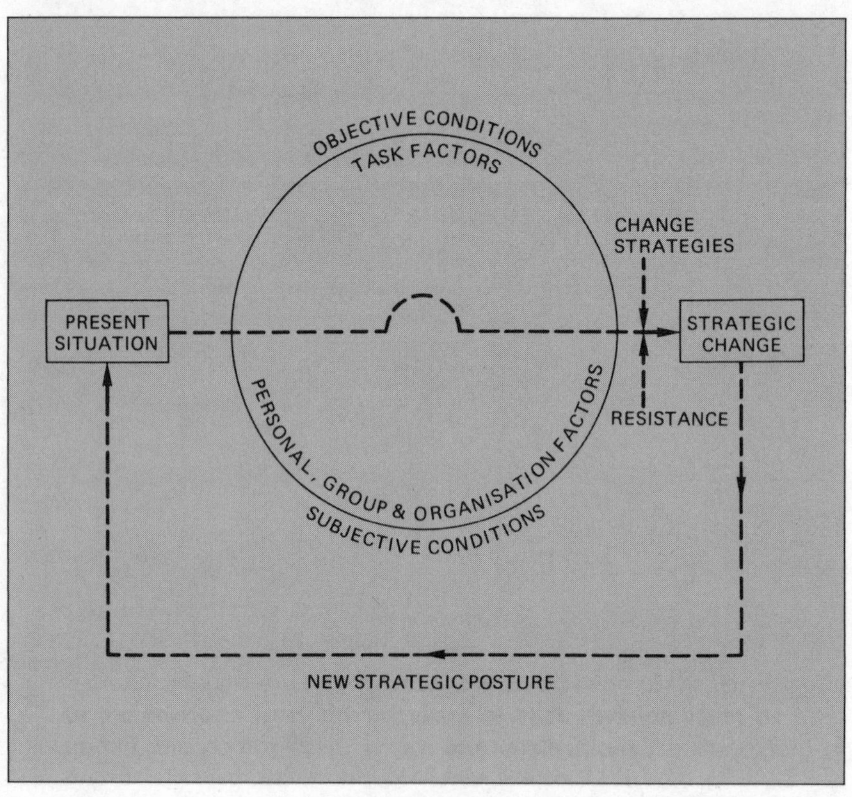

10.1 Introduction

Implementing strategic decisions inevitably involves changes within the organisation. Changes in strategy, technology and/or structure, are vital if the firm is to anticipate and respond to changes in its environment. Successful organisational change has at least three critical components:

1. *A new strategic vision*, translated into detailed operating strategies.
2. *New organisational skills*, to make the new vision work.
3. *Commitment of key people in the organisation*, to the new vision and the development of new skills (Philips, 1983).

In this chapter, we concentrate on the last component, since without the commitment of those involved, real organisational change cannot take place. The chapter is divided into three parts. In the first we look at how people respond to change, and at the factors that influence their reactions. In the second, we analyse popular strategies for managing change and present a contingency approach. In the third we examine the phenomenon of resistance to change, and its causes.

I RESPONSES TO ORGANISATIONAL CHANGE

10.2 Resistance to change reconsidered

Much of the early literature on organisational change perpetuated the idea that employees inevitably resist attempts to get them to behave differently. There was little consideration of the idea that employees may respond positively to change or indeed, initiate it themselves. This sort of expectation that people will resist change, can become a self-fulfilling prophecy. Lawrence (1954) points out:

> It is curious but true that the staff man who goes into his job with the conviction that people are going to resist any idea he presents with blind stubbornness is likely to find them responding just the way he thinks they will. The process is clear: whenever he treats the people who are supposed to buy his ideas as if they were bull-headed, he changes the way they are used to being treated, and they will be bull-headed in resisting that change. (Lawrence, 1954).

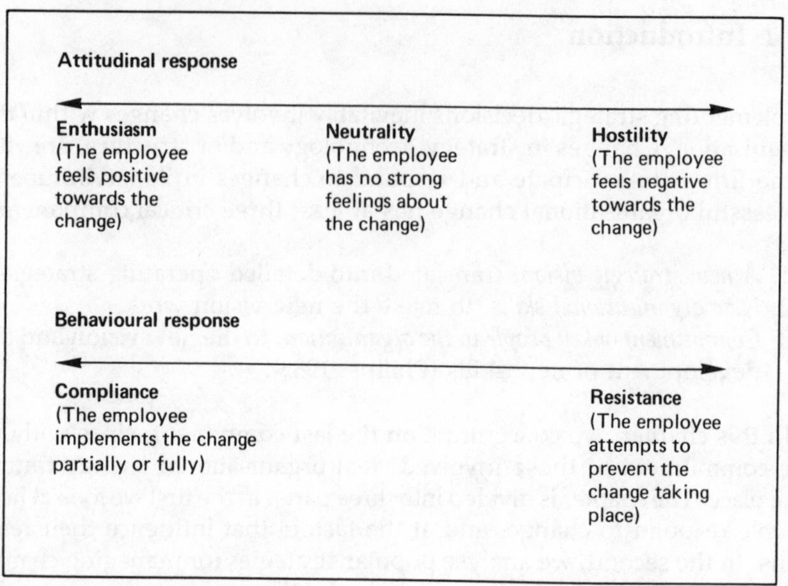

FIGURE 10.1 Employee responses to change

The dangers of automatically expecting resistance to change, are now more widely appreciated, and the idea that employees may welcome change, has gained credence (see Powell and Posner, 1978). However, preconceptions of any kind are best avoided when considering reactions to change. We are not suggesting that one should not envisage certain responses in relation to *specific* change initiatives, but that one should not *automatically* expect a particular kind of response regardless of the situation.

The range of employee responses to change can be represented on two continuums, as shown in Figure 10.1. We distinguish between *attitudinal* and *behavioural* responses, since the two do not always correspond.

An *attitude* of hostility, for instance, will not necessarily be translated into resistance *behaviour*. For example, a manager instructed to set up quality circles within his department, may feel hostile to the idea but complies because he does not want to prejudice his promotion prospects. An individual who has no strong personal feelings about a particular change may join a strike against it, because of union pressure to do so. In many cases, of course, the mental and behavioural response *will* correspond. However, the change agent (we use the terms 'change agent' and 'change manager' to refer to anyone, inside or outside the organisation, attempting to create change within it) needs to be aware of both types of response so that he can decide whether any discrepancy between the two is important and, if so, select a suitable change-strategy to deal with it. Going back to our first example, the change agent may decide that although the manager is likely to comply with an instruction to implement quality circles, the scheme will be unsuccessful unless the manager *feels* more positive about it. Suppose the change agent discovers that the hostility is based on a misunderstanding of the nature and purpose of quality circles. He may decide that rather than simply instructing the manager to implement the scheme, a programme of education would help him to see the logic of quality circles, and move his responses, on both continuums, further toward the left. This example shows the importance of understanding the reasons underlying the responses to change-initiatives. It is only by discovering why the manager feels hostile to quality circles, that a suitable change-strategy can be selected. Wherever possible, those responsible for managing change should analyse the factors influencing employees' responses, and base their change-strategy on that analysis.

Factors influencing responses to change

People react to change in general, and to specific changes. We are interested in the latter – reaction to changes resulting from strategic decisions. We shall, however, discuss reaction to change *per se*, in so far as it affects the response to particular changes. Behavioural and attitudinal responses to change depend on two main factors:

1. *The individual's perception of the change and its effects* Each individual actively processes and interprets information in a unique way. This means that perceptions of the change will vary depending on the factors shown in Figure 10.2.
2. *The individual's perception of responses and their effects* Employee reaction to a change not only depends on perception of the change itself, but also on perception of the range of responses available, and their likely effects.

This helps to explain the point made earlier, that an individual's feelings about a proposed change may not produce the expected behaviour with regard to that change. Someone who perceives a change as misguided, may at the same time perceive that resistance is futile and therefore decide to implement the change. Figure 10.2 outlines factors which influence perception of change and responses to it.

A. CHANGE FACTORS – content and effects of change, speed and method of implementation

B. PERSONAL FACTORS – general attitudes, personality, self-confidence, tolerance of ambiguity

C. GROUP FACTORS – group norms, group cohesiveness, superior's reaction

D. ORGANISATIONAL FACTORS – change history, organisational structure and climate

FIGURE 10.2 Factors influencing perceptions of change and responses

10.3 Change factors

These factors are concerned with the *specific* change being initiated. From the individual employee's point of view, there are two main types of change resulting from strategic decisions:

1. *Technical changes* connected with the job itself: changes in pay, hours of work, conditions of service, promotion prospects, type of work, and so on.
2. *Social changes* affecting the employee's social relationships with others in the organisation: changes in social status, work group, supervisor and so on.

It has been argued that it is of social, rather than technical changes that employees are most wary (Lawrence, 1954). So, for example, an employee may turn down a request that he move to a different position with improved pay and conditions (the technical aspect) because he does not want to move from a familiar work group to an unfamiliar one (the social aspect).

The manner and speed of implementation will also affect the way a specific change is perceived. A change that is imposed on people quickly and without consultation, may well be seen as undesirable, simply because they have not been given a chance to discuss it. On the other hand, the same change may be enthusiastically received, if introduced gradually and with the participation of those affected by it. Coch and French (1948) carried out a classic study confirming the influence of methods of implementation on responses to change. In their study of changes in work procedures in a clothing factory they observed that management could reduce or remove hostility and resistance to changes in work methods, by ensuring that those affected by the change participate in planning it.

Personal factors

An individual's perception of a change, and his or her responses to it will to some extent depend on factors such as his or her general attitudes and personality. Attitudes towards change in general, are obviously linked to attitudes towards specific changes. An employee who has been badly affected by past organisational change, may well develop negative attitudes towards change in general, and thus resist any new proposals regardless of their content or effects. Similarly, attitudes towards authority, management, and co-operation will also affect the employee's responses to change. Other aspects of personality such as level of self-confidence and tolerance of uncertainty will play a part in determining reactions to change. Individuals with low levels of confidence and low tolerance of ambiguity may doubt their ability to cope with the demands of change, and may be unable to cope with the uncertainties produced by change. The ability to tolerate change may also be affected by age. Rogers and Stanfield (1966) demonstrated that innovativeness tends to be, amongst other things, a function of age, and tends to decline as one gets older.

Group factors

Membership of groups, within the organisation, will play a part in determining the individual's response to change-initiatives. It is common for distinctions to be drawn between formal and informal groups in organisations (see Boot *et al*, 1977). Formal groups, such as project teams are created to accomplish a specific task or meet an organisational goal. They tend to have a formally-specified membership, structure and rules, and may be permanent or temporary.

Informal groups are not explicitly set up by management but arise spontaneously. They tend to be based on shared interests or friendship. In practice there are overlaps between the two types of groups. People who work together in a formal group may well develop informal relationships within it.

The presence of other people has been shown by many researchers, to affect the individual's behaviour. Asch's experiments demonstrate that social pressure can persuade an individual to behave in a way he would not otherwise have done (Asch, 1952). This study and the Hawthorne studies (see Pugh, 1984, p. 279) have shown how individuals are influenced by groups and may conform to norms of behaviour established by the group. The extent to which an employee conforms very much depends on the group's cohesiveness, that is, the attractiveness of the group to its members and the extent to which they will make sacrifices to maintain its existence. The more cohesive the group, the higher the level of conformity to group norms.

This has obvious implications for the individual's response to change-initiatives, which may be strongly influenced by the reaction of the group. Just as an individual's reaction may be affected by *group* norms, it may also be influenced by other *individuals* within the organisation. So, for example, an employee may concur with his superior's view of a change in order to keep in favour with him.

Organisational factors

The organisation's record of change will affect the way that current change proposal's are received by employees. This includes, not only the success of any past attempts at change, but also their effects on employees, the way they were implemented and the way employees' reactions were dealt with. For example, in an organisation with a history of rapid change, introduced successfully, employees may be more receptive to any *new* change-initiatives. In an organisation with a past history of unsuccessful change efforts, half-heartedly implemented, new change proposals may be greeted with some scepticism.

The organisation's structure may influence responses to change. Burns and Stalker's study of the Scottish electronics industry (see Pugh, 1984, p. 40) demonstrated the difficulty of initiating and implementing change in mechanistic structures. Highly bureaucratic organisations may inhibit employees' ability to initiate or implement change, even where they see it as desirable (see Chapter 11).

Management style may also affect the way that employees respond to change. The influence of very authoritarian management, for example, could be two-way. It may inhibit resistance or, under certain circumstances, actually provoke it.

It is clear that the individual's reaction to change is a function of a number of relatively fixed factors (*B–D* on Figure 10.2) and of the change and change-strategy itself. Those responsible for managing change have little or no control over factors such as the individual's personality, group norms, or the organisation's structure, at least not in the short term. The only factors they may be able to control are the content of the change and the strategy for implementing it. In circumstances where the change agent is responsible for planning *and* implementation, he may have the freedom to alter both.

In many instances, however, the change manager will only have control over the strategy for implementation, since the *nature* of the change itself, will already have been decided on. Wherever possible then, the change strategy should not be seen as a fixed variable which is decided on the basis of a preconceived idea of how employees react to change, since how they react depends partly on that strategy itself. Rather, the change strategy should be seen as one of many variables which affects the way that employees react to change. Different change strategies will result in different responses to change.

II STRATEGIES FOR MANAGING CHANGE

In this section we examine a number of different strategies for managing change and outline the advantages and disadvantages of each. We finish by suggesting a contingency approach to the problem of deciding which one(s) to use.

10.4 Strategies of participation

Mumford and Pettigrew (1975) comment that the acceptability of a technical change is often related to the extent to which those affected can *participate* in the decision processes concerning the proposed installation. 'Participation' means different things to different people. At one end of the scale are those who see it as management keeping employees informed about the decisions *they* are taking (to us that is communication rather than participation). At the opposite end of the scale are those who see it as giving complete responsibility for decision-making to subordinates. We use the term 'participation' widely to describe strategies that *involve* those affected by the change in some or all aspects of its design or implementation. Thus participative strategies can be seen to lie on a continuum with strategies that verge on consultation at one end and those that give complete responsibility for designing and implementing the change to subordinates, at the other.

In recent years, participative change strategies have frequently taken the form of 'Organisational Development' or OD. OD is a long-term programme of intervention into the organisation's social processes, using the principles and practices of behavioural science, to create attitudinal and behavioural changes, leading to increased organisational effectiveness. An OD programme is normally undertaken at the request of management and can be carried out by a change agent from inside or outside the organisation, provided that he or she is not part of the prevailing organisational culture. OD interventions can take many forms and Illustration 10.1 summarises some of the main ones.

Organisational development differs from more traditional change programmes in which an outside expert is called in to study the situation and make recommendations. In OD efforts the change agent helps members of the organisation to diagnose and solve the organisation's problems themselves.

Strategies of participation are necessary if the change manager does not himself possess all the necessary information to design and implement the change, and where others are expected to resist the change. Its major advantages are that, in many cases, it leads to real commitment to the changes decided on, and to a 'better' decision since all relevant sources of information have been used. Participation, however, can be a very lengthy process, involving much time and effort, and may result in a poor decision, if not properly managed.

All our comments so far, have referred to genuine strategies of participation. However 'participation' is sometimes used as a way of manipulating people. An individual may be invited to 'take part' in planning a change, to give him the impression that his views are being taken into account, when in fact a decision has already been made. This sort of strategy inevitably leads to scepticism about participation and may make genuine attempts to involve subordinates in the planning of change unworkable.

10.5 Strategies of education and communication

Zaltman and Duncan (1977) define this sort of strategy as one in which 'the relatively unbiased presentation of fact is intended to provide a rational justification for action'.

The presentation of the change and reasons for it, may be in the form of reports, memos, discussions, etc., on an individual or group basis. A change strategy of education and communication is based on the assumption that if people are given the rationale for change, they will see the need for it and therefore accept it. This assumes that because the change agent sees the change as rational and justified, it will be seen in the same light by others. This is obviously not always the case. Where there is a clash of interests between parties in the organisation, what represents a rational change for one group may prevent another from reaching *its* goal. In a case like this is an educative strategy is unlikely to

ILLUSTRATION 10.1 Typical OD Techniques

Confrontation meeting

A meeting of managerial level personnel, whose aim is to bring into the open and find ways of resolving, conflict within the organisation. Groups of managers from different levels and functions identify the problems that prevent them, as individuals, from achieving their goals. Typical problems are lack of clear goals, poor attitudes, procedures, etc. The lists are then circulated to all at the meeting. Participants then form into groups based on the way they are normally organised at work, and headed by the most senior manager present. Their tasks are:

1. To identify problems relating to *their* work area and decide on steps to overcome them.
2. To identify the problems they think top management should work on.
3. To decide on the best way to communicate the results of the meeting to subordinates.

Confrontation meetings have the advantage of being easy and quick to carry out, and are claimed to lead to rapid organisational improvements in problem-solving and communication. The danger is that decisions made in haste at such meetings are suboptimal, and that leaving non-management out of the process results in a one-sided view of problems and lack of commitment from employees not taking part. Despite these drawbacks, confrontation can be a useful technique when time is short, and changes are needed rapidly (See Beckhard, 1967).

Management by objectives (MBO)

The process begins with top management setting corporate objectives, which are then translated into departmental objectives after discussion with departmental managers. Individual managers then meet with their subordinates to agree mutually upon the subordinates' targets which will contribute towards achievement of the company's overall objectives. The level of support and training necessary to achieve those targets is agreed upon and dates set for assessment of results achieved. Where targets have not been met, the reasons are identified and necessary remedial action taken – again by mutual agreement between manager and subordinate.

ILLUSTRATION 10.1 *continued*

The assumption behind MBO is that individuals will be more motivated to achieve objectives on which they themselves have agreed. The system has a number of shortcomings. In the short term it can be very time-consuming and involve a lot of administration. It can also encourage a narrow view in which employees are judged purely on achievement of quantifiable objectives. Employees may be tempted deliberately to set themselves low objectives to ensure that they are achievable. In organisations with a tradition of authoritarianism, employees may be unenthusiastic about MBO, with the result that decision-making is not really shared. However, if carried out skilfully and with commitment in an atmosphere of trust between management and subordinates, MBO can be powerful change mechanism.

Open systems planning

A process in which key management personnel identify the organisation's 'core mission', and analyse the internal and external environment in terms of how they affect the organisation's ability to achieve its goals. Organisational systems are then modified so that it can adapt better to environmental demands. Like MBO, open systems planning demands a lot of effort and commitment, and may not result in commitment from those not involved in the process. It is a relatively new and undeveloped technique but appears to be useful when major changes are to be made.

Process consultation

'A set of activities on the part of the consultant which help the client to perceive, understand, and act upon process events which occur in the client's environment' (Tichy, 1983). These 'process events' are interpersonal relationships in the organisation. They may be communications, group roles and norms, decision-making, authority, delegation, and leadership, for example – in fact any human actions which occur between people in the organisation. The outside consultant helps the organisation diagnose the strengths and weaknesses of its own processes, and suggests alternative solutions. The *client*, however, must decide which solutions to try. To clarify the nature of process consultation Schein compares it with two more traditional consultation models – the 'purchase model' and the 'doctor–patient' model. In the 'purchase model' the *organisation* defines its need – perhaps for an employee attitude survey and hires a consultant to carry it out. In the 'doctor–patient' model the consultant is invited into the organisation to diagnose the client's problem and he then recommends a solution. Process consultation, in contrast, is about *joint* diagnosis and the passing on of diagnostic skills to the client. It is vital that the client recognises the problem for itself and plays an active role in deciding on the remedy. Process consultation is a useful way of solving interpersonal problems, and is intended to enable the client to identify future problems and solutions for himself.

Sensitivity training

Sometimes described as T groups (training groups), sensitivity training is designed to help individuals become more perceptive about their own feelings and behaviour, and those of other people. The idea is to teach employees more about group dynamics and group norms, so that they can become more adept at interpersonal relations. A T group consists of about a dozen people with a professional leader to act as a catalyst and facilitator. The group meets without a structure or an agenda for periods ranging from a few days to a fortnight. The focus of discussion is the interaction and behaviour of members of the group during the session. Although a commonly-used technique in the early days of OD, it has met with mixed success and is used less often now. The major problem with the technique is that it affects only the individual, not the whole social system. As a result individuals often find it difficult to sustain any change in their behaviour on their return to their normal work situation. Because of this it has now largely been replaced by techniques such as 'team building'.

Team building

Team building, or team development is a technique that affects both organisational processes and people. Its aim is to increase the effectiveness of work teams within the organisation. Work teams spend a few days together, with a change agent, away from the work situation. Led by the change agent, the team agrees on a written statement of its purpose, and on performance objectives which can be used to measure its success. They then decide on the role of each member in achieving the team's goals. The final stage involves the development of team communication, and decision-making processes, and mechanisms for managing interpersonal relations and conflict between members of the team (Tichy, 1983).

work since the change is *irrational* from the point of view of some of those affected by it.

A programme of education and communication may be useful when resistance, based on inadequate or inaccurate information, is anticipated. Such programmes, however, can be both time-consuming and expensive, and require a relationship of trust between change agent and those affected by the change. If there is no trust the message is unlikely to be believed.

10.6 Power strategies

In an organisational context, power is the *capacity* to effect or affect organisational actions. According to Mintzberg (1983) power has three main bases:

1. *Control of something essential to those over whom one has power*, for example information or financial reward.
2. *Formal authority*, that is, power vested in office, or the ability to get things done, by virtue of one's position. People usually concede the right of those in formal authority to give instructions, having been conditioned, by the socialisation process, to accept it as the norm.
3. *Access to people who can rely on 1 or 2.*

A change agent may use a power strategy to bring about change if he possesses any of the above bases of power. It involves effecting a change by virtue of one's power over others in the organisation. The power does not have to be explicitly used, in order to be effective in bringing about change. In the first instance, formal authority is normally relied on to gain compliance from subordinates. It is only when this fails that the first-mentioned basis of power is likely to be used. So subordinates may implement a change, simply because 'the boss' tells them to do so. However, if the instruction to change is resisted, the change agent may resort to coercion, by implicitly or explicitly threatening loss of jobs, promotion prospects and so on. He may actually sack or transfer those who refuse to co-operate, as a way of bringing others into line. Finally, change may be brought about by a change agent who has the ear of someone else in a position of power. His instructions may be complied with because of his known access to other powerful individuals.

Closely allied to power strategies, are what we call *'personal power'* strategies, in which power is based on possession of personal qualities such as charisma or physical strength. Personal power, of this kind, is often vested in informal leaders within the organisation. In some cases, those in possession of formal authority may well choose not to use their own power, to bring about change, since this approach may be resisted by subordinates. Instead they may rely on those people with 'personal power' to do the job for them, since this may meet with less resistance.

Power strategies are useful in situations where the change must be quickly implemented, and few resources are available for programmes of education or strategies of negotiation. Power is best used when the commitment of those affected is not necessary for implementation of the change, or when little resistance is expected since, if resistance is crushed by force, it can create problems later. That is not to say it cannot be used successfully to overpower resistance, merely that the change manager should be aware of its risks. (Other aspects of power relationships within the organisation are considered in the second part of Chapter 13.)

Strategies of manipulation

A strategy of manipulation involves the conscious structuring of events so that others behave in the way the manipulator wishes (MacMillan, 1978). In the context of organisational change, such a strategy could be used to get others in the organisation to feel enthusiastic about, or at least to comply with, a request to change.

MacMillan suggests two ways in which an individual can manipulate others:

1. *Situational* He can restructure the *situation* so that the subject decides on a course of action he would otherwise not have done.
2. *Intentional* He can alter the subject's perception of the existing situation, so that he/she changes his/her *intentions*, and decides on a new course of action.

MacMillan goes on to suggest that manipulation may be in one of two modes:

1. *Positive mode of manipulation* The subject feels better off as a result of the manipulation.
2. *Negative mode of manipulation* The subject feels worse off as a result of the manipulation.

These two dimensions can be combined to produce four manipulation tactics:

	Situational	*Intentional*
Positive	Inducement	Persuasion
Negative	Coercion	Obligation

The following example illustrates each method of manipulation, and is an adaptation of MacMillan's illustration:

A manufacturing organisation wishes to get one of its sales managers to take over a different territory which will mean him moving to a new location. A strategy of manipulation could be used to bring about this change, and would involve the use of one or more of the following tactics:

Inducement
The manipulator restructures the *situation* so that the subject's circumstances are *improved* if he selects the desired course of action.

- The employer could offer the sales manager a generous relocation allowance, and a salary increase in order to get him to move and take over the new territory. If the manager does move, it will be in response to the above offers, and he will feel better off because he has done so. His attitude towards the manipulation will be *positive*.

Coercion
The manipulator restructures the *situation* so that the subject's situation is *worsened* by not selecting the desired alternative.

- The employer could threaten to block the sales manager's promotion prospects within the organisation if he does not take over the new territory. If the manager does decide to move, he will feel worse off than before and will have *negative* feelings towards the manipulation.

Persuasion
The manipulator attempts to change the subject's *perception* of the situation, by persuading him he'll be *better off* by carrying out the required course of action.

- The employer might persuade the sales manager to move by telling him that in the past mobility has been rewarded by rapid promotion in the organisation. If the manager is persuaded to move by this argument he will feel he has benefited by the decision and will feel *positive* about the manipulation.

Obligation
The manipulator attempts to make the subject feel obliged to do what the manipulator wishes.

- The employer could try to make the sales manager feel guilty about not moving, by reminding him of all the money the company has spent on training him in skills which the take-over of the new territory will demand. The sales manager may then feel obliged to move but will feel *negative* about it.

Although these four tactics of manipulation have been presented separately, in practice a combination of all four could be used to bring about change. In certain circumstances, a manipulative strategy can be a cheap and easy way of getting people to implement a change. It costs less than negotiation for example, and is quicker and easier than participation, or a full-scale programme of education. However, if a negative form of manipulation is used, and the individual feels he has been tricked into accepting a change, it may create problems later.

10.7 Strategies of negotiation

A common way of implementing change is by negotiation. Negotiation is where people whose interests conflict come to an agreement about how they will behave with respect to one another. For example, a union may negotiate a productivity deal with management, whereby employees gain bonus payments in return for higher output.

The following illustration is drawn from MacMillan's example. Suppose an employee is negotiating with an employer for a lump-sum payment, in return for taking early retirement. The employee will have a lower limit in mind, below which he will not go. This is the employee's *bargaining base*. Let us suppose it is £25 000. He will not accept a payment of less than this. The employee will also have an upper limit in mind which he feels is the best offer he is likely to get. This is the employee's *aspiration base*, let us suppose it is £35 000.

The employer, of course, will also have an aspiration base, but this is the lowest sum he thinks the employee will accept – say £20 000. The employer will also have a bargaining base – the highest sum he is prepared to offer – say £30 000. This may result in a situation like that shown in figure 10.3. We can see from the diagram that the two bargaining bases must overlap if there is to be a deal. If a deal is struck it will be somewhere between £25 000 and £30 000.

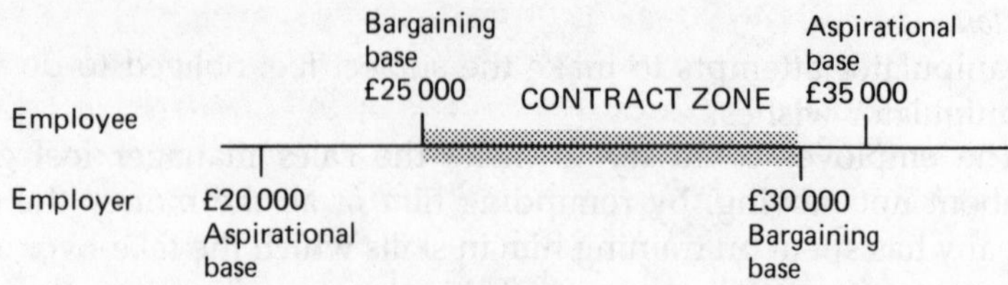

FIGURE 10.3 Employee/employer bargaining

Source: Based on MacMillan (1978).

Negotiation is useful when it is obvious there are going to be losers as a result of a change, and where those losers are likely to resist. Although negotiation may sometimes be the only way to manage change, its drawback is that its use can lead to a situation where change is only possible by negotiation.

Strategies of facilitation

Facilitative strategies are those which make the implementation of change easier, among or by, the change target (Zaltman and Duncan, 1977). Facilitation may involve providing training in the new skills demanded by the change, providing counselling and support for those affected by the change, or providing the necessary environmental conditions (equipment, space, etc.) for the individual to change.

Facilitative strategies are helpful when a proposed change is likely to produce anxiety on the part of those affected by it. Facilitation is such that it can only be used with people who recognise that the change is necessary and are willing and able to make use of the assistance and support offered. The only major drawback to this sort of strategy is its cost in terms of time and money.

Multiple strategies

Although we have presented these strategies separately, in reality, a number of them are likely to be used in combination to bring about change. In some circumstances it may be appropriate to use two or more strategies simultaneously, with different change targets. For example, a change agent introducing a system of flexible working hours into an organisation, may find it necessary to use two strategies at the same time. It may be enough to use a power approach on people who have worked with flexible working hours in other organisations, since they understand how it works and the benefits it offers. For other people who are not familiar with the system, a strategy of education and communication may be used to explain how it works and the advantages it offers. In other circumstances two or more strategies may be used consecutively. For example, after a power strategy has been used to implement a change, it may be followed by a strategy of facilitation to help those affected to cope with the effects of the change.

10.8 Selecting strategies for change – a contingency approach

The change manager obviously has a wide range of strategies from which to choose when planning and implementing change. Over the past fifteen years or so, change agents have tended to favour participative strategies, particularly those such as organisational development (OD) which use the techniques and theories of behavioural science. Lorsch (1976) points out that this is partly because OD approaches have been developed by academics, consultants and staff personnel, all of whom have skills and values which favour power-sharing approaches to management. He adds that participative strategies can be very effective, *'where they fit the people, tasks and traditions of a particular situation'*.

The danger is that the change manager automatically selects one particular strategy or group of strategies regardless of their suitability to the particular situation he faces. What should happen is that the change agent analyses the particular situation with which he is faced, and *then* decides on the most suitable strategy to cope with it. There is no 'best' change strategy; some are simply more appropriate in certain situations than others. The analysis should take into account a number of situational factors, which can be categorised as task or non-task factors:

Task factors are those that are directly related to the *particular* change programme in question.

Non-task factors are those that are not directly related to any particular change programme, and are relatively fixed, at least in the short term.

Task factors

1. THE LOCUS OF RELEVANT DATA FOR DESIGNING AND IMPLEMENTING THE CHANGE

   If the change agent does not possess all the information necessary to design and implement the change, but requires data from other people, he will have to follow a strategy which allows some degree of participation. (Kotter and Schlesinger, 1979) The smaller the change agent's need for information from others, the more he *can* move away from participation towards the other strategies.

2. SPEED OF INTRODUCTION
If the change must be introduced quickly, power or manipulative approaches may be indicated, since strategies involving participation, education and negotiation can be very time-consuming.

3. RESOURCES AVAILABLE
If resources are limited, the change agent will have to take into account the cost of the various strategies. Strategies of participation, education, negotiation and facilitation can prove extremely costly, if large numbers of people are involved. However, the cost of any strategy has to be weighed against the possible costs of resistance which may be brought about by the use of other strategies.

4. AMOUNT OF COMMITMENT REQUIRED
Not all changes need the commitment of those affected in order to be successful. In some cases compliance is all that is required. For instance a change in the kind of machine used to do a particular job, may not require the machine operatives' commitment or enthusiasm, to be effective. Some changes, however, do require the commitment of those implementing them, in order to be effective. Our earlier example of a quality-circles experiment is relevant here. Such an experiment is unlikely to work properly, without the commitment of all concerned. In most cases, participative or educative strategies are more likely to gain commitment than are strategies of power or manipulation. However, this is not always the case, and where compliance is all that is required a participative approach may be a waste of time and effort.

5. ANTICIPATED REACTION TO CHANGE
We have already stressed the dangers of *automatically* expecting a particular response to change initiatives. However, having taken into account the factors outlined in the first part of this chapter (see Figure 10.2) the change agent will, in most cases form an opinion of likely reactions to a *particular* change proposal. If he envisages support for and compliance with the change, a power strategy is probably the quickest and cheapest method of implementation. This may be backed up by a strategy of facilitation to increase efficiency of adoption. Where resistance or hostility is expected, however, other strategies *may* be more appropriate. Participation may help to gain commitment to the change, but if this is not possible and resistance is based on ignorance or misinformation, a

strategy of education and communication may be the next best thing. Where resistance is expected because some people are losing out as a result of the change, negotiation may be the best policy. Facilitation may work if resistance is based on fear of ability to cope with the change. Where none of the above are feasible, manipulation may be used, as a last resort. We do not rule out a power strategy, where resistance is anticipated, but the change agent should be aware of the risks involved in quashing resistance in this way.

Non-task factors

1. EXISTING NORMS ABOUT INVOLVEMENT
If there are strong organisational norms favouring involvement in decision-making, employees will expect a participative approach to the management of change; and may resent changes they have not helped to plan. On the other hand, if norms lead employees to expect top management to make all the decisions, then non-participative approaches will be more consistent with expectations. As Lorsch (1976) points out, to use an approach which is inconsistent with existing norms is, in effect, implementing a change. This may be a desirable part of the required change, in which case such a strategy is appropriate; if not, a strategy more in keeping with expectations is preferable.

2. RELATIONSHIP OF CHANGE AGENT TO CHANGE TARGETS
The amount of power the change agent has over the change target is an important determinant of change strategy. If the change agent is in a powerful position *vis à vis* the change target, he has the *option* to use a power strategy, although he may not necessarily choose to do so. The less power the change agent has, the more he will be forced towards non-power approaches. The amount of trust the change targets have in the change agent, should also affect the choice of change strategy. If the level of trust is high, participative or educative approaches may be successful. Where the relationship is characterised by mistrust however, attempts to involve or educate subordinates may meet with suspicion and hostility.

3. LEADERSHIP STYLE
The change strategy chosen must be consistent with the change agent's leadership style. For instance, if the change manager is skilled at, and feels comfortable with a participative approach, its use is likely to be appreciated by subordinates. If the change agent uses a participative approach, when he is unskilled and uncomfortable with it,

subordinates may sense his lack of confidence in the strategy and see it as false and manipulative.

Consideration of all these factors should provide the change manager with clues as to the most appropriate change strategy. However, this sort of analysis will not always result in a clear answer to the problem of choosing a strategy for change. Take, for example, the manager who has very little time in which to institute a change, and yet needs information from a lot of people before he can decide what to do. In this situation, a compromise will be necessary. The manager will need to consult with others but will have to make do with representatives of different organisational groups, rather than all group members, as he would have liked. In many instances, consideration of all these factors will point to the use of multiple strategies.

10.9 Planning the change process

Successful design and implementation of change may be made easier, by going through the following process (Kotter and Schlesinger, 1979).

1. ANALYSIS OF CURRENT SITUATION
   An analysis of the organisation's problems and opportunities. This should identify, where possible, causes of the problems and the speed with which they must be resolved. It should also identify ways in which opportunities can be exploited, and then outline any changes necessary as well as their effects and implications.
2. ANALYSIS OF SITUATIONAL FACTORS
   This should focus on the task and non-task factors outlined earlier.
3. SELECTION OF CHANGE STRATEGY
   This should be based on the above analysis. A plan for implementation of the change should specify when it is to take place, the degree of involvement of others, and specific tactics such as retraining and communication programmes. It is vital that the strategy chosen should be consistent with the previous analysis.
4. MONITORING IMPLEMENTATION
   This step involves monitoring the implementation. There are two reasons for this. First, it enables unexpected problems to be quickly identified and rectified, and second, it means the success of the change strategy can be judged, and lessons learned for use in future change programmes.

III RESISTANCE TO CHANGE

10.10 Outcomes of hostility

In spite of a carefully-planned change-programme, based on the sort of analysis outlined, there may still be hostility towards it. Hostility will not necessarily be translated into active resistance, but it may still have damaging outcomes. A negative attitude towards a change may lead to half-hearted implementation. As we mentioned earlier this will not always affect the efficiency of implementation, but in many cases (such as the introduction of an MBO programme), it will. Where hostility does not prevent the change being carried out, it may surface in other equally damaging ways. Reduced morale, lack of commitment to the organisation, absenteeism, and high labour turnover, may be the indirect result of hostility towards organisational change.

In some cases hostility *is* translated into active resistance behaviour. This can take many forms – strikes, withdrawal of co-operation, reduction in output, or sabotage, all of which are damaging for the organisation.

Resistance to change – irrational or rational?

Sometimes it is easy to see why a particular change is being resisted – if jobs are threatened, for instance. On many occasions, however, resistance appears irrational to outsiders or to those initiating the change. As such it is seen as harmful and as something to be overcome. In fact, hostility and resistance to a change is usually entirely rational *from the point of view of those resisting* and is based on a number of reasons:

1. FEAR OF LOSING CURRENT SATISFACTIONS
   People may fear, rightly or wrongly that they will lose something of value, because of a change. It may appear to threaten any current satisfaction, from jobs and promotion prospects to valued social relationships and status.
2. FEAR OF INADEQUACY
   A change may be resisted because people fear it will demand things of them, they feel unable to deliver. New skills, new behaviour patterns or attitudes, different ways of thinking or relating to people, may be required. Individuals who doubt their ability to meet these new demands, may resist the change that makes them necessary.

3. RELUCTANCE TO ADMIT WEAKNESS
   To accept that a change is necessary, is to admit that there is something wrong with the *status quo*. An individual who has invested time, energy and reputation in something, may not welcome suggestions that it be changed.

4. PARTICULAR CHANGE CONSIDERED UNDESIRABLE OR IMPOSSIBLE
   A change may be resisted, not because of personal reasons such as those above, but because it is considered bad for the organisation, or others affected by it. The change itself may be seen as desirable, but unworkable, because of lack of resources, for example.

5. RELATIONSHIP WITH CHANGE AGENT
   Suspicion of the change agent may lead to hostility towards any changes he proposes – regardless of their content. If the change agent is an outsider or a newcomer to the organisation, it may be felt that he does not understand the organisation's values, problems or objectives, or that he does not have its best interests at heart.

Any of these reasons may apply to the individual or to groups within the organisation. In situations where a group of people have reasons to resist a change, other individuals within the group may comply with group norms and engage in resistance behaviour, regardless of their personal feelings about the change.

Hostility or resistance to change is therefore, usually entirely logical from the point of view of those against it. Seen in this light it should not always be regarded as something to be quashed, but as a symptom, signalling that something is wrong. Lawrence (1954) draws a useful analogy between resistance in the organisation and pain in the body. Resistance is useful to the organisation in the same way that pain is to the body. It does not tell us *what* is wrong, only that some thing *is* wrong. It makes no more sense to try to overcome such resistance than it does to take a pain-killer without diagnosing the ailment.

Change agents should be aware that resistance can be a healthy phenomenon, and can be used constructively. Those opposing the change usually have something of value to say and their objections should be given consideration. When the reasons underlying resistance are identified, those advocating change may find their proposals are not, after all, in the best interests of the organisation. Resistance may generate alternative proposals or lead to useful modifications. Thus resistance can often be used positively by change agents. By resisting, people are communicating important information to the manager of change.

This sort of information, about the resistors' values, attitudes and objectives as well as their resources and capabilities, should always be taken into consideration, by those planning and implementing change.

10.11 Summary

1. Attitudinal responses to change (for example, hostility) need not necessarily be translated into resistance behaviour as there are other considerations which might determine the response (for example, resistance may harm promotion prospects).
2. Behavioural and attitudinal responses to change depend on the individual's *perception* of the change and of the range of responses available and their likely effects.
3. 'Social' changes (to groups, status, supervision) are often perceived to be more disruptive than 'technical' changes (pay, conditions of service, type of work, equipment).
4. Personal factors (such as age, self-confidence, attitudes to authority), group factors (norms, cohesiveness) and organisation factors (record of past changes, structure, management style) are important and relatively stable influences in the change process.
5. Participative change strategies are particularly effective where management needs the active co-operation of staff, but 'participation' can be regarded sceptically and with suspicion if it is used manipulatively.
6. Power strategies are appropriate where change must be rapidly introduced and where the commitment of those affected is not necessary for successful implementation.
7. Manipulation involves the conscious structuring of events so that others behave in the way the manipulator wishes. The manipulator can either restructure the situation, or alter the subject's perception of the existing situation.
8. Negotiation is useful where there are likely to be losers as a result of a change, and where the losers can disrupt the implementation of the change.
9. A contingency approach suggests that the relevant factors in the situation (both those specific to the change itself, and those that are relatively permanent features of the organisation) should be considered before selecting the appropriate change strategy.

Further reading

Mumford and Pettigrew (1975) provide fascinating insights into the processes of strategic change through an empirical study of an actual change situation. MacMillan (1978) provides an interesting framework for understanding change strategies.

References

Asch, Solomon E. (1952) *Social Psychology* (Englewood Cliffs, New Jersey: Prentice-Hall).

Beckhard, R. (1967) 'The Confrontation Meeting', *Harvard Business Review*, XLV.

Boot, R. L., Cowling, A. G. and Stanworth, M. J. K. (1977) *Behavioural Sciences for Managers* (Leeds: Arnold).

Coch, Lester and French, John R. P. (1948) 'Overcoming Resistance to Change', *Human Relations*, I.

Kotter, John P. and Schlesinger, Leonard A. (1979) 'Choosing Strategies for Change', *Harvard Business Review*, March/April.

Lawrence, Paul R. (1954) 'How to Deal with Resistance to Change', *Harvard Business Review*, May/June.

Lorsch, Jay (1976) 'Managing Effective Change Strategies', *Harvard Business School Note, HBS Case Studies*.

MacMillan, Ian C. (1978) *Strategy Formulation: Political Concepts* (St Paul, Minnesota: West).

Mintzberg, Henry (1983) *Power in and around Organisations* (Englewood Cliffs, New Jersey: Prentice-Hall).

Mumford, Enid and Pettigrew, Andrew (1975) *Implementing Strategic Decisions* (London: Longman).

Philips, Julien R. (1983) 'Enhancing the Effectiveness of Organisational Change Management', *Human Resource Management*, 22, Spring/Summer.

Powell, Gary and Posner, Barry Z. (1978) 'Resistance to Change Reconsidered: Implications for Managers', *Human Resource Management*, 17, Spring.

Pugh, D. S. (1984) *Organization Theory* (Harmondsworth: Penguin) p. 279.

Rogers, Everett and Stanfield, J. David (1966) 'Adoption and Diffusion of New Products: Emerging Generalisations and Hypotheses', paper presented at the Conference on the Application of Sciences to Marketing Management, Purdue University, July, 1966.

Tichy, Noel M. (1983) 'The Confrontation Meeting', *Harvard Business Review*, XLV.

Zaltman, G. and Duncan, R. (1977) *Strategies for Planned Change* (Chichester: Wiley).

CHAPTER 11

Strategy and structure

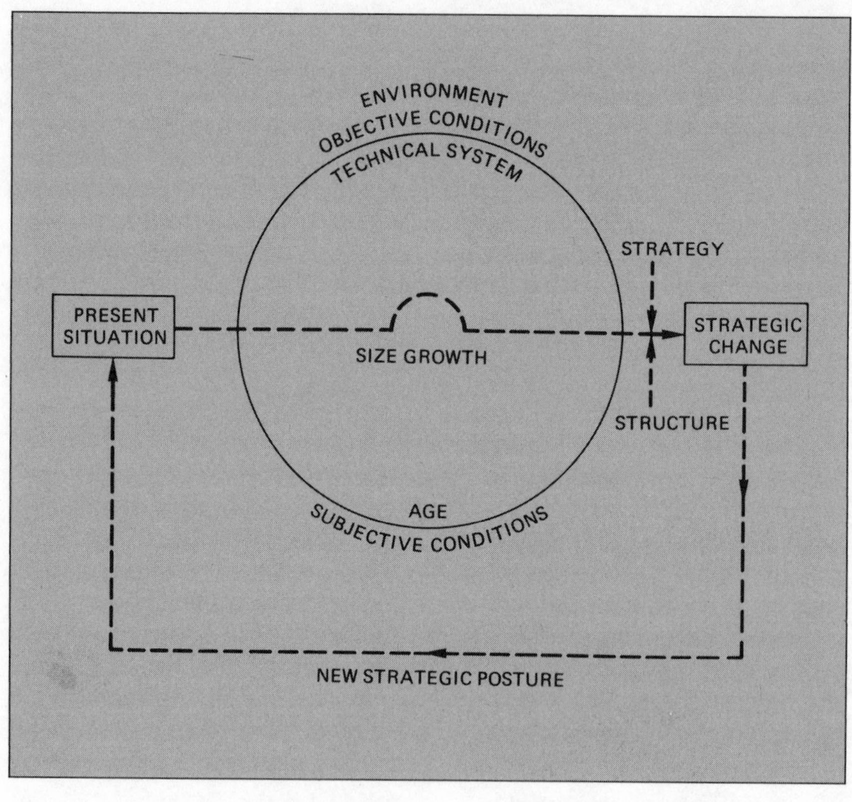

11.1 Introduction

In this chapter we examine the *contingency factors* which influence the structuring of organisations. These factors, which can be regarded for the moment as independent variables, have a significant impact on the design of the organisation. Effective structuring requires a degree of congruence between the contingency factors and the organisation's structures and processes. Four categories of contingency factors will be considered in this chapter: age and size; growth; the technical system and the environment. A fifth, power, is considered separately in Chapter 13.

In the appendix to this chapter we have included a brief summary of Mintzberg's model of the five parts of an organisation, and the five co-ordinating mechanisms. Readers who are unfamiliar with this approach are advised to read this appendix as the particular terminology is used to explore structural issues in this and subsequent chapters. We would also strongly recommend Mintzberg's *Structure in Fives* (Prentice-Hall, 1983) as a masterly and coherent framework for exploring structural issues.

11.2 Age and size

Here, we explore two 'static' contingency factors, age and size. Growth is treated as a separate dynamic factor, although there are clear links between growth, age and size. Five general relationships between age and size and structure have been identified, supported by empirical evidence:

1. *The older the organisation, the more formalised its behaviour*
   Repetition of a task leads to predictability, which in turn permits the introduction of routines and procedures, thus formalising behaviour.
2. *The larger the organisation, the more elaborate its structure*
   Size usually leads to increasing specialisation and differentiation. The administrative component (which controls the operating core) becomes more significant, and as Lawrence and Lorsch's (1967) research reveals, with increasing differentiation comes an increased need for co-ordination. This is effected through a range of devices: a larger hierarchy which can co-ordinate through direct supervision, standardisation of work processes and outputs (through the

development of planning and control systems) and through the use of liaison devices to assist the process of 'mutual adjustment' (where work is co-ordinated through direct informal communication between the people doing the job).

3. *The larger the organisation, the larger the size of its average unit*
   As the firm grows and specialisation develops, wider spans of control can be tolerated, as it is possible to supervise large groups of people doing a standardised, specialised task. Rapid growth tends to increase unit size as the creation of *new* units is a discrete step which requires a deliberate policy decision to effect, whereas adding more people to the existing unit structure can be achieved through a continuous, incremental process.
4. *The larger the organisation, the more formalised its behaviour*
   As the organisation grows, more behaviours are repeated, which leads to increasing predictability thereby making formalisation easier. A rather more negative aspect to size is the increasing isolation and reduced morale of the individual employee. This often results in the need to *control* behaviour through rules, procedures and the exercise of authority.
5. A fifth relationship has been suggested: *as size increases the proportion of administrative staff increases* through the need to maintain the increasingly elaborating superstructure). However, although extensive research has been undertaken in this area, no clear relationship has been convincingly established.

11.3 Growth

Chandler's thesis

There does, however, appear to be a good deal of evidence to suggest that as organisations grow they go through structural transitions, changes in *kind* rather than degree. Chandler's Thesis, for example, consists of four elements:

1. The structure of the firm follows its growth strategy.
2. Structure and strategy develop through a particular sequence.
3. Structures are not adapted until pressure of inefficiency *forces* a change.
4. The formulator of strategies is rarely the person who creates structures.

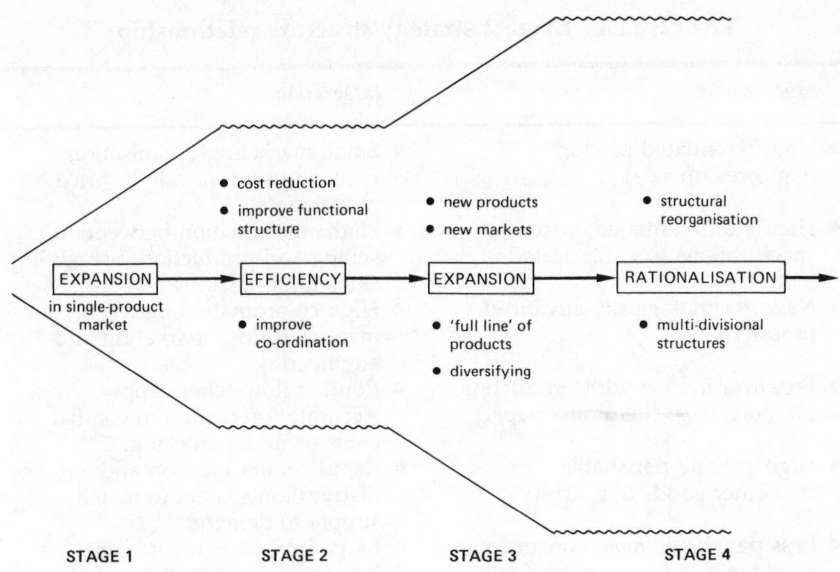

FIGURE 11.1 Chandler's four stages of development

Chandler identified four stages of development which are illustrated in Figure 11.1.

STAGE 1 THE INITIAL EXPANSION AND ACCUMMULATION OF RESOURCES

Here the strategic task facing the firm is to meet the expanding demand. This implies a need to enlarge the scale of operations and the creation of distribution networks and new marketing organisations. The key structural changes required are a move to a functionally-differentiated structure and the possibility of vertically integrating forwards or backwards.

STAGE 2 RATIONALISING THE USE OF RESOURCES

Two major strategic tasks face the organisation: the need to reduce unit costs, and the need to *integrate* functional activities to enable the firm to respond to market fluctuations. Unit-cost reduction requires the following structural responses:

- clearer definition of lines of authority and communication channels within a single functional area;
- the need to systematise and improve the processes and techniques of marketing, manufacturing and materials procurement.

TABLE 11.1 Stage 2 strategy/structure relationships

Product/market	*Integration*
• Undifferentiated product (e.g. ores, metals)	• Small marketing organisation. Flow adjusted quickly to price movements
• Highly differentiated, customer specifications (e.g. fabricated metals)	• High co-ordination between selling and production. Scheduling skills important
• New, technologically advanced products	• High co-ordination between manufacturing, marketing and engineering
• Producer market with production for stock (e.g. chemicals, paper)	• Routine flow-scheduling Accurate forecasting to combat over- or under-stocking.
• High volume perishable consumer goods (e.g. fruit)	• Rapid communication and distribution system to match supply to demand
• Less perishable mass consumer goods (e.g. tobacco, some foods)	• Large inventory investment, long- and short-term forecasting. Co-ordination of product flows
• Consumer durables	• Critical importance of forecasting, formal budgeting and capital allocation techniques

The second strategic task, integration, demands different structural responses depending on the product/market served by the firm (see Table 11.1).

STAGE 3 CONTINUED GROWTH THROUGH EXPANSION INTO NEW PRODUCTS AND NEW MARKETS

As existing markets are saturated there are fewer cost-cutting opportunities. The key strategic tasks are:

- the development of a 'full line' of comparable products
- expansion at home and abroad.

Chandler identified different patterns of expansion depending on the orientation of the firm. Firms with a product/market orientation tended to diversify into related products and related markets; whereas, firms with a technological orientation moved into diverse product/markets but into areas with a related technology. The structural changes involved at Stage 3 are the move to setting-up marketing and often manufacturing organisations in new geographic areas (either distant parts of one country or abroad).

STAGE 4 RATIONALISING THE USE OF EXPANDING RESOURCES

Although in Stage 3 the firm expanded its resources it did not ensure their efficient employment. Structural reorganisation is required to ensure a better 'fit' between the new tasks facing the firm and its organisational arrangements. Chandler's research established that initially firms attempted to deal with the Stage 3 diversification through either:

- forming a larger, functionally departmentalised structure,
  or
- setting up almost completely independent subsidiaries.

The latter development is a form of 'holding company' structure where the central HQ adopts a 'hands-off' approach to the quasi-autonomous subsidiaries, except to establish broad financial targets and to act as a supplier of investment capital. However, Chandler noted an increasing tendency to adopt the multi-divisional structure to manage diversified corporations. Figure 11.2 shows a simplified multi-divisional structure.

In a multi-divisional structure the divisions are responsible for short/medium term 'operating' decisions, whereas 'strategic' decisions would be made in the central office. Of course, in these large corporations strategic decisions and operating decisions tend to take on different meanings from our understanding of a typical small/medium-sized firm.

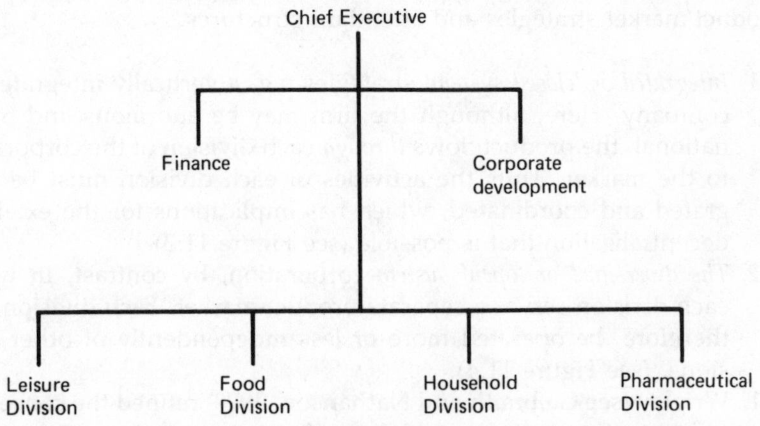

FIGURE 11.2 A simplified multi-divisional structure

For example, whereas in a small firm the decision to launch a new product would clearly be strategic, in a multi-divisional corporation this decision may well be made at the divisional level. Strategic decisions at the headquarters in the multi-divisional structure would involve decisions, for example, about the size of the pharmaceutical business or whether a new division should be established to handle industrial customers.

In many US divisionalised corporations reward systems are linked to division performance, and this management technique is gaining ground in the UK as well. The central office can also act as a surrogate capital market where divisions compete for a share of the capital available for expansion. In this respect, it is likely that this form of structure reverses the trend towards satisficing and non-profit ('managerial') objectives being pursued (which were discussed in Chapter 2). As the size of the corporation increases and shareholders become less and less influential in the goal-setting process, Galbraith (1967) and others have argued that profitability becomes a secondary objective; however, the multi-divisional structure may result in the re-establishment of the goal of profitability through the way each division is managed.

Chandler also cites case evidence for parts (3) and (4) of his thesis: that structures are not adapted until pressure of inefficiency forces the change, and that this change process is usually a painful one, which is often carried out by a different chief executive from the one who masterminded the Stage 3 entrepreneurial changes.

Chandler's classic study has subsequently been elaborated, and has also been applied to other countries. Before we look in a little detail at UK evidence for his thesis, we should consider some important developments of the strategy/structure relationship.

B. R. Scott (see Galbraith and Nathanson, 1978) identifies two types of product/market strategies and attendant structures:

1. *Integrated or 'closed system'* strategies e.g. a vertically integrated oil company. Here, although the firm may be enormous and multinational, the product flows *through* each division of the corporation to the market. Thus the activities of each division must be integrated and coordinated, which has implications for the extent of decentralisation that is possible (see Figure 11.3).
2. *The diversified or 'open' system* corporation, by contrast, in which each division serves a separate product-market. Each division can, therefore, be operated more or less independently of other divisions. (see Figure 11.4).

L. Wrigley (see Galbraith and Nathanson, 1978) refined the concept of diversification into four types of diversification strategies:

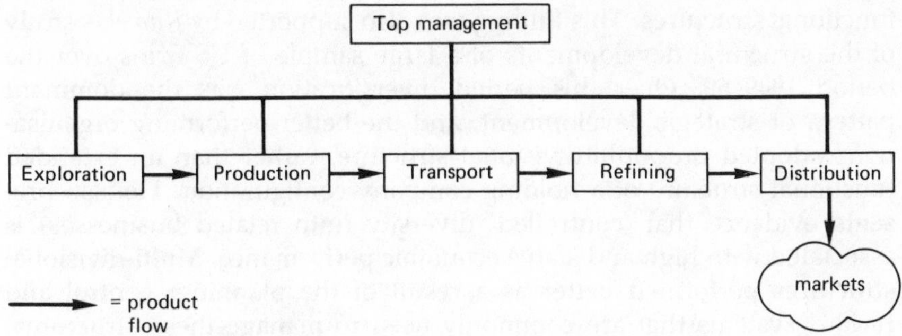

FIGURE 11.3 Integrated structure

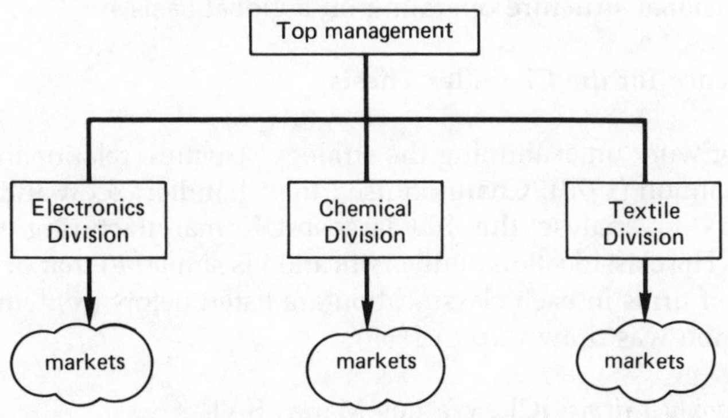

FIGURE 11.4 Diversified structure

- *single-product* businesses (more than 95 per cent sales accounted for by one product)
- *dominant-product* businesses (where one product accounts for between 70 and 95 per cent of sales)
- *related-businesses* (where more than 30 per cent of sales are outside the main business, but these businesses are related by customer, distribution channel, 'core skills' or technology)
- *unrelated business* (where more than 30 per cent is outside the main business but there are *no* connections between the diversified activities).

Wrigley found that the more diversified the strategy the greater the move towards divisional autonomy. He also confirmed the Chandler findings that single and dominant-product businesses tend to have functional structures. This finding was also supported by *Rumelt's* study of the structural developments of a large sample of US firms over the period 1949–69. Over this period diversification was the dominant pattern of strategic development, and the better-performing organisations adopted the multi-divisional structure, rather than an extended functional structure of a holding company configuration. He also presents evidence that 'controlled' diversity (into related businesses) is associated with high and stable economic performance. Multi-divisional structures performed better as a result of the planning, control and reward systems that are commonly used to manage these structures, and because the corporate management did not feel under any pressure to invest in marginal activities related to a single or dominant business, they were more or less free to invest in or abandon activities purely on the basis of their relative yields. (See Illustration 11.1 for an example of a multi-divisional structure operating on a global basis.)

UK Evidence for the Chandler Thesis

The major work on examining the strategy/structure relationship in the UK is Channon (1973). Channon used the Chandler, Scott and Wrigley framework to analyse the 100 largest UK manufacturing firms (in 1969–70). His classification of diversification is similar to that of Wrigley; example of firms in each classification are listed below (remember, this classification was drawn up in *1969*):

Single-product firms: ICL, Watney Mann, BAT
Dominant-product firms: ALCAN, British Steel Corporation, Tate & Lyle, BP, Burton
Related-product firms: Cadbury/Schweppes, Heinz, Unilever, Dunlop, Glaxo, Tube Investments.
Unrelated-Products: Rank, Reckitt & Coleman, Thomas Tilling, Standard Telephones and Cables.

The number and direction of strategy changes over the period 1950–70 are shown in Figure 11.5. The major moves were from single and dominant products to related diversifications. These moves were accompanied initially by moves from functional structures to the holding-company form, as this form is less sophisticated in terms of planning and controlling systems than the multi-divisional form. Howevers, most firms then moved from the holding-company form (that is, extreme decentralisation of decision-making) to the multi-divisional structure (some recentralisation). Channon categorised the extent and type of diversification into three groups:

ILLUSTRATION 11.1 Allied Go Global

Allied became a multinational company in 1983 with its $1.8 billion take-over of **Bendix**, a maker of, among other things, spark plugs, aircraft landing-gear and piping for nuclear-power plants. Until then Allied was a sluggish, second-league company, nearly all-American, with interests in chemicals, oil and gas. Allied wants to develop into Europe in a variety of areas: North Sea oil exploration, car brakes, typesetting machinery, chemicals, speciality chemicals, medical-diagnostic equipment and aero space. The Chief Executive, Mr Edward Hennessy is ready to spend $1 billion on the right buys.

In becoming 'global', Allied has reorganised itself centrally at its New Jersey headquarters into five core businesses: chemicals, oil and gas, car components, aerospace, and industrial technology. But it has not found a satisfactory answer to the conflict between its ambitions to organise globally and the demands of European managers for some local autonomy for European operations that take in 20 000 (mostly former Bendix) employees spread across 84 plants and sales and R & D offices. The European businesses now report to the five divisions of New Jersey. They have no overall European management to guide them.

The advantages of neatness are obvious. A disadvantage is that it is hard to motivate managers when the big decisions come to them from New Jersey over the telephone. So Mr Hennessy has been sounding out his European managers in London and Frankfurt on how Allied can delegate powers to them without losing the cohesion that it is seeking in organising itself as a global rather than a multinational company.

One possible compromise is what is known in Allied as the **Canada model**. This gives **Allied Canada** authority to organise and administer the groups' operations in Canada but requires each of the product-line managers to report to the five divisions in New Jersey. Varying the Canada model, a central European management organisation could, for example, be responsible for common purchasing, transport and training.

Meanwhile, Mr Hennessy is trying to keep everybody happy. His previous incarnation as an executive with **ITT** in Brussels taught him, he says, that local management knows best what's

ILLUSTRATION 11.1 *continued*

going on in Europe. And he promises to delegate as much authority as possible, eventually to the point of setting up a separate European board of directors. Just how that will fit in with the global structure is still anybody's guess.

(Source: *The Economist*, 12 May 1984)

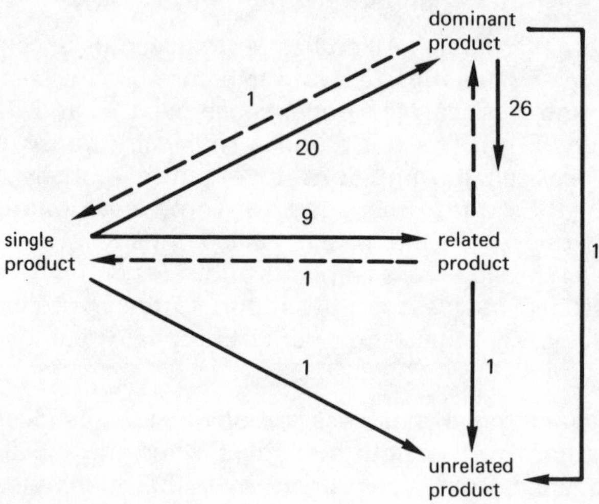

FIGURE 11.5 Number and direction of strategy changes 1950–70

Source: Channon (1973).

- *the undiversified enterprises* (for example, those firms in the drink, tobacco, power machinery, oil and metals industries)
- *the technological diversifiers*: where diversification is based on related technology or core skill (for example, chemical and engineering industries)
- *the acquisitive diversifiers*: firms that have diversified chiefly through acquisition (for example, communications, food, packaging, paper and textile industries).

For each enterprise classification Channon identified general strategic characteristics of firms in these industries and the structural features related to these characteristics.

UNDIVERSIFIED ENTERPRISES

General strategic characteristics

- High levels of concentration in the industry, achieved mainly through the acquisition of weaker competitors.
- Low industry growth, and low average profitability.
- Significant entry barriers (due to technology, capital requirements, brand loyalty, access to raw material).
- A low level of transferable technology, that is, the technology employed in the industry is not easily applied to new products.

These conditions have led to slow strategic change in these industries.

Structural features

- Most firms had multi-divisional structures based on the needs of different market segments (remember that Channon was studying *large* corporations).
- But there often existed significant interconnecting and product flows between divisions (Scott's closed system corporation).
- Integration between these connected divisions was effected through a strong central functional co-ordination.
- Many firms were vertically integrated, which has led in some to a narrowing of management perspectives, and a heavy commitment of resources to a single product.
- The moves to concentration through acquisition were initially controlled through a holding-company structure. But this was often changed to a multi-divisional structure after a change in leadership, and a decline in performance.

Thus the experience of these undiversified enterprises tends to support the Chandler thesis.

THE TECHNOLOGICAL DIVERSIFIERS

General strategic characteristics

- Initial moves to diversification were through acquisitions.
- Many companies institutionalised the strategy of diversification through engaging in extensive R & D activities.

- Although these firms' industries had low entry-barriers (through the wide range of markets served) their performance was above the average for all firms in the sample over the study period.
- A strategy of specialisation in specific market segments was common.
- Competition has increased through new entrants from home companies and imports.

Structural features

- Most firms had moved to the multi-divisional structure.
- This structural reform was frequently associated with a change in leadership or a decline in profits.
- Structural (as opposed to strategic) change was often resisted as it disturbed existing power structures.

THE ACQUISITIVE DIVERSIFIERS

General strategic characteristics

- Some firms acquired other firms because they were unable to develop new products internally.
- Some diversified because vertical integration had failed to protect their existing markets.
- Metals firms diversified to escape dependency on a narrow product range.
- Industry growth rates were generally low, as were entry barriers, which led to a high level of competition.

Structural features

- These attempts at diversification rarely led to improve profit performance because of deficiencies in structure, skills and controls.
- Therefore, the holding-company structure usually gave way to the multi-divisional structure.
- But most firms still had relatively small headquarters and less than adequate planning and control systems (especially in firms with a dominant personality as chief executive).

Channon's general conclusions were as follows:

1. Competition has increased in the UK since 1950 (because of the break-up cartels, the entry of foreign companies, imports, the

dissolution of captive colonial markets and new technologies leading to new products and markets).
2. The response to increasing competition has been concentration (for example, aircrafts, cars, brewing) and diversification.
3. The functional form is inadequate for managing diversity; and the initial response to diversifiction – the holding-company structure is also inadequate (because of a lack of central guidance, unnecessary internal rivalry, duplication and inefficiency).
4. The multi-divisional form has been increasingly adopted: 8 per cent of top 100 firms in 1950, 70 per cent in 1970.
5. There has not, as yet, been a wholesale adoption of the US style of divisional structure: there is little use of performance-related rewards, some functions are still centralised (for instance, marketing) and there is little generation of internal competition to allow the headquarters to act as a capital market. However, Channon expects the full US style of multi-divisional structure to be adopted as competitive pressures force companies to adopt the best 'fit' between strategy and structure.

Similar studies to Channon's have been carried out in other European countries: Pooley-Dyas in France, Thanheiser in Germany and Pavan in Italy (see Galbraith and Nathanson 1978). All these studies confirm the trend to increasing diversification, but the adoption of the multi-divisional structure has not been undertaken at a uniform rate in all countries. In France, for example, although firms have diversified there has not been a large-scale move to adopt the multi-divisional structure. Franko, (1974) who specifically studied multi-national companies found that many European multi-nationals stayed with a functional structure. These results would seem to contradict Chandler's thesis. However, the key variable that is absent in situations where the move to multi-divisional form has not beeen adopted is *competition*. Where firms are diversifying under quasi-monopoly conditions the *status quo* structure offers the solution with the least resistance. And, where firms continue to be profitable there is no pressure to reorganise the structure to 'fit' the new situation. Hence, these studies have added an important postscript to the Chandler thesis: structure follows strategy only when structure makes a difference to performance. In the absence of declining performance, the existing (inefficient) structure will prevail. The relationship between strategy, structure and performance that these studies have thrown up are described schematically in Figure 11.6.

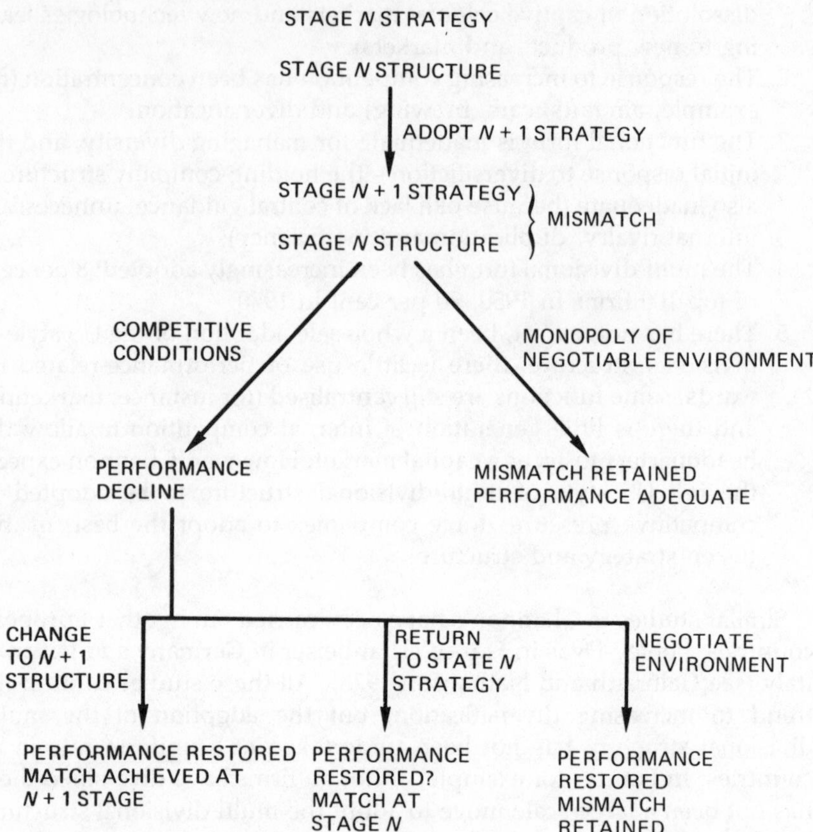

FIGURE 11.6 Schematic of possible strategy, structure and performance relations

Source: Galbraith and Nathanson (1978).

11.4 Greiner's developmental model

Greiner (1972) has devised a model relating growth rate, age and size to five stages of structural and process development which a firm must pass through to sustain appropriate performance levels. Hence, his model serves both a descriptive and prescriptive function. He identifies five dimensions of organisation development.

1. *Age* – the important impact of age is the increasing tendency, as time passes, for attitudes and behaviour to become institutionalised, thus building up resistance to change.

2. *Size* – Considerable organisational problems of communication, co-ordination and interdependence.
3. *Stages of evolution* – these are patterns of management which remain more or less stable and where only small changes occur, 'fine tuning' management processes to the tasks facing the firm.
4. *Stages of revolution* – these are periods of substantial turbulence and considerable upheaval in the organisation, where old practices are put under pressure by new demands created by increasing size and age. The crisis is either resolved, whereupon the firm proceeds to further growth, or it is unresolved, leading to stagnation or maybe even the organisation's death.
5. *Growth rate of the industry* – high industry growth increases the rate of change in the firm, and, where industry growth has led to substantial profitability, an evolutionary stage can be extended. This concept is similar to the situation of the firm facing a 'monopoly of its negotiable environment' in Figure 11.6 – in this instance, a mismatch between size and structure can be tolerated because of high profitability. However, if the firm's structure moved onto a matched strategy – structure situation profitability may be increased even further.

Figure 11.7 illustrates the five phases of growth, and the evolutionary and revolutionary stages related to the age and size of the firm. The growth rate of the industry is represented by the slope of the line – the steeper the slope the higher the growth rate. Each evolutionary period has a *dominant management style* which is used to achieve growth (such as delegation in phase 3) and each revolutionary period has a *dominant management problem* that must be resolved for growth to continue (for instance, the crisis of control at the end of phase 3). Each phase is both an *effect* of the previous phase, and a *cause* of the next. Briefly, the evolutionary and revolutionary concerns at each phase are:

Phase 1 *Growth through creativity*

Energies directed to product development and selling. Close-knit, committed team with control exerted through immediate customer feedback.

Crisis of leadership

As size increases, employees cannot be managed through informal processes. Need for manufacturing and financial expertise. Leader under stress.

Phase 2 *Growth through direction*

Crisis of leadership resolved through 'professionalising' the organisation: specialisation, functional structure; systems for

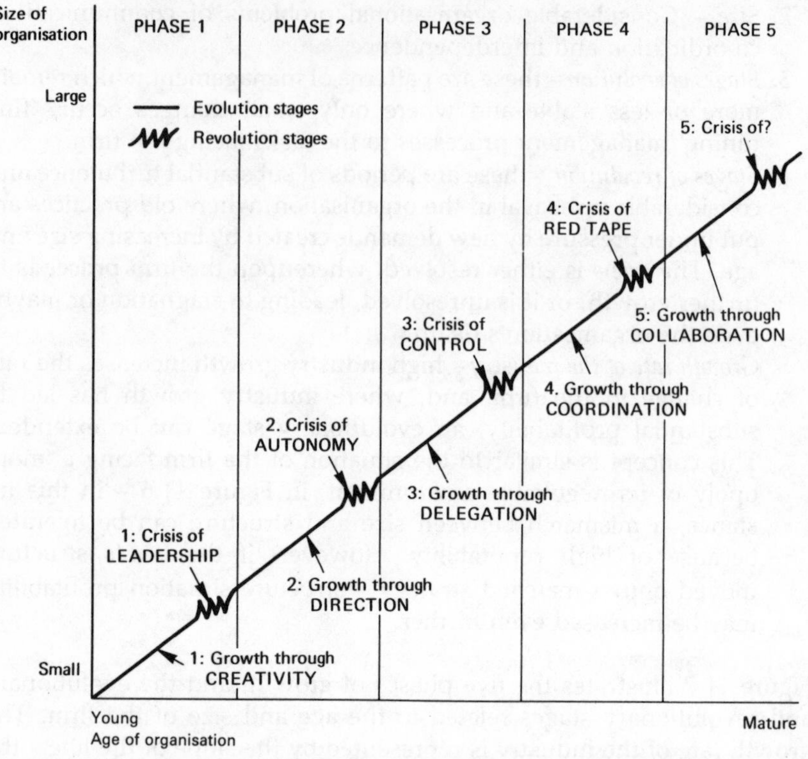

FIGURE 11.7 The five phases of growth

Source: Greiner (1972) p. 38.

budgeting and inventory; work standards adopted; formalising communication; decision-making moves up the expanding hierarchy.

Autonomy crisis

Employees feel restricted by hierarchy, the over-centralisation of decision-making and the inability to exercise initiative.

Phase 3 *Growth through delegation*

A move to decentralisation: more responsibility to plant managers and sales managers; profit centres and bonuses used to motivate; top management reduced to 'management by exception' and strategic issues.

Control crisis

Top executives feel they are losing control, and parochial attitudes are growing in sub-divisions.

Phase 4 *Growth through co-ordination*

Formal systems for achieving greater co-ordination are adopted: merge decentralised units into products groups; formal planning procedures (such as corporate planning); increase in staff concerned with company-wide control; managers encouraged to take a corporate perspective.

Crisis of red tape

A lack of confidence between staff ('out of touch') and line ('unco-operative'), and between headquarters and field units; a proliferation of systems; innovation stifled.

Phase 5 *Growth through collaboration*

Red tape crisis overcome through strong interpersonal collaboration; social control and self-discipline replace formal, external control; teams and matrix structures; real-time information systems.

Greiner anticipates that phase 5 may be concluded by a crisis of 'psychological saturation' where employees are exhausted by teamwork demands and the need for innovation. He flies a phase-6 kite which may involve a dual organisation structure – a 'habit' structure for daily work routines, and a 'reflective' structure for stimulating perspectives and personal enrichment (including flexible hours, revolving jobs, sabbaticals, relaxation and sport activities).

The model can have a prescriptive role to play. For example, managers may be able to anticipate the structural and process features of the next phase of growth, and encourage the development of key skills and strengths which will be required in that phase. Moreover, progression from one phase to the next is not automatic, managers must consciously act to move the organisation through the revolutionary stage to the higher phase of evolution. Perhaps the organisation may benefit from encouraging diversity in skills and processes, which although not obviously related to the current phase of development may well be vital for future success. See Illustration 11.2 for an example of the evolution of organisation structures in the aerospace industry.

11.5 The technical system

The third contingency factor, the technical system, refers to the techniques, processes, equipment and skills employed in the operating core. We would, presumably, expect the structures and processes *within* the core to be determined to a large extent by the technical system, but there is evidence to suggest that the influence of the technical system on structure reaches all parts of the organisation.

Trist and Bamforth's study of changes in the technical system in the UK coal industry (see Pugh, 1984, p. 394) from the 'hand-got' method,

ILLUSTRATION 11.2 Task and Structure Relationships in the Aerospace Industry

Task	*Structure*
Rudimentary aircraft (Wright Flyer)	Simple structure. Simultaneous design and production of aircraft. *Size: 2*
Aircraft become more complex	Separation of design from production with the chief designer in overall control. Still a small and informal organisation. *Size: 10*
Problems with particular aspects of design	Emergence of specialists in structures, aerodynamics and weights. Also specialist supplies of engines and materials. Chief designer requires competence in all aspects of project. *Size: 50–100*
Second World War brings need for mass production. Developments in jet and rocket propulsion. Concern for reliability	Mass production techniques required: developments in jig and tool design, quality control, value engineering, production engineering, liaison engineers. Designers no longer omnicompetent — loss of status and authority. Problems of recruiting specialists, increasing dependence on specialists. Coordination problems of a large functional organisation. *Size: 500–1000*
Multiple projects	Sequential nature of design process replaced by management of many simultaneous projects. Matrix structure solution: multi-specialist project teams led by designer. Problems of dual authority and supply of designers with sufficient breadth of experience for effective leadership. *Size: 1000–5000*

Rapidly accelerating project costs. Increasing international competition.	Mergers and concentration in the industry to share development costs. Need to integrate merged companies: initially a holding-company approach with relatively autonomous divisions; then to the 'true' multidivisional structure. Co-ordination problems: harmonisation of practices, project leadership, duplication. Emergence of specialist sectors: aircraft, engines, helicopters, guided weapons, space engineering
Massive increases in project development costs and aircraft complexity. Need for standardisation and interoperability of equipment	Need for international collaboration. Requires negotiated agreements; clear, precise task definition; good interpersonal relationships Problems of suspicion, dependence, fear of losing engineering capabilities Some solutions: Co-location of international teams; supernational bodies to provide international standards; CAD/CAM facilities intersite communication and reintegration of design and production

(Source: Stamper, J. T., 1984)

using picks and shovels, to the 'long wall' system of large-scale cutting-machines) revealed the complex interrelationships between the technical system and the social system. And, following their study, Joan Woodward (see Pugh, 1984, p. 52) undertook a survey of 100 manufacturing firms in Essex, in an attempt to determine relationships between structural variables (for example, span of control, extent of formalisation, proportion of administrative staff) and performance. She established that variability in structural variables is strongly correlated with production technology, and that high performing firms had structures close to the median of all firms (in the survey) in that type of industry. Production systems can be classified as follows:

Unit and small batch production

1. Production of units to consumer requirements
2. Production of prototypes
3. Fabrication of large equipments in stages
4. Production of small batches to order

Large batch and mass production

5. Production of large batches
6. Production of large batches on assembly line
7. Mass production

Process production

8. Intermittent production of chemicals in multi-process plant
9. Continuous-flow production of liquids, gases, etc.

Production systems with higher numbers in this classification have increasingly impersonal control mechanisms. In unit-production control is exercised by managers directly in touch with operatives (or by the operatives themselves); impersonal systems devised by analysts in the technostructure prevail in the mass-production organisations; and in process-industries control mechanisms are built into the process machinery. Moreover, the control problems facing the lower numbered production systems are more complex because of the nature of the tasks undertaken: novel problems, the need to co-ordinate diverse activities, the inability to schedule for smooth production runs.

Woodward also identified another control dimension in addition to the personal–impersonal continuum, the degree of fragmentation in the control system (see Pugh, 1984). At one extreme (in process industries, for example) we would find a single, integrated control system, at the other extreme would be the situation often experienced in batch and mass production industries where there is a variety of often conflicting control influences. Demands on production personnel to reduce costs, improve quality, shorten delivery dates are often not reconcilable, hence these fragmented systems can generate considerable conflict within the organisation. These two control system dimensions can be related to production technology, as in Table 11.2.

Particular relationships were established by Woodward between the production technology and the structure and processes of the organisation:

Unit and small batch production Firms using these technologies were often engaged in the production of *ad hoc* and non-standard products. They tended to have organic structures, with small work teams and first-line management working closely together. Co-ordination was

Table 11.2 Types of control system related to production technology

	Integrated System	Fragmented System
Personal Control	*Entrepreneurial unit, and small batch organisations* Control conflicts reconciled by owner/manager	*Batch and mass production in small organisations* More people involved in setting control criteria
Impersonal Control	*Process production* Controls built into system	*Large batch and mass production in large organisations* Controls set by technostructure and other functional interests, remote from operating core.

effected through mutual adjustment between operators, or by direct supervision and, because of the need for close liaison between sales, product development and production activities there tended to be little evidence of narrow functional specialisation with, for example, sales people possessing considerable technical expertise. Thus, to use Mintzberg's classification, these firms had very short middle-lines and small (or non-existent) technostructures.

Large batch and mass production In firms with these technologies, standardisation (of work, skills and outputs) was extensive. Control was achieved through designing highly routinised and low-skill jobs, hence supervisors were capable of controlling large numbers of operators. As a consequence, these firms had highly-developed technostructures. It is in these firms that Woodward found most of the 'classical' principles of organisation put into practice (for instance, well-defined job descriptions, clear hierarchies, written communication, unity of command, clear separation of line and staff). Because of the extreme degree of standardisation achieved in mass-production firms, the major task of the management is to deal with the few exceptional circumstances that disturb the smooth running of the systems and procedures devised by the technostructure.

Woodward identified three areas of conflict in mass production firms:

1. Conflict between the demands of the technical system and the social needs of the people who work the system.

2. Conflict between the short-term views of production managers, and the longer-term perspectives of the strategic apex.
3. Conflict between line personnel (who are at the heart of the organisation, and have power and information) and staff personnel (who possess expertise, but lack formal power and some vital pieces of information).

As a result of these conflicts (especially the first source) mass-production firms are obsessed with controlling workers – through direct supervision, threats and punishments. And because of the domination of the operating core in these firms, this control mentality spills upwards to infect other parts of the superstructure. The strength of this influence on the rest of the structure can be seen where organisations have been able to *automate* their operating core: in these firms, as the major source of conflict has been removed, the concern for controls, rules and regulations can give way to more informal and organic structural forms. Process firms illustrate the point very well.

Process production Process production technology is found in firms engaged in the continuous production of, for example, steel, chemicals, gases, petroleum. The key organisational feature of these firms is the almost complete absence of workers tied directly to the pace of production, in fact if one visits process firms the immediate impression is that of an abandoned plant! The operating core is almost totally automated – and whereas in mass-production firms rules, standards and control systems are applied to people, in process technology they are applied to machinery. This fundamental difference in the nature of the operating core transforms the superstructure dramatically:

- Unskilled workers in the core are replaced by much fewer skilled technicians who maintain the technical system.
- Line or staff distinctions become blurred, as there is no obvious 'line'-management function of controlling workers in the operating core.
- The technostructure is concerned with designing the technical system, rather than the control of the work of others.
- The structures tend to be organic, with small teams and more intimate and informal relationships between managers and managed.
- Because of the highly skilled nature of the jobs in process firms, they tend to engage in extensive training.
- Co-ordination is mainly achieved through mutual adjustment and the use of liaison devices.
- Decision-making power is decentralised to the experts.

Burack (cited in Mintzberg, 1979) suggests that in advanced production systems there is an increasing tendency toward *managerial* innovations rather than technological innovation, increasing technical complexity leads to increasing organisational complexity (more specialisation, control technologies and support functions). Moreover, *Thompson and Bates* (see Mintzberg, 1979) demonstrate that automation (increasing technical complexity and, more critically, specificity) increased the speed and precision of tasks at the expense of increased rigidity. Processes that are automated are less able to tolerate disturbances.

J. D. Thompson

Thompson's book *Organisations in Action* (Thompson, 1967) develops his earlier work with Bates. We consider his views here as they provide a link between technology as a contingency factor, and the impact of the firm's environment on its structure. Thompson proposes that:

> *Organisations under norms of rationality seek to place their boundaries around those activities which if left to the task environment would be crucial contingencies.*

That is, organisations often include within their areas of responsibility, activities which could be performed by outside agencies, without 'damage to the major mission of the organisation'.

Thus, for example, a hotel's major purpose would be the provision of rooms and meals, and laundry would be expected to be sent outside; however, many hotels operate their own laundry, to ensure an efficient service and a regular supply of clean linen.

Thompson makes this point to show the direction in which a lot of 'domains' are expanding. He then takes this point further by saying that we can be even more precise about the direction of expansion of organisations, depending on the type of technology. He proposes that:

> *Organisations employing long-linked technologies seek to expand their domains through vertical integration.*

Vertical integration refers to the combination within a single organisation of successive stages of production, which could be incorporated in a separate organisation. Thompson gives the example of car manufacturers developing mass production, then going to establish channels for mass distribution, and acquiring capacity to make parts and accessories, so they could be sure of having supplies. He points out that although vertical integration is most feasible in manufacuring industries, it does happen in other organisations such as hospitals, which not only provide health care, but also train medical personnel for the future.

Thompson recognises the limitiations of vertical integration – the most important one being when the activities before, or after major mission 'fan out'. For example, it would be extremely difficult for Woolworths to manufacture all the products sold in its stores.
Thompson's next proposition is that:

> *Organisations employing mediating technologies, seek to expand their domains by increasing the populations served.*

He gives the example of insurance companies who must find enough clients to prevent any one loss from destroying the coverage of the others. Sears Roebuck started out by using mail order only, then went into retailing operations when the population moved into urban areas and ceased to be dependent on catalogue shopping.
The next proposition is that:

> *Organisations employing intensive technologies . . . seek to expand their domains by incorporating the object worked on.*

So where the technology is expected to produce a change in the client, in for instance a drug-dependency unit, the organisation seeks to place its boundaries around the client, by keeping him within its own environment. This reduces the possibility of contamination of the client by outside factors which reduce or negate the effectiveness of the organisation's efforts. In extreme cases, such as in mental hospitals, these boundaries completely surround the client, and the organisation becomes an institution.

Having shown how organisations incorporate what would otherwise be serious contingencies, Thompson goes on to look at the question of balance. He argues that organisations often find that they have acquired capacity in excess of what is needed to fulfil their main purpose. The problem arises because all the capacities acquired are not necessarily 'continuously divisible'. Vertically-integrated organisations, for instance, may have greater capacity of some production stages than at others. This could be because of a merger with another company not geared up to the same rate of operations, or because bigger-than necessary production units are needed to produce the required number of units in a given time. So for example, to have a machine which will make fifty units on time, may mean having one capable of producing 200. There is also the problem that the costs of acquiring these capacities are so great that the organisation must commit itself to using them in the future. This again, can lead to imbalance in capacity. This leads to his next proposition that:

> *Multicomponent organisations . . .will seek to grow until the least reducible component is approximately fully occupied.*

So for example, car manufacturers with distributive capacity in excess of output, will increase output. As Thompson points out, this assumes that the market will take this increase in output, and he recognises that there must be a balanced output and demand.

Thompson then goes on to say that:

> *Organisations with capacity in excess of what the task environment supports will seek to enlarge their domains.*

A widespread response to excess capacity is diversification – the development of new products and services, in other words, the expansion of domain.

Thompson accepts that some organisations do not need to incorporate vital activities, because they have the power to ensure availability when needed. Another reason why firms may not expand their domains in this way, is because they lack the resources to do so – all methods of incorporation tend to be extremely expensive. Thompson recognises that integration may not happen or be slow to happen, simply because the necessary redesign of the organisation may be 'slow and halting'.

Thompson identifies three types of interdependence between units or activities in an organisation. The most straightforward type of interdependence is *pooled*, where two units share the same pool of resources (money, space, management expertise). The second type is *sequential* interdependence where work moves in a sequence from one unit to the next. This is a more critical relationship than pooled interdependence, moreover, sequentially interdependent units also display pooled interdependence. The third and most critical type is *reciprocal* interdependence, where, for example, components are required to move from unit *A* to unit *B* and back to unit *A* again. Reciprocal interdependence incorporates both pooled and sequential interdependence. So, firms will seek to control receiprocal interdependencies first, then sequential and then the less critical pooled interdependencies. Thompson offers this theory as an explanation of Chandler's three stages of development:

Stage I The unifunctional firm incorporates the reciprocal interdependencies within the organisation.

Stage II Sequentially interdependent activities are incorporated through vertical integration.

Stage III Excess capacity caused by the high investment into critical functions leads to diversification into new domains which can share the under-utilised technology. Diversification creates pooled interdependence among units sharing a common technology or distribution channel.

11.6 Environment

Lawrence and Lorsch's research was aimed at determining what kind of organisation deals successfully with different environmental conditions (Lawrence and Lorsch, 1976). They employed two central concepts in their analysis:

Differentiation: A difference in cognitive and emotional orientation between managers. The four dimensions of differentiation being: time-orientation; the orientation to particular goals; interpersonal orientation; and formality of structure.
Integration: The state of collaboration that exists among departments that are required to achieve unity of effort by the demands of the environment.

The task facing an orgnisation is to facilitate integration without sacrificing the degree of differentiation required to succeed in the environment. In their study Lawrence and Lorsch compared companies competing in different industries (plastics, containers, foods) to see how integration and differentiation were achieved and to establish which firms proved to be more successful than others in their industry. For example, firms in the plastics industry faced considerable technical uncertainty about products and processes because of continually-emerging scientific developments. The functions within the firm which were more vulnerable to this uncertainty were fundamental research and applied research. They discovered that these functions were significantly differentiated from the sales and production fuctions on the four dimensions of differentiation (for example, fundamental researchers work to a long time-horizon, sales people to a short).

Most successful firms achieved a degree of differentiation that matched, or fitted, the requirements of the environment. Greater environmental diversity and uncertainty demand greater differentiation. And firms (such as the container industry) facing less uncertain environments were required to display the least amount of differentiation.

Success demands not only the required levels of differentiation, but also the appropriate degree of integration. Integrating processes include 'good' relations between functions and effective procedures for consultation. They found that forcing a decision was more effective than

TABLE 11.3 A two-dimensional categorisation of environments and organization structures

	Stable	*Dynamic*
Complex	Decentralised Bureaucratic (standardisation of skills) 1	Decentralised Organic (mutual adjustment) 2
Simple	Centralised Bureaucratic (standardisation of work processes) 3	Centralised Organic (direct supervision) 4

Source: H. Mintzberg, *Structure in Fives: Designing Effective Organisations*, p. 144.

smoothing over differences when conflicting views arose. Those firms that valued the maintenance of good relations above the need to make good decisions demonstrated below-average performance. (See Chapter 12 on Groupthink).

Lawrence and Lorsch also ascertained that the locus of influence to resolve conflict should be at the level where the required knowledge about the environment is available. The more uncertain the environment, the lower in the organisation structure this locus tended to be. Hence, environmental uncertainty demands a degree of decentralisation of decision-making. Finally – a point about power in the organisation – they observed that the influence of fuctions varies depending upon which function is vitally involved in the dominant issues posed by the environment.

Mintzberg has developed Lawrence and Lorsch's findings, and has attempted to synthesise their and other writers' work (for example, the work of Burns, Child, Hunt, Chandler and Galbraith) on the relationship between structure and environment. He uses two environmental dimensions: complexity and stability to generate the four states of the environment shown in Table 11.3. *A dynamic* environment exerts unexpected, unanticipated circumstances upon the firm. It makes the firm's work uncertain or unpredictable. A *stable* environment is highly predictable, thus permitting a great deal of standardisation (of work processes, skills and/or outputs) to take place within the organisation.

An environment is *complex* to the extent that it requires the organisation to have a great deal of sophisticated knowledge about products, customers, etc. It becomes *simple* when that knowledge can be broken down into easily comprehended components. Mintzberg presents a set of hypotheses about the environment which are supported, to a greater or lesser extent, by empirical research:

1. *The more dynamic the environment, the more organic the structure.* This is supported by the research of Burns and Stalker, Lawrence and Lorsch, Chandler and Sayles, and others. In a stable environment, the firm can standardise ('bureaucratise' or 'mechanise') its operating core, and in extremely stable circumstances, standardisation can spread upwards, away from the core to all parts of the structure (see Table 11.3, quadrants 1 and 3).

   Unpredictability, however, means that the firm cannot rely on standardisation as a co-ordinating mechanism, instead mutual adjustment and direct supervision must be used. There is evidence to suggest that the demands of a dynamic environment will drive the structure towards an organic state even when other contingency factors (large size, a regulating technical system) are pulling the firm towards a bureaucratic structure (see Table 11.3, quadrants 2 and 4).

2. *The more complex the environment, the more decentralised the structure.* Lawrence and Lorsch's plastics firms faced a complex and dynamic environment, as do Boeing, the subject of Galbraith's study (see Galbraith and Nathanson,1978 p. 49–51). Complexity, as Galbraith points out, means that one brain cannot cope with all the information needed to make all the decisions. So the chief executive must pass on some decision-making power to subordinates. If the firm is facing a complex but *stable* environment, then, as stability tends to lead to bureaucracy, we would expect to find a particular type of decentralisation emerging. These firms will use standardisation of skills (see Table 11.3, quadrant 1) as the prime co-ordinating mechanism, for example, in the professional bureaucracy (a hospital). However, if the environment is complex and *dynamic*, an organic means of co-ordination is required – that is, mutual adjustment (Table 11.3 quadrant 2).

   See Illustrations 11.2 and 11.3 for examples of environment/structure relationships.

11.7 Congruence or 'fit'

For an organisation to be effectively structured the structures and processes should *fit* the contingency factors. Furthermore, the organisational design parameters themselves should be internally consistent,

ILLUSTRATION 11.3 Restructuring in the Computer Industry

A. *Changes at Hewlett-Packard*

Hewlett-Packard, one of America's largest and most innovative electronics companies, is shuffling its top management to make selling its products as important as dreaming up new ones. The company's board has just agreed to form a new marketing group on a par with H-P's other groups, now shrunk from five to three, and organised more in tune with markets than machines.

Marketing matters more to computer companies now because of the switch in demand from large, expensive machines understood only by experts to mass-produced personal and portable computers. Companies run by engineers and innovators, like Hewlett-Packard and **Digital Equipment Corporation**, found the change painful. They were slow to give marketing people more power.

H-P began to pull its rambling computer operations together in late 1982. Without a lead from the top, different parts of the company had developed their own small computers. Salesmen pushing these products got in each other's way and customers often found that new machines were not compatible with other H-P products.

Hewlett-Packard's shuffle, the first since 1970, is meant to make it easier to market computers in conjunction with the company's electronics instruments. Though the company says that its two founders, Mr David Packard (Chairman) and Mr William Hewlett (Vice-Chairman), are not planning to retire yet, the latest reshuffle makes this look more likely.

(Source: *The Economist*, 21 July 1984)

B. *NCR*

In 1972, **NCR** lost $60m and was saved from going to the wall by Mr William Anderson, then Chairman, who retired in April 1984. Like the Swiss watchmakers who allowed Japanese companies to steal the digital-watch market, NCR failed to switch quickly enough from mechanical cash registers (in which it led the world) to the new electronics.

ILLUSTRATION 11.3 *continued*

Mr Anderson forced NCR into electronics. He cut the workforce from 90 000 to 63 000 and in 1976 he hired Charles Exley from **Burroughs**, a big rival, as his heir-apparent. Together they squeezed everything to improve margins, sold off unwanted old businesses like office paper, and started acquiring new expertise. NCR aims to deliver a new generation for virtually every main product line by 1985. They also aim to become the industry's most cost-effective producer.

New savings can come only from more efficient management, collaborating with other producers on standard equipment and buying in components when it makes commercial sense. To this end, NCR has been reorganised into seventeen profit centres, reporting to a four-man office of the chief executive responsible for overall strategy. This decentralisation aims to encourage in-house entrepreneurs and to speed new products to the market. It used to take NCR up to two years to turn an idea into a commercial product.

(Source: *The Economist*, 27 October 1984)

they should match each other. Particular combinations of design parameters appear to relate consistently enough together to enable us to identify commonly occurring configurations, such as Burns and Stalker's mechanistic and organic structures, the traditional bureaucracy, the divisionalised structure, the 'professional bureaucracy', the matrix structure. But these structural types may prove to be too generalised to provide specific guidance for resolving particular strategy – structure issues. So, although we would not recommend a piecemeal approach to the solution of structural problems, there is an argument for searching for local consistency among design parameters, and for adjusting the structure in an incremental way (as indeed most strategic changes tend to be of an incremental nature). Illustration 11.4 explores some structural issues resulting from a strategic decision to improve product quality.

Mintzberg has postulated four 'intermediate variables' which can help in cutting through the complexities of the relationships between contingency factors and the design parameters.

1. *Comprehensibility of the work* – how easy is it to understand the organisation's work:

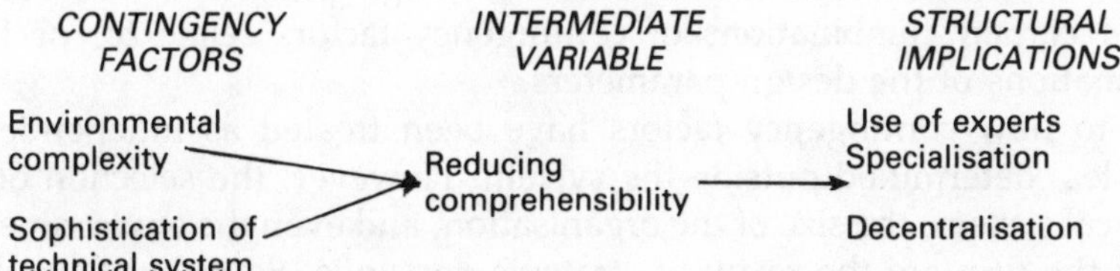

2. *Predictability of the work* – prior knowledge of the work the organisation must do:

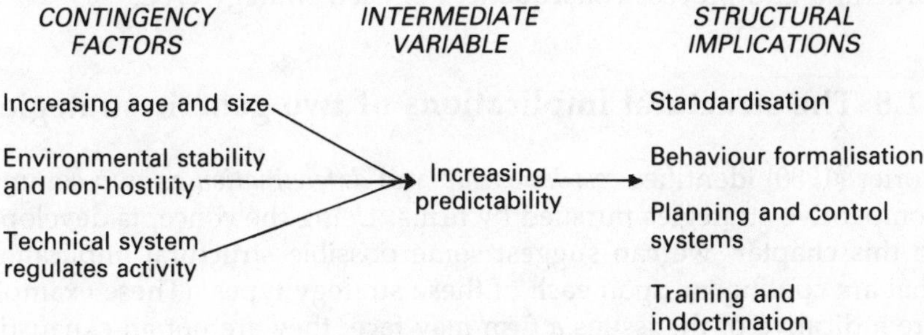

3. *Diversity of work* –the variety of the work the organisation has to do:

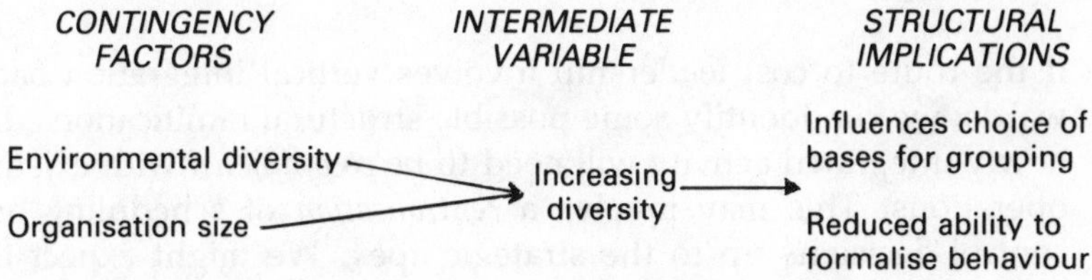

4. *Speed of Response* – how quickly the organisation most respond to the environment in order to survive:

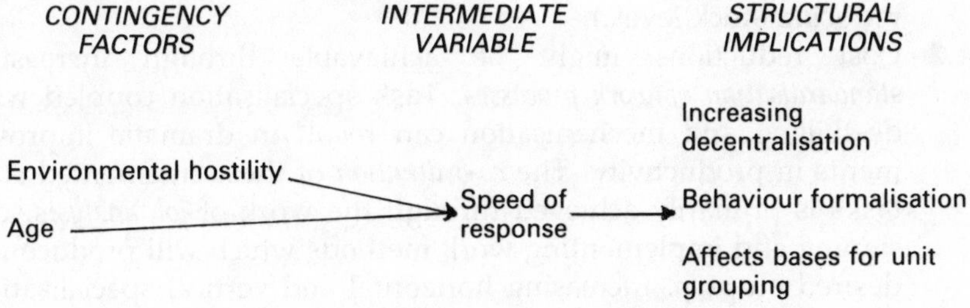

So each intermediate variable is determined by particular configurations of the contingency factors and, in turn, the state of the intermediate variable determines the state of the design parameters. In other words, certain combinations of contingency factors relate to, or fit, combinations of the design parameters.

Up to now contingency factors have been treated as independent variables, determined outside the system. However, the selection of a technical system, the size of the organisation, and even the environment facing the firm are the result of strategic decisions. So rather than the contingency factors being outside the control of the management, they can be viewed as an output of past strategic decisions.

We shall now consider two general strategic thrusts and the possible structural and process consequences of each strategy type.

11.8 The structural implications of two generic strategies

Porter (1980) identifies *cost leadership* and *differentiation* as two common competitive strategies pursued by firms. Using the concepts developed in this chapter, we can suggest some possible structural implications that are contingent upon each of these strategy types. (These examples are indicative of the issues a firm may face; they are not an exhaustive treatment).

Cost leadership

- If the route to cost leadership involves vertical integration backwards, we can identify some possible structural ramifications: the newly-integrated activity will need to be *co-ordinated* with existing operations. This may involve a *centralisation* of scheduling and control decisions up to the strategic apex. We might expect the introduction of *standardised* procedures for controlling the flow of material from one stage to the next, and the stability of the relationship between the *sequentially interdependent* process should permit the introduction of cost-reducing systems (for example reducing stock levels).
- Cost reductions might be achievable through increasing *standardisation of work processes*. Task specialisation coupled with de-skilling and mechanisation can result in dramatic improvements in productivity. The *co-ordination* of these fragmented subtasks is primarily achieved through the work of *job analysts*, designing and implementing work methods which will produce the desired outputs. Increasing horizontal and vertical specialisation

ILLUSTRATION 11.4 Structural Implications of a Strategic Decision

We now consider how this framework for analysing structure can help in the implementation of strategies. As we have seen in this chapter, much of the literature on the relationship of structure to strategy focuses on the more 'macro' issues such as growth (including multi-divisional structures, and the multinational operations). However, we have also seen that strategic decisions are part and parcel of all firms regardless of their size and complexity; that strategic decisions can take many forms, and that they are not just about product–market relationships. So, in this section, we shall explore the structural implications of a fairly straightforward decision. We will explore in a little detail some of the structural options open to a firm considering a strategy of improving product quality.

Having decided that quality improvement is desirable, the management must then decided upon the means to reach this objective. Suppose that two alternative approaches were considered, one we will call the mechanistic approach, the other the organic approach. There is considerable disagreement among the management group about which alternative to select.

The table below describes the existing structure in terms of the design parameters. A picture emerges of a rather traditional structure in which the workers in the operating core are controlled by procedures and the exercise of authority, and where they are actively discouraged from communicating. Quality is controlled by a separate group inspecting the workers' output; a 'safety net' control system which tries to ensure that even if the workers do make a lot of rubbish, only 'quality' products should reach the customer.

Quality improvement *within* this existing structure may involve some of the following measures:

1. Tightening up inspection procedures. Perhaps increase sample sizes, perhaps introduce more in-process quality checks (for instance, inspect the product at more stages in its manufacture).
2. Redirect the payment-by-results system to one based on quality as well as quantity produced.

ILLUSTRATION 11.4 *continued*

3. Examine work instructions and specifications in order to identify any errors.
4. Separate out the inspection department to make it independent of the production manager. This would avoid pressures being put on the inspection staff to give concessions on sub-standard items in order to achieve a production deadline.

These and other possible measures are merely extensions of the existing state of the design parameters. They are likely, therefore, to meet with little resistance as they are congruent with the prevailing organisation culture.

However, suppose that a group of 'Young Turks' see this strategic problem as a means to change the organisation's structure, processes and culture towards a more organic form. Improving quality through non-mechanistic means may involve changes to certain key design parameters. These changes are listed in the right-hand column below.

This 'organic' approach represents a major shift in most of the design parameters. Moreover, it is likely that these changes cannot be made in a piecemeal fashion for the approach to work. Therefore, in seeking such a radical shift our 'Young Turks' are likely to meet massive resistance from entrenched customs, attitudes, systems and general organisational inertia.

CONTRASTING APPROACHES TO QUALITY

Structural Variable	*Existing Structure*	*'Organic' Solution*
Co-ordinating Mechanisms	Standardisation of work Standardisation of outputs	Same, plus some mutual adjustment
Specialisation	Extensive horizontal and vertical specialisation	Move away from specialisation to introduce quality control activities within the operative's job description
Training and Indoctrination	Largely semi- and unskilled work in operating core.	Required for acceptance of new work practices;

	Little indoctrination	changing attitudes of operatives towards quality responsibility; changing supervisors attitudes towards operatives
Behaviour Formalisation	Extensive. Rigidly defined jobs, methods, etc.	A relaxation of rigidities in job demarcations required
Grouping	Functional specialisation. Operating core split into: machine shop, treatments, fabrication, stores, inspection	Requires dispersal of 'inspection' department, staff to machine shops, etc. Establishment of 'Quality Assurance' department
Unit Size	Large groupings with wide spans of control in operating core	Creation of smaller groups to tackle quality problems
Planning and Control Systems	Separate production planning and control department, Inspection department, controls quality	Requires a shift in quality control philosophy from inspecting *products* to assessing the *systems* that produce the products
Liaison Devices	Few needed for co-ordination	Project leaders required to co-ordinate cross-functional product-related quality action teams
Decentralisation	Limited	A shift in quality decision-making from specialists to operatives and first-line managers
Informal Communication	Officially discouraged	An acknowledgement of the value of informal communication in improving the quality of decision-making, morale and the atmosphere of the organisation

also has the effect of *formalising* and *bureaucratising* the structure. Perhaps a small *informally* managed structure may develop into a rigid, highly authoritarian *mechanistic* structure as the operating core is transformed from *small batch* production to *mass production*.

- Cost-reduction in *process* industries may only be achievable through operating the optimum size of plant at somewhere near maximum utilisation. So the emphasis shifts to the *technostructure* where forecasting skills (to ensure that capacity matches future demand) and process-engineering expertise are required to achieve economical operation. A highly sophisticated *integrated control system* is required, which may well be designed into the plant. In process industries, where the *operating core* can be automated, high and sustained capacity utilisation can be achieved without the need for intense supervision of labour (and the ramifications of such a 'control mentality' for the rest of the superstructure).
- Cost reduction achieved through *standardisation of outputs* require close *liaison* between designers, engineers and production management. Liaison may be effected through the use of *integrating managers* or the setting up of *product teams*.
- Cost savings may be secured through the accumulation of experience over time. Good practices must be retained in the organisation through effective record-keeping and through *training* and *indoctrination*. Staff must be encouraged to stay with the organisation, which may involve designing career structures and maintaining an attractive working environment (including appropriate *management styles*, *decentralisation* of decision-making, *delegation*, etc).

Differentiation

- A route to product differentiation for a particular firm might be to engage in fundamental and applied research. We would expect these departments to be highly *differentiated* from other functional areas such as production, and marketing, which then poses the problem of *integrating* these diverse activities so as to achieve the overall task. Hence, strong *co-ordination* may be required between the research departments and the marketing people to ensure that the developing products will meet a perceived niche in the market. *Project teams* can aid this process, or the firm might even formalise the relationship between functions/divisions and product teams by implementing a *matrix* structure.

- Our firm may differentiate on the basis of customer service: instead of supplying a severely limited range of low-cost items to the customer, we may decide to focus upon a smaller segment which would be prepared to pay for an individual, customised product. This may require a move from *standardisation of products* (the only way to compete on cost terms) to a *'professionalisation'* of the organisation. Here, the client is served individually by skilled professionals, who are able to conduct a technical dialogue with the client. The structure may well require a radical transformation: *decentralising* decision-making power to the locus of information and knowledge, the 'professionals'; a shift from bureaucratic controls towards a more *informal, organic* non-authoritarian structure; the use of subjective *measurement of performance* and *negotiated objectives* rather than imposed, quantitative targets. The firm will also need to design a structure which will attract and motivate gifted individuals.
- As product/markets develop, a strategy of differentiation may result in a firm supplying a wide range of products to an increasingly segmented total market. The management may then discover that a *functional* structure is no longer appropriate for managing such a diverse range of products. They may decide to reorganise the grouping of jobs into new *units*, based upon geography, customer types (industrial, consumer), product types (solvents, adhesives) or production technology (extruded products, injection moulded products). These new groupings may then form separate divisions in a *multi-divisional structure*, each division operating semi-autonomously with central control taking the form of *performance standards* (for example, return on capital, gross profits) and control over the allocation of capital.

11.9 Summary

1. In this chapter we examined the contingency factors which influence the structuring of organisations. Four factors were considered: age and size, growth, the technical system and the environment.
2. Older and larger organisations tend to be more formalised. Larger size also leads to more elaborate structures and larger unit sizes.
3. Chandler's thesis suggests that structure follows growth strategy and that most firms move through definite stages of growth.
4. The Chandler thesis was extended to considerations of diversification (Wrigley, Scott) and performance (Rumelt, Channon).

5. Greiner's growth model identifies five dimensions of organisation development: age, size, stages of evolution, stages of revolution, and the growth rate of the industry. Firms move through alternate phases of growth and crisis.
6. Woodward's work highlighted the important influence of the technical system on the organisation's structure.
7. Thompson's propositions provide us with insights into the motives behind strategic moves into vertical integration and expansion.
8. The impact of the firm's environment on structure was explored along two environmental dimensions: complex – simple; and dynamic – stable. Dynamic environments push the organisation towards organic structures, complexity forces decentralisation.

Appendix: The five coordinating mechanisms

Mintzberg defines the structure of an organisation as 'the sum total of the ways in which it divides its labour into distinct tasks and then achieves co-ordination among them' (Mintzberg, 1979). This definition neatly encapsulates the organisation's dilemma. Because of the size and/or the complexity of the task facing the firm, it is necessary to divide the whole task into smaller sub-tasks. This confers the benefits of specialisation and the division of labour, but in order to accomplish the *total* task, all these sub-tasks must be integrated and co-ordinated. The superstructure, and processes within the superstructure, are the mechanisms which attempt to achieve this co-ordination.

Co-ordinating mechanisms

Mintzberg identifies five co-ordinating mechanisms:

1. *Mutual adjustment* Work is co-ordinated through direct informal communication between the people doing the job.
2. *Direct supervision* One individual takes responsibility for the work of others, issuing instructions and monitoring their actions.
3. *Standardisation of work processes* The *contents* of the work are specified or programmed (e.g. through detailed job instructions).
4. *Standardisation of outputs* The *results* of the work are specified (e.g. its dimensions, its performance).
5. *Standardisation of skills* This is accomplished through specifying the *training* required to do a particular job.

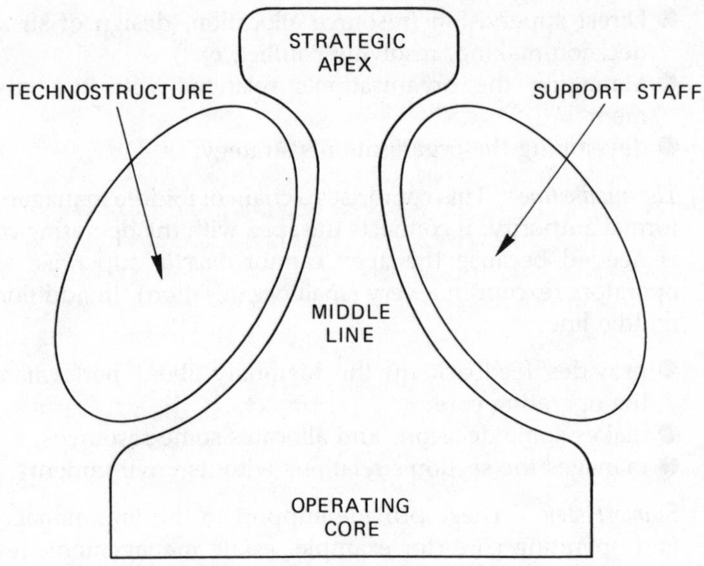

Figure 11.8 Five basic parts of the organisation

The five basic parts of the organisation

Mintzberg suggests that an organisation consists of five basic parts which vary in relative size and importance. These are illustrated in Figure 11.8.

(i) *The operating core* The operating core consists of those members who perform the basic work of the organisation, that which is related directly to the production of products/services. It carries out four prime functions:

- securing inputs
- transforming inputs into outputs
- distributing outputs
- providing *direct* support to the production process (for instance, plant maintenance).

(ii) *The strategic apex* These are the people charged with overall responsibility for the organisation. They are required to manage the organisation so as to achieve the aims of those who control it. Their prime functions are:

- Direct supervision (resource allocation, design of structure, decision-making, resolving conflict, etc.)
- Managing the organisation's relations with the environment
- developing the organisation's strategy.

(iii) *The middle line* This comprises a chain of middle managers with formal authority. It connects the apex with the operating core. It is needed because the apex cannot *directly* supervise all the operators (except in a very small organisation). In addition, the middle line:

- provides feedback up the hierarchy about performance in the operating core
- makes some decisions and allocates some resources
- manages the section's relations with its environment.

(iv) *Support staff* These provide support to the line management and operating core (for example, estate management, restaurant, sports club, cleaners, industrial and public relations, payroll, reception, R & D). Support staff are often there as a result of the organisation's attempts to encompass and control more 'boundary activities' to reduce uncertainty. (that is, to prevent the firm being damaged by the non-performance of some critical activity not under the firm's control).

Support activities are usually only loosely coupled to the core (unlike, for example, maintenance) and they can be located at various levels in the hierarchy.

(v) *The technostructure* The technostructure consists of analysts who affect the work of others. Many are control analysts who attempt to effect standardisation in the organisation. Increasing standardisation can result in a reduction in the skill level required in the operating core. There are three types of control analysts:

(a) work study analysts (these standardise work processes)
(b) planning and control analysts (who standardise output), for example, planning, budgeting, quality system designers.
(c) personnel analysts (who standardise *skills*) for example, trainers, recruiting staff.

Depending upon the type of organisation which in turn is influenced by contingency factors like age, size, technical system and environment, each basic part of the structure differs in its size and importance. In Chapter 14 (Models of Strategic Decision-making) we explore different structural types using this basic framework.

Further reading

A concise survey of the strategy–structure field is provided by Galbraith and Nathanson (1978). Mintzberg (1979) summarises and synthesises the relevant organisation theories.

References

Chandler, A. D. (1962) *Strategy and Structure* (Boston, Massachusetts: MIT).

Channon, D. (1973) *The Strategy and Structure of British Enterprise* (London: Macmillan).

Franko, L. (1974) 'The Move Towards a Multi-Divisional Structure in European Organisations', *Administrative Science Quarterly*, 19.

Galbraith, J. K. (1967) *The New Industrial State* (London: Hamish Hamilton).

Galbraith, J. R. and Nathanson, D. A. (1978) *Strategy Implementation: The Role of Structure and Process* (St Paul, Minnesota: West) pp. 90–1.

Greiner, L. E. (1972) 'Evolution and Revolution as Organisations Grow', *Harvard Business Review*, July–August.

Lawrence, P. R. and Lorsh, J. W. (1967) *Organisation and Environment* (Cambridge, Massachusetts: Harvard).

Mintzberg, H. (1979) *The Structuring of Organisations* (Englewood Cliffs, New Jersey: Prentice-Hall).

Porter, M. E. (1980) *Competitive Strategy* (New York: Free Press).

Pugh, D. S. (ed.) (1984) *Organisation Theory* (Harmondsworth: Penguin) pp. 394–416.

Rumelt, R. (1974) *Strategy, Structure and Economic Performance* (Cambridge, Massachusetts: Harvard).

Stamper, J. T. (1984) 'Evolution in Aerospace Engineering Organisation', *Aerospace*, April.

Thompson, J. D. (1967) *Organisations in Action* (New York: McGraw-Hill).

CHAPTER 12

Social and psychological influences

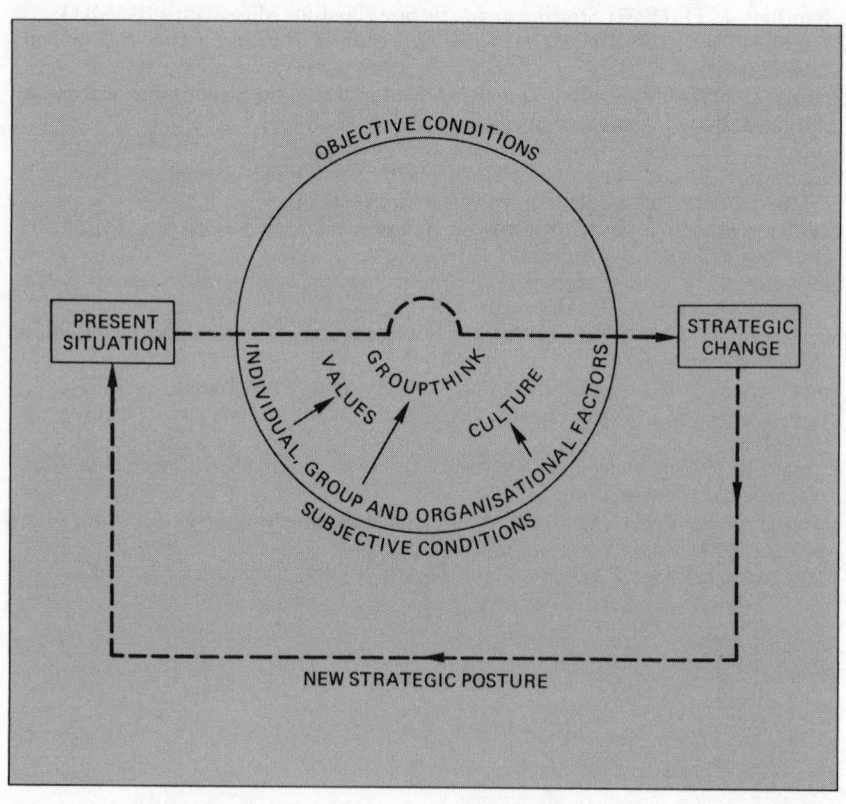

12.1 Introduction

In Chapter 1 we emphasised the distinction between *descriptive* and *prescriptive* approaches to strategy-making. In our exploration of systematic approaches to strategy-formulation (Chapters 3–8) a variety of tools and techniques have been presented which theorists and practitioners believe can help firms to make better strategic decisions. In this chapter we consider a range of social psychological factors that may affect decision-making within the firm. These influences are grouped into individual, group and organisational factors, but before we consider these, some general points should be made.

What is a 'good decision'?

One view would be that this judgement can only be made with hindsight, that is, when the effects of the decision can be evaluated in the light of post-decision events. A contrary view would be that a good decision is one based upon a sound and logical assessment of all the factors, decision options and possible outcomes. In other words, this judgement could be made at the point of decision. For example, Janis and Mann (1979) suggest that high-quality decisions are more likely to emerge if the decision-maker:

1. thoroughly canvasses a wide range of alternative courses of action;
2. surveys the full range of objectives to be fulfilled and the values implicated by the choice;
3. carefully weighs whatever he knows about the costs and risks of negative consequences, as well as the positive consequences, that could flow from each alternative;
4. intensively searches for new information relevant to further evaluation of the alternatives;
5. correctly assimilates and takes account of any new information or expert judgement to which he is exposed, even when the information or judgement does not support the course of action he initially prefers;
6. re-examines the positive and negative consequences all known alternatives, including those originally regarded as unacceptable, before making a final choice.

This rational and comprehensive approach would appear to exclude a 'hunch' or 'seat-of-the-pants' or intuitive decision which nevertheless may result, for instance, in the introduction of a very successful product.

Systematic, logical decision-making

One of the dangers in an over-reliance on systematic approaches to decision-making (of which the corporate planning process is one variant) is that it can stifle flair, intuition, inspiration and creativity in favour of rather dull but highly justifiable, 'logical' decisions. The ideal solution might be to devise a decision process which incorporates the best features of both approaches, that is, the comprehensiveness of the sytematic approach combined with a capacity for generating and incorporating novelty and ingenuity into the process.

A critical perspective

A danger in a chapter of this nature is that attention is inevitably concentrated on the fallible aspects of human beings and their institutions. We should, however, bear in mind that any firm about which we can level criticisms with regard to the decision-making processes used, exists *as a result of* decisions made in the past, so, the fact that the firm is there at all is a tribute to someone's decision-making abilities. This leads to our last introductory point:

Challenging past decisions

The products, processes, structures, manning levels, policies, procedures and the colour of the office walls are all the result of past decisions. An awareness of the many factors that can operate on the decision-making process, some of which will be considered here, should give people working in organisations some encouragement to question the *status quo*. As we pointed out in Chapter 11, where there are few pressures on organisations, or parts of an organisation, which could test the appropriateness of existing arrangements, the results of poor past decisions can linger on indefinitely, to the detriment of efficient operations and increased profitability.

12.2 Individual factors

Whether strategic decisions are made by individuals or by people working together in groups, there are factors affecting individuals which may help us to understand why particular decisions are reached.

Figure 12.1 shows the stages in a stylised decision process at which the individual factors are likely to have most impact on the decision.

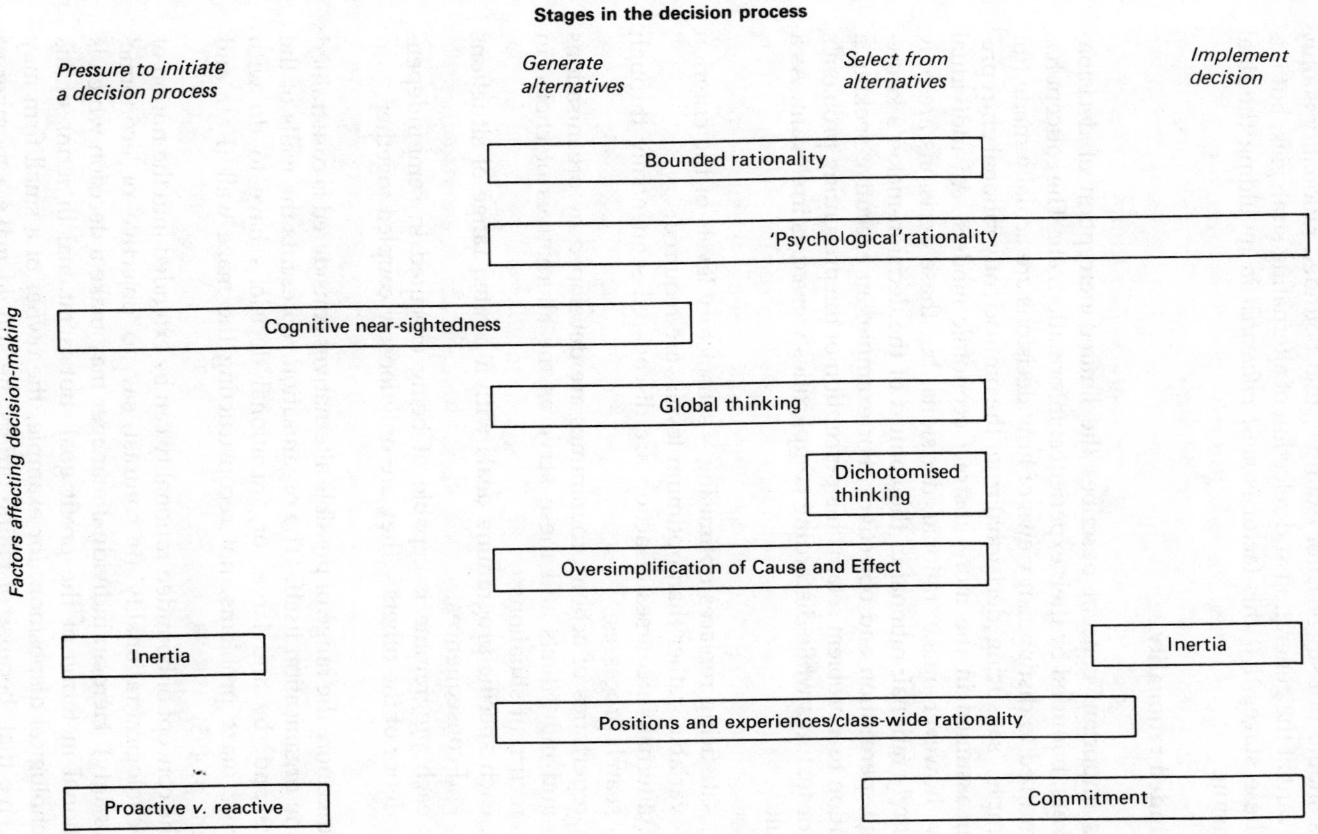

FIGURE 12.1 Issues in individual decision-making

This should not suggest, for example, that bounded rationality is only relevant at the generation and selection of alternating strategies, but it is at these stages that this factor is *most influential* in moulding the final decision.

Bounded rationality

This important concept describes the limited perception of decision-makers, bounded by their experience, information, etc. The concept has been used to distinguish views of how decisions are actually made (for example, 'satisficing' decisions) from the omnisciently rational entrepreneur assumed in the more abstract economic models. An individual may, however, make 'rational' decisions, but these decisions are only *relatively* rational; rational in the context of the decision-maker's knowledge, perception and objectives. For example, an executive seeking a solution to a problem retains his perception of the presenting problem's major features while discarding complexities viewed as irrelevant. As a result:

1. satisficing replaces optimising – satisfactory levels of the criterion variable, rather than optimum levels, are required;
2. alternative courses of action are discovered sequentially through search processes;
3. repertories of action programmes are developed by organisations and individuals and these serve as the alternatives of choice in recurrent situations;
4. each specific programme deals with a limited range of situations and consequences;
5. each programme is capable of being executed in semi-independence of the others – they are only loosely coupled together.

Furthermore the range of possible alternatives considered is constrained by the organisation itself. 'The organisation represents the walls of the maze and, by and large, organizational decisions have to do with solving maze problems, not reconstructing the maze wall.'(Katz and Kahn, p. 495)

The concept of bounded rationality can be extended into the notion of 'psychological rationality' (in contrast, say, to 'objective' or 'economic' rationality). Here an individual manager may make a decision which is irrational in terms of the profit goal, but is rational in terms of his psychological disposition; for example, the owner of a small firm may perceive that, because of falling orders, he should make a member of staff redundant, otherwise profit levels will be reduced. Now, to keep the member of staff could actually be justified as being 'economically rational' (on grounds of maintaining profitability) if, for instance:

(a) an upturn in orders is anticipated;
(b) sacking a member of staff may seriously reduce morale, leading to lower output and poorer quality.

But let us assume that our owner-manager has decided not to make this employee redundant because the interview with him or her would be extremely painful. So the manager has implicitly traded off profits for peace of mind and a quiet life. Thus when we use the term 'rational' pertaining to decisions we should be aware of the frame of reference against which we are assessing 'rational' behaviour.

Perceptual biases and distortions

These tendencies stem largely from the need to simplify complexity, to make information and experiences manageable. A brief description of these biases and distortions is attempted here, the interested reader is referred to Katz and Kahn's *The Social Psychology of Organizations*.

COGNITIVE NEARSIGHTEDNESS

This is the tendency to pay more attention to physical, quantitative, visible and immediate factors at the expense of intangibles and dimensions of the problem that are remote in time and place. This bias to 'the bits you can kick' can seriously distort decision-making. The use of quantitative techniques, in forecasting, for example, often exacerbates this tendency.

Managers who are able to free themselves from this phenomenon then face the problem of persuading their more-myopic colleagues to accept their point of view.

GLOBAL THINKING

On way of simplifying the world is to create a few categories (the fewer the better) and lump people and things into them, for example, all men like sport; all women like babies; all Russians are communists. Prevailing attitudes in the 1950s and 1960s reflected the view that Japanese products were cheap and nasty imitations of Western products. Prejudice is one aspect of this tendency, literally pre-judging on the basis of some inappropriate categorisation, and the more psychologically remote a group is, the more susceptible it is to these distorted perceptions.

DICHOTOMISED THINKING

Or 'black and white' thinking – something is either all good or all bad, there are no in-between, curates'-egg positions. In reality, almost any problem concerning people introduces a fuzzy, unsatisfactory collection of contradictory factors which, if they are ignored in favour of a quick and easy assessment using extremes will result in valuable information being lost in the decision process.

OVERSIMPLIFICATION OF CAUSE AND EFFECT

A problem of logical, 'straight-line' thinking is the tendency to search for one-way connections between variables: *x* causes *y* – whereas, not only may *z* affect *y*, but *y* may affect *x*. Again, in an effort to cut through complexity, we can oversimplify our analysis of the situation.

POSITIONS AND EXPERIENCES

We tend to view the world from our positions in 'social space' (that is, class, income, culture, education, job) and from our place within the organisation. If we change our role in the organisation (for instance, on promotion) not only is our overt behaviour likely to change, but the way we think may change as well.

We can also tend to assume that everyone thinks like we do. For example, a manager might assume that a subordinate would be motivated by a prospect of promotion just because *he* is.

Because each of us can only enjoy a severely limited range of experiences, our perceptions must be limited accordingly. And unless a conscious effort is made to reverse this tendency, career and life-styles may lead to a narrowing of experiences. A senior manager may be isolated from attitudes and concerns on the factory floor, may live in a suburb of like-minded individuals, and may filter the media in such a way that he is only exposed to information which is congruent with his existing attitudes.

Values

Guth and Tagiuri (1965) identified the importance of the personal values of top management in the determination of strategy. They see values as the 'guidance system' which a person uses when faced with choices. Values are stable features of a manager's personality, especially if some values clearly dominate over others. Guth and Tagiuri employed a value classification system, which when applied to different professional groups revealed that senior executives exhibit a particular value-system where economic, theoretical (rational, logical) and political values are predominant; social values (altruism, love of people) rated lowest.

Guth and Tagiuri suggest that, even if an executive is not very conscious or articulate about his values, they will impose themselves no less forcefully on his actual choices. Problems and conflicts arise when there are marked differences between executives' value-systems, or where other, usually economic imperatives, forced executives into decisions which ran counter to their value-preferences. They conclude with the interesting assertion that managers should bear in mind that corporate strategy must ultimately inspire personal commitment or else it will not be implemented.

Values can, of course, be encouraged, modified or undermined by deliberate managerial actions. Training courses, informal pressures and organisational myths, legends and traditions can be employed to bring about a consistent set of values in the organisation. Illustration 12.1 gives an example of how one organisation tries to inculcate a set of values.

Class-wide rationality

Michael Useem, in his article on 'Classwide Rationality' (Useem, 1982) suggests that the senior executives in large corporations in the USA and UK owe their primary allegiance to their *class* rather than to the particular organisation for which they work:

> The classwide principle asserts that membership in the corporate elite is primarily determined by position in a set of interrelated networks transecting virtually all large corporations. Acquaintanceship circles, interlocking directorates, webs of ownerships, and major business associations are among the central strands of these networks . . . The participants in this network are prone to favour government programmes coincident with the common and longer range concerns of most large corporations. The advocacy of classwide policies is sure to be opposed by many if not most corporate managers when these policies adversely affect their own firms, but the classwide principle asserts that there will be a segment of the corporate elite with at least a nascent capacity to provide the broader needs of big business, to act as political leadership for the entire corporate elite (*Administrative Science Quarterly*, June 1982, p. 202).

Useem presents a considerable amount of evidence (original and secondary sources) to support the thesis that class-wide rationality is a powerful influence in corporate decision-making.

His conclusion also questions the validity of many 'managerial theor-

ILLUSTRATION 12.1 Values in Securicor

Keith Erskine, when he was in charge of Securicor, proclaimed that 'Securicor cares'. This was translated into a broad philosophy for the whole company.

1. 'We eliminated the conflict of interest by the mutual company. All profits over the safe minimum go to the workers and customers.
2. We respect the Dignity of Man.
3. We rebuke prejudice, whether of race, class, religion, rank or sex.
4. We judge merit by character, rather than slickness.
5. We regard self-discipline as ennobling, enforced discipline as degrading.
6. We treat our men as educated and adult, capable, with a little help and guidance, of running their own show.
7. We lift motivation, whether for employers or employees, above the lowest common denominator of greed or necessity – men we have found will join together in a "common effort to a noble end". So we have introduced the theme of Caring for the Common Good . . .
8. Men do not want to be managed – they want to be helped. But the need for leadership and for inspiration is as vital as before, only of a more quiet, patient and unselfish kind, giving credit to the men. Human relations pose a challenge as exciting and rewarding as music, art or writing. They demand the same dedication.'

(Source: Case Clearing House, *Securicor Limited*, prepared by D. F. Channon)

ies of the firm' (see Chapter 2) which are based on the premise that the divorce of ownership from control results in managers pursuing non-profit related objectives. If class-wide rationality does underpin higher level corporate decision-making, then we can hypothesise that decisions will be made in the long-term interests of corporations as a whole.

Channon (1979) found some links between the socio-economic backgrounds of the UK executives and the growth strategies of their firms. 'Entrepreneurial' firms (characterised by diversification, mainly through acquisition) tended to be run by men with fairly humble origins, with only a secondary school education. On the other hand 'professional' firms (with low acquisition rates) and 'family-led' firms (the least diversified firms in the survey) were run by people with a traditional upper-class background – public school (often Eton), then Oxford or Cambridge, service in a famous regiment, and membership of London clubs.

Proactive *v* reactive

Many management writers advocate that managerial work should consist of planning, organising, motivating, communicating and controlling (or some other permutation of these and similar laudable activities). In reality too many managers could best describe their jobs as fire-fighting of one form or another. The management role is often seen as having to deal with problems, disturbances, interruptions to routine with which staff feel unable to deal (or the manager thinks they are not capable of doing so). 'Management by exception' elevates this situation to the status of a prescriptive theory of management. So a 'good day' is when the telephone never rings, and no one knocks on the door!

It is not surprising, therefore, that the essentially reactive nature of much managerial work does not encourage the development of positive attitudes towards planning and changing. Most change is viewed as risky and muddled, and it is perhaps not surprising that a strong leaning towards the *status quo* may be encountered in many managers. This inertia tendency may be countered by other motivations:

(a) the desire to solve the manager's overriding problem (obsolete machinery, insufficient budgets, an unco-operative staff member);
(b) the willingness to support the need for changes to other areas of the organisation, not his or her own area.

This last point introduces another aspect of inertia and that is a resistance to 'improvements' suggested *to* the managers by other individuals, divisions or planning department teams. Ideas that *we* think up are likely to be much more acceptable to us than those advanced by 'non-specialists'. Moreover, there may be a perception of implied criticism behind these suggestions, in as far as the manager perhaps should have thought of them himself.

Commitment

The extent to which a person will be bound to the decision which he or she takes (either legally or psychologically) will affect decision-making behaviour. A strong feeling of commitment will motivate the individual to engage in a high degree of pre-decisional search activity and it will also influence the degree to which the individual will 'stick' to the decision which he or she takes. Strong commitment will impel the individual to maintain a course of action in the face of adverse feedback and criticism.

Information preferences

Mintzberg (1973) identified the manager's preference for 'live' information:

1. Managers place greater reliance on up-to-date information even if it may not be thoroughly verified.
2. Managers tend to favour verbal information, telephone conversations, formal and informal meetings.

As a consequence, much of the information upon which decisions are made is undocumented and of a qualitative nature. This information tends to set up a resistance to decision-making techniques which rely mainly on amassing large amounts of dated, quantitative information. And, because vital qualitative information is locked in the manager's head, this information can only be incorporated in the decision if the particular manager is actively engaged in the decision-making process. This phenomenon works against the management scientists' efforts, because no matter how sophisticated the techniques used, say, to forecast demand, may be, if a vital piece of qualitative information is not available to the analyst the conclusions are likely to be rejected.

Assumptions

The decision-maker never has 'complete' information upon which a sound decision can be based. Where information is not available, assumptions must be made in order to proceed with the decision process. Most decisions involve implicit assumptions, and a way of improving decision-making would be to make these assumptions *explicit*.

In the preparation of reports on complex problems, assumptions are inevitable. However, even if the analyst himself is aware of these assumptions the user of the report may be unaware of them, as simplifying assumptions are usually buried in text or appendices. Moreover, if the analyst is poorly briefed he may make an assumption that he regards as of peripheral importance, whereas the commissioning manager may perceive the area as critical.

We might suggest that while assumptions are indeed necessary, an awareness of assumptions made is of equal importance.

Unprogrammed decision-making

Peer Soelberg (1972) researched the job-selection decision made by post graduate MBAs at Sloan School of Management. This decision, he felt, represented an excellent opportunity to analyse unprogrammed decision-making. The students had no previous experience of making this type of decision, the decision was seen as vitally important and the decision process extended over a lengthy period. Moreover, he thought that of any group of people, these students were most likely to employ logical, systematic methods in reaching the decision. Most of his research relied upon interviews with the students over a five-month period during which the final decision was being formulated.

He found that some very interesting processes were at work in this type of unprogrammed decision:

(a) The student defines the career problem by deriving an *ideal solution* to it; this guides his planning of a set of *operational criteria* for evaluating specific job alternatives.
(b) The student *believes* he will weigh up all the factors before making his decision, but in fact he does not do this. If this happens at all, it occurs *after* the decision has been taken.
(c) The student searches *in parallel* for alternatives (rather than sequentially).
(d) He evaluates each alternative along a number of *non-comparable goal dimensions*. There is no evidence of factor-weighting at this stage.
(e) It appears that the student makes his decision *implicitly* long before he *explicitly communicates* it to others. The decision is usually based on a consideration of only one or two 'primary goal attributes'.
(f) During the confirmation process a great deal of perceptual and interpretational *distortion* takes place in favour of the implicit choice. Choice is reduced to *two* alternatives: the preferred alternative and a 'confirmation candidate' introduced for comparative purposes.

So because the selection process is painful (he has to reject possible better alternatives) the student implicitly selects a favourable alternative *prior to* the overt selection process; and he then constructs the selection criteria so that the favourite will emerge. In this confirmation process only one or two criteria are used ('primary goal attributes') and it is usually reduced to a *pro* and *con* argument about only two alternatives (one of which, the decision-maker ensures, stands no chance of being selected). He has then constructed for himself a very simple decision rule which enables him to explain and justify his choice to others.

Some implications of these findings might be:

(i) be honest with yourself: stop the decision-making process when you know you have really ceased to consider alternative options;
(ii) if you want *your* alternatives to be selected by a senior manager, you must make sure it is available to the decision-maker *before* his implicit selection criteria have been established;
(iii) because of the way the decision rules are arrived at (that is, selected to fit the 'favourite') it makes it extremely difficult to get decisions reversed and other alternatives considered (to get the decision changed you have to get the decision *rules* changed first).

12.3 Group factors

There are several ways of making a set of strategic decisions, ranging from *ad hoc*, impulsive policy shifts directed by the chief executive to a thorough, systematic group-decision process. Argenti, for example, advocates the creation of a cross-functional team, with an organising, collating and co-ordinating activity undertaken by a corporate planning manager (Argenti, 1980). The advantages of such a team approach are:

(a) An increase in the range of ideas and perspectives that can be brought into the decision-making process.
(b) A more rigorous testing of the feasibility of alternative strategies as each manager can examine the ramifications of a strategy for his area in detail.
(c) A commitment to the resulting decisions.
(d) An improved corporate perspective and corporate identification on behalf of participating managers.

However, there are problems as well as benefits associated with group decision-making, some of which we will explore in this section.

Groupthink

The group cohesion which may result can be viewed as a positive by-product of strategic decision-making teams, but it may also produce counter-productive processes which can seriously impair the critical faculties of group members. Janis has labelled this suspension of critical judgement that results from the individuals' effort to maintain group cohesion as 'groupthink'. In an effort not to rock the boat and be seen as a poor group-member, doubts and criticisms which the individual may have about the decisions the group is taking are held in check.

Symptoms of the groupthink phenomenon are:

1. an illusion of invulnerability, shared by most or all of the members, which creates excessive optimism and encourages the taking of extreme risks;
2. collective efforts to rationalise in order to discount warnings which might lead the members to reconsider their assumptions before they recommit themselves to their past policy decisions;
3. an unquestioned belief in the group's inherent morality, inclining the members to ignore the ethical or moral consequences of their decisions;
4. stereotyped views of rivals and enemies as too evil to warrant genuine attempts to negotiate, or as too weak or stupid to counter whatever risky attempts are made to defeat their purposes;
5. direct pressure on any member who expresses strong arguments against any of the group's stereotypes, illusions or commitments, making clear that such dissent is contrary to what is expected of all loyal members;
6. self-censorship of deviations from the apparent group consensus, reflecting each member's inclination to minimise to himself the importance of his doubts and counter-arguments;
7. a shared illusion of unanimity, partly resulting from this self-censorship and augmented by the false assumption that silence implies consent;
8. the emergence of self-appointed "mindguards" – members who protect the group from adverse information that might shatter their shared complacency about the effectiveness and morality of their decisions. (Janis and Mann (1979) p. 130).

Figure 12.2 depicts the stages of groupthink from the antecedent conditions, through the symptoms of groupthink just described, to the symptoms of defective decision-making that result.

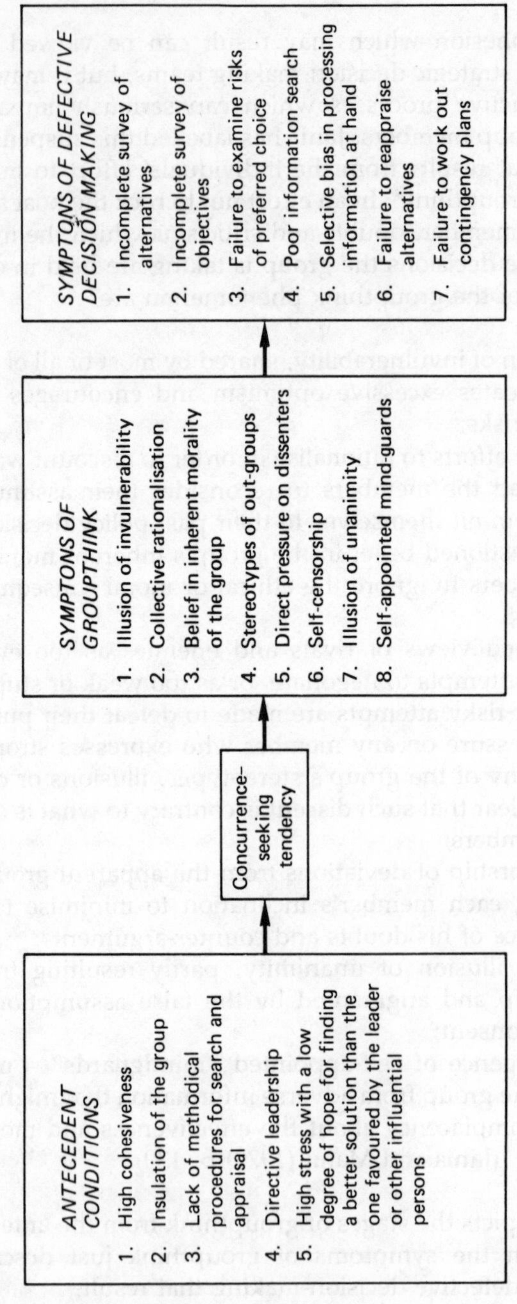

ANTECEDENT CONDITIONS
1. High cohesiveness
2. Insulation of the group
3. Lack of methodical procedures for search and appraisal
4. Directive leadership
5. High stress with a low degree of hope for finding a better solution than the one favoured by the leader or other influential persons
Concurrence-seeking tendency
SYMPTONS OF GROUPTHINK
1. Illusion of invulnerability
2. Collective rationalisation
3. Belief in inherent morality of the group
4. Stereotypes of out-groups
5. Direct pressure on dissenters
6. Self-censorship
7. Illusion of unanimity
8. Self-appointed mind-guards
SYMPTONS OF DEFECTIVE DECISION MAKING
1. Incomplete survey of alternatives
2. Incomplete survey of objectives
3. Failure to examine risks of preferred choice
4. Poor information search
5. Selective bias in processing information at hand
6. Failure to reappraise alternatives
7. Failure to work out contingency plans

FIGURE 12.2 Analysis of Groupthink

Source: Janis and Mann (1977) p. 132.

Janis has suggested some ways of overcoming groupthink:

(a) the leader of the group assigns the role of critical evaluator to each member, including himself. Doubts and criticisms are positively encouraged within the group. However, this suggestion may be rather hard to implement as nobody relishes criticism.
(b) the leader should not bias the group towards a particular decision, wittingly or unwittingly, by the way that guidance as to what is to be accomplished and how it is to be accomplished, is initially given. A group can easily become sensitive to the wishes of the leader, thus producing the 'right' decision.
(c) members of the group should seek advice from trusted colleagues who are outside the group. Fresh perspectives can thus be introduced.
(d) A devil's advocate role should be assigned to a group member (or members). The role should have high status in the group and it should preferably be rotated.
(e) a 'second chance' meeting should be held to permit members to express any residual doubts he or she has about the consensus the group has reached.

Huseman and Driver (1979) have suggested a further technique which overcomes the problems of groupthink. They advocate a dialectical approach to decision-making. The thesis and antithesis of a situation (or the pros and cons) are presented by staff assistants recruited from outside the group, the decision-making team are then able to derive the synthesis (solution) to the problem. The advantage of this technique is that members of the group do not have to endanger cohesiveness by expressing arguments against group commitments; the arguments are made by outsiders.

Some other group-related problems

1. *Risky shift*
   This term describes a tendency for groups to make riskier decisions than individuals, because of factors such as: dispersed responsibility; influential members having more extreme views; the tendency for individuals to become more extreme in their views when placed on the defensive; 'moderate' members remaining silent.
2. *Interaction problems*
   Here we are referring to the behaviour of group-members which acts to impair the working of the group: sniping at others; adopting hidden agendas (for example, criticising someone's ideas as a way

of putting them down); over-talking; ignoring 'low status' contributors; protecting personal interests and reputations; distorting or withholding information.

3. *Procedural problems*
The way meetings are arranged and conducted can either oil the decision-making wheels or make them grind to a halt. Some examples:

(a) an overlong gap between meetings results in members forgetting what happened, losing interest and probably not thinking or doing anything in the time between meetings;
(b) minutes not taken, badly taken, not circulated, circulated half an hour before the meeting;
(c) a mass of information circulated before the meeting which is unlikely to be read;
(d) complex documents tabled at the meeting;
(e) over-formal meetings procedures can stifle a degree of spontaneity that a less formal approach might encourage. Moreover, a climate of fear in a meeting can severely inhibit group members;
(f) poor control of discussion – can lead to members becoming disillusioned and viewing the meetings as a waste of time;
(g) tiredness and non-attendance at critical sessions;
(h) sticking too rigidly to earlier decisions. The strategic decision-making process should produce an evolving awareness of the firms' situation which may render earlier judgements inappropriate;
(i) crowded agendas leading to rushed decisions;
(j) biased presentations and poor presentations.

Of course, many of the above factors have been creatively exploited by managers for their own ends!

12.4 Organisation factors

In this section we shall be looking at some particular features of organisations which impinge upon strategic decision-making.

Structure

The relationship between strategy and structure was explored in depth in Chapter 11. Here we will be selecting certain aspects of organisational structures which have an impact on the type and quality of strategic decisions made by a firm.

(1) SIZE

Clearly, in every large organisations decision-making processes can become unwieldy. *Centralisation* of decision-making, usually at the top of the firm, overcomes some of the problems of co-ordination of decisions, but has disadvantages:

1. decisions can be made without a fuller knowledge of 'local' circumstances;
2. lower management levels may be upset as a result of their lack of involvement in decisions;
3. centralised decisions can tend to stifle initiative at lower organisational levels.

Decentralised decision-making gives managers a degree of autonomy and permits the apex of the structure to concentrate on 'larger' strategic issues. We are assuming here that there is a continuum of decision-making ranging from operating decisions, through tactical decisions to strategic decisions. Our view is that many tactical decisions (and even some operating decisions) have a critical strategic component. This is explored in more depth in Chapter 14.

(2) ORGANISATION CULTURE

Elements of culture will range from attitudes and opinions endorsed by senior management through to the canteen facilities, hence it is a difficult concept to define. Perhaps the reader may more readily identify with the changes, both obvious and subtle, that he or she has experienced when moving between departments within the same organisation, or by joining another organisation.
Handy suggests that there are four possible types of culture found in organisations: power, role, task and person.

Power culture

1. Typically found in small entrepreneurial organisations, controlled by a central, powerful individual.
2. Few rules and procedures, with decisions often reflecting the power relationships between influential members.
3. Successful members have the following characteristics: power-orientated, risk-taking, not security-minded, self-confident as individuals (not 'team' people), thick-skinned.

Role culture

1. Typically a bureaucracy, with well-defined functional specialisms, problems, authority systems, and communication channels.
2. Offers security and predictability, and successful adapters to the culture tend to be 'satisficers' who are happy to fill a role, applying the accepted methodology.

Task culture

1. Typically job-or project-orientated, can be a matrix structure, but is always adaptable.
2. Influence based on expert power, and commitment to the team's task. Obliterates individual objectives, status and style differences.
3. Members need to be confident in their own expertise, adaptable, good co-ordinators and team persons.

Person culture

1. The organisation exists to enable individuals to serve their own interests (for example, barristers, architects, consultants). But, more importantly, individuals with this outlook can be found in one of the other three types of culture – they are usually specialists on whom the organisation is dependent (computer experts, medical consultants, professors).
2. Individuals with this cultural preference tend to be difficult to manage as they are unresponsive to the more typical power systems of the organisation (position power, expert power, personal power).

There is a good deal of similarity between these cultural categories and Mintzberg's structure types (for example, power culture: simple structure; role culture: machine bureaucracy; task culture: adhocracy; person culture; some aspects of professional bureaucracies). We consider some of the ramifications on strategic decision-making of the Mintzberg structural configuration in Chapter 14.

(3) PROACTIVE *V* REACTIVE ORGANISATIONS

The reactive management style may not only characterise the behaviour of an individual manager, it may be the dominant style in the organisation. In a situation where most people are rushing around fighting fires it is difficult to introduce a reflective analytical and planning activity. It is

ILLUSTRATION 12.2 Corporate Cultures

Bank of America

Bank of America is struggling to tackle a traditional culture which is typical of large banks. Its vice-chairman describes the problem as:

> A paternalistic organization where mediocrity is condoned, with a rigid hierarchy and people of similar rank paid about equal regardless of results, where there is no incentive to be innovative . . . where the emphasis is on tactical rather than strategic thinking (*The Economist*, 24 March 1984).

Woolworth

John Beckett, Chairman of Woolworth UK, joined the company from **British Sugar**. Beckett knows he does not know all the answers to Woolworth's problems. His brand of management is not proven in the instinctive, flair-fired world of retailing. As one rival put it 'There must be a throb of excitement with buyers, designers and advertisers hyped up and wound up'. Such a scenario hardly applies at Woolworth where 'operation facelift' – a lick of paint – and various market-research studies and experiments with different retail formulae have had little perceptible impact on the chain.

Beckett says, 'We must have time – another three years at least. We are not talking about merely changing merchandise and display. We are changing attitudes and in-bred cultures in this business'.

(The *Observer*, 9 December 1984).

Virgin

Richard Branson's company is heading for an annual turnover of £150m. His flamboyant style seems to pervade the organisation's strategy:

1. Virgin has a policy of low overheads. There are eight small and chaotic offices in West London, miles in style from the high-rent corporate headquarters of the City.
2. Encourage entrepreneurship. In the music business, Virgin's policy is to set up new labels in order to keep close to

ILLUSTRATION 12.2 *continued*

its bands and their markets. Too large a company, it reckons, would lose touch with the trends which have so far been the key to Virgin's success.

3. Never move far from the core market, pop-music. Virgin have entertainment centres which look and feel different, brighter and louder. Virgin Atlantic has trendy cabin staff and taped music aimed at a younger market. 'Pop' entertainers are offered free passage if they agree to do their stuff for the amusement of the passengers.

(Source: *The Economist*, 24 November 1984)

often vitally important to be seen to be busy; consequently, sitting back, looking at a blank wall and actually *thinking* can be perceived as idleness.

The nature of the task facing some organisations often determines that this reactive style is the only way to accomplish the work, but in many circumstances where reactive management is in evidence it is as a result of poor organisation.

Some examples:

1. A poorly structured firm may lead to managers being overburdened with operating decisions which could easily be delegated.
2. Inadequate management development can lead to managers, insecure in their new positions, filling their days doing the work they used to do in a subordinate position.
3. A lack of policy clarification, proceduralisation and systems can result in low level decisions being pushed up the hierarchy.

One way to introduce some planning activity into reactive climates is to set up separate planning/management services type departments. The problem associated with this approach is that these staff personnel are likely to be excluded from vital, current information in the possession of line management, and so the quality of their researches will suffer in execution and acceptance.

(4) CROWDING OUT

The sense of the immediate, often bordering on panic, which can be detected in some organisations necessarily results in short-term considerations crowding-out longer-term changes. So even where the time and effort has been expended in making some longer-term strategic decisions, they may well not be implemented as more 'urgent' problems appear to dominate the managers' time.

Senior executives can be instrumental in setting a climate where crowding-out is positively encouraged. An ethos which values 'action', 'seat-of-the-pants', gut-feel decision-making can result in a more reflective, analytical approach to decisions being regarded as dithering and indecisiveness.

Also, the chief executive can demonstrate other behaviours which mitigate against a comprehensive approach to decisions. A strong functional bias can set the critical boundaries to a decision in such a way as to exclude important considerations emanating from other functional areas.

(5) NARROWING ORGANISATION THINKING

A narrowing of thinking can result from certain policies pursued by an organisation. For example, some large firms follow a policy of filling managerial positions from within the organisation. Although this might have beneficial effects in reducing staff turnover through improved promotion prospects, and in ensuring that management at all levels have experience of the 'coal face', a major drawback is the effect which such a policy has on organisational decisions. Junior employees looking to the firm to provide a career, soon detect the attitudes, values (and even political tendencies) that are 'right', and they discard (or at least do not mention) 'wrong' opinions that they might hold. It is less painful for the individual if he manages to internalise the right views, thus suffering no dissonance that would be experienced by an individual saying one thing and believing the opposite.

This process results in a narrowing of perspectives in the organisation which, we would argue, must affect the quality of decisions. The phenomenon is likely to be most noticeable in organisations like the police, armed services and very large corporations which invariably promote from within. It is reinforced by the ridiculing of incongruent views and opinions and by the exclusion of dissidents from decision-making (and, sometimes, exclusion from the organisation).

An over-conservative promotion and appointments policy can also lead to senior positions being dominated by 'men of sound judgement' rather than people with ideas. Internal promotion may implicitly be based on how successfully a manager manages a *status quo*, through implementing policies and procedures designed by someone else. Initiative is often discouraged, being perceived as 'rocking the boat'.

Moreover, even if a manager was inclined towards change, because change usually entails an element of risk, and as it is easier to place the blame for current problems on decisions taken by the previous incumbent, it may be safer to pursue a *laissez-faire* policy.

Decisions based on precedents can avoid wasting time and effort going over old ground and are justifiable as long as the dimensions of the present problem are identical to the previous situation. In dynamic organisational environments this is unlikely to obtain, and an over-reliance on what went before will result in making inappropriate decisions.

A final aspect of this problem results from the dominance that a particular specialist group may have achieved in the organisation. The group can influence strategic thinking by restricting the scope of analysis to issues within its sphere of competence, and can exclude other groups and opinions from effective participation by restricting access to specialised information (either by actually withholding information, or by deliberately obfuscating or complicating information).

12.5 A typology of organisations

Miles and Snow (1978) have identified various features of organisations' strategies, structures and processes which enable them to draw up a fourfold typology of organisations. Before we present this typology we should briefly consider their basic theses. They suggest that organisational adaptation can be conceptualised as a *cycle of adjustment*, potentially requiring the simultaneous solution of three major problems:

(a) the entrepreneurial problem (defining the organisation's domain: its products and target markets);
(b) the engineering problem (putting into operation the management's solution to the entrepreneurial problem);
(c) the administrative problem (rationalising the existing systems, formulating and implementing processes which enable the organisation to innovate).

Important features of this adaptative cycle are:

(a) it is concerned with the organisation *as a whole*;
(b) the three adaptative problems are intricately interwoven;
(c) adaptation frequently occurs in sequence (see Figure 12.3), but the cycle can be triggered at any one of these three problem points.

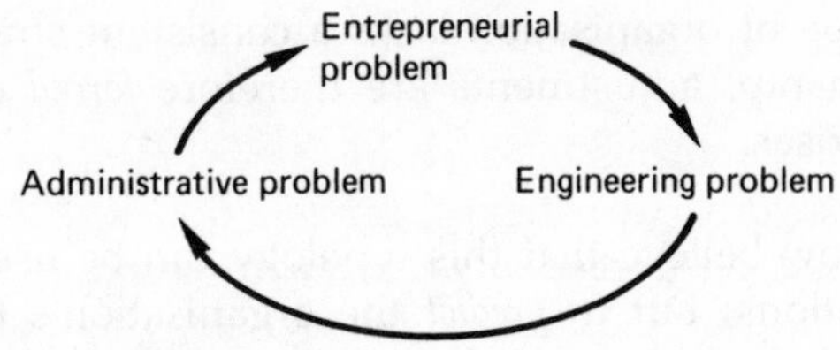

FIGURE 12.3 The adaptive cycle

(d) Adaptive decisions made today tend to harden and become aspects of tomorrow's structure which can then constrain management's choices during the next cycle of adaptation.

In their research into strategy and structure Miles and Snow have identified a fourfold typology of organisation. They adopt the 'structure follows strategy' thesis and are able to categorise most organisations as being in one of the following groups:

(a) *Defenders*, which display the following characteristics:
- narrow product market domains;
- management expertise is limited in scope, but they are highly expert in the firm's specialism;
- little concern with searching for alternative strategies, therefore no need to make major changes to technology, operations or structure;
- attention focused on improving the efficiency of present operations.

(b) *Prospectors*, with these characteristics:
- continual search for market opportunities;
- they often create change and uncertainty to which competitors must respond;
- concern with product/market issues deflects attention from improving efficiency.

(c) *Analysers*:
- operate in two types of domain: one relatively stable, the other changing;
- in the stable area the use of formalised structures and processes leads to efficiency;
- in the changing domain they watch competitor actions and rapidly adopt the most promising ideas.

(d) *Reactors*:
- management perceives change and uncertainty in the environment, but is unable to respond effectively;

- this type of organisation lacks a consistent strategy–structure relationship, adjustments are therefore *forced* on the firm to avert crises.

Miles and Snow believe that this typology can be used, not only to *classify* organisations, but to *predict* the organisation's behaviour. For example, the 'defender' type of organisation faces the engineering problem of trying to improve efficiency. Possible solutions are:

1. to use cost-efficient technology;
2. a move towards vertical integration.

But this strategy may well involve heavy investment which, in turn, (for the investment to be a success) requires that the technological problems remain familiar and predictable for a long time-period. Similarly, Miles and Snow point to the tendency of defenders to adopt rather rigid, mechanistic structures; these are fine for cost-reduction and centralised control, but are not appropriate to changing market circumstances.

Miles and Snow develop their thesis by identifying the characteristic entrepreneurial, engineering and administrative problems facing each of the four types of organisation, exploring typical solutions to these problems and the costs and benefits associated with these strategies.

Their work provides an interesting and challenging framework for the exploration of strategy and structure issues. By highlighting the costs and benefits of particular strategy–structure mixes the contradictions and dilemmas inherent in a firm's strategy can thus be expressed and managed in an explicit and conscious way.

12.6 Summary

1. The chapter explored social and psychological factors which influence decision-making in the organisation. Factors at the individual, group and organisational level were considered.
2. Individual factors included various perceptual biases and distortions which stem essentially from the need to simplify complexity.
3. A brief look at management values, social and class orientations helped us to flesh out the managerial theories of objectives introduced in Chapter 2.
4. Groupthink is a phenomenon of cohesive decision-making groups that interferes with critical judgement. Some solutions to the problem were presented.

5. Other group-related problems considered included risky shift and problems stemming from the poor management and conduct of meetings.
6. Particular aspects of organisation culture and style, can lead to the crowding-out of strategic considerations by short-term thinking, and to a narrowing of perspectives.
7. The Miles and Snow typology of organisations links strategy with the culture and structure of the organisation. Miles and Snow identify four types of organisation: defenders, prospectors, analysers and reactors.

Further reading

For a fuller discussion of group and individual factors dip into Katz and Kahn (1966) and Janis and Mann (1979). To get the real flavour of Miles and Snow's novel approach you should read the original (Miles and Snow, 1978).

References

Argenti, J. (1980) *Practical Corporate Planning* (London: Allen & Unwin).

Channon, D. (1979) 'Leadership and Corporate Performance in the Service Industries', *Journal of Management Studies*, 16, pp. 185–201.

Guth, W. D. and Taguiri, R. (1965) 'Personal Values and Corporate Strategy', *Harvard Business Review*, September.

Handy, C. B. (1981) *Understanding Organizations* (Harmondsworth: Penguin) pp. 177–85.

Huseman, R. C. and Driver, R. W. (1979) 'Groupthink: Implications for Small Group Decision-making in Business' in Huseman, R. C. and Carroll, A. B. (eds) *Readings in Organisational Behaviour* (Boston, Mass.: Allyn & Bacon).

Janis, I. L. and Mann, L. (1979) *Decision Making* (New York: Free Press).

Katz, D. and Kahn, R. L. (1966) *The Social Psychology of Organisations* (Chichester: Wiley).

Miles, R. E. and Snow, C. C. (1978) *Organizational Strategy, Structure and Process* (New York: McGraw Hill).

Mintzberg, H. (1973) *The Nature of Managerial Work* (London: Harper & Row).

Soelberg, P. (1972) 'Unprogrammed Decision Making', reprinted in Turner, J. H., Filley, A. C. and House, R. J. (1972) *Studies in Managerial Process and Organizational Behaviour* (Glenview, Ill.: Scott, Foresman and Company).

Useem, M. (1982) 'Class-wide Rationality', *Administrative Science Quarterly*, June.

CHAPTER 13

Power

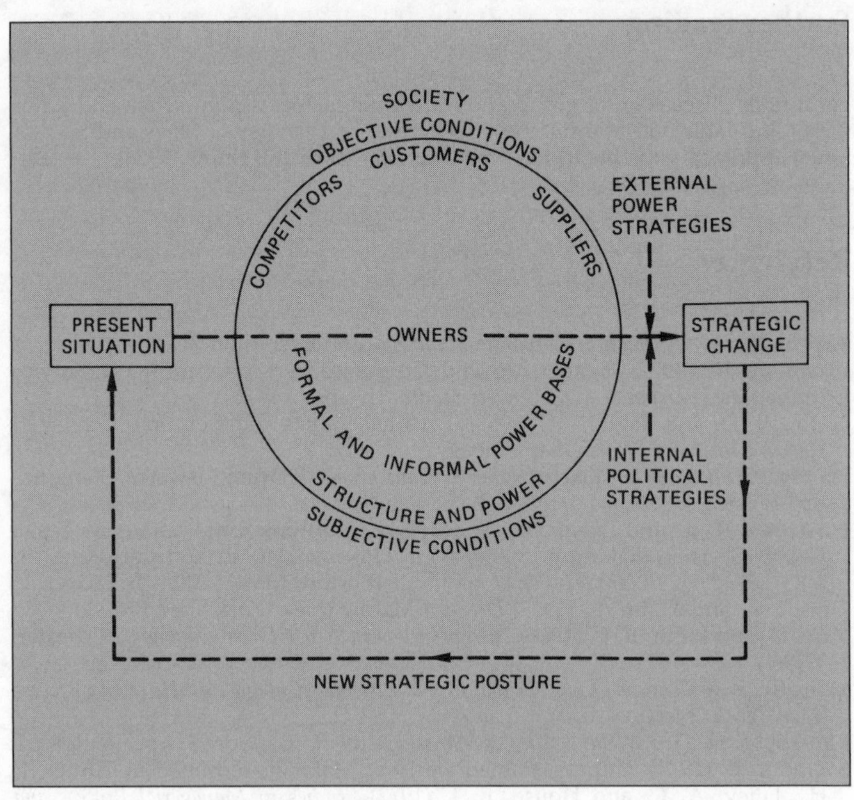

13.1 Introduction

An understanding of power relationships between the firm and external groupings, and power relationships within the firm's structure can help us to explain many aspects of strategic decision-making, and the implementation of these decisions. An insight into power structures is particularly helpful in explaining decisions and behaviours that, on the face of it, seem irrational. The chapter is divided into two parts. First, we will be exploring the power relationships between the firm and external actors such as owners, customers, suppliers and other groups in the wider society. Second, we will examine power relationships *within* the firm, seeking explanations as to why certain groups seem to wield more power than others, why people resort to 'political' activity, how power effects strategic decision-making and how power and structure are related.

I EXTERNAL POWER RELATIONSHIPS

13.2 The power of external groups over the firm

Power can be defined as the capacity to effect or affect organisational actions (Mintzberg, 1983, p. 4). Power relationships between the firm and external groups stem from *resource dependencies*. Mintzberg makes three propositions concerning these power relationships:

1. The more *essential* the resource supplied to the firm the more power the supplier has over the firm.
2. The more *concentrated* the suppliers or customers the greater their power over the firm.
3. The more *dependent* the external group on the firm the more effort it makes to influence the firm.

The ability of external groups to influence the firm can therefore vary from weak (for example, the most imperceptible effect of an individual customer's decisions to switch from one brand of frozen peas to another) to direct power over the firm (such as a bank foreclosing a mortgage).

We will consider four different groups of external influences, the bases of their power over the firm, and their means of influencing the management of the firm. The power relationships between the firm and its owners, customers, suppliers and society at large will be examined. The power relationships between the firm and its employees will be considered in the second part of the chapter.

Owners

Types of ownership range from personal ownership, through institutional ownership (that is, where one organisation owns another) to dispersed ownership (where many people hold shares in the firm). Clearly, in the first two types the owners would be able to exert more direct influence over the firm's management than where ownership is dispersed. (The problem of the separation of ownership from control has been mentioned already in Chapter 2.) Where a significant proportion of shares is owned by one individual (even if this represents as little as 5 percent of the total stock), that individual can exert considerable power over the firm's management; or where a number of shareholders decide to act together, a similar degree of influence can be effected.

For many corporations, shares have been dispersed among large numbers of individuals, and the power of these shareholders lies in their ability to exert *indirect* influence over the firm's management. They cannot voice their opinions directly but they can 'vote with their feet', by selling their shares. The likelihood of substantial numbers of shareholders selling their shares, and thus depressing the share price, exerts a continuing influence over the management of most companies. At the very least, it persuades managers to include the shareholders' interests (dividends, and growth in the value of their shareholding) at some point in their strategic deliberations.

The most direct channel of influence over the firm is via the Board of Directors. The Board stands between the owners and the members of the organisation. It is usually made up of both insiders and external influencers. Although the Board is formally required to look after the interests of the owners of the firm, membership of the Board and the behaviour of individuals who become members is subject to influence, negotiation, individual needs and external pressures.

The Board has the legal power to control the organisation, but this power is usually delegated in the first instance to the Chief Executive Officer (CEO) appointed by the Board. So it could be agreed that the power of the Board expresses itself most concretely in the appointment or dismissal of the CEO. However, there is evidence that the decision to appoint a successor to a retiring CEO is usually made by the CEO himself. (Mintzberg, 1983, pp. 71–3)

The Board often takes direct control over the firm in times of crises (the CEO dies, the firm is facing bankruptcy), but its usual role is the ability to review managerial decisions and performance. Key strategic decisions (to take over another company, to launch a new product, etc.) are commonly referred to the Board for authorisation. But this power can be seriously reduced through lack of information available to the Board members (especially 'external' Board members) and their lack of expertise. Board members are often appointed for public relations or status-enhancing reasons, and the tradition of the 'gifted amateur' is unfortunately too apparent in the Boardrooms of many UK companies.

The net result is that Boards often act merely in a rubber-stamping role, approving the vast majority of the 'decisions' presented to them by the CEO and the senior management group. However, there are certain contingent factors which can increase the power of the Board:

1. Concentrated ownership.
2. Dependency of the firm on the directors themselves for financial support.
3. The director's knowledge of the firm's operations.
4. Times of crisis or transition.
5. A small Board membership.

Customers

The firm's customers can exert influence over the above market relationship between the firm and the consumer. Where the customers are concentrated (or where they choose to act in concert) they are in a position to withhold a vital resource from the firm, that is, sales revenue. For example, when the Ministry of Defence wants to buy tanks from a firm it is able to exert considerable indirect power over the firm. In order to ensure that the firm sticks to the agreed standards of manufacture the MOD can insist on implanting its own Quality Assurance Representative inside the firm, with the power to inspect organisational systems, structures and documentation.

Where a direct dialogue between customer and supplier is possible, special conditions and specifications can be laid down by the client (these circumstances can be found in many organisations ranging from a bespoke tailor to a supplier of satellites). However, the firm can choose to ignore these conditions if the client's business does not constitute a major proportion of total sales. Customers also enjoy a degree of legal power over the firm, enshrined in consumer protection legislation.

Suppliers

Suppliers to the firm may well be in a position to dictate terms, especially if they supply a vital component to the firm and there are no other sources of supplier. They may be able to determine, to a great extent, the price charged, the timing of delivery, the particular features of the product and the payment conditions. For example, during the 1973–4 oil crisis, oil companies used their ability to control the severely limited petrol stocks as a way of achieving much more favourable terms of trade with the garage owners: whereas, prior to the crisis garage proprietors enjoyed extensive credit terms, many of them were coerced into accepting direct-debit agreements. (The proprietors did, however, use the crisis to get rid of Green Shield Stamps – who needs to offer an inducement to sell petrol when demand massively exceeds supply?)

When an airline, for example, is considering re-equipping its aircraft fleet, aircraft manufacturers may well employ various strategies, other then merely detailing the aircraft's strengths and informing the airline of the price. Influencing strategies can range from a fairly innocuous 'business lunch' through to the paying of 'commissions' to key influencers inside the firm.

Suppliers of loan capital (such as banks) may also be in a position to exercise power over the management of a firm, through the threat of withdrawing funds, and through day-to-day involvement with the managers.

Figure 13.1 describes the concept of a power balance between the firm and the supplier and the conditions tending to shift power to one or the other. Figure 13.2 describes the factors which determine the degree of effort the supplier is likely to exert to influence the firm. (See also Illustration 13.1 as an example of the firm's power over suppliers).

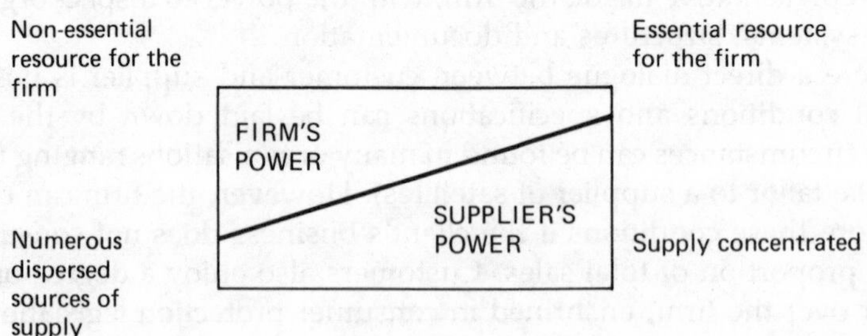

FIGURE 13.1 Power balance between the firm and the supplier

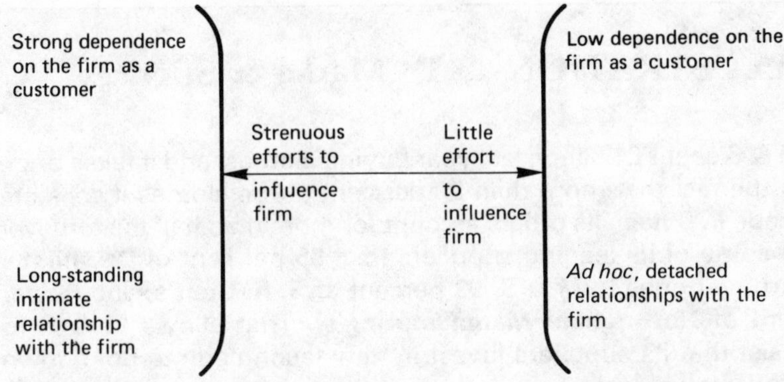

FIGURE 13.2 Degree of effort supplier uses to influence firm

Society

Society at large exerts a variety of direct and indirect influences on the firm. These means of influence can be ranked on three dimensions. (See Figure 13.3). We will consider each means of influence in order, the least direct and powerful (social norms) first, through to the focused, powerful influence of direct controls.(Mintzberg, 1983, Ch. 5).

Social norms are generally accepted standards of conduct (values, ethics) which filter into the organisation through every participant. They are continually evolving, so behaviours which were once unacceptable become perfectly respectable. Different influencers can seek to press contradictory norms on the firm.

Formal constraints can be regarded as social norms made official. They are legally imposed by an external influence and are usually backed by some form of official sanction. For example, while an individual car manufacturer may be unwilling to introduce pollution control equipment unilaterally (because of the cost-penalty involved), passing a law could ensure that all manufacturers were equally disadvantaged, thus preserving the competitive balance within the industry.

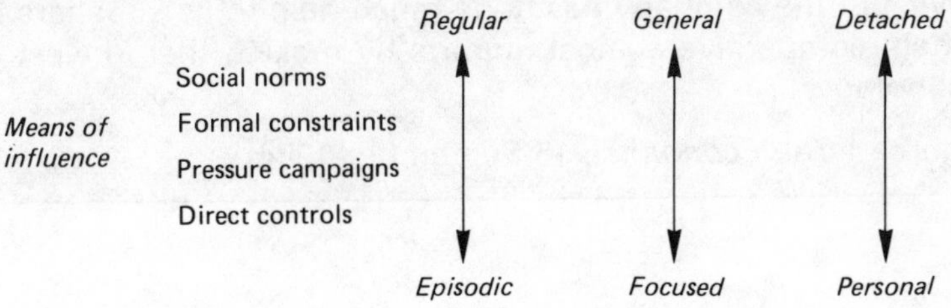

FIGURE 13.3 Societal influences

ILLUSTRATION 13.1 Marks & Spencer

M & S spent £1 billion last year buying clothes, and it takes pride in the fact that more than 90 per cent of the clothes it sells are made in Britain. Its orders account for more than half the turnover of some of its leading suppliers (e.g. 95 per cent of **Dewhirst's** turnover goes to M & S, 92 percent of **S. R. Gent's**, and 62 per cent of **Nottingham Manufacturing's**). That allows M & S to insist that its suppliers invest in new technology to hold down Marks' own costs.

To support its new strategy, M & S is also giving suppliers tighter deadlines for getting more stylish clothes into the shops. Knitwear, for instance, that used to be delivered 13–14 weeks after an order had been placed, will have to arrive within days. Fast delivery is important because Marks is switching to three fashion seasons a year instead of two.

Suppliers face another pressure: they can no longer count on Marks to buy any clothes made over and above those ordered under contract. Previously firms made, say, an extra run of dresses so that if the style did well in the shops they would be ready to fulfil a rush repeat order. If the dresses proved a failure, Marks was often ready to buy the extras at reduced price.

As well as making its suppliers bear its technology costs, Marks now wants them to shoulder some of its design costs, too. S. R. Gent, which has the largest styling department in Britain, is already sending Marks some 250 new design ideas a week.

Suppliers that are unable to live up to Marks' expectations will be given the push, even if they have sold to the company for years. British clothing manufacturers may balk at Marks' hard ways, but the company has done much help to its suppliers to remain competitive against imports by making them invest in technology.

(Source : *The Economist*, 15 September 1984)

Pressure campaigns are usually adopted by groups who wish to change the organisation's behaviour, usually on one specific issue. The campaign can take a variety of forms: boycotts, press attacks, sabotage. It can act as a catalyst translating an emerging social norm into a formal constraint on the firm (see Illustration 13.2).
Direct controls can take several forms:

1. direct access to decision-makers in the firm;
2. temporary membership of an internal decision-making group;
3. implanting a full-time representative inside the firm;

ILLUSTRATION 13.2 The External Coalition

Brock Fireworks

Brock – which sells more than £2m of fireworks a year – obtained an injunction banning further distribution of a press release by the British Society for Social Responsibility in Science (BSSRS), criticising the firm for making plastic bullets, and urging local authorities to break contracts for fireworks supplies with the company.

Brock say the press release was defamatory. In court, it did not dispute making plastic bullets for the Government, but said it had no control over design or use.

(Source : The *Observer*, 4 November 1984).

Shares to suit God and Mammon

Two big names in the investment industry, **Shearson–American Express** and the **Calvert Group**, are to launch unit trusts which plough investors' money into 'socially responsible' companies. To qualify for funds, companies must promote smooth union–management relations, hire on the basis of equal opportunity, and steer clear of befouling the environment. Both funds have also ruled that companies which profit from South African apartheid should be excluded. The Calvert group go further by excluding from its investment portfolio the giants of the $60 billion a year weapons industry, and nuclear power companies.

(Source : The *Guardian*, 20 November 1982)

4. the power to authorise certain of the firm's decisions;
5. the power to impose a decision on the firm.

In Chapter 15 we shall see how direct controls (particularly (4) and (5) above) are used by the external influences to interfere in the decision processes of the non-profit organisation.

13.3 The firm's power over external groups

MacMillan (1978) developing an idea of Chamberlain's (Chamberlain, 1955), suggests that external actors can be classified as *symbionts* or *commensals*. The firm depends on symbionts for inputs, and the symbionts in turn depend on the firm to take their outputs. For example, component suppliers, employees and customers would all be symbionts. As the firm and the symbiont both need each other in order to survive they must *co-operate* with each other. However, they are also in conflict over the *terms* of the exchange relationship (for example, prices, wages).

Commensals seek to attract the firm's symbionts. Hence any organisation that competes with the firm in attracting customers, employees or suppliers is a commensal. As commensals do not need one another in order to survive, the relationships between them tend to be much more competitive. McMillan goes on to demonstrate the relationship between the firm and the external actors and how an organisation might 'manage' the situation to its own advantage.

Strategic power resources

In order to restructure a situation, the actor requires resources, and as power is situation-specific the power resources are similarly specific. The resource must therefore be applicable to the situation. For example, the ability of the NUM to control the movement of coal from pits to power-station is only a power resource if the power-stations are short of coal. Generally, a resource is a strategic power resource when there is an under-supply of it, *and* when it is difficult or costly for those dependent on the resource to find an alternative, so the more alternatives a firm has available relative to its opponents, the more power it has.

Power and dependency

We have seen that power can be viewed as the possession of resources which enable the firm to gain compliance. If two parties are *mutually* dependent on one another in the exchange relationship, then the power relationship would be equalised. Power of one organisation *over* another results from an *asymmetrical* dependence relationship. Aldrich (1979) examined the ways in which a social service organisation deals with this power dependency problem. Four alternatives were suggested:

1. The organisation can build up its own resource base and thus reduce dependence.
2. The organisation can seek alternative sources, thus limiting dependence.
3. The organisation can use coercive force to make the other organisation give up resources without complying with its demands.
4. The organisation can withdraw from the dependency relationship by modifying its goals or technologies.

This interesting set of alternative strategies can be developed into a matrix of power strategies applicable to the firm, but before we attempt to derive such a matrix it is worth considering a transaction-or exchange-based theory of interorganisational behaviour which has been developed from an economic perspective.

THE MARKETS AND HIERARCHIES PARADIGM

Williamson (Francis *et al.*, 1983) has formulated a theory which purports to explain the comparative advantages of markets and organisational hierarchies as forms of economic organisation. His 'markets and hierarchies' theory bridges a gap between the mainstream economic theory of the firm, and organisational theory approached from socio-psychological perspectives. The fundamental point of departure from both of these traditions is that his theory takes *transactions*, rather than the firm or market as the basic unit of analysis. The approach stems from studies Williamson undertook into *vertical integration*, and into situations where the market had 'failed' as an efficient allocating mechanism. He found that the same human and environmental conditions kept reappearing in these studies, namely:

1. *Bounded rationality*: the 'hyper-rationality' of neo-classical economics is unrealistic and non-operational in trying to unravel organisational complexities, hence the adoption of the assumption of bounded rationality (see Chapter 12).
2. *Opportunism*: this extends the usual economic assumption of the pursuit of self-interest to include *guile*, for example, conning people, cutting corners, etc.

Faced with these two factors the basic organisational design problem reduces to this: 'organise transactions in such a way as to economise on bounded rationality while simultaneously safeguarding those transactions against the hazards of opportunism'.

In practice, firms engaging in recurring, uncertain, idiosyncratic (that is, specialised) transactions have a strong interest in preserving the exchange relation. This interest will result in a move away from the market towards making these transactions *internal* to the organisation. Thus, in the pursuit of efficiency the firm will attempt to restructure, or vertically integrate. Williamson interprets a study of vertical integration undertaken by Chandler (1977) using the markets and hierarchies paradigm. Where firms began mass-producing consumer-and producer-durables in the USA, their relationships with distributors became problematic. Distributors would have to be induced to make product and brand specific (idiosyncratic) investments (in, for example, demonstrating equipment, after-sales service) and, once these investments were made, manufacturers and distributors would be dealing with each other in a bilateral exchange arrangement. Given the hazards of opportunism that could arise in such circumstances, the market relationship was abandoned in favour of vertical integration (for example, sewing machines, farm machinery).

The move to multidivisional structures has similarly been interpreted in terms of Williamson's theory. The functional structure presented opportunities for managers to engage in opportunistic pursuit of their own, function-related sub-goals, and, at the same time, senior executives were excessively constrained by day-to-day problems in making strategic decisions. Hence, the change to the multi-divisional structure serves to economise on bounded rationality by permitting the headquarters executive to concentrate on strategic issues, and moreover, the divisional managers are deflected from opportunism by the requirement to operate profitable divisions. Here, then, we see a move *from hierarchy to the market* where the HQ acts as a type of capital market, and each division is a separate 'firm'.

The markets and hierarchies paradigm, the work of J. D. Thompson (1967) (see Chapter 11) and the references we have made to MacMillan and Aldrich contain a consistent thread, and that is the tendency for the organisation to try to control critical contingencies. We can use the insights provided by these writers to construct a matrix of power-strategies for the firm.

DERIVING THE POWER STRATEGY MATRIX

We assume, first, that the firm is in business to make profits, and that the profit-making process is not automatic and totally controllable. There are a number of *sources of instability* which stem from the inability of the firm to control all the stages in the profit-making process directly. We can group these instabilities into those stemming from the firm's

ILLUSTRATION 13.3 Sinclair

Sir Clive Sinclair, Britain's favourite high-technology businessman, is moving too fast for his suppliers – and possibly for his own good. **Sinclair Research** launched its £299 QL personal computer in Britain in January 1984 with the promise of mail-order delivery within 28 days. Sinclair withdrew early advertisements which made that promise, and has now said that, because of an unspecified development problem, nobody ordering the QL today (March 1984) will get it until June. Thorn EMI is making the QL for Sinclair; Sinclair has yet to announce the second manufacturing source promised for late this year.

Each of Sinclair's three previous computers (all cheaper and much less ambitious than the QL) has encountered its share of production or distribution difficulties. So, at one point, did the pocket calculator that Sir Clive invented in the 1970s, and his digital wristwatch.

(Source : The *Economist*, 3 March 1984)

Sir Clive **Sinclair** is battling to salvage his two inch flat-screen television, which has proved a spectacular flop since its launch in September 1983, amid a blaze of publicity. The £79.95 television, hailed as 'a major breakthrough', is the latest in a long line of projects which potential customers have been unable to lay their hands on.

Production of the TV, which was claimed at the time of the launch to be less than one-third the price of its nearest competitor, is split between four companies. **Timex** makes the low power consumption tube; **Ferranti** the novel chip; **AB Electronics** the sophisticated tuner; and **Thorn EMI's Ferguson** and **Timex** are responsible for final assembly.

(Source : The *Observer*, 24 June 1984)

relationships with: (i) the market, (ii) suppliers, (iii) employees, and (iv)society and government.

Some examples of sources of instability are:

Market: consumers switching to a competitor's brand; a decline in the total market; aggressive moves by competitors; retailers not merchandising the firm's product effectively.

Suppliers: interruption in supply; poor quality of supplied components; increasing raw material prices (see Illustration 13.3).
Employees: collective withdrawal of labour; over-reliance on key professionals; unco-operative staff.
Society and government: imposition of pollution regulations; pressure groups campaigns; tax increases.

It is because the firm's owners are not in direct control of these (and many other) destabilising factors that the profit-making process involves a high element of risk. Indeed, even the delegation of power from the owners of the firm to professional managers introduces the risk that the managers may act in *their* interests rather than those of the shareholders.

The four major sources of instability form one side of the matrix, the other side consists of a power dimension. The firm can adopt a range of responses to these destabilising elements which can be classified by the degree of control that is effected over the source of the instability.

Type A response: the firm acts so as to control the source of instability directly.
Type B response: the firm acts to increase the dependency of the source of instability upon it, thereby increasing the firm's power.
Type C response: the firm restructures its relationships with external agencies so as to reduce its dependence.
Type D response: the firm attempts to reduce the impact of external shocks by modifying its internal systems.

So, Type *A* responses can be viewed as the most aggressive power strategies (which may also be the most expensive and risky options to pursue) and Type *D* responses are the weakest (but they may also be the cheapest and least risky options). Type *D* responses do not rely on any direct exertion of power or influence over the source of instability. They conform most closely to the notion of the small firm in a highly competitive market where exchange relationships with external actors are typically anonymous. The firm has to adapt to survive the incessant buffeting from the environment.

The four responses can be arranged in a power hierarchy:

Increasing power over sources of instability ↑		
	Type A	Direct control
	Type B	Increase symbiont's dependence
	Type C	Reduce firm's dependence
	Type D	Adapt internally to cope with instabilities

The complete matrix (Table 13.1) includes a selection of strategies in each cell to illustrate the variety of potential power responses theoretically available to the firm.

TABLE 13.1 The power strategy matrix

Response type	Market based	Suppliers	Employees	Society and government
	Source of Instability			
Type A Direct control	1. Vertical integration forwards to control distribution channels	1. Vertical integration backwards to take over supplier	1. Use legal controls e.g. contracts	1. Direct control of media
	2. Horizontal integration (by merger or take over) to control competition	2. Establish own source of supply	2. Use of authority, indoctrination and coercion to gain compliance	2. Direct access to political power
	3. Establishing a monopoly (e.g. through cost leadership via capacity expansion)	3. Place quality assurance representatives in the supplier firm·		
Type B Increase symbionts dependence	1. Establish captive market segment through product differentiation, advertising, new products	1. Use small suppliers so your business accounts for a large proportion of suppliers total sales	1. Move staff around to increase their dependence	1. Offering inducements to politicians, officials etc.
	2. Threaten distributors and smaller competitors to maintain a favourable market position	2. Demand customised products so supplier has to dedicate capacity to your firm	2. Encourage non-marketable specialisations	2. Financial support to political organisations
	3. Collude with erstwhile competitors to control conditions of sale	3. Negotiate long-term contracts	3. Offer low-interest loans to increase dependence	3. Threaten e.g. to close factories to extract favourable conditions from governments

Continued on page 320

Response type	*Source of Instability*			
	Market based	*Suppliers*	*Employees*	*Society and government*
Type C Reduce firm's dependence	1. Diversify: new markets; new products; acquisitions 2. Widen channels to existing markets to reduce dependence on too few routes	1. Increase number of suppliers 2. Change technology to reduce need for particular, specialised supplies 3. Increase stocks of components	1. Reduce dependence on key skills, staff, by training replacements 2. Automate where feasible	1. Avoid products and markets likely to arouse intervention by governments
Type D Adapt Internally	Improve flexibility to respond to changing market circumstances: • more flexible production processes • more organic structures • improve market intelligence gathering • reduce financial and operational gearing • reduce costs to better withstand falling prices	1. Develop contingency plans to cope with interruptions in supply 2. Use standard components 3. Buy, not lease, equipment	1. Exclude unions 2. Proceduralise tasks to improve substitutability of staff 3. Store information in files, not heads 4. Keep staff happy and loyal	Improve political intelligence gathering

II INTERNAL POWER RELATIONSHIPS

13.4 Power systems

People, units or organisations are powerful or powerless in specific circumstances – 'power is context- or relationship-specific (Pfeffer, 1981, p. 3). *Authority* is formal, legitimate power vested in the office a person holds. Authority in a firm originates with the power of the owners and is delegated to the Chief Executive Officer (CEO). The CEO then (in theory) designs the superstructure and chooses to delegate authority to subordinate positions. The authority structure includes reward and punishment systems designed to ensure compliance. However, if control over subordinates could only be achieved by manipulating rewards and punishments, the authority structure would degenerate into an expensive exercise of explicit power. In most firms, most of the time, subordinates do not weigh up their power relationships with the boss. They accept their superior's authority, and right to give orders, even though in reality the boss may find it difficult to fire, punish or promote the subordinate. Whereas the exercise of 'raw' power involves costs, authority does not: in fact, its exercise can *enhance* it.

Clegg and Dunkerley (1980) see the acceptance by subordinates of management power as part of a 'structure of control, hegemony, rule and domination which continues to be *the* natural convention. It is only when control slips, taken-for-grantedness fails, routines lapse and problems appear that the overt exercise of power is necessary' (Clegg and Dunkerley, 1980, p. 481).

The system of authority involves the exercise of *personal control*, which can take the form of direct orders, setting decision guidelines, reviewing decisions and setting resource constraints (budgets), and *bureaucratic control* or impersonal control over people. Here *systems* designed by analysts are used to control behaviour, for example, work instructions, procedures, payment-by-results system, MBO. Where a high degree of uncertainty, complexity and instability exists in the tasks facing the firm, senior management are required to pass decision-making power down the hierarchy to middle and junior levels.

Informal power systems can be deliberately employed to enhance the working of formal, authority systems. For example, the system of *ideology* in the firm can be fostered by the senior management as a means of controlling employee behaviours:

1. by positive references to past triumphs, myths and traditions;

2. by recruiting and promoting only those who display the 'right' attitudes;
3. by exerting informal pressures on deviant individuals.

So far we have considered the systems of authority and ideology that are at work in the firm's hierarchy. In the next section we consider other sources of power in the firm that can lead to individuals or groups being able to influence events, even though they may possess little or no formal power.

13.5 Informal power bases

We saw in the discussion about the firm's power relationships with external groups that *dependence* relationships underlie power relationships. If we exclude legal powers that particular employees may be able to invoke (for instance, Health and Safety representatives) we find that different forms of dependence relationships also underpin the informal power structures in the firm. However, the power base only becomes operational if the holders of power exercise their will and political skill in making the dependence relationship work in their interests.

Coping with uncertainty

Power bases can stem from the firm's dependence on a critical resource or expertise. Specialisation confers power if the resource which the individual or group controls is critical and non-substitutable. But the specialist's power also severely limits the individual who possesses it: his power is *constrained* by his expertise; it is not absolute power, but is relative to the prevailing circumstances. If these circumstances change (if the printing firm no longer needs skilled compositors) then the power base withers away.

An informal power base can be enjoyed by individuals or groups who are currently engaged in the firm's critical problem areas. *Uncertainty* is a weakness that groups who are able to cope with it can exploit to their advantage. Crozier (see Mintzberg, 1983, p. 167) found that the maintenance men in a highly routinised state-run tobacco firm possessed considerable informal power through the firm's dependence on their will and skill to keep the plant functioning. Firms try to reduce uncertainty by *standardisation* and *forecasting* but, especially where a firm faces a turbulent environment, there will always be some uncertainty. Hinings, *et al* , (1974) in an extended study of a number of firms, found that groups who were coping with uncertainties were seen as the most powerful, followed by those engaged in activities in the direct work-flow of the firm (the operating core).

A group or individual's power base can be enhanced by ensuring that no low-cost substitutes exist. This can be effected by developing specialised language and techniques, by storing information in heads, rather than files and by keeping the management ignorant of potential internal or external substitutes (such as consultants).

If the critical contingencies facing the firm change, then the power bases shift accordingly. But there is a danger in assuming a one-way causal relationship between strategic contingencies (changes in the environment or technology, for example) and resultant power relationships. To do so would be to take as 'given' situations which may well not be exogenously determined. Suppose the consumer-products division faces more uncertainty than the industrial division, and it has increased power because of its ability to cope with these critical contingencies. Can we presume a one-way relationship between the environmental conditions and the internal power relationships between the divisions? Who decided to move into, stay in, and expand the consumer products business? Decisions about the structure and how to differentiate the organisation cannot be assumed to be entirely determined by outside forces. For example, the management may choose to centralise data processing, which may in turn result in the emergence of a new source of informal power in the organisation.

The power to affect decision processes

Members of the firm who are in a position to influence the decision *processes* can thereby have an affect on the decision *outcomes*. This can be achieved through:

(i) control over constraints, values and objectives employed in the decision processes (for instance, a manager could invoke 'the Board's wishes' in an effort to block a strategic option: 'The Board would never accept any scheme which reduced market share in the south-east');
(ii) control over the alternatives considered. This can be effected through membership of study groups and planning committees;
(iii) control of information *about* alternatives;
(iv) an understanding of the power distributions and where to exert influence and political skills.

Pfeffer suggests that a unit's power can be enhanced by its possession of 'technological certainty'. This refers to the degree of consensus that exists among the group's members about paradigms, models and cause–effect relationships. If the group is certain about a particular strategy then it is likely to be in a good position to convince others.

Assessing informal power

It is no easy matter to uncover the informal power relationships in an organisation. If power is to do with overcoming opposition or resistance, we need to be able to identify what would have happened *without* the exercise of power. We might be able to assess the power distribution by examining actual decisions – if we know who got their way in budget allocations and strategic decisions we could infer that they have the power.

It could be assessed by identifying the *symbols* of power – titles, the 'best' offices, named car-parking spaces, etc. Or we could simply ask people in the firm to tell us who has the power. For this to work, we must assume that people are able to detect informal power and are prepared to be truthful in their reported assessments. A way of assessing relative functional power is to discover which functions are represented on the most important decision-making committees, and which function most often supplies the firm's Chief Executive Officer.

Conditions for the use of power

Pfeffer's model of the conditions producing the use of power and politics in decision-making is depicted in Figure 13.4. The elements in the top half of the model combine to produce a situation of *conflict*. *Differentiation* in the structure leads to *interdependence* between organisation members, where the actions of one person affect others. This leads to interaction between members and acts as a potential basis for conflict. Differentiation can also result in the emergence of *heterogeneous goals*, and *heterogeneous beliefs about 'technology'* (means–end relationships). *Scarcity* of resources increases the potential for conflict. The greater the scarcity compared with the demand, the greater the power and the effort that will be expended in resolving the decision.

The conditions of interdependence, heterogeneity of goals and beliefs about technology and scarcity, taken together produce conflict. Whether the conflict results in political activity depends on the two conditions in the lower half of the model. The first condition is the *importance* of the decision issue, or resource. A trivial issue is unlikely to warrant an elaborate political effort. The second condition is the *distribution of power* in the structure. If power is *centralised* political activity is unlikely to emerge. It is in structures where power is *dispersed* that political bargaining and coalition formation are most likely to be found.

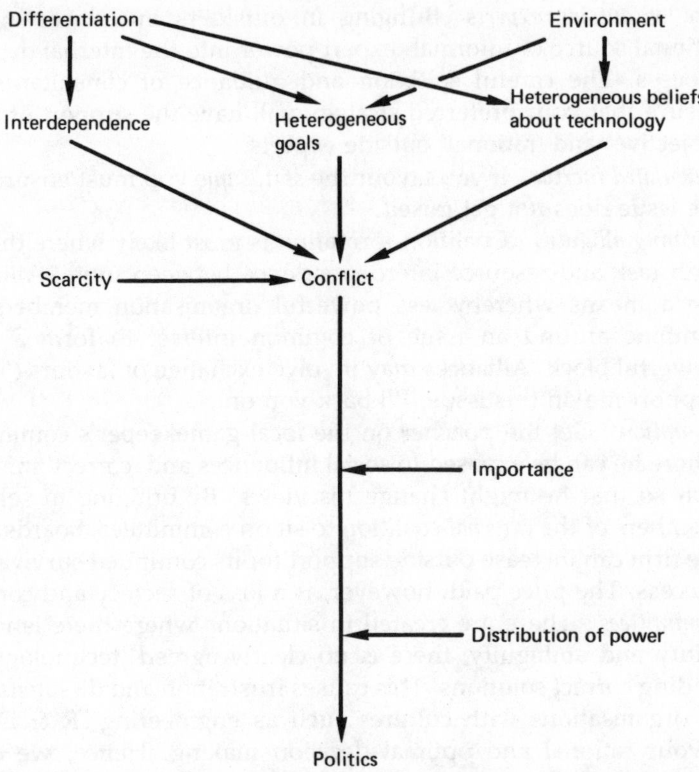

FIGURE 13.4 A model of the conditions producing the use of power and politics in organisational decision-making

Source: Pfeffer (1981).

13.6 Political strategies

Power is most effective when it is deployed unobtrusively, thus a good deal of political activity may be difficult to detect. The exercise of informal power often underlies changes in strategic decisions, which are overtly presented as 'rational' policy adjustments. Some examples of political strategies and tactics should illustrate the scope and subtlety of the exercise of informal power:

1. *Selective use of objective criteria* Rather than coming out in the open and declaring support for a particular strategy, you advocate and stress *criteria* for evaluating strategies which will inevitably result in your preferred outcome being adopted.

2. *Use of outside experts* Bringing in outsiders introduces an additional source of informal, expert power into the internal decision process. The careful selection and guidance of consultants can ensure that your preferred strategy will have the support of these 'objective' and 'rational' outside experts.
3. *Calculated inertia* If you favour the *status quo* you must ensure that the issue does not get raised.
4. *Forming alliances* Coalition-formation is most likely where there is high task-and-resource interdependence between units. Alliances are a means whereby less powerful organisation members can combine around an issue of common interest to form a more powerful block. Alliances may involve exchange of favours ('if you support me on this issue, I'll back you on . . .').
5. *Co-option* Get the poacher on the local gamekeeper's committee, where he can be exposed to social influences and 'correct' information so that he might change his views. By bringing in selected members of the *external* coalition to sit on committees, boards, etc., the firm can increase outside support for its continued survival and success. The price paid, however, is a loss of secrecy and control.
6. *Committees* These are created in situations where there is uncertainty and ambiguity; there is no clearly agreed 'technology' for finding correct solutions. This causes frustration and dissatisfaction in organisations with cultures such as engineering, R & D that favour rational and optimal decision making. Hence, we could expect to find committees proliferating in highly differentiated firms (with multiple, heterogeneous sub-unit goals).
7. *Sponsorship* Here the individual attaches himself or herself to an important member of the firm, and, in return for a share of power, the subordinate supports the sponsor. Sponsors make vital strategic information available to the chosen subordinate, and, through a form of reflected power, other members of the firm can be made aware of the politically 'correct' horses to back. This process clearly influences the degree of support a particular strategic thrust can generate within the higher reaches of the organisation.
8. *Empire building* One route to personal advancement is to collect subordinates and sub-units as a way of enhancing one's power base. These political manoeuvres can act so as to deflect strategic decisions away from the explicit goals of, for example, profitability. If large staffs equals power, then power-seeking managers will argue for, and support decisions which increase the size of their departments.
9. *The strategic candidates game* Because of the unstructured and ambiguous nature of strategic decision-making, it can be viewed as a

highly political process. A manager may have a pet project which needs support to get implemented. The manager seeks support from influential members of the firm, and if successful a 'critical mass' of support is reached. Once this stage is attained a bandwagon effect takes over, as the previously uncommitted members judge the way the wind is blowing and rush to be associated with the idea.

Political language and symbols

> Language, symbols, rituals and ceremonies are used to manage the process by which actions and events are given meaning. The process is managed in such a way as to provide legitimation and a supporting structure for the desired behaviours and actions which are to be carried out within the organisation (Pfeffer, 1981, p. 180).

This approach takes the view that organisational 'reality' is socially constructed, and one consequence of it is the possibility of affecting *feelings* about decisions and actions independently of the actions themselves. Some examples of the use of political language and symbols include:

- Making decisions *prior to* the development of explanations or justifications. So 'strategic planning' may often be used to justify a strategy chosen for political reasons. This is a form of 'retrospective rationality'.
- Beliefs in the value and efficiency of analysis and planning constitute *ideologies* which are rarely questioned and are often used to mask the use of power. Analysis, especially quantified analysis gives an appearance of value-free rationality. Another aspect of ideology is the way that the pursuit of profit and the legitimate right of managers to give orders are beliefs which are rarely challenged by organisation members.
- Symbolic responses include the creation of an administrative structure or procedure to satisfy, cosmetically, an aggrieved group; for example, setting up a 'Customer Relations Department' in response to a pressure group's activities.
- Ritual political activity includes, for example, firing the manager 'responsible' for the problem, crisis, decision; for instance, sacking the team manager after losing a run of games.
- Language can be used to evoke support by, for instance, presenting a dominant value in the form of a simple phrase: 'careless work can kill'.
- By changing or enhancing the setting management can convey that something new and important is going on.

TABLE 13.2 Strategies for avoiding the use of power and politics in decision-making

Strategy	*Costs*
1. Slack or excess resources, including additional positions and titles (reduces *scarcity*)	Inventory costs, costs of excess capacity and personnel
2. Achieve homogeneity in goals and beliefs about technology through: • recruitment practices • socialisation • use of rewards and sanctions	Fewer points of view therefore less diverse information represented in decision-making ('Groupthink', see Chapter 12).
3. Make decisions appear less important	Decision may be avoided to the detriment of the firm Subterfuge may be discovered.

Before we leave the consideration of internal power strategies, Table 13.2 suggests some strategies that can reduce the incidence of political activity. The strategies operate on the problems causing political behaviour described in Figure 13.4. The costs of each strategy are also included in the table.

13.7 Politics and structure

Structure can be viewed as an evolving system, adapting to meet changing environmental, technical, growth and size variables; the problem being how to derive the most efficient configuration (see Chapter 11). However, an alternative view put forward by Pfeffer looks at structure as being the outcome of a political contest for control within the organisation, which also provides organisation members with further political advantages by virtue of their structural positions. Some aspects of this approach considered here are differentiation, mergers, centralisation, routinisation and the role of information systems.

1. *Differentiation* Creating additional specialised sub-units confers formal status on an activity. This can help to reduce the amount of informal, political activity in which a particular group (not officially recognised) needs to engage to promote its interests.
2. *Mergers* and take-overs can result in debilitating political struggles

between the duplicated sub-units with the perceived 'senior' partners in the combination holding the psychological advantage.

3. *Centralisation* Child (1972) has argued that neither size, technology nor environmental requirements are so binding in most organisations as to remove the potential for choice of the structural arrangements by those in power in the organisation. Thus, if the ownership of the firm is concentrated, it is likely that decision-making power will be centralised, perhaps in the CEO, closely controlled by the Board, where the senior management's power is consequently reduced.
4. *Routinisation* and mechanisation can render operatives and professionals much less powerful, as they no longer control a critical resource. Hence, power can tend to move away from those groups either to new critical sub-units, or to the apex. In functions where work is routinised and specifiable (as in production) decision-making power tends to be concentrated at the top of the function; in contrast, in functions like sales, or personnel where standardisation is difficult, power tends to be more dispersed.
5. *Information systems*: As information is an important source of power, the design and location of information systems may well be determined by power struggles, rather than 'rational' criteria.

Finally, we shall look at the powers of the members of the internal coalition, using Mintzberg's categorisation of the different parts of the firm's structure (see the appendix to Chapter 11).

The internal coalition is made up of full-time employees, who are committed to the firm (because of their dependence on its wellbeing), who are extremely knowledgeable about the firm and who make the decisions within the firm.

The power of the CEO

The power of the Board is funnelled through the CEO into the organisation structure. the CEO clearly is the person in the position of greatest authority. The CEO, as the Board's trustee, has sweeping formal powers over the firm, the power to:

- hire and fire;
- impose decisions on subordinates;
- veto and over-rule other's decisions;
- set salaries.

The CEO usually has informal powers, in addition to the formidable formal powers:

- leadership, through the establishment of organisational values and ideology;
- charisma;
- skills of persuasion and negotiation;
- access to strategic information (from inside and outside the firm).

CEOs, having often spent years climbing to the top of the firm are heavily committed to the organisation. And, as the status of a CEO is associated with the *size* of the firm, growth is an important goal for the CEO. Hence survival and growth are key concerns for the CEO. So we could conclude that if the shareholders are a weak influence over the firm, survival and growth – subject to a minimum profit constraint (see Chapter 2) – are likely to emerge as the real goals of the senior management.

As it is unlikely that the CEO will actively seek to surround himself with people trying to oppose him, executive selection (including the replacement of the CEO upon retirement) is likely to reflect the CEO's interests. The new CEO can either *replace* non-sympathetic staff with his loyal supporters (which can be difficult), or he can *expand* the number of staff by adding *his* people and gradually shift power to them.

The power of line managers

The closer managers are to the CEO the more they are able to share in the CEO's power. However, because of their number and their limited access to informal sources of power (such as information) they enjoy only a fraction of the CEO's power. Line managers have *delegated authority* over the unit for which they are responsible, and they can develop their own informal powers based on expertise, information and personality to augment their formal power. The fundamental difference between being a CEO, and being in charge of a department within the organisation, is that the departmental manager is subject to direct personal control by his superior; the CEO, especially where the external influencers are dispersed, is not subject to such close scrutiny and control.

Line managers usually share the CEO's goals of growth and survival and particularly ambitious managers see empire-building as a route to increasing status, power and other rewards. But line managers can also pursue *autonomy* as a goal, to reduce dependence on other parts of the firm which they cannot control and to free themselves from interference from above.

The power of the operatives

As they are usually remote from the external influencers, the operatives are often the members of the firm least interested in the goals or demands of the owners. They are often virtually powerless as individuals, hence the attempt to enhance their power through collective action. Professional operatives, however, possess critical knowledge and skills which can be used to influence other members of the firm.

Trade unions are part of the external influencers, and are used to pursue the operatives' interests, particularly in regard to wages, jobs, safety and working conditions. However, informal groups can form and use their power to obstruct imposed changes, particularly when existing social relationships (which may provide the operatives with a great deal of support and satisfaction at work) are threatened (see Chapter 10).

Professional operatives can group together to pursue goals which derive from the nature of their work:

- protection of the group's autonomy;
- enhancement of the group's prestige and resources;
- professional excellence (regardless of the level of excellence commercially demanded).

The power of the analysts

Staff groupings, like technical specialists are, by definition, outside the line of authority, which stretches down from the CEO, through the middle line, to the operating core. They are supposed only to advise the line management. Analysts are employed, generally, to replace personal controls with bureaucratic systems. For example, the speed at which an operative works could be controlled directly by the formal, direct supervision of his line manager; or the pace of work could be controlled by a piece-rate payment system designed by work-study analysts. Similarly, production planners and budget officers can take away from the line manager decision-making power over the determination of work schedules, and the allocation of resources.

Firms that rely heavily on bureaucratic systems of control (for example, those with mass production technologies) tend to have powerful technostructures. The analysts' power derives initially from their expertise, but as we have seen, they can gradually erode the authority of line managers. They use their power to increase the deployment of their technocratic systems in the firm. Their loyalties tend to be to their profession rather than to the firm. Although they are interested in changing the organisation through increasing technocratic control, in order to achieve bureaucratic standardisation a considerable degree of task stability is required within the organisation. So they seek to increase the firm's control over the sources of instability facing it.

The power of support staff

Unskilled support staff are usually in a very weak position in the firm. Whereas unskilled workers in the operating core can seriously disrupt the firm, support staff may merely find themselves replaced by an outside contract agency (such as office cleaners). Professional support staff (for example, public relations) do have some power deriving from their expertise, but, like the cleaners, they can be replaced by using the services of other organisations. Hence they seek to *involve* themselves in the key decision processes taking place in the upper middle line and the apex.

13.8 Summary

1. The study of power relationships between the firm and external groupings, and with the structure of the firm itself can provide us with valuable insights into strategic management.
2. Power relationships between the firm and external groups stem from resource dependencies: the more essential and concentrated the supply of the resource, the more power the group has over the firm.
3. The interests of the owners of the firm are legally represented by the board. However, the board can often lack the information and expertise effectively to influence the management of the firm.
4. Society at large exerts a range of influences over the firm: from regular, general and detached influences (like social norms) through to the focused influence of direct personal intervention in the decision-making process.
5. The firm's power over external groups was explored in terms of dependence relationships. The discussion introduced the concepts of symbionts and commensals (MacMillan), and the markets and hierarchies paradigm (Williamson).
6. A power-strategy matrix can be drawn up with external sources of instability (from markets, suppliers, employees, society and government) forming one side of the matrix and power responses the other. These range from direct control over the source of instability through to a modification of internal systems to cope with external shocks.

7. Internal power relationships were the subject of the second part of the chapter. The authority system forms the basis of formal power in the organisation. There are, however, informal power bases, stemming from internal dependence relationships. Bases of informal power considered were: the ability to cope with uncertainty, and the power to affect decision processes.
8. Various political strategies were considered, (for example, calculated inertia, forming alliances, empire-building). Political language and symbols can be used to affect individuals' perception of organisational reality.
9. The chapter ends with an overview of the relative power of the five parts of the structure: the apex, the line managers, the operatives, the analysts in the technostructure, and the support staff.

Further reading

The most readable and comprehensive text on power is Mintzberg (1983). Pfeffer (1981) uses some interesting examples (especially of not-for-profit organisations) but it concentrates on *internal* power structures.

References

Aldrich, H. E. (1979) *Organizations and Environment* (Englewood Cliffs, New Jersey: Prentice-Hall).

Chamberlain, N. W. (1955) *A General Theory of Economic Process* (London: Harper & Row).

Chandler, A. D. (1977) *The Visible Hand: The Managerial Revolution in American Business* (Cambridge, Massachusetts: Harvard University Press).

Child, J. (1972) 'Organization Structure, Environment and Performance: The Role of Strategic Choice', *Sociology*,6.

Clegg, S. and Dunkerley, D. (1980) *Organization, Class and Control* (London: Routledge & Kegan Paul).

Francis, A., Turke, J. and Willman, S. P. (1983) *Power, Efficiency ,and Institutions* (London: Heinemann).

Hinings, C. R., Hickson, D. J., Pennings, J. M. and Schneck, R. E. (1974) 'Structural Conditions of Intraorganizational Power', *Administrative Science Quarterly*.

MacMillan, I. C. (1978) *Strategy Formulation: Political Concepts* (St Paul, Minnesota: West).

Mintzberg, H. (1983) *Power In and Around Organizations* (Englewood Cliffs, New Jersey: Prentice-Hall).

Pfeffer, J. (1981) *Power in Organizations* (London: Pitman).

Thompson, J. D. (1967) *Organizations in Action* (New York: McGraw-Hill).

CHAPTER 14

Models of strategic decision-making

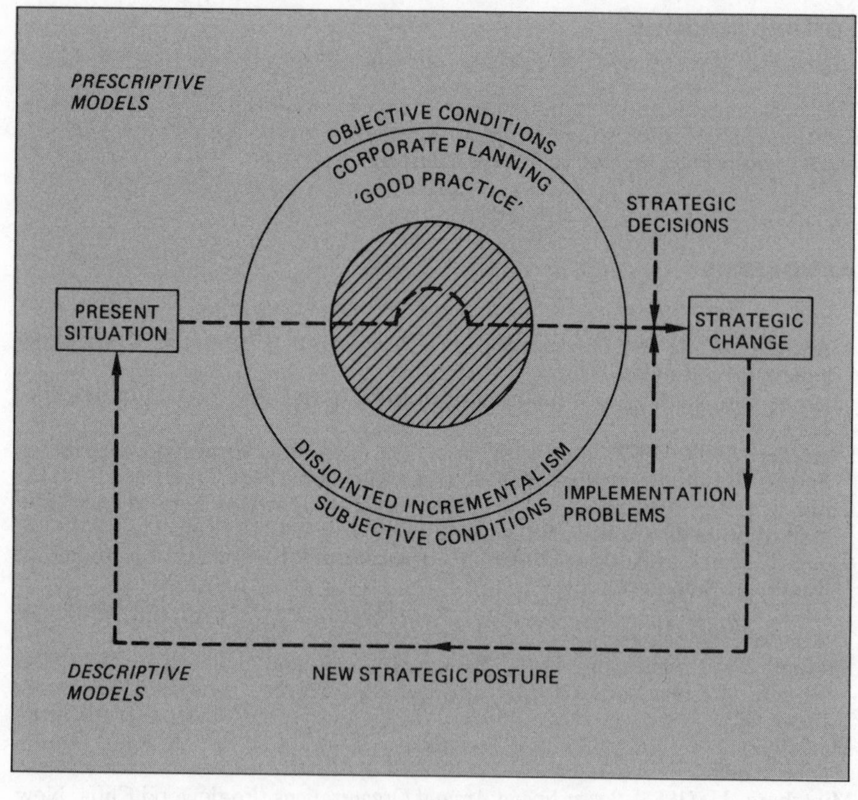

14.1 Introduction

In this chapter we set out to explore a range of different approaches to strategic decision-making. We examine incremental models, a decision-process model and a number of studies which focus more on the content of strategic decisions. We end the chapter with some suggestions for the development of a contingency theory of strategic decision-making, but first of all we consider some criticisms of rational approaches to strategy-formulation.

14.2 Criticisms of corporate planning

Rational planning approaches, of which corporate planning is probably the best known, and possibly the most widely applied form, have been subjected to a number of criticisms. In this section we will list the more important criticisms which, taken together, pose a strong argument against an organisation adopting corporate planning. (Figure 14.1 describes a typically systematic corporate planning process.)

(i) For many firms, the dynamic nature of the environment makes the corporate plan rapidly redundant unless it is couched in the most generalised terms.
(ii) Information is never available in the quantity and quality required to undertake a comprehensive analysis of the internal and external environment, or to permit an exhaustive exploration of alternative strategies.
(iii) Decision-makers are not capable of comprehending much more than a very limited and simplified set of interrelated variables. In fact, decision-makers deliberately employ devices to simplify complexity, for example, breaking the problem down into discrete, manageable chunks, which are dealt with in sequence.
(iv) Systematic, formal planning activities can stifle the emergence of radical, 'maverick', but potentially successful ideas.
(v) Where the corporate plan is drawn up by specialist planners, line managers (who have to implement the plan) often display resistance to decisions in which they have not been involved. In addition, staff planners often lack access to vital information held by line managers. (See Illustration 14.1).
(vi) Peters and Waterman (1982) point out that fewer than one in ten US companies produce a corporate strategy that is achieving its goals.

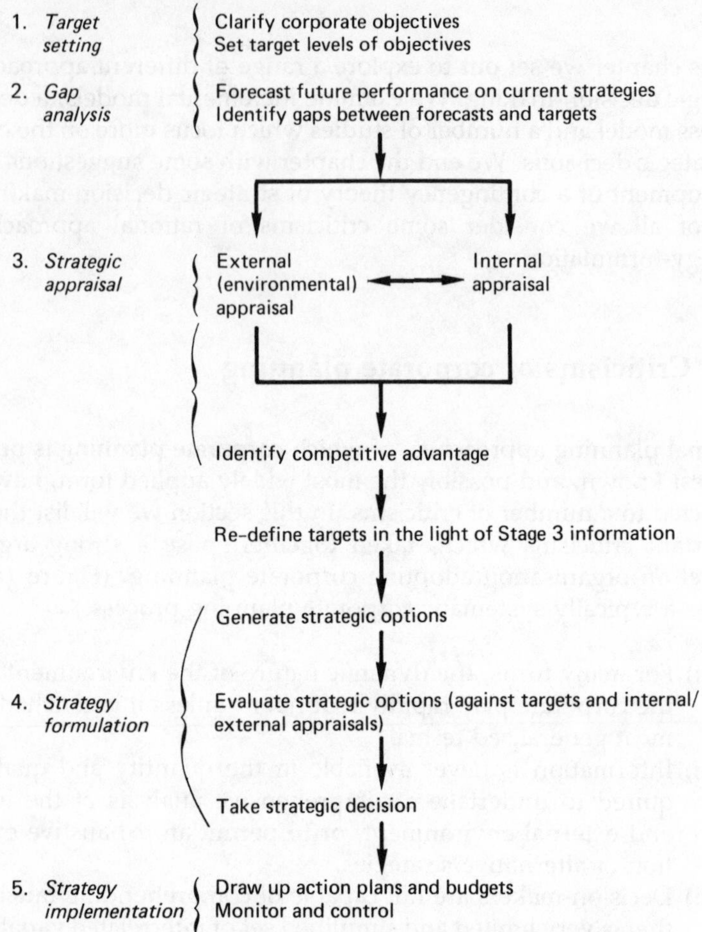

FIGURE 14.1 A corporate planning process in outline

Source: Adapted form Argenti (1980).

(vii) Many problems with corporate planning crop up at the implementation stage:

- implementation of changes proposed in the plan always seem to take longer than expected.
- unforeseen big problems surface
- competing activities and, especially, *crises* within the firm deflect attention from implementing the plan.

(viii) Problems often arise in the introduction of the corporate plan-

ILLUSTRATION 14.1 Corporate Planning Reconsidered

In 1970 85 per cent of Japan's leading companies were practicising corporate planning; by 1975 only 20 per cent were. What has gone wrong with corporate planning?

1. The oil crisis of 1973 forced executives into short-term, rapid and drastic decisions. Hence corporate planning, along with other new management techniques (programme budgeting, MBO, critical path, exponential smoothing) fell right out of favour.
2. Corporate planning became over-blown with abstruse terminology, computer modelling, probability-estimating and over-sophisticated forecasting methods. This left many line-managers confused and resentful of this all powerful technique.
3. Specialist planners drew up the plan and tried to sell it to senior executives, who, increasingly in the 1970s, did not buy it.
4. The stability of the 1960s led people to believe in long range forecasting and planning. The shocks of 1973–4 and 1979 produced a state of turmoil to render most pre-oil-crisis forecasts hopelessly inaccurate.
5. The style of management in large and medium-sized companies was moving towards a far more participative pattern, away from executives handing difficult problems over to specialists, back towards taking responsibility on their own shoulders.

The lesson is clear: you can plan in *detail* over short periods and you can plan in *outline* over long ones, but what you absolutely cannot do is plan in detail over long periods.

Instead of highly detailed, comprehensive plans produced by specialist planners, the top executives should plan themselves, agreeing on a few *broad statements* of policy (for example, 'we will move into speciality chemicals'; 'we will break the group into semi-autonomous profit centres'), with the assistance of an intelligent person to make calculations, take notes, make forecasts, etc. – this could be done by a senior accountant.

(Source: John Argenti, 'Don't let planners meddle with your strategy', *Accountancy*, April 1984, p. 152.)

ning process. Like many eagerly grasped management panaceas (for example, MBO, quality circles, management audits) insufficient attention is paid to developing the organisation and the management in preparation for the successful introduction of the new planning system.

Having listed some of the major disadvantages associated with corporate planning, we should try to balance the discussion with a brief description of the benefits that can be derived from the *process* of corporate planning, even if the *outcome* from the process (the recommended strategy) is not wholly adopted:

- 'rational' techniques can *assist* choice even if (because of the pressure of complex qualitative variables) they cannot *make* the choice;
- systematic planning can encourage an orderly approach to the study of strategic problems;
- an analytical approach can help in defining the strategic problem;
- the process of rational analysis can generate useful information which can shed light on 'softer', more value-laden issues;
- rational analysis can force the decision-makers to confront the value judgements that need to be made.

We can represent the corporate planning approach to strategic decision-making in our model of the process of strategic management described in Chapter 1. (See Figure 14.2).

To recap, briefly, the objective conditions include the present and future states of the firm's environment and its internal resource deployments. The subjective conditions refer to the social, structural, psychological, cultural and political variables extant in the organisation. The corporate planning process is designed to develop successful strategies by a systematic analysis of the objective conditions. However, judging by some of the criticisms of the technique already listed, an explanation of the failure or partial failure of systematic planning is that it takes too little account of the subjective conditions. Although the quality of the *content* of the strategic decisions may be relatively high, the quality of the decision *process* may be low. Thus 'good' decisions may not be implemented. We can represent corporate planning in our model depicted in Figure 14.3.

In contrast to the systematic, rational technique of corporate planning, Lindblom (1959, in Pugh 1984) describes the actual process of the practice of policy-making as an incremental, 'muddling through' process. We shall consider his model, and two more prescriptive adaptations of incrementalism in the following section.

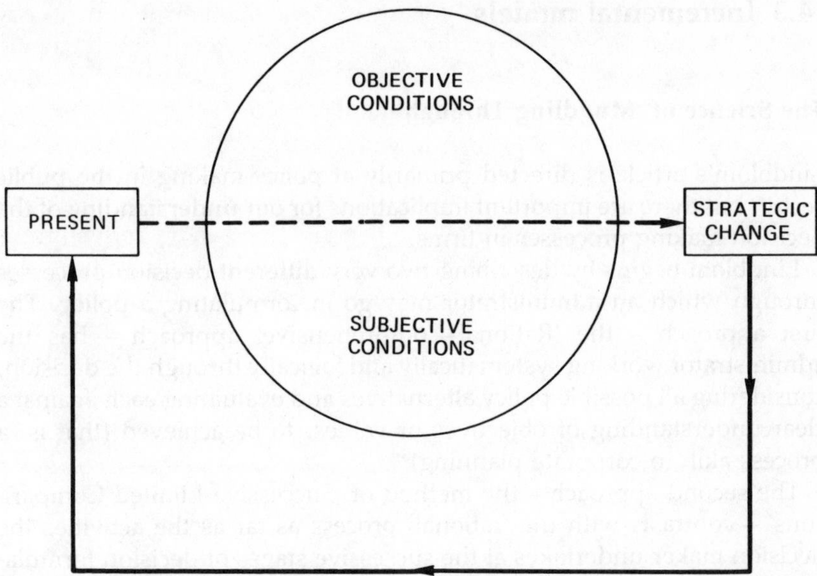

FIGURE 14.2 The process of strategic management

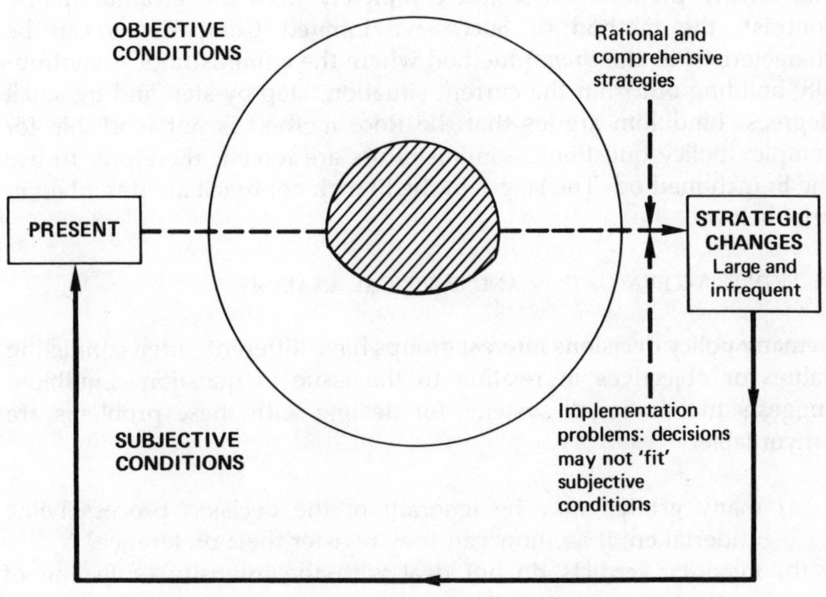

FIGURE 14.3 Corporate Planning

14.3 Incremental models

The Science of 'Muddling Through'

Lindblom's article is directed primarily at policy-making in the public sector, but there are important implications for our understanding of the decision-making processes in firms.

Lindblom begins by describing two very different decision processes through which an administrator may go in formulating a policy. The first approach – the 'Rational–Comprehensive' approach – has the administrator working systematically and logically through the decision, considering all possible policy alternatives and evaluating each against a clear understanding of objectives or values, to be achieved (that is, a process akin to corporate planning).

The second approach – the method of 'Successive Limited Comparisons' – contrasts with the 'rational' process as far as the activities the decision maker undertakes at the successive stages of decision formulation.

Lindblom subtitles the rational–comprehensive approach the *Root* method as the decision-maker is starting anew from fundamentals each time, building on the past only as experience is embodied in a theory, and always prepared to restart completely from the ground up. By contrast, the method of Successive Limited Comparisons can be characterised as the *Branch* method where the administrator is continually building out from the current situation, step-by-step and by small degrees. Lindblom argues that the Root method is not workable for complex policy questions; administrators are forced, therefore, to use the Branch method. The stages in the Branch approach are described in brief below.

INTERTWINING EVALUATION AND EMPIRICAL ANALYSIS

In many policy decisions interest groups have different, often conflicting values or objectives in relation to the issue in question. Lindblom suggests that 'rational' systems for dealing with these problems are unworkable:

(a) many groups may be ignorant of the decision process being undertaken; if so, how can they register their preference?
(b) majority verdicts do not deal with the intensity of feeling of particular groups.

(c) when values conflict with one another, how can a ranking of preference be determined?
(d) the relative importance of different values changes as the problem or circumstance under consideration changes.

He adds:

> Even if all administrators had at hand an agreed set of values, objectives and constraints, and an agreed ranking of these values, objectives and constraints, their marginal values in actual choice situations would be impossible to formulate (Lindblom, 1959, p. 244).

So, as the administrator is unable to formulate the relevant values first and *then* choose among policies to achieve them, he must choose directly among alternative policies that offer, for example, different marginal combinations of values. Assume an administrator was confronted with two policy options, *X* and *Y*, which offer the same degree of attainment of objectives *a*, *b*, *c* and *d*, but differ with regard to attainment of *e* and *f* as follows:

Policy	*Objective attainment*
X	More *e* than policy *Y*
Y	More *f* than policy *X*

In choosing *X*, say, the administrator is valuing the marginal increment in *e* as being more desirable than the marginal increment in *f*. The only values that are relevant to his choice are the increments by which the two policies differ, and, when he chooses between the two marginal values he does so by making a choice between *policies*. So his concern with values need only involve information and evaluation of the *marginal differences* between different options.

RELATIONS BETWEEN MEANS AND ENDS

The Root method advocates working from a statement of desired ends or objectives, through to a generation and evaluation of alternative means to those ends. But, in the processes just described in the first stage of the Branch method, this separation of ends and means does not take place; means and ends are chosen *simultaneously* through the selection of a particular, preferred policy option. But the 'Branch' process creates problems of policy evaluation. If we have no clear, agreed idea about objectives, how can we judge whether one policy is better than another?

THE TEST OF A 'GOOD' POLICY

Under the 'rational' Root method, a clear statement of objectives, for instance, 15 per cent Return on Shareholder's Capital, can be used as the criterion against which policy alternatives can be judged. But with the simultaneous selection of means and ends in the Branch approach such an evaluation is impossible. To show that a policy is wrong one cannot point to an agreed objective or set of objectives that are not being achieved. Instead one must argue that another policy (and its implicit objectives) is more desirable. Moreover, the Branch approach permits agreement on *policies* to take place among interest groups, whereas their particular values or objectives may differ widely. For example, in a recent debate in the House of Commons on British Citizenship the Government's proposals were opposed by both the Opposition and certain elements in the governing party. Clearly, the two groups differed widely in their general aims and values, yet they could agree on a particular policy issue.

So a 'good' policy is one that gets a wide measure of agreement. This is no less 'rational' than the Root method, because, after all, that approach merely forces agreement at the earlier, objective setting stage of the decision process. The method of successive limited comparisons at least enables the policy-formulation process to advance to a stage where some measure of agreement is likely, whereas in the Root method, unless 100 per cent agreement of objectives is achieved at the outset, the process cannot continue.

In a sense, then, the Root method, as applied to complex administrative decisions, requires a degree of decision-making and reconciliation to take place even *before* the process proper has begun.

NON-COMPREHENSIVE ANALYSIS

Drastic simplification is often necessary when dealing with complex issues. It is impossible to deal with a truly comprehensive analysis of a given situation; the information is just not available and there are limits to the intellectual capacity required to accommodate an exhaustive array of options.

In the Branch approach simplification is achieved in two principal ways:

(a) a limitation of policy comparisons with those policies that differ in relatively small degree from policies at present in effect. Therefore, it is not necessary to undertake fundamental inquiry into alternatives and consequences; one only needs to examine those areas where the proposed alternative differs from the *status quo*.

(b) by ignoring important possible consequences of possible policies as well as the values attached to the neglected consequences. Although this might be seen as a rather damning condemnation of the Branch approach, Lindblom believes that in a society which has a multi-faceted and comprehensive array of policy-making structures and agencies such that most interest-groups and values are represented somewhere, the incremental approach works to the advantage of that society.

SUCCESSION OF COMPARISONS

Comparisons, together, with the policy choice proceed in a chronological series:

> Policy is not made once and for all; it is made and re-made endlessly. Policy-making is a process of successive approximation to some desired objectives in which what is desired itself continues to change under reconsideration (Lindblom, 1959, p. 250).

If the administrator proceeds through a succession of incremental changes serious lasting mistakes can be avoided:

(a) past sequences of policy steps provide him with knowledge about further similar steps;
(b) big jumps towards the 'ultimate' objectives are not necessary as he never expects his policy to be a final resolution of the problem;
(c) he is in effect able to test his previous predictions as he moves on to each further step;
(d) past errors can often be remedied fairly quickly with this approach.

See Illustration 14.2 for a personal decision viewed from the Root-and-Branch perspectives.

Support for incrementalism

1. Mintzberg (1983) suggests that there are forces acting to preserve the stability of the organisation's goal system:

   (a) a strong organisational ideology;
   (b) precedents as a form of organisational memory – past decisions and budget allocations become institutionalised into almost permanent features;

ILLUSTRATION 14.2 A Personal 'Strategic' Decision

An Example Comparing the Root-and-Branch Approaches

A young married couple, with no children, are looking for a house to buy in London. Claire is an economist for a leading commercial bank and her husband, Philip, works for an employment agency. Both are located in the City. At present they live in a rented flat in Kennington.

Claire suggests that they ought to approach this problem in a systematic manner. She suggests they list their objectives with regard to their ideal house and proceed accordingly. Philip agrees and, before they have even looked into an estate agent's window, they draw up the following list:

1. *Price* : between £70 000 and £78 000
2. *Location* : South London
3. *Transport* : within 10 minutes walk of a tube or train station
4. *Size* : two or three bedrooms
5. *Garden* : small but secluded

On sifting the local South London press Claire finds three houses which fit their requirements. According to the advertisements all three meet the five objectives. However, after seeing the houses in a hectic sprint around south-east London, Claire and Philip find themselves rather deflated, sitting in a cafe trying to decide what to do. This was how they now reviewed each house:

House A : looked dingy and was right next to a primary school.

House B : had been on the market for two years and required a considerable amount of renovation.

House C : had a roomy and airy 'feel' to it but was at the top end of their price range.

They agreed that the initial list of objectives was far too narrow, since, having looked at available properties, there were obviously many other factors that were important in the decision. Philip suggested that rather than try and expand their list of objectives (or go for a points-rating system that Claire proposed) they would be better off simply comparing the houses that came onto the market, one with another.

Postscript

They ended up buying a two-bedroomed maisonette with no garden. When asked why they decided upon this particular property they gave their reasons:

(i) Although they were the first people to see it, the sellers had five offers above the price agreed with Philip and Claire that the sellers felt obliged to turn down. In Claire's words 'the house is definitely sellable if we decide to move at short notice'.
(ii) The lounge at the rear has a good view over a golf course.
(iii) Although it takes them fifteen minutes to cycle to the station each morning, 'it's worth it' said Philip 'as this was the only house we looked at where we really felt that we could relax and feel "at home"!'

(c) the problems and costs associated with changing agreed goals, which induces a type of organisational inertia;
(d) the presence of 'slack' resources which can be used to deal with temporary shifts in the relative powers of members of the coalition without unduly disturbing the goal system.

2. Donaldson and Lorsch's research leads them to conclude that 'Major shifts in strategy do not occur suddenly or rapidly. On the contrary, the process of strategic change is basically an incremental one, and each step is relatively small' (Donaldson and Lorsch, 1983, p. 9). They believe that the Branch method is a more accurate description of top management decision-making than the Root method, although the CEOs, because of their wish to see the firm succeed, impose an underlying pattern on the means-end relationship. Therefore we can distinguish ends from means because 'it is the corporate managers' *belief system* that ultimately directs their strategic decisions by restricting the outcomes, values, and options considered' (Donaldson and Lorsch, 1983, p. 201).

The incremental process appears to be a more 'natural' decision-making approach compared with the highly prescriptive corporate planning model. However, although the process seems to emerge from the subjective conditions extant in the organisation, and hence it blends

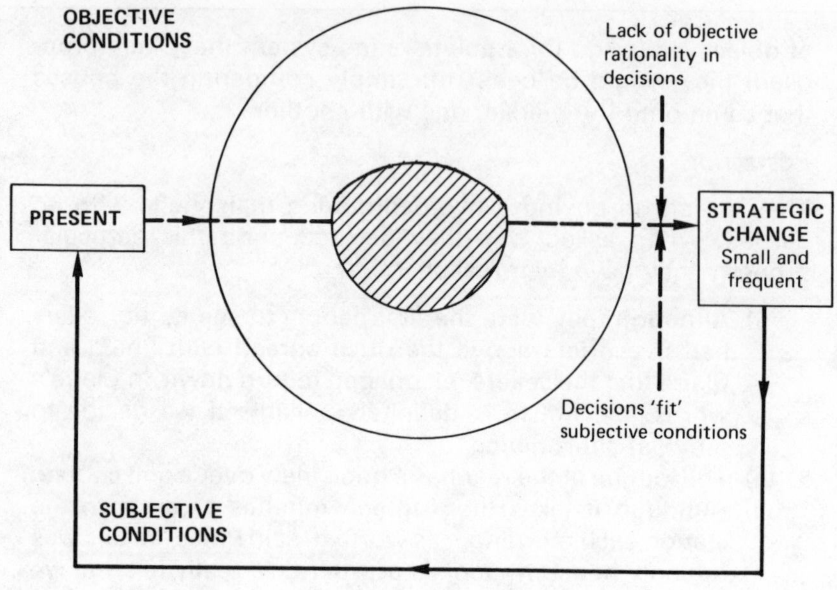

FIGURE 14.4 Disjointed incrementalism

quite happily into the structure, the rather *ad hoc* and partial consideration given to the objective conditions may result in a poor quality of decision content. (See Figure 14.4)

14.4 Mixed scanning

Etzioni (1967) offers a compromise between (or perhaps a synthesis of) the rational comprehensive model and disjointed incrementalism, which he calls 'mixed scanning'. According to Etzioni mixed scanning is:

not so: exact
Utopian
unrealistic } as rationalism

and is

not so: constricting in its perspective
conservative
myopic
non-innovatory } as incrementalism

The process he describes operates at two levels:

Level 1 being a broad overview
Level 2 consisting of detailed analysis within the overview.

Different aspects of the two levels are listed in Table 14.1.

TABLE 14.1 The two levels of mixed scanning

Level 1	*Level 2*
Values and goals Fundamental decisions Fundamental policy formulation: sets basic directions	Objectives Incremental decisions Incremental process which prepares for fundamental decisions and revises them after they have been made

Fundamental decisions are concerned with a variety of interrelated aspects:

(i) definition of major problem areas;
(ii) selection of the main overall alternative to be pursued;
(iii) allocation of time and resources for high level (1) and low level (2) scanning;
(iv) decisions about whether to drop existing courses of action
(v) decisions about reformulating goals.

So Level 1 decision activity concerns decisions about goals, planning strategies and action strategies. Etzioni gives detailed guidance on how to use the mixed scanning technique which could be summarised as in Figure 14.5. The major contribution which Etzioni makes is the explicit recognition that implementation is an integral part of planning and decision-making. Planning is a *continuous process*.

Camhis (1979) criticises Etzioni's claim that mixed scanning combines more or less equally the features of rationalism and incrementalism. He argues that, because Etzioni assumes that goals and values can be identified and ranked, this places mixed scanning firmly towards the rationalist end of the continuum. But, whereas in social-policy-formulation we could agree with Camhis' criticism, in the case of applying mixed scanning to strategic decision-making in firms, we believe that goal-identification is much simplified. We argued in Chapter 2 that there is an overriding objective facing the firm – the need to

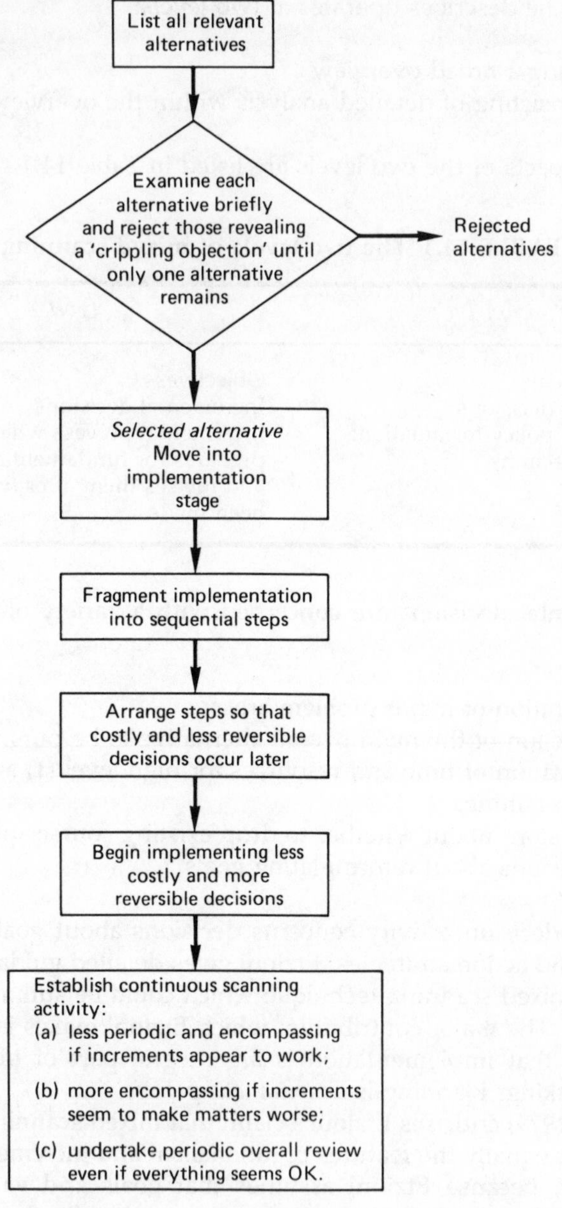

FIGURE 14.5 The mixed scanning process

make some level of profit. Thus Camhis' misgivings about mixed scanning in the policy field are not so applicable to the use of the technique in business organisations.

14.5 Logical incrementalism

Quinn's book *Strategies for Change: Logical Incrementalism* (Quinn, 1980) is another attempt at deriving an approach to strategy which acknowledges the realities of organisational decision-making. In his planning research he observed three tendencies:

1. the planning activity often tended to become a bureaucraticised, rigid and costly paper-shuffling exercise;
2. most major strategic decisions seemed to be made outside the formal planning structure, even in organisations with well-accepted planning cultures, but especially so in smaller and entrepreneurial companies;
3. management literature on planning seemed to be producing more and more sophisticated but unworkable models.

Using an interview technique Quinn attempted to:

1. identify some common patterns of strategic action;
2. understand better how managers in complex situations really did act;
3. obtain their insights as to why they acted as they did;
4. compare their actions and perceptions with the viewpoints expressed in prevailing theories.

> Strategies may be looked at as either *a priori* statements to guide action or *a posteriori* results of actual decision behaviour. . . One, therefore, must look at the actual emerging pattern of the enterprise's operant goals, policies and major programmes to see what its true strategy is. Whether it is consciously set forth in advance or is simply a widely-held understanding resulting from a stream of decisions, this pattern becomes the real strategy of the enterprise (Quinn, 1980, pp. 9–10).

Whereas formal, logical planning models seemed not to be followed in practice, Quinn does not hold that the major descriptive theoretical alternative 'muddling through' is an adequate explanation of actual strategic behaviour. Managers *purposely* blend different processes (labelled behavioural, power-dynamic and formal analytical) together to improve both the quality of the decisions and the effectiveness of their implementation. His studies show that:

1. Effective strategies tend to emerge from a series of strategic formulation *subsystems*. Each subsystem involves a somewhat different set of players, information needs and time imperatives. Each attacks a specific issue of corporate-wide importance, (e.g. product positioning, innovation, acquisition, reorganisation) in a disciplined way. Optimal strategies tended to demand incrementalism and opportunism in their formulation.
2. There are powerful 'logic patterns' in the formulation of effective strategies for each subsystem, but the timing and pacing of the decision processes differ from subsystem to subsystem.
3. Because each subsystem had its own cognitive limits and process limits, its strategies tend to be arrived at logically and incrementally. Consequently, the total enterprise strategy (which has to deal with the interactions of all the subsystem strategies) is arrived at through a process of 'logical incrementalism'.
4. In the hands of a skilful manager this is *not muddling*. It is a purposeful, effective, productive management technique for improving and integrating both the analytical and the behavioural aspects of strategy formulation.

He concludes that:

1. The most effective strategies tend to emerge step by step from an iterative process in which the organistion probes the future, experiments and learns from a series of partial (incremental) commitments rather than through global formulations of total strategies.
2. Logical incrementalism is a synthesis of logical, global analysis (e.g. corporate planning) and political or power-behavioural decision making which operates through a process which:
   (a) improves the quality of available information;
   (b) establishes critical elements of political power and credibility;
   (c) creates needed participation and commitment;
   thus enhancing decision quality and the likelihood of successful implementation.
3. The quality of each sub-system's strategy is improved if executives move forward incrementally, modifying their conclusions from broad conceptions towards specifics as more information, confidence and personal commitment are achieved.
4. As each sub-system 'pulses' forward it *interacts* with the strategies of other subsystems creating:

new opportunities
new demands
new constraints for all sub-systems.

5. Because of this continuing complexity and uncertainty executives *should* manage each sub-system incrementally in keeping with its own imperatives.
6. Therefore effective strategic managers try to *shape* the development of both sub-system and total enterprise strategies productively in a logically incremental fashion. Thus they:
   (a) accept ambiguity
   (b) ensure that the sub-systems do not work at cross purposes
   (c) define overall strategy in such a way as to encourage movement in the 'right' directions
   (d) consciously avoid overspecifics which might impair flexibility or commitment

Formal integration of different strategies was rarely achieved other than in the minds of individual executives:

> But the kinds of strategic consensus one could observe appeared much like giant river systems, constantly in flux and flow with many more or less discrete tributaries contributing to its strength. The system's central thrusts might be quite clear, but its specific boundaries and currents would rarely be completely perceivable in their totality (Quinn, 1980, p. 58).

On *goals*, he suggests that effective top executives typically announce only a *few broad goals;* they encourage other sections of the organisation to propose some: and they allow others to emerge from informal processes. Strategic goals are developed through a complicated, largely political consensus-building process.

Quinn sees the major obstacle to successful strategic planning as the trap of thinking of strategy-formulation and implementation as separate sequential processes: '(Executives) have relied on the awesome rationality of their formally derived strategies and the inherent power of their positions to cause their organisations to respond', whereas, successful managers build the seeds of understanding, identity and commitment into the very processes that create their strategies. By the time the strategy begins to crystallise in focus, pieces of it are already being implemented. 'Constantly integrating the simultaneous incremental processes of strategy formulation and implementation is the central art of effective strategic management (Quinn, 1980, p. 145). We could represent logical incrementalism in our model (see Figure 14.6). Note

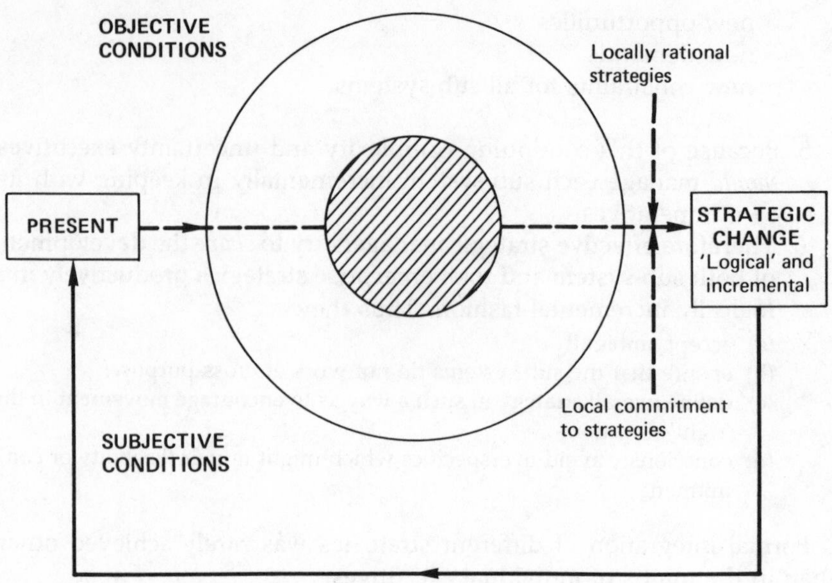

FIGURE 14.6 Logical incrementalism

that the shaded area spans both the objective and subjective conditions equally (but obviously, not completely).

14.6 A managerial incremental model

The incremental models considered so far have concentrated exclusively on the *processes* of strategic decision making. Donaldson and Lorsch (1983) present a managerial model which, whilst being clearly associated with the incrementalist group of models, includes some suggestions as to the *content* and thrust of strategic decisions in firms. Their model is derived from an empirical analysis of twelve successful US industrial corporations. It highlights the importance of survival as a goal pursued by CEOs and the psychological and 'objective' constraints on the strategic choices open to the top executive. They maintain that the CEO is committed to the survival and growth of the corporation in which he has invested so much of himself over the years. In making decisions these CEOs are not only concerned with the reactions and expectations of investors. They strive to reach decisions which will maintain or enhance their market positions as well as meeting the expectations of their colleagues for stability and career opportunities.

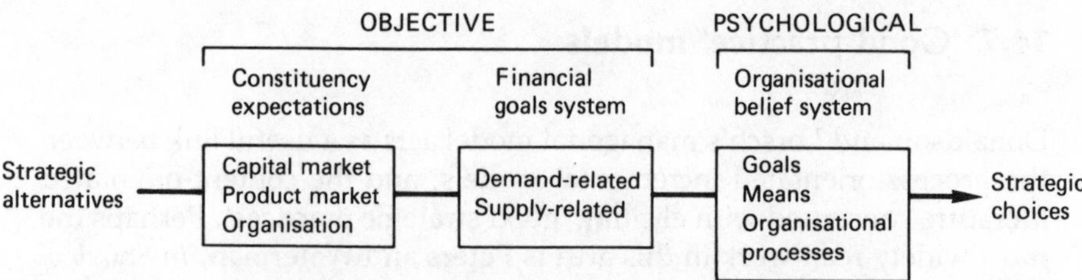

FIGURE 14.7 Constraints on strategic choice

Source: Donaldson and Lorsch, 1983

Beliefs about what consumers want and the way to compete with rival firms tend to figure strongly in the CEOs' strategic thinking. However, if the market conditions alter they are often unable to readjust, preferring instead to stick with policies which led to past successes. Their research supports incremental views of strategy-making, hence major strategic changes are accomplished by gradual adjustments over many years.

Figure 14.7 is a diagrammatic representation of the model. The objective contraints on the CEO consist of the expectations of the investors, the product markets and the people surrounding him in the organisation, and the need to balance the supply of and demand for funds. The psychological constraints or beliefs which the CEO holds, consist of:

- a view about the firm's distinctive competences
- the risks they are willing to take
- the degree of self-sufficiency they desire.

The model leads to a set of underlying objectives which the corporate managers strive to achieve:

1. to become financially independent of the capital market;
2. to reduce dependence on existing product markets through diversification;
3. to develop a committed and loyal workforce to minimise the chance of dominance from the organisation constituency.

Although CEOs do not rely on 'pure' theory (contained in economics, organisation or strategic-planning texts) they do rely on theories derived from the collective experience of themselves and their predecessors as it has been incorporated into their belief system.

14.7 'Good practice' models

Donaldson and Lorsch's managerial model acts as a useful link between the process-orientated incremental models, and the content-orientated literature concerned with eliciting 'good strategic practices'. Perhaps the most widely-read work in this area is Peters and Waterman, *In Search of Excellence* (Peters and Waterman, 1982). This stimulating book emerged from some applied research into organisational effectiveness instigated by McKinsey and Co in 1977. Peters and Waterman were interested in discovering what it was about certain very large companies that made them continually successful. In particular, did a code of good practice exist across these companies, which may be successfully implemented by the not-so-successful company? They synthesise a variety of policies, values, beliefs and systems into a set of eight attributes which tend to characterise and distinguish the excellent companies from the rest:

1. *A bias for action* Even in very large companies that are analytical in their approach to decision-making, there is an emphasis on trying out new ideas quickly, rather than waiting for the results of an exhaustive series of tests. These excellent companies work hard at maintaining fluid, responsive organisations; there is an emphasis on informal communication and mutual adjustment as the co-ordinating mechanism. Task forces are usually *temporary* (rather than being enshrined in a bureaucratic matrix structure), *small*, with *voluntary* membership and display a concern for *tangible results* rather than formal reports. In fact, the bias for action rules out lengthy research reports and memos (there is a 'rule' at Procter & Gamble that no memo should exceed one page!)
2. *Close to the customer* The excellent companies listen to the customer. They place great importance on service, quality and reliability. Service and quality standards are set almost unrealistically high, but resources and management effort are extensively deployed to back up these commitments. Reward ceremonies, quality circles, and some rather corny but effective US-style razzmatazz are all employed in the drive to get the message over. And by listening to the customer, the excellent companies are better placed to tailor products to particular market segments.
3. *Autonomy and entrepreneurship* Innovative companies encourage local initiative. They encourage practical risk-taking and support good tries, believing in the maxim 'the man who never makes a mistake, will never make anything'. They foster 'mavericks' and competing groups duplicating research effort. Once again, 'doers' –

people with the energy and commitment to get an idea off the ground – are encouraged even if they function outside the recognised formal systems and structures. Successful innovation requires intense communication – which is facilitated by flexible, informal structures.

4. *Productivity through people* The successful companies recognise the value of people. Concrete expressions of the concern for the individual include: policies of no-redundancy; excellent training; the use of first names; managers in regular informal contact with staff; performance evaluation orientated around peer review rather than management control systems. Other, less obvious expressions of the concern for people include: the fostering of a 'we-feeling', a feeling of the firm as an extended family; the apparent absence of a rigidly-followed chain of command; fewer management layers; a wide availability of information; treating people as adults; breaking up large units into many smaller ones.
5. *Hands-on, value-driven* Virtually all of the excellent companies had a well-defined set of guiding beliefs. The values are rarely expressed as quantifiable profit-type objectives (which are unlikely to motivate those outside the apex of the organisation). Leadership in these companies involves the perpetration of these values often through the use of corporate legends and myths. Leaders assist in this process by inspiring staff with ambitious visions, and by getting out and meeting staff on their own ground. Beliefs commonly held include: being the 'best'; the importance of getting the nuts and bolts of the job right; people at all levels have ideas.
6. *Stick to the knitting* Never acquire a business you don't know how to run. Diversifications should relate to the core strength of the company (for example 3M's skills in coating-and-bonding technology). Hands-on, value-driven leadership styles rely on the credibility of management which derives in large part from a knowledge and experience of the technical problems of the jobs with which employees are coping. This credibility is hard to sustain if senior management are ignorant of the technicalities of a newly-acquired, unrelated company.
7. *Simple form, lean staff* None of the excellent companies were run with a matrix structure. Structural forms tended to be simple, with small corporate headquarters even in the largest companies. The authors' main criticisms of matrix structures are the complexity of operating them, and the confusion of objectives, or values caused by a structure which says that everything is equally important. They suggest that one dimension (the function, project or region) must have primacy. The excellent companies used management

policies which mean that structural change is not the great upheaval experienced by many large, complex organisations. For example, job security, training and a policy which encourages staff to treat organisational units as having flexible, permeable membranes rather than brick walls means that change is not such a big deal. Decentralisation and small unit size also seem to be successful policies. Johnson & Johnson, for instance, has 150 divisions, each with its own R & D, personnel and finance functions. Pushing authority down the line and preserving autonomy for as many people as is practical were further expressions of the desire for organisational simplicity.

8. *Simultaneous loose–tight properties* This last feature perhaps summarises the major thrust of their argument. Excellent companies are prepared to push decision-making way down the structure, they are prepared to tolerate duplication of effort, flexible and informal structures, and they foster a climate of lower level initiative, but at the same time they jealously guard a small number of key *values*. Using the Mintzberg design parameters, co-ordination – ensuring that the right things are being done throughout a large and complex organisation – is effected largely through standardisation of skills, through forms of training and indoctrination which imbue all staff with these core values. Lower-level co-ordination seems to rely on combinations of the other four co-ordinating mechanisms, but informal mutual adjustment seems to be the favoured means. These key values invariably involve paying close attention to the customer, to quality and to innovation. These values are positive rather than the constraining checks and controls common to many large bureaucracies. And because these values are stable and enduring, staff are free to innovate within these value parameters – they know broadly what is required, they are not constantly jumping from objective to objective as the boss's overriding problem, or whim, changes.

Peters and Waterman's book is just one of a number of recently published 'good practice' texts. Hugh Marlow, a British consultant has produced a UK version called *Success*. He has suggested (in a paper delivered to the UK Institute of Personnel Managers Conference 1984) that *In Search of Excellence* rightly criticises the US trends to over-simplification and over-reliance on techniques, but that these criticisms do not necessarily apply to the UK firms which rarely suffer from an excess of professional management systems and approaches. He makes the interesting point that European culture has a greater tolerance of ambiguity and change and has a greater historical perspective on which to draw. Consequently, the paths to success for US firms cannot simply be transferred to the UK without recognising the difference in cultures.

Goldsmith and Clutterbruck (1984) present three necessary prerequisites to successful management:

Innovation

- absence or removal of barriers to change
- a natural curiosity about how things are done elsewhere
- an international perspective
- strong support for innovation from the CEO.

Integrity

- towards customers to foster their trust in the firm
- towards employees
- towards suppliers.

Involvement

- instilling pride in the organization in employees
- communication both downwards and upwards
- high pay, promotion prospects, and good training.

Solman and Friedman's very readable *Life and Death on the Corporate Battlefield: How Companies, Win, Lose, Survive* highlights the importance of establishing a competitive difference: 'Size is not necessarily the key to success and survival on the corporate battlefield . . . *difference* is. A tiny twenty-four-hour convenience store can't compete with Safeway, but then Safeway can't compete with the convenience store either' (Solman and Friedman, 1982, p. 47). They also present evidence of the use of political influence by large corporations in achieving their aims (see also Sampson, 1973).

14.8 Decision process models

Mintzberg, Raisinghani and Theoret's analysis of twenty-five strategic-decision processes resulted in the construction of a sophisticated and comprehensive descriptive model of strategic decision-making (Mintzberg *et al.*, 1976). Their work suggests, first that the strategic decision process is characterised by:

1. novelty;
2. complexity;
3. open-endedness.

Only by groping through a recursive, discontinuous process involving many difficult steps and a host of dynamic factors over a considerable period of time is a final choice made, (Mintzberg *et al.*, 1976, pp 250–1). They were able to categorise these twenty-five decisions in three ways:

1. By the *stimuli* that evoked them:

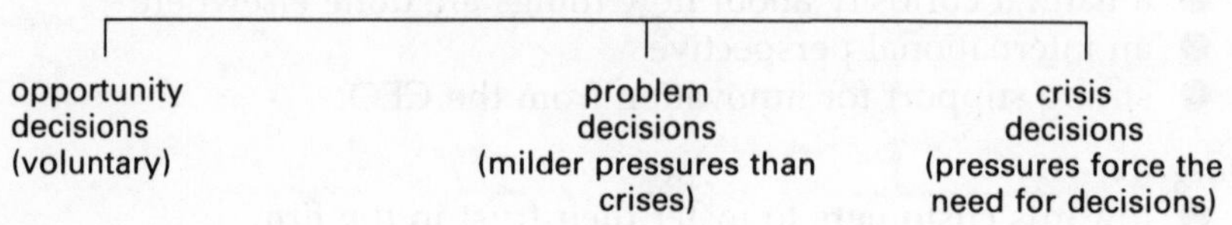

During the development of a solution a given decision process can move along this continuum because of a delay or a managerial action: opportunities missed can result in a problem; a crisis can be used as an opportunity to innovate.

2. By the *solution*:

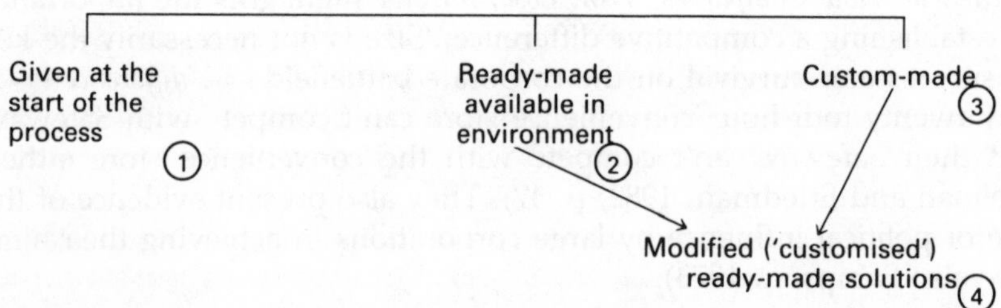

3. By the *process* used to arrive at them.

This method of categorisation is developed at length in their paper. They suggest that the decision process can be broken down into three basic phases:

(i) the *identification* phase;
(ii) the *development* phase;
(iii) the *selection* phase.

This breakdown is not dissimilar to Simon's 'intelligence–design–choice' model. Within each of these phases Mintzberg *et al.* identify various *routines* which we will now examine.

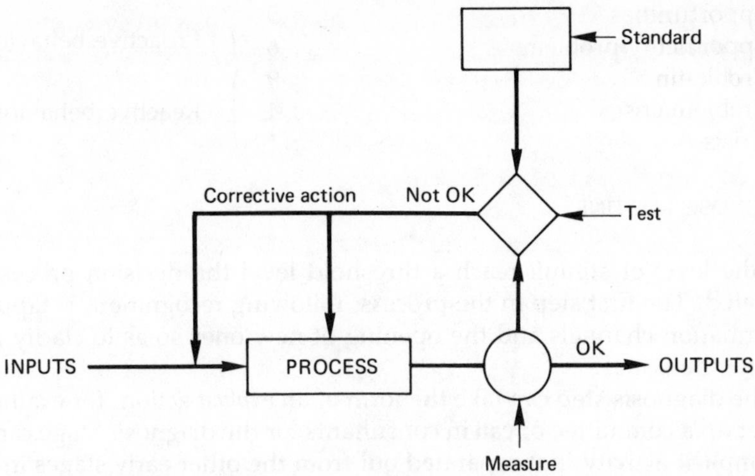

FIGURE 14.8 A simple control system

The identification phase

DECISION RECOGNITION ROUTINE

Most strategic decisions do not present themselves to the decision-maker in a convenient and obvious way. The need for a decision can be identified as a difference between information about an actual situation and some expected standard, rather like the simple control system model depicted in Figure 14.8.

The signals from the internal and external environments indicating the existence of problems or crises vary in intensity. Mintzberg *et al.* offer some interesting hypotheses concerning the cumulative amplitude of various stimuli and the threshold which, when reached, triggers action. They make two important points:

1. *Matching* A decision-maker may be reluctant to act on a problem for which he sees no apparent solution. He may also decide not to use a new idea which does not deal with a perceived difficulty. But when an opportunity is matched with a problem, a manager is more likely to initiate decision-making action.
2. *Proactive or reactive* This issue was raised in Chapter 12. Their contribution, resulting from the analysis of the twenty-five decisions, is that the view that organisations tend to react to problems rather than seek opportunities is not entirely accurate. They classified the twenty-five decisions as follows:

opportunities	: 5	Proactive behaviour
opportunity/problems	: 6	
Problem	: 9	Reactive behaviour
Problem/crises	: 4	
Crisis	: 1	

DIAGNOSIS ROUTINE

As the level of stimuli reach a threshold level the decision process is initiated. The first step in the process, following recognition, is tapping information channels and the opening of new ones so as to clarify and define the issues.

The diagnosis step can take the form of an *explicit* action, for example, to set up a committee or call in consultants; or the diagnosis stage can be an implicit activity, not separated out from the other early stages in the decision-making process. Most overt diagnostic activity takes place in the mild 'problem'-type decision categories: crises tend to pressurise decision-makers into skipping a formal diagnostic stage; and opportunities presumably do not demand much investigation as there is nothing to correct.

The development phase

This phase accounts for the bulk of time and other resources devoted to the decision-making process. There are two basic routines: search, and design. The two routines are fundamentally different:

Search activity: seeking ready-made solutions (looking for a needle in a haystack = covergent thinking)
Design activity: developing custom-made solutions or modifying ready made solutions
(writing a novel = divergent thinking)

SEARCH ROUTINE

Types of search activity include:

(a) *Memory search*: scanning the organisation's existing memory
(b) *Passive search*: waiting for unsolicited alternatives to appear
(c) *Trap search*: activating 'search generators' to produce alternatives
(d) *Active search*: directly seeking alternatives through scanning widely or focusing narrowly

Mintzberg *et al.* suggest that, on the basis of their study, search is a step-wise process, beginning with the 'easiest' source of solution (memory) through to active search for alternatives. If no ready-made solution exists the organisation is forced into design activity.

DESIGN ROUTINE

Mintzberg *et al.* draw a highly significant conclusion from their research into design activity:

> Apparently, because design of custom-made solutions is expensive and time-consuming, organisations are unwilling to spend the resources on more than one alternative. In contrast, the cost of generating extra alternatives during the *search* routine is small, and when relatively little design is involved, as in modified solutions, organisations are prepared to fully develop a second solution to compare it with the first (Mintzberg *et al.*, 1976, p. 256) (our emphasis) (see also Chapter 12).

The design of a custom-made solution is a complex, iterative process consuming much time and energy. The complex problem is often broke down into a sequence of sub-decisions with a limited number of alternatives to consider at each decision node. The solution is built brick by brick, the designers not knowing what the end-product will look like until it is finished.

This finding clearly has serious implications for 'rational – comprehensive' planning models. Strategic problems are, almost by definition, unstructured and non-programmable. According to this evidence, any decision-making technique which includes the generation (and subsequent evaluation) of a *wide range of alternatives*, most of those alternatives being in some sense 'unique' and purpose-built for the organisation, is 'forcing the organisation in a direction which is opposite to its "natural" tendency'.

The selection phase

Rather than selection following on in an orderly fashion from the development phase, selection activities are often intertwined within the development phase, especially where a design routine is being followed. Selection is typically a multistage, iterative process involving a progressively deepening investigation of alternatives. Mintzberg *et al.* identify three routines in this phase: (i) screen routine; (ii) evaluation-choice routine, and (iii) authorisation routine. Two multistage patterns of these three routines were discerned in the study (See Figure 14.9).

A SELECTION ROUTINES APPLIED SEQUENTIALLY TO A SINGLE CHOICE

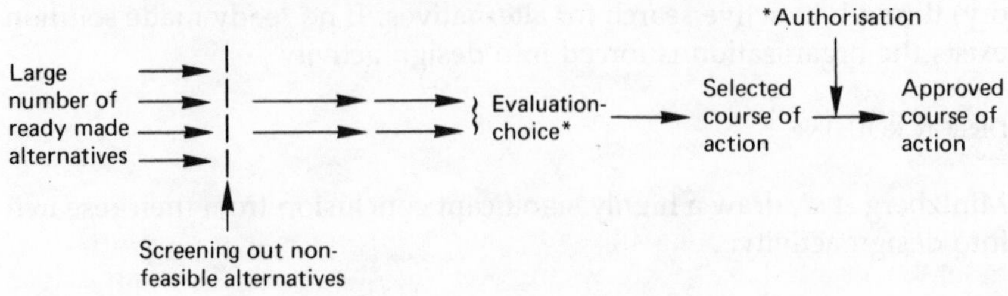

FIGURE 14.9 Selection routines

B SINGLE SELECTION STEP IS MULTISTAGE OR NESTED

Here the alternative may be evaluated in a general way, then in succeedingly more intense ways. Or one choice can be subjected to authorisation at successively higher levels in the organisation. So in *Figure 14.9* the stages marked * are extended.

SCREEN ROUTINE

This is a superficial routine more concerned with eliminating non-feasible alternatives than with determining what is appropriate.

EVALUATION–CHOICE ROUTINE

Although this part of the decision process is dealt with at length in the literature on strategic decision-making, Mintzberg *et al.* found that it did not form a particularly significant role in the actual decisions under investigation. They found little evidence of the use of analytical, objective approaches in this stage; in fact judgement and the consideration of 'soft' non-quantitative variables proved to be much more significant.

The problem of information overload and the complexity and dynamic nature of many strategic decisions can place a severe cognitive strain on the decision-maker. This can be coped with by:

1. using proxy means of choice (for example, precedent, tradition, imitation);
2. evaluating the sponsor of the alternative instead of the alternative itself (judging the singer, not the song);
3. setting up a limited number of primary goals and secondary con-

straints. The secondary constraints are used to *reject* alternatives, the primary-goal dimensions are used to compare possible alternatives (see Chapter 12).

AUTHORISATION ROUTINE

Where the individual making the choice does not have the authority to commit the organisation to a particular course of action, authorisation must be granted by positions further up the hierarchy. Difficulties experienced at this phase include:

1. authorisers limiting their considerations either to total acceptance or to total rejection of the alternative;
2. authorisers lacking the required depth of knowledge of the problem and solution to put them.

Supporting routines and dynamic factors

Three sets of routines support the three central phases of identification, selection and development. Decision control routines guide the decision process itself, communication routines provide the information for decision-making, and political routines enable the decision-maker to cope with the political forces operating both inside and outside the organisation. In addition to these supporting routines, the dynamic nature of strategic decision-making is reflected in six groups of dynamic factors:

1. *interrupts* – caused by environmental forces;
2. *scheduling delays, timing delays* and *speed-ups* which are deliberately invoked by the decision-maker;
3. *feedback delays* – awaiting the result of a previous decision;
4. *comprehensive cycles* – cycling back to an earlier phase to improve understanding of a complex issue;
5. *failure recycles* – cycling back, for example, to the development phase having failed to find an acceptable solution.

A simplified version of the complete model is presented in Figure 14.10.

In a recent paper Mintzberg and Waters (1985) suggest a typology of strategies. *Intended* strategies are distinguished from *realised* strategies – the former being the management's planned strategy, the latter being

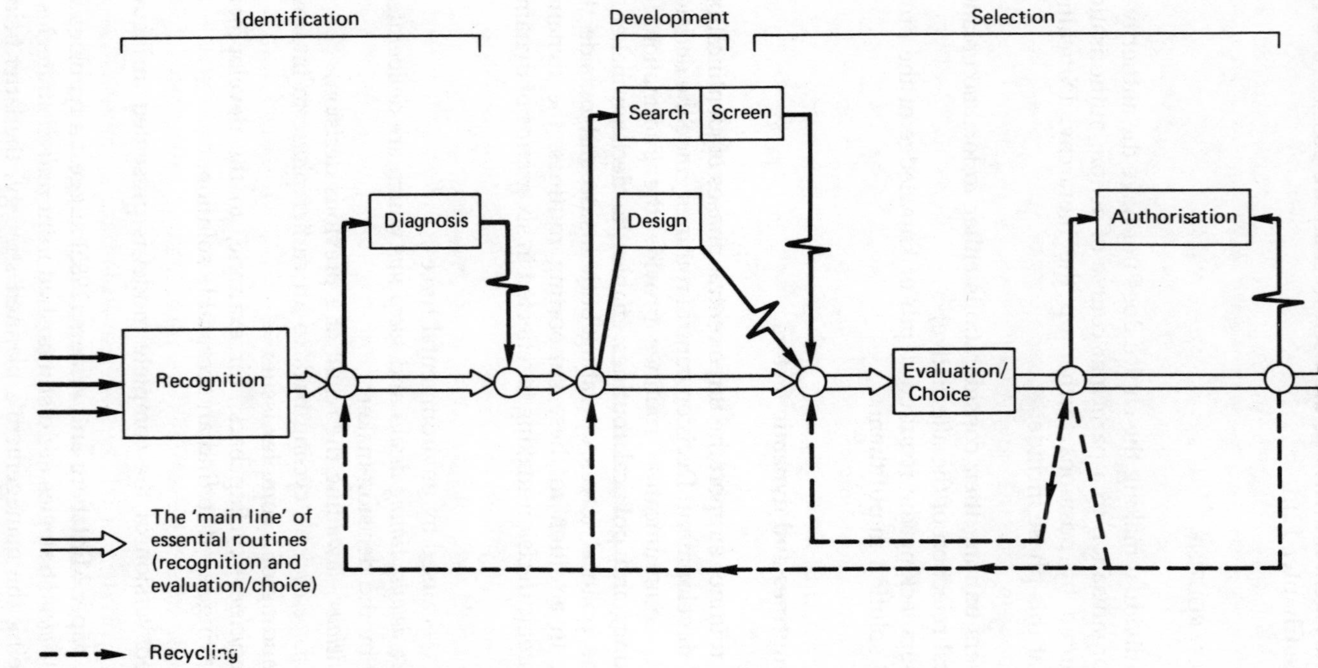

FIGURE 14.10 Mintzberg *et al.*'s general model of the strategic decision-making process (simplified)

Source: Mintzberg *et al.* (1976).

what the organisation actually did. So *deliberate* strategies are those that are realised as intended, and *emergent* strategies are patterns or consistencies in streams of actions realised despite, or in the absence of, intentions (see Figure 14.11). A summary of the eight strategy types can be found in Table 14.2.

14.9 Towards a contingency theory of strategic decision-making

Corporate planning on the one hand, and Quinn and Etzioni's incrementally-based models on the other can be regarded as attempts to derive coherent and implementable prescriptive approaches to strategic decision-making. Whereas, Mintzberg *et al.*'s model is essentially descriptive in nature; it is not intended as an attempt to design a 'better' decision-making system. For those looking for ways to improve their organisation's decision-making processes there is a danger of opting for a decision system which is not suited to the particular circumstances of their organisation.

We have seen in, for example, the literature on management style, the dangers of promoting a single approach as a solution to all situations. Similarly, in organisation theory we have moved from the advocacy of a set of 'rules' for good organisation (such as, well-defined job descriptions, 'one-man-one-boss', limited spans of control) to an acknowledgement that different situations – environment, technology – demand particular organisational structures and processes. So, it seems reasonable to suppose that one type of decision-making process (such as corporate planning) will not be suitable for every organisation.

In Chapter 11 we explored how contingency factors affected the structure of the organisation. We looked at how the age, size, environment, and technical system of the firm might be connected to its structure and internal processes, and in Chapter 13 the power relationships within the firm, and the power links between the firm and its environment were also considered. So one way of working towards a contingency approach to strategic decision-making might be to take these five contingency factors and examine how the various states of each factor might affect the strategic decision-making processes.

This approach is likely to be extremely complex (though that is not a reason to abandon it) as it will be necessary to examine many states of each contingency variable. Moreover, combinations of states of each variable would need to be considered because of the interrelationships that might exist within each particular combination. Such an exhaustive

TABLE 14.2 Types of strategies

Strategy	*Major features*
Planned	Strategies originate in formal plans: precise intentions exist, formulated and articulated by central leadership, backed up by formal controls to ensure surprise-free implementation in benign, controllable or predictable environment; strategies mostly deliberate
Entrepreneurial	Strategies originate in central vision: intentions exist as personal, unarticulated vision of single leader, and so are adaptable to new opportunities; organisation under personal control of leader and located in protected niche in environment; strategies relatively deliberate but can emerge
Ideological	Strategies originate in shared beliefs: intentions exist as collective vision of all actors, in inspirational form and relatively immutable, controlled normatively through indoctrination and/or socialisation: organisation often proactive *vis-à-vis* environment; strategies rather deliberate
Umbrella	Strategies originate in constraints: leadership, in partial control of organisational actions, defines strategic boundaries or targets within which other actors respond to own forces or to complex, perhaps also unpredictable environment; strategies partly deliberate, partly emergent and deliberately emergent
Process	Strategies originate in process: leadership controls process aspects of strategy (hiring, structure, etc.) leaving content aspects to other actors; strategies partly deliberate, partly emergent (and, again, deliberately emergent)
Unconnected	Strategies originate in enclaves: actor(s) loosely coupled to rest of organisation produce(s) patterns in own actions in absence of, or in direct contradiction to, central or common intentions; strategies organisationally emergent whether or not deliberate for actor(s)
Consensus	Strategies originate in consensus: through mutual adjustment, actors converge on patterns that become pervasive in absence of central or common intentions; strategies rather emergent
Imposed	Strategies originate in environment: environment dictates patterns in actions either through direct imposition or through implicitly pre-empting or bounding organisational choice; strategies mostly emergent, although may be internalised by organisation and made deliberate.

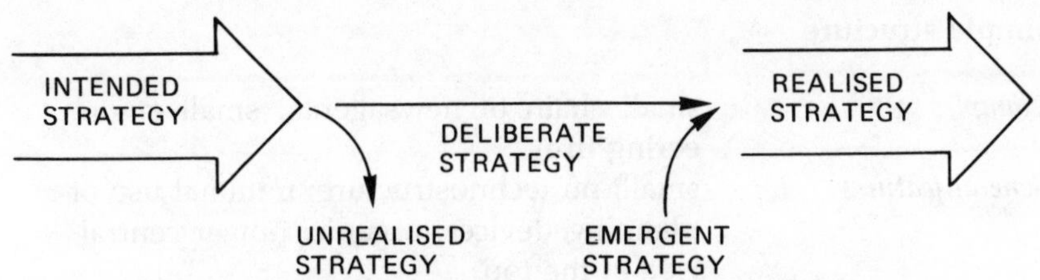

FIGURE 14.11 Deliberate and emergent strategies

Source: Mintzberg and Waters (1985).

study is outside the scope of this book, but we can suggest a less comprehensive theory if we accept that it is possible to identify a limited number of commonly-found combinations of contingency variables. These combinations would form coherent gestalts where there were congruent relationships between the contingency variables.

Fortunately, the hard work has already been done by Mintzberg, who puts forward five structural configurations which seem adequately to represent the situations of a large number of organisations. So rather than examining all the states of each contingency variable, we can use these configurations as generalised models of commonly-occurring combinations of the states of our contingency variables. The five configurations are:

the *simple structure*
the *machine bureaucracy*
the *professional bureaucracy*
the *divisionalised structure*
the *adhocracy*.

We have identified, for each of these configurations, its general features and the contingent conditions which have influenced the development of each configuration. We have concentrated attention on the implications for strategic decision-making which emerge from each configuration, and we have highlighted some of the potential problem areas posed by the structure.

Simple structure

Examples	small chain of newsagents, small engineering firm
General features	small; no technostructure; minimal use of planning devices; organic; power centralised at the top
Strategic decision-making	• flexible, rapid, co-ordination is relatively easy, • sole responsibility of CEO • intuitive, not analytical, entrepreneurial, opportunistic • extension of CEOs values and personality

CONTINGENT CONDITIONS

Environment	simple – comprehended by one person dynamic – unpredictable which makes standardisation difficult
Technical system	non-sophisticated and non-regulating*
Age	usually young firms which have not had time to elaborate the structure
Size	small
Power	• autocratic and/or charismatic leadership • owner-controlled

PROBLEMS

1. Operating problems crowd out strategic considerations
2. Total reliance on one individual, therefore it is vulnerable
3. Exclusion of other viewpoints can lead to poor decisions and demotivated staff.

NOTE

* regulation refers to the extent to which the technical system controls the operator's work e.g. the pace of work, the discretion the operator can exercise.

Machine bureaucracy

Examples	large car manufacturer, food processing, TV assembly
General features	Operating work is routine; processes are standardised; highly formalised structure; powerful technostructures; an obsession with control
Strategic decision-making	• only the apex can take a general, strategic perspective, therefore decision-making is a top–down process • belief in rationality of decisions • apex makes strategy; the middle-line and operating core implement it

CONTINGENT CONDITIONS

Environment	simple and stable
Technical system	regulating; not automated (to the extent, for example, of a chemical-processing plant); mass production
Age	mature
Size	large
Power	centralised at the apex, though some informal power resides with analysts in the technostructure. Often subject to strong external control

PROBLEMS

1. Apex often too concerned with improving efficiency (productivity, cost-reduction) and dealing with conflicts (such as strikes) to devote sufficient time and energy to strategic issues.
2. Rigid structures and over-formal communication channels stifle the flow of ideas and initiatives.
3. In the event of disturbances and instabilities the apex becomes even more overloaded (see Burns and Stalker 1966).
4. Long communication lines lead to distortions, delays and non-availability of strategic information at the apex.
5. The formulators of strategy are not the implementers, and, as most strategies need adaption at the implementation stage, the results are often (a) the wrong strategy being forced through, or (b) the whole plan being abandoned because one part is inappropriate, or (c) long delays as the plan is passed upstairs to be redrawn.

Professional bureaucracy

Examples	school, college, hospital, construction, craft work
General features	bureaucratic but not centralised. Stable but complex operating work leads to standardisation of skills and decentralisation. Power is based on professional expertise not hierarchy (as in machine bureaucracy). Small technostructure, short middle line, large operating core and support staff.
Strategic decision-making	• highly decentralised structure • organisation often has a set of unmeasurable, unagreed goals which complicate SDM • strong influence asserted by external professional bodies • strategy is best viewed as emerging from the initiatives of individual professionals • initiatives from the operating core are managed through committee structures by administrators • administrators need to rely on the use of informal power and persuasion to effect strategic changes.

CONTINGENT CONDITIONS

Environment	complex and stable
Technical system	*not* highly regulating, sophisticated or automated (although the work of individuals may be highly complex, the technical *system* of the operating core as a whole is not)
Age	varies
Size	varies
Power	resides with the professionals in the operating core who have a great deal of autonomy

PROBLEMS

1. Co-ordination of activity in order to achieve a coherent strategy is often thwarted because of the relative autonomy of the professionals.
2. The problems of measuring performance lead to vagueness and indecision in SDM.
3. The structure is inherently inflexible in so far as the task of the organisation has been subdivided into rigid specialities.

Divisionalised structures

Examples	Trafalgar House, Reckitt & Colman, ICI
General features	a set of relatively autonomous units coupled together by a central administrative structure (the headquarters). Divisions are usually able to function without needing to co-ordinate their activities with other divisions. Most often found superimposed upon machine bureaucratic structures.
Strategic decision-making	• usually divisions have the power to make decisions concerning their own operations (markets, products, etc.), but because the general manager of the division is held responsible for the division's performance, decision-making can tend to be centralised *within* the division. • headquarters controls divisions through quantifiable performance targets – profits, ROCE, Sales. (Standardisation of outputs). • detailed strategy cannot be made at headquarters as this undermines divisional autonomy, and moreover, the headquarters staff rarely possess the information and specialised expertise to make specific strategic decisions. • headquarters tries to control SDM through the training, indoctrination and development of the divisional managers. • headquarters strategic activities include: (i) managing the portfolio of *divisions* (whereas the division manages a portfolio of *products*) (ii) allocating finance, authorising capital projects (iii) designing the performance control system (sets the targets, review periods, planning and budgeting systems) (iv) replacing and appointing divisional managers (v) certain critical functions may be

centralised at the headquarters (for example, purchasing in a large retail chain; marketing in a multinational selling a standardised product such as Coca Cola.

CONTINGENT CONDITIONS

Environment product and market diversity (often competition forces divisionalisation as a way to improve efficiency)
Technical system needs to be divisible to permit divisional autonomy
Age tend to be mature organisations
Size usually large
Power power located at headquarters and centralised at the apex of each division.

PROBLEMS

1. Conglomerate structures deny the shareholder flexibility to move capital between different industries as their perceived performance and risk profiles change. Thus conglomerates can delay (but not eliminate) the forces determining the ebb and flow of particular businesses to the detriment of economic efficiency, for example, a successful division unable to grow as its profits are used to subsidise a loss-making division. (However, this may not be an inevitable outcome of conglomerate structures – see Chapter 2)
2. Divisional managers are not wholly autonomous, they can lean on (and be leaned on by) the headquarters management. Maybe, as a result, the development of their general management (or strategic) perspective is hindered.
3. The performance control system can tend to encourage only *incremental* strategic decision-making (if the divisional manager is judged on a year-by-year basis). Hence, the longer-term, riskier strategic leaps may be consciously avoided by these managers.
4. Headquarters management may try to centralise (to avoid duplication; to gain control) which may reduce the efficiency of the divisions. Information at headquarters level is often too generalised and quantified to be reliable for making what should really be divisional strategic decisions.
5. Because of the emphasis on quantifiable performance controls, strategically significant qualitative issues (such as social relationships) may be ignored.

The 'Adhocracy'

Examples	NASA, management consultants, the editorial part of a newspaper, chemical processing
General features	highly organic, little formalisation, innovative with teams of specialists and selective decentralisation. Almost an anti-bureaucracy, a sophisticated and flexible form of organisation, heavily reliant on liaison devices to effect co-ordination. Often uses a matrix form.
Strategic decision-making	• the decision-making power resides largely with the highly-trained professionals who are dispersed throughout the structure, not just in the operating core (as in the professional bureaucracy). • thus strategy *emerges* from individuals making separate decisions. The dichotomy between formulation of strategy and its subsequent implementation does not, therefore, apply. • strategic decision-making power is often located in loosely-structured work constellations. • because the means to achieving the organisation's ends are not well-defined, only general and flexible guidelines can be given to constellations. • senior management need to devote time to resolving conflicts between groups (without resorting to the use of formal authority) and to liaising with the external environment (getting more projects, for example).

CONTINGENT CONDITIONS

Environment	dynamic and complex (often requiring frequent product changes)
Technical system	can have simple, non-regulating technical systems, or highly sophisticated, automated operating cores (as in some process firms)

Age	tends to be a youthful form of organisation as there are usually pressures to formalise the structure
Size	tend to be small, but can be very large
Power	power of decision-making can flow to anyone with expertise, regardless of position

PROBLEMS

1. Ambiguity and a lack of structure can result in a highly political decision-making environment.
2. Loose control from the apex can result in staff pursuing non-organisational goals.
3. Decision-making can involve considerable time and effort, resolving differences, canvassing support, dealing, liaising, consulting, etc.

These five models are ideal types, probably no organisation exhibits these features precisely. Moreover, hybrid forms exist which contain the essential features of two structural types. For example, a newspaper might have an 'adhocracy' type of structure to tackle the creative, editorial task, and a machine bureaucratic structure to manage the printing side of the business.

Nevertheless, although these are models they are not so generalised that it is impossible to see strong parallels between any given firm's structure and one of the five structural types. If we accept that this is the case, this initial attempt at a contingency theory of strategic decision-making leads to two important conclusions:

1. it is not useful to force a particular approach to strategic decision-making (for example, corporate planning) onto a structure which is inherently unsuited to it;
2. strategic decision processes that emerge from a particular structural configuration may be improved upon, but it is likely that only incremental adjustments are feasible, those that fit the contingent conditions.

14.10 Summary

1. Models of strategic decision-making range from the prescriptive (such as corporate planning) to the descriptive (disjointed incrementalism).

2. Corporate planning has been criticised as: being inflexible; being incompatible with the cognitive and informational limitations of managers; stifling initiative; causing implementation difficulties where it has been adopted.
3. Disjointed incrementalism describes a decision process in which means and ends are chosen simultaneously through a succession of limited comparisons of policy options. This process seems a more naturally emergent decision-making system which fits the subjective conditions of the organisation.
4. Logical incrementalism describes a decision process in which strategic sub-systems in the organisation formulate partial strategies in a logical but incremental way. As such it can be regarded as a synthesis of rational, comprehensive analysis and power–behavioural decision-making. The sub-systems operate within a few broad guidelines set by senior management, and as they 'pulse' forwards strategy is both formulated and implemented incrementally.
5. 'Good practice' models are prescriptions for better strategic management. Successful enterprises adopt similar postures towards productivity, customers, staff and structure.
6. Decision process models describe actual strategic decisions. Strategic decisions have an identification phase, a development phase and a selection phase.
7. Strategies can be categorised as being either deliberate (where the strategy is realised as intended by the management) or emergent (where strategies are realised despite, or in the absence of, intentions).
8. A contingency approach to strategic decision-making can be derived using Mintzberg's five structural configurations: simple structure, machine bureaucracy, professional bureaucracy, divisionalised structure and adhocracy.

Further reading

Peters and Waterman (1982) is a readable, common-sense handbook of good strategic management practice. Of the more academic texts, Quinn (1980) makes good use of empirical evidence in supporting his synthesis of rational comprehensive and power-behavioural approaches to strategy-making. Mintzberg and Waters (1985) is concise, and suggests directions which the study of strategic management might take in the future.

References

Argenti, J. (1980) *Practical Corporate Planning* (London: Allen & Unwin).

Burns, T. and Stalker, G. M. (1966) *The Management of Innovation* (London: Tavistock).

Camhis, M. (1979) *Planning Theroy and Philosophy* (London: Tavistock).

Donaldson, G. and Lorsch (1983) *Decision Making at the Top* (New York: Basic Books).

Etzioni, A. (1967) 'Mixed-scanning: a third approach to decision-making', *Public Administration Review*, vol. 27, December.

Goldsmith, W. and Clutterbuck, D. (1984) *The Winning Streak* (London: Weidenfeld & Nicolson).

Lindblom, C. E. (1959) 'The Science of Muddling Through', reprinted in Pugh, D. S.(ed.) *Organization Theory* (Harmondsworth: Penguin) 2nd edn.

Marlow, H. (1984) *Success* (London: IPM).

Mintzberg, H. (1983) *Power In and Around Organizations* (Englewood Cliffs, New Jersey: Prentice-Hall).

Mintzberg, H., Raisinghani, D. and Theoret, A. (1976) 'The Structure of "Unstructured" Decision Processes', *Administrative Science Quarterly*, June.

Mintzberg, H. and Waters, J. A. (1985) 'Of Strategies, Deliberate and Emergent', *Strategic Management Journal*, vol. 6.

Peters, T. J. and Waterman, R. H. (1982) *In Search of Excellence* (London: Harper & Row).

Quinn, J. B. (1980) *Strategies for Change: Logical Incrementalism* (Homewood, Illinois: Irwin).

Sampson, A. (1973) *The Sovereign State: The Secret History of ITT* (London: Coronet).

Solman, P. and Friedman, T. (1982) *Life and Death on the Corporate Battlefield* (New York: Signet).

CHAPTER 15

Not-for-profit organisations

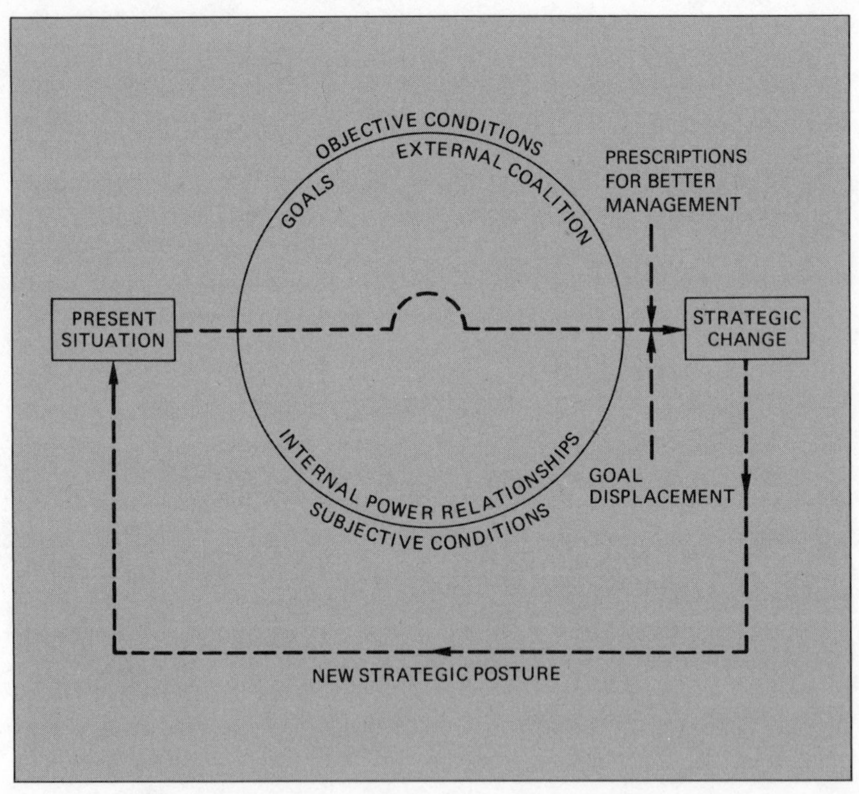

15.1 Introduction

In Chapter 2 on objectives we suggested that, while in many respects not-for-profit organisations (NFPs) displayed similar characteristics to the profit-seeking firm, there were fundamental differences between the two types of organisation. As this book is primarily concerned with strategic decision-making in the firm we make no apologies about the overwhelming emphasis on private sector organisations. However, in this chapter we shall attempt to go some way towards redressing the balance by explicitly focusing on the distinctive features, and strategic management issues that are peculiar to NFPs. Other writers have taken a view that NFPs are not sufficiently different from firms to warrant much more than a passing reference to them (see, for example, Johnson and Scholes, 1984). In contrast, we believe that NFPs require special treatment in a book on strategic management, and that to fail to make clear the distinctive features of NFPs is to invite confusion in strategic thinking.

We shall begin the chapter with a comparison of firms and NFPs on three broad dimensions: goals, funding and external influence, and internal power relationships. We then consider power structures, and issues in the strategic management of NFPs. We end the chapter with a consideration of a particular type of NFP – the nationalised industry, and a brief exploration of some aspects of inter-organisational relationships.

15.2 Firms and NFPs: a comparison

It seems rather glib to define an NFP as any organisation that does *not* have the pursuit of profits as its primary goal, but as a working definition it should suit our purposes in this chapter. So this definition would include the Navy, Market Weighton Lawn Tennis Club, Oxfam, the GLC, British Rail and Liverpool University. Such a broad definition will inevitably prevent us from making anything other than very general points that *may* apply to *some* NFPs. Although one benefit of addressing this diverse range of organisations is that it should make us very wary of attempting a straightforward transplanting of concepts, decision-making systems and control mechanisms from the firm to NFPs in general. Let us first compare firms and NFPs on one fundamental dimension: the purpose of the organisation, its goals.

TABLE 15.1 Comparing firms and NFPs: goals

Firms	NFPs
Quantitative	Qualitative
Unchanging	Variable
Consistent	Conflicting
Unified	Complex
Operational	Non-operational
Clarity	Ambiguity
Measurable	Non-measurable

15.3 Goals

Table 15.1, summarises some of the more important differences between firms and NFPs in respect of their goals. However, we are not suggesting that *all* NFPs goal-structures display *all* these features, merely that these are features of many NFPs goal-systems.

Although we would not argue that firms are profit-*maximising* organisations they clearly have to make some level of profits otherwise they will cease to exist. As we explained in Chapter 2, other so-called objectives (like increasing market share, being technically innovative, caring for the environment) can more usefully be regarded as *strategies*, *means* to an end rather than ends in themselves. So the firm has the advantage of goal clarity: profits must be made, performance can be measured, and alternative strategies can be evaluated against this overriding objective.

In contrast, most NFPs have goals which are often qualitative in nature, that are often conflicting, changing and open to different interpretations. For example, the National Park Service of the USA has its objectives spelled out in legislation:

> To conserve the scenery and the national and historic objects and the wildlife therein and to provide for the enjoyment of the same in such manner and by such means as will leave them unimpaired for the enjoyment of future generations. (William C. Everhart, *The National Park Service*, Praeger Publishing, 1972, p. 21).

On the face of it this appears straightforward enough, and, unlike many NFPs, at least the National Park Service has some concrete guidance. However, there is a built-in dilemma in these guidelines, between public access to the wonders of nature, and the preservation of them for future generations. This dilemma is a very real one for members of the parks service. Some resolve the problem by organising the two objectives into a definite hierarchy: preservation first, access second. Others see it as a problem which is present even in very low level decisions, for example, how many camp-site places to offer the public in a given area of a National Park. So the tension between these often contradictory objectives is acted out in the day-to-day decisions of many members of the organisation.

Sequential attention to goals

Conflicting goals can be coped with by a process of shifting priorities over time. Instead of trying to reconcile conflicting goals the NFP pursues one goal until such time as pressures (internal and/or external) force a change of direction in favour of another goal. A similar process can occur in politics: concern for welfare and meeting social needs forming the predominant complexion of governments, until such time as pressure from voters and political lobbies forces a shift towards policies striving for 'efficiency' and fiscal responsibility.

Such shifts of emphasis often reflect a divided external power structure controlling the organisation, where no one group in the external coalition is able to secure an enduring dominant position.

Goal succession

If we agree that firms are basically in business to make money then the concept of goal achievement does not really apply. One cannot envisage the senior management of a firm instructing the workforce to take the rest of the year off, 'because we've made enough profit already this year'! If we see goal structures as constraints of some form (maybe as maze walls which *guide* the direction the organisation takes rather than completely determining it) then the profit-goal is a wall which, if you push against it, will keep moving away. In contrast, many NFPs are established to achieve concrete and achievable goals, for example, a group of residents campaigning for a by-pass to their town; once the by-pass is built to their satisfaction the goal of the organisation is achieved. Another problem might then face those members of the organisation who, for a variety of reasons, gained satisfaction from working in and belonging to the group, which were in addition to the stated shared cause. These 'system goals' – personal goals that organisation members satisfy merely through membership of the organisation (such as companionship and status) – might encourage members to seek a new goal for the organisation, one to replace the achieved goal. Thus goal succession can be a problem for NFPs: we have the rather strange phenomenon of an established organisation looking for something to do!

15.4 Performance measurement

If there is a lack of clarity in the objectives of the NFP, and, moreover, even if the goals are clear but achievement of them is not measurable, then assessing the performance of the organisation becomes extremely difficult. The authority structure can be weakened if there is no objective way of determining the performance of a particular department. This problem is not, of course, unique to NFPs. In all but the smallest firms, differentiation and departmentalisation present performance measurement problems (how do you assess the performance of the Personnel Department?) The problem is exacerbated in many NFPs because there is no 'bottom line' of ultimate performance (profitability) which can be used to reinforce the authority structure.

Proxy measures and goal displacement

One way around the problem is to measure some aspect of the task which *can* be measured in the hope that 'good' performance on this criterion will reflect the achievement of the unmeasurable 'true' objectives. If the purpose of schools was to educate and prepare children to take a useful place in society, a goal which cannot be directly measured, we would have to rely on indirect measures of goal achievement in order to assess the performance of an individual school. We *can* measure exam pass rates and use these as a yardstick to compare one school with another. (However, even this 'objective' measure needs to be treated with caution: if the intake to each school, the resources, the parental support, etc., are not the same then is it legitimate to use this measure in isolation?)

One unfortunate consequence of using proxy measures is that the measurement system can distort the efforts of people within the NFP in favour of the measurable objective. So our school might be producing neurotic, socially-inept school-leavers who are incapable of constructively using their leisure time, but who nevertheless have a string of exam passes.

Schools and other professional bureaucracies are often reluctant to disclose proxy measures of performance, believing that they will be interpreted in a simplistic and unfavourable way. Hospitals avoid the publication of mortality statistics, police forces are seldom willing to publicise their success rates in solving crime. When pressured into disclosing information, the professionals are more likely to release information about *inputs* rather than *outputs* – for example, staff/student ratios, direct/indirect employee ratios.

Efficiency

So, because of problems with measuring outputs, emphasis shifts to the measurement and control of input costs. *Efficiency* usually refers to the utilisation of the *means* (the resources), whereas *effectiveness* relates to the *goals* of the organisation. Thus an organisation could be very efficient but totally ineffective. For example, consider a firm making mechanical adding-machines: through the utilisation of the most advanced production methods it might be achieving very low unit costs compared with any other comparable firm (it is therefore efficient), but because no one wants to buy mechanical calculators any more it is not making any profits (it is therefore ineffective). In contrast, an effective organisation might be a mountain rescue team which, through the skilled and courageous application of human and material resources, is able to rescue an injured climber. It is effective because it has achieved its objective, it could only be judged efficient if we were able to assure ourselves that no unnecessary resources were employed in the rescue. So, in a sense, efficiency is a value-free concept: we might argue about the goals of the organisation, but, once we turn our attention to the use of resources in achieving the goals some reasonably objective observations are possible.

Efficiency has, however, acquired negative connotations. Because costs are typically more easily measured than benefits, efficiency is all too often interpreted as simply 'economy'. And the more unquantifiable the benefits the more vulnerable the activity can be to economising cuts. (Some departments and budgets in firms, for example, advertising market research suffer in this regard). See Illustration 15.1.

15.5 Funding and the external coalition

NFPs are often influenced by a fragmented external coalition made up of a variety of individuals and organisations, each with a different axe to grind. For example, a College or Polytechnic is subject to a variety of controlling influences: the local authority, the Department of Education and Science, the Board of Governors, the CNAA, the lecturer's union

ILLUSTRATION 15.1 Management in the Health Service

Mr Norman Fowler will shortly announce new plans for injecting a management ethos into the **National Health Service**. It will be the third attempt in ten years to shake up the administration of the service.

The main idea is to run the NHS more like an ordinary business or, with luck, like a good business. Decisions at every level should be taken swiftly by general managers, rather than agonised over by the existing system of 'consensus management'. At present, management teams are made up of representatives from the various health service professions and each member has a right of veto. The team's proposals are then passed to the district and regional health authorities, part-time boards of outsiders who meet about once a month and practically all of whose information comes from the management teams.

The enquiry into NHS management looked askance not only at the slowness of this procedure, but also at the fact that ideas strongly opposed by one group might never be brought up. They found a morass of unclaimed responsibilities and merry disorganisation. They also found an absence of any systematic attempt to set goals and monitor progress towards them, and recommended that output should be measured more methodically.

But the problem with output measures in health, as in education, is that nobody agrees on exactly what the output is supposed to be, let alone how to measure it. The sort of performance indicators now used can provide pat answers to questions in parliament, but not much else. They are, for the most part, crude measures of turnover with no reference to quality. In terms of these measures, the most efficient hospital could be one which admitted people, whether well or ill, gave them no treatment and discharged them the next day. Since there is no accepted idea of what efficiency in the health service is, health service workers, including doctors, tend to see efficiency-minded managers as people who go around switching off life-support machines to save electricity.

(Source: The *Economist*, 24 March 1984).

NATFHE, the NUS and so on. If no one external influencer holds an enduring dominant position, the College is likely to be facing a divided external coalition. Sometimes influencers will be trying to push the College in more or less the same direction, at other times it will be subject to conflicting demands being made upon it. Obviously, a critical resource for an NFP is cash, and, not surprisingly, those who provide most of the funds for the NFP are likely to have more power to influence NFP decisions.

NFPs can obtain funding from a variety of sources: clients, national and local governments, membership subscriptions, donations. One useful distinction that can be made between different sources of funds is between those that are provided by the customers and/or clients, and those provided by the 'sponsors' of the NFP. A firm tends to be heavily dependent on sales of products/services to customers for income and it will therefore tend to be very interested in pleasing the customer in its strategic deliberations. However, the client, or recipient of the NFPs services, typically pays only a small proportion (if any) of the cost of providing the service. Hence, the client influence over the NFP, or more importantly, the degree to which the client's interests will be of paramount importance in strategic decision-making may well be small. However, we must be cautious in pushing this argument too far, as there are many other factors operating within and without the organisation which may in effect be driving the NFP to take especial account of the client's interests (as, for example, the professionalism of the doctors and nurses in a hospital).

Pfeffer (1981) has observed an interesting aspect of sponsor's power over the NFP stemming from the incremental nature of most funding decisions. He suggests that organisations can be taken over by discretionary control over not more than 10 per cent of the organisation's total budget (Pfeffer, 1981, p. 106). The process works like this:

Year 0

NFP Budget determined by some form of rule such as number of pupils/ patients x £*x*; or last year's budget + inflation. This is the fixed or non-discretionary proportion of the budget.

Year 1

The Fixed Budget is augmented by a discretionary increment which permits change, adaption, problem solving, opportunities to excel.

Year 2

The increment, as far as the members of the NFP are concerned, has now been absorbed into the organisation as an essential part of the total

ILLUSTRATION 15.2 Funding Problems Facing NFPs

The following examples illustrate problems that many NFPs have to wrestle with when faced with funding problems:

1. A legal aid group must decide whether it will begin to charge clients a modest fee in order to generate much-needed earned income (the mission statement talks about providing free legal aid).
2. A church must decide whether to take a stand on abortion. Regardless of the position it takes, it risks alienating a large number of church members. Yet the minister believes that the mission of the church is to provide guidance on moral issues.
3. An all-male school, responding to decreasing enrolments, has been advised by a marketing consultant to go co-educational. Yet the staff and old boys feel that the original mission to offer a quality education to young men is still valid.
4. A symphony orchestra, organised to improve the quality of the musical life of its city must decide whether to increase the number of 'pops' concerts and decrease its regular subscription concerts of classical music. The programming change would assist the organisation in meeting its payroll but would compromise the mission of the organisation.
5. A women's health organisation, founded as a collective, must decide whether it will reorganise around more conventional management lines in order to increase efficiency and professionalism. Several of the organisation's founders believe that 'collective' management is central to the organisation's mission.

(Source: Thomas Wolf, *The Non-profit Organisation* (Englewood Cliffs, New Jersey: Prentice-Hall, 1984)

budget. This gives the provider of the increment considerable power through the threat of withdrawing these additional funds.

Pfeffer concludes that this sort of political skill in the manipulation of funds means that 'he who has the gold makes the rules, but it takes less gold if you know the rules' (Pfeffer, 1981, p. 109). See Illustration 15.2.

15.6 Power structures in NFPs

The formal power structures of firms (discussed in Chapter 13) tend in general to flow from the shareholders' ownership of the firm, their control of the Board, who then appoint the CEO. The CEO is thus usually the most powerful individual in the firm, and he or she delegates formal power to subordinate managers. However, we also identified a variety of organisational circumstances which tended to fudge this clear picture of the firm's power structure (for example, the informal power of some experts, the power to influence decisions indirectly by influencing decision *processes*). In general, though, the hierarchical nature of the power structure of most firms is easily discerned by the members of the organisation.

In contrast, NFPs display a wide variety of power structures. A useful starting-point is the nature of the commitment of the individual to the NFP. Whereas most employees in most firms have more of a calculative or utilitarian involvement with the organisation, some NFPs evoke strong ideological or normative commitment from their members. Some political and religious organisations demand and receive an almost complete integration of the individual's goals with those of the organisation. This form of NFP has been characterised by Mintzberg as the 'Missionary' type (see Mintzberg, 1983, ch. 21).

The Missionary

MAIN CHARACTERISTICS

- often volunteer organisations (charities, religious and political organisations)
- *strong* loyalty to the organisation's mission
- mission can be clear, if not operational
- standardisation of norms
- can be started by charismatic leader.

STRATEGIC RAMIFICATIONS

- strong ideology leads to strong resistance to change
- freedom of action is severely constrained
- can be highly *decentralised* as control is internalised through the acceptance of the ideology
- relatively autonomous: not subject to external pressures
- because of goal clarity, Missionaries suffer from little internal politicking.

Moving away from the missionary form towards the more selective identification of the organisational participants with the goals of the NFP, we would locate the various forms of professional organisations that Mintzberg dubs Meritocracies (Mintzberg, 1983, ch. 22).

The meritocracy

MAIN CHARACTERISTICS

- hospitals, universities and other professional bureaucracies
- power resides with the experts in the operating core: experts owe allegiance to their profession rather than the particular organisation
- complex mission leads to weak CEO power and displacement of organisational goals by the goals of the experts (autonomy, excellence).

STRATEGIC RAMIFICATIONS

- NFP often dependent on scarce, highly-mobile professionals
- NFP can be indirectly controlled externally by the professional's associations
- political behaviour encouraged by goal ambiguity and performance measurement problems: budgets allocated in part on the basis of the perceived power of departments
- professional bodies can act through their members to impede the introduction of strategic changes (rigidity in defence of professional norms)
- strategic change usually comes about through persuasion and negotiation.

We suggested earlier that whilst client-influence over the meritocracy might be minimal in terms of funding power, professional commitment to serving the client's interests may override this factor. In some circumstances this commitment to the client can place the professional in the position of actively working against the management's wishes.

A university provides a good example of a meritocratic power structure. Pfeffer and Moore (1980) have suggested that power in universities is determined by the department's ability to provide two critical resources: student enrolments and external funding. The enhanced status of the providing department enables it to influence budgeting, promotion and other resource-allocation decisions which, in their turn, continue to increase the department's power. So, as long as the department continues to deal with the major source of uncertainty facing the university, it will continue to perpetuate its relative power position.

15.7 Strategic management in NFPs : The role of the board

Unterman and Davis (1982) surveyed 103 NFPs in the USA with respect to their policy-making characteristics and in particular the role of the Board of Trustees. They compared NFP structures with the typical corporation and identified some important differences.

1. *Size of Boards* Whereas most firms would have Boards of about ten to fifteen, NFPs usually have upward of thirty members. Large Boards tend to confuse the signals about objectives reaching the NFP management, with the result that often the CEO is able to enforce his own value-system, the conflicting signals acting so as to neutralise the Board's effectiveness.
2. *Use of Insiders* In contrast to the corporation's Board, there is often only one insider on the NFP Board, the CEO. This often results in only limited information reaching the Board, which is compounded by a lack of specific managerial expertise being brought to bear on policy decisions.
3. *Continuity of Service* Most NFP Boards have fixed terms for membership, often with a rotating chairmanship, the average length of service being significantly less than the Board of the corporation. This can lead to a short-term focus of the Board and a risk that the Board's relative ignorance of the organisation's workings is perpetuated.

The diversity of interests and ambiguity of purpose stemming from the composition of the NFP Board indirectly affects the internal decision processes. Lack of goal clarity and strategic direction positively invites internal political behaviour.

Decision-making processes

Pfeffer has isolated four decision-making models which are summarised in Table 15.2. Of the four, the picture emerging from our discussion so far would seem to rule out the rational model. Some NFPs may tend towards the bureaucratic model where a high degree of goal clarity

TABLE 15.2 A summary of four decision-making models

	Model			
Dimension	*Rational*	*Bureaucratic*	*Decision Process*	*Political Power*
Goals, preferences	Consistent within and across social actors	Reasonably consistent	Unclear, ambiguous may be constructed *ex post* to rationalise action	Consistent within social actors; inconsistent, pluralistic within the organisation
Power and control	Centralised	Less centralised with greater reliance on rules	Very decentralised anarchic	Shifting coalitions and interest groups
Decision process	Orderly, substantively rational	Procedural rationality embodied in programmes and standard operating procedures	*Ad hoc*	Disorderly, characterised by push and pull of interests
Information computational requirements	Extensive, systematic	Reduced by the use rules and procedures	Haphazard collection and use of information	Information used and witheld strategically
Decisions	Follow from value-maximising choice	Follow from programmes and routines	Not linked to intention, result of intersection of persons, solutions, problems	Result of bargaining and interplay among interests

Source : Pfeffer (1981) p.31 (abbreviated).

exists. The decision process/organised anarchy model is a relatively recent formulation which not only eschews rationality (by removing the assumption of consistent overall objectives), but also removes the assumption of predefined, known preferences held by the various social actors. Choice is determined by the situation in which the decision-maker finds himself. This model goes further than Lindblom's model of disjointed incrementalism (see Chapter 14); here preference is not only revealed by choice, it is *determined* by choice. Intentions, 'observed' by organisation researchers according to decision-process theorists, are more likely to be imputed to the actors by the observers than being a characteristic of the organisation being researched. Pfeffer, however, criticises this approach as not providing us with a great amount of predictive power. He clearly favours a political model where interest groups (or individuals) are able to influence decisions through their possession of some form of power over other actors in the organisation. Conflict is endemic in the organisation and decision outcomes often reflect the compromises flowing from bargaining processes rather than simply the preferences of the 'winners'.

We would not press the case for any one of the four models as being a consistently superior representation of organisational decision-making. A model is useful in so far as it helps us understand a complex situation. As such, a model does not have to have a weight of empirical evidence supporting it for it to be useful.

Managing NFPs

We now turn our attention to problems of strategic management in NFPs. As many NFPs are subject to a great deal of external interference, and are dependent (for funding, licences, etc.) on powerful external groups, a critical role of the CEO is external liaison. CEOs therefore need expertise in a 'buffer' role, acting between the NFP and its sponsors. One tendency that can emerge from this willingness to please sponsors is a form of defensive centralisation. The top management try to retain decision-making authority to avoid any actions by lower levels which might upset the sponsors. However, we have seen that in some NFPs decision-making power naturally flows to the professionals in the operating core (for example, in hospitals) and attempts at centralisation may lead to poorer quality decisions, and demotivated professionals. On the positive side, skill in the liaison role may help in reinforcing the personal power of the CEO as, typically, the formal authority of the CEO position is weak relative to the power of his or her counterpart in a firm.

Weak position power means that the CEO has to rely on tactics other than the exercise of formal authority to control and influence other members of the organisation. Political skills – persuading, cajoling, forming alliances, bargaining – are of considerable importance, as are the personal qualities of the leader. One hesitates to use the term 'charisma' as it is a difficult concept to specify, but certainly a leader with strong values and a clear sense of direction is more likely to gain the confidence of the other members of the organisation. Strong leadership can only be exercised where there are people looking to be led, and in many NFPs, because of the lack of goal clarity, many members *are* looking for a sense of purpose and direction which can be provided by the CEO.

On the negative side, strong leadership can, first, make the organisation too dependent on a particular individual, thus raising management succession problems; and second, over-direction from the apex can stifle initiative at lower levels.

Many established bureaucratic NFPs are managed more by rules and regulations than by people. The hazards here are familiar: inappropriate measures of performance leading to a distortion of effort; goal displacement where adherence to the rule-book assumes more importance than exercising common sense and initiative; frustration caused through rigidity and inflexibility in the control systems.

Prescriptions for improved management of NFPs

In this section we shall look briefly at two prescriptive techniques designed to improve the control and performance of NFPs. Then we consider cost–benefit analysis as a technique designed to aid public-sector decision-making. All three were first applied in the USA, and only cost–benefit analysis has had significant exposure in the UK.

PLANNING, PROGRAMMING, BUDGETING SYSTEM (PPBS)

This system was developed by the US Department of Defense to assist administrators in choosing among alternative programmes. It follows a step-wise procedure:

1. specify objectives as far as possible in measurable terms;
2. analyse *actual* output for the NFP in terms of these specified objectives;
3. measure the cost of the particular programme;
4. analyse alternatives and search for those that have the greatest effectiveness in achieving the objectives;
5. establish the process in a systematic way so that it continues to occur over time (Keating, 1980).

The parallels with systematic corporate planning are clear, but whereas the firm's objectives are amenable to quantification, PPBS stands or falls on the ability to assign meaningful quantitative objectives to areas like education, health and defence.

ZERO BASE BUDGETING (ZBB)

ZBB is an attack on the insidious process of incrementalism. It is designed to avoid the tendency of NFP budgets to creep ever upwards, where next year's budget is largely a function of this year's budget. With ZBB nothing is taken for granted – *all* of the budget must be justified each year, not just the marginal increment.

COST–BENEFIT ANALYSIS (CBA)

CBA is an attempt to introduce some 'objective' economic analysis into major public-policy decisions, the most well-known applications of the technique in the UK being the Roskill Commission inquiry into the siting of the third London Airport, and earlier in the 1960s, the Victoria Line study. Put very simply, CBA tries to account for all the significant costs and benefits resulting from each policy option, and summing them (usually over a period of future years) the analysis provides an 'objective', quantified assessment for each option.

If we use an example of a road by-pass to a town it might help explain some of the features of the technique. Let us assume that there are two possible routes. Each route has different advantages and disadvantages, proponents and opponents, so there is no unanimously agreed route. Certain costs of each route, such as the actual costs of constructing the road are reasonably amenable to quantification. However, CBA should take the perspective of the society as a whole, so we need to consider a much wider spread of costs and benefits than the simple construction costs:

Costs

- Loss of agricultural land
- Destruction of some houses
- Increasing travel costs for some road users
- Spoiling an area of scenic beauty.

Benefits

- Marked reduction in traffic noise in town centre
- Travel time savings for some road users
- Fewer road accidents and pedestrian injuries
- Creation of a pleasant, traffic-free town centre.

There will also be spin-off (or 'ripple') effects on road-users elsewhere in the country, as traffic-flows are disturbed as a result of the construction of the by-pass.

Clearly, some of these costs and benefits are not directly measurable in money terms, and ingenious proxy measures and indications have been derived to overcome these difficulties. Other problems with the analysis are listed below:

1. How do we treat *future* costs and benefits? Are they regarded as equally valuable as today's costs? If we discount future costs and benefits, what discount rate reflects *society's* preferences for present over future benefits?
2. When do we stop including ripple effects? And how far ahead is it feasible to look?
3. How do we value saved lives? Thirteenth-century churches? A pleasant view? Peace and quiet? Air pollution? Saved time?

In addition to these difficulties there are serious issues concerning the theoretical underpinnings of the technique. CBA is rooted in a branch of welfare economics which is not without its critics. For example, the 'societal perspective' of CBA appears relatively uncontroversial, until one considers some ramifications of this seemingly apolitical, neutral standpoint. At the heart of the theoretical framework of CBA is the compensation principle, which regards a change that makes group *A* better off, but group *B* worse off, as an improvement in society as a whole, as long as group *A* could compensate group *B* and still be better off. In other words, group *B* would be no better or worse off than before the change, and group *A* would be better off. However, according to the welfare economists supporting CBA, the compensation need not be paid in practice – there would still be a net gain to *society as a whole* as a result of the change.

To put this argument in a real context, the CBA justification for locating a new airport on the edge of a city is masking the fact that the saving of twenty minutes of a business-man's time is 'worth' more to society than subjecting the local residents to noise pollution. A technique which purports to add up construction costs with noise pollution 'costs', time savings with sites of special scientific interest is likely to be wide open to criticism. CBA displays many of the worst features of 'rational analysis' masking and obfuscating the political, social and moral issues in a decision. CBA is usually applied to major (and usually controversial) public-sector decisions; decisions which are naturally political. In practice, the results of a CBA will be enthusiastically invoked by those who like the conclusions of the analysis, and will be

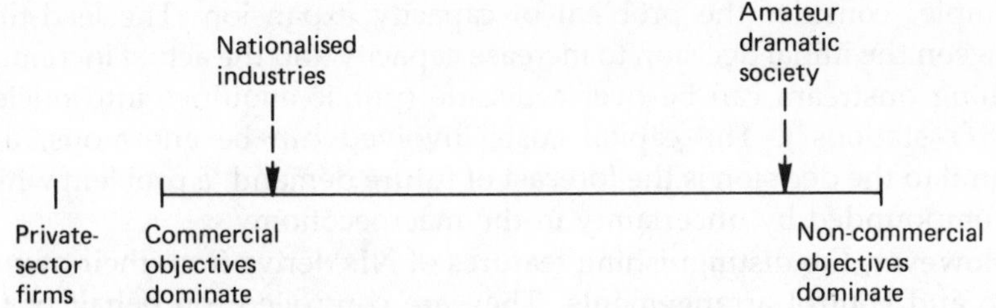

FIGURE 15.1 NFP objectives

reviled by those who do not. In practice, 'real' costs (like concrete and wages) are likely to be given a greater weight than 'notional' costs (like noise pollution and waiting time). At best CBA can provide some supporting analysis and evidence to the decision-taker (who is familiar with the limitations of CBA). At worst, it can be used to give a gloss of objective rationality and legitimacy to a covertly political decision.

15.8 Nationalised industries in the UK

Nationalised industries still occupy a commanding position in the economy of the UK, despite recent enthusiasm from the Conservative government for privatisation. We do not have the space to explore these particular organisations in detail, but these NFPs deserve some consideration as they occupy a grey area between the purely private-sector firm, and the 'obvious' NFP organisation (such as a charity). One way of classifying Nationalised Industries (e.g. British Rail, NCB, Post Office) is to locate them on the continuum drawn in Figure 15.1. The figure suggests that, no matter how commercially-orientated the board of the nationalised industry might be, it is still a fundamentally different form of organisation from the private-sector firm. Nationalised industries (NIs) have special problems with regard to strategic management, some of which stem from the nature of the industry itself, but most result from the nature of the relationship between the NI and the government.

Taking the industry-related issues first, many NIs are 'natural' monopolies. Either through the existence of scale economies, or through a wish to avoid wasteful duplication, we have sole suppliers of rail services, gas, water and electricity. These large, monopolistic and often capital-intensive industries would face peculiar strategic problems irrespective of the form of ownership. To take one important aspect as an example, consider the problem of capacity expansion. The lead-time between the initial decision to increase capacity and the actual increment coming onstream can be over a decade (public enquiries into nuclear power stations?). The capital costs involved can be enormous, and central to the decision is the forecast of future demand, a problem which is compounded by uncertainty in the macroeconomy.

However, the distinguishing features of NIs derive from their ownership and control arrangements. They are controlled, on behalf of the nation, by the government of the day, through the appropriate sponsoring ministry. We shall focus on two key problem-areas stemming from this form of ownership: objective setting, and interference in strategic decision-making.

(1) *Objectives*

These ostensibly flow from Acts of Parliament establishing the NI, and subsequent White Papers dealing with nationalised industries. In general, NIs are required to provide a particular good or service (which can constrain both divestment of 'unprofitable' sections of the business, and diversification). NIs have been subject to varying types of financial targetting: some aimed at overall performance, some directed to more efficient use of new capital. Objectives and targets can change within the lifetime of a government, and more usually between governments of different complexions.

(2) *Interference in strategic decision-making*

Both Labour and Conservative governments have interfered directly in the decision-making processes of NIs. Governments have used NIs as instruments of macroeconomic policy:

- to reduce unemployment (through subsidies)
- to stimulate growth (through investment)
- to reduce price inflation (by holding down prices)
- to control wage increases (by setting a public sector 'example')
- to support private sector firms (for example, BEA's purchase of Trident aircraft)
- to subsidise rural dwellers (through flat-rate charging policies)
- to reduce the public sector borrowing requirement (PSBR)

Recently, Ministries have insisted on reviewing (and approving or rejecting) the NIs corporate plans, as well as engaging in formal performance reviews of the industry. Corporate plans for ministerial consumption often have 'shadow' counterparts for internal use which reflect a more realistic picture of the industry's future (see Smith, 1984). As far as pricing policies, where appropriate, are concerned, NIs that sell a product or service to the public should be pricing at 'marginal cost'. This requirement, reasonably understandable in theory, raises a whole host of problems when attempts are made to apply it in practice. Also, government economists are generally opposed to cross-subsidisation, which if followed through in the pricing policy of, for example, the Electricity Boards, would mean country-dwellers paying considerably more for their electricity than town-dwellers.

Privatisation shifts the NI from being a commercially-orientated NFP into being a fully-fledged private-sector firm. However, where the NI is a natural monopoly, an unfettered pursuit of profits may lead to a deterioration in the service provided to some (or maybe to all) consumers. Prospects for making profits if you are (realistically) the sole provider of an essential service must be rather good; this point was underlined by the huge jump in British Telecom's share price on the first day of trading in the newly privatised company (see Illustration 15.3).

15.9 Inter-organisational relationships

Interconnections with other organisations can be of central importance to some types of NFP. We have already considered a broader, power-orientated view of interconnections between firms and other profit and not-for-profit organisations (Chapter 13); in this section we shall expand a little on the bases and forms of inter-organisational interactions experienced by some NFPs. A good example of the types of NFP with which we are concerned here would be social/welfare agencies. An individual organisation, say a social work agency, has to interact with other organisations such as the police, the Courts, the probation service, hospitals, schools, the housing Department, etc., on a regular basis, in order to deal with the clients' problems.

These interconnections can take many forms, from being simple information exchanges between one NFP and another, to complex formal and informal interlocking networks limited by client, resource and information flows. For some NFPs, then, the management of these interrelationships is of critical importance to the achievement of the organisation's mission. We will consider some of the issues involved under two headings: situational factors, and forms of interaction (see Hall, 1982).

ILLUSTRATION 15.3 Controlling the Nationalised Industries

How are those nationalised industries not suitable for privatisation to be controlled? The Chancellor, **Mr Lawson**, is fed up with allowing them to make large losses while pleading freedom from government interference. If they are going to continue to draw on public funds, he says, then they will have to be more accountable to government both financially and politically. Mr Lawson wants to tighten their accounting methods, improve monitoring of their efficiency and be able to sack their boards. He recognises that some of them, like gas and electricity, are natural nationwide monopolies whose price mechanisms and investment levels may always involve government decisions. Others – such as railways, coal and posts – could be made more subject to competition, and may indeed be put in the private sector one day, but at present they provide a service which the public expects to be in part social and for which it supplies a subsidy.

The Treasury proposals require ministers to lay down clear objectives to which nationalised industry chairmen should work. They require the boards to publish performance indicators by which they may be judged and their annual borrowing and subsidy levels determined. If chairmen do not like them, they can resign or be fired. The government wants to make more explicit its role as representative of the public's shareholding and as the industries' banker. By doing so, Whitehall should be better able to resist day-to-day meddling in the industries' affairs.

(Source: The *Economist*, 29 September 1984)

Situational factors

ENVIRONMENT

Generally, the turbulence and complexity of the environment facing the organizations will tend to increase the need for inter-organisational relations. Task complexity usually militates against standardised responses, so problems need to be resolved by discussion between specialists. The need to interact with other agencies is facilitated by geographical proximity – the closer the organisations are, the easier it is to 'mutually adjust'. Also, the organisation's level of awareness of other organisations in its 'field' will affect the level of inter-organisational interaction.

DOMAIN CONSENSUS

The simplest form of domain consensus is a general agreement amongst interacting organisations about the scope of the 'catchment area' of each and all the organisations. A more important consensus is the level of agreement about role or task differentiation among the organisations – obviously disagreement here will lead to conflict, or maybe to clients falling between two agencies' perceived domains. At a more philosophical level, consensus relates to the compatibility of goals and ideologies, for instance, the 'treatment ideology' of the police with regard to young offenders, compared with that of the social work organisation.

Forms of interaction

Interactions can be *ad hoc*, or highly formalised and standardised. Interactions can be voluntary and co-operative in nature, or forced upon the organisation by laws and regulations. Dependency (for resources, information, clients) of one organisation on another often forms the basis of the interaction, and so an understanding of power relationships stemming from dependence will help us to tune into some issues of conflict and co-operation between these types of organisations. Where there is mutual dependence, organisations will try to maintain co-operative relationships, where dependence is asymmetrical, power strategies can be employed. Generally, organisations will act so as to minimise their dependence on other organisations by a variety of strategies (see Chapter 13).

We should not forget in this context, the importance of the individual actor's *perceptions* of the power relationship – these can vary even within the same organisation, but are crucial in determining the style of interaction conducted on an interpersonal basis.

15.10 Summary

1. NFPs were compared with firms on three broad dimensions: goals; funding and external influence; and internal power relationships.

2. NFP goals tend to be qualitative, variable, complex and often conflicting. Conflicting goals can be attended to in sequence.
3. Measuring the performance of NFPs can cause problems of goal displacement if inappropriate proxy measures are used.
4. As the 'client' of the NFP often pays little or nothing for the service rendered, the client's interests can be subordinated to those people and organisations that provide the funds for the NFP.
5. Particular internal power structures can be found in NFPs, in particular the Missionary form, and the Meritocracy were considered.
6. Decision-making processes in NFPs tend to be bureaucratic, and/or political in nature. CEOs need well developed political skills in order to steer the organisation in the desired direction.
7. Prescriptive techniques for more efficient strategic management of NFPs have been applied in the US, and to a lesser extent in the UK (for example, PPBS, ZBB, CBA).
8. Interference in nationalised industries by succesive governments has caused them to have strategic-management problems peculiar to themselves.
9. Some NFPs have strong interconnections with other NFPs : these interrelationships were considered in terms of situational factors (environment, domain consensus) and forms of interaction.

References

Hall, R. H. (1982) *Organisations: Structure and Process* (Englewood Cliffs, New Jersey: Prentice-Hall).

Johnson, G. and Scholes, K. (1984) *Exploring Corporate Strategy* (Englewood Cliffs, New Jersey: Prentice-Hall).

Keating, B. P. and M. O. (1980) *Not-for-Profit* (Glen Ridge, New Jersey: Horton).

Mintzberg, H. (1983) *Power in and Around Organisations* (Englewood Cliffs, New Jersey: Prentice-Hall).

Pfeffer, J. (1981) *Power in Organisations* (London: Pitman)

Pfeffer, J. and Moore, W. L. (1980) 'Power and Politics in University Budgeting', Administrative Science Quarterly.

Smith, J. Grieve (1984) *Strategic Planning in Nationalised Industries* (London: Macmillan).

Unterman, I. and Davis, R. H. (1982) 'The Strategy Gap in Not-for-Profits *Harvard Business Review* (May–June).

Index